GRAPHIC DESIGN

HISTORY
IN THE WRITING

(1983–2011)

WITHDRAWN

CONTENTS

CONTENTS

This reader seeks to trace the history of graphic design over the past thirty years – its generally accepted life span as a distinctive field. The selected essays address the origins and purposes of graphic design's history, its theory and methods, its relation to other areas of inquiry and links with practice, as well as its role in education. Our aim – as an editorial team composed of a practising graphic designer and a graphic design theorist – was to choose only texts published in English that consider the work of the historian, making this reader first and foremost a historiography. Through extremely diverse styles of writing on the subject, this collection attempts to sketch a history's history: the first to date about graphic design.

Like all compilations, this one falls short. First, because we limited our choice to texts published in English. While this reflects, to some degree, the status of English as an international language, it also, and quite glaringly, contradicts one of this reader's main arguments: that more needs to be written about graphic design history from more varied perspectives – including linguistic, social and political. We felt it was important to start, if not from scratch, then from what exists in English but was dispersed across numerous sources (journals, books, even blogs), much of it hard to access: call it a survey, or a map, with many areas in need of further cartography.

Second, because this reader is the fruit of research and conversations specific to a time and place: originally meant to accompany a conference we co-organised in May 2011 at St Bride Library, London, entitled 'Graphic Design: History in the Making', the reader took (much) longer to produce than initially planned, as one text lead to another, and another, the pool of potential essays expanding insatiably. This expansion accelerated thanks to the input of students from the Royal College of Art in London and the École cantonale d'art de Lausanne who alerted us to the significance for them of certain texts.

As mentioned at the outset, we restricted ourselves to the history of graphic design, leaving out articles devoted to the history of design in general, however influential some of these may be. This restriction allowed us to foreground the question of the autonomy of graphic design history, while remaining alert to the dangers of constituting, through a reader such as this one, something like a canon. If our starting point was that graphic design has its 'own' history, the resulting reader suggests that this possessiveness is very much in dispute, and has been from the start.

Another one of our presuppositions was that graphic design historiography indeed has a 'start' – here 1983 – and can be told in linear fashion. This, too, is a shared point of contention throughout the following essays, and although we opted to organise the reader chronologically, we were pleased to observe the recurrence of non-linear (circular, jagged-edged) patterns, with texts continuously referring to each other and reprising arguments that had appeared settled. We began with the image of the reader as a timeline; the end product, to our relief, reads more like a cluster of discontinuous lines. To respect this quality of a site under construction, we chose to keep our editorial interventions to a minimum, maintaining the texts' grammatical and editorial idiosyncrasies while removing the occasional references to their original context of publication.

Finally, a word about words: calling this book a 'reader' was for us a way to underscore the theoretical and discursive potential of graphic design, and to argue that its history needs not only to be exhibited and illustrated, but also produced and debated 'in the writing'.

Sara De Bondt and Catherine de Smet

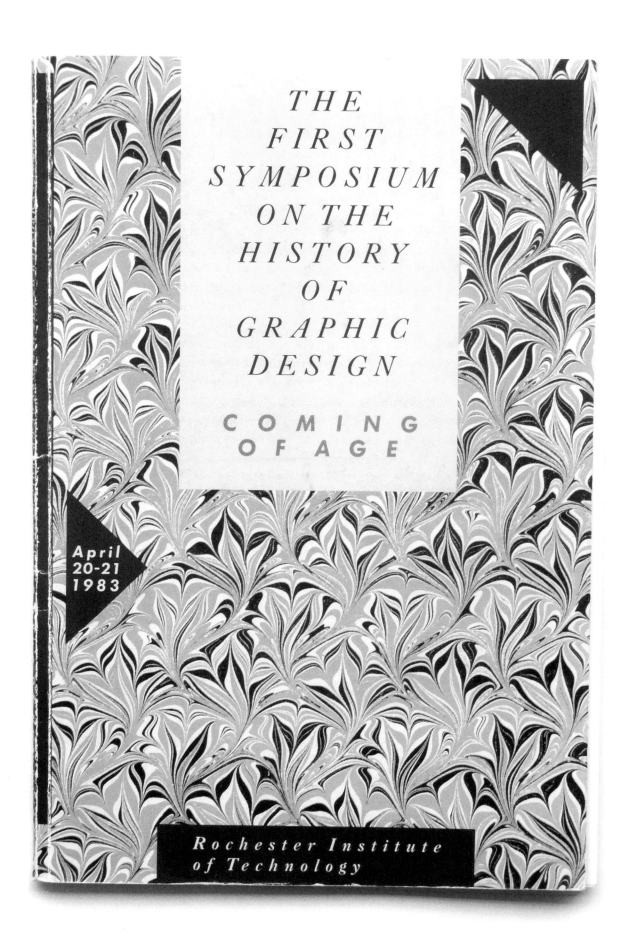

THE FIRST SYMPOSIUM ON THE HISTORY OF GRAPHIC DESIGN

COMING OF AGE

April
20-21
1983

Rochester Institute
of Technology

KEYNOTE ADDRESS

MASSIMO VIGNELLI
1983

This symposium on the history of graphic design is definitely a historical event. That is a rhetorical way of saying, 'Thank God, it was about time. We need it!' I don't know why it took so long. I just can't believe that for centuries, certainly for decades, graphic designers have been happy and content with simply producing and looking at pretty pictures. Perhaps that attitude of the here and now is the heritage of the modern movement; but even before that, there seems to have been very little engagement with and study about the meaning of graphic design.

I have with me a shopping list of needs that we have. One of them is to find out more about the history of graphic design. We need to find out what the Romans were doing during Roman times. Why did we start with Helvetica? We need to know more about graphics in the Middle Ages. We need to find out more about the beautiful graphics of the Renaissance; for example, the marvelous typefaces we see in the buildings of that time. We need to know more about what kind of relationship there was among the graphic designers who were doing books after Gutenberg, the architects, the environment, and the philosophy of the time. Graphic design has been kept in the dark. We need a little flashlight, if not a floodlight, cast on history. We need to know a little more about the strong currents of the eighteenth century, the emergence of the Enlightenment, the impact of its meaning as reflected in the design publications of that time, the contrasts and the contradictions implied in the periods of cultural transformations, and the origin of modern times, communication, and industrialization.

We need to study what happened to graphic design with the invention of advertising which had a powerful influence on our profession. We need to find out more about all these things through the ages that had an impact on our graphic design.

We need to investigate more about communication theories. It is certain that until we have theory we will not have a profession. We cannot continue to talk about how nice a picture is, or how nice the work of one or another designer is. I want to know why it was done, how, what motivated it all. As professionals we can no longer continue in this state of ignorance in which we have been going thus far.

Criticism is the other thing which we need tremendously. We need to produce continuous criticism which will push us forward into the right place, showing us the appropriate directions. Other professions like architecture, to name one, are really sustained and forwarded by criticism. There are plenty of magazines on architecture and interiors. They criticize architecture to death, but we're never doing that. If you open a graphics magazine from the last thirty years, there never seems to be a page of criticism, just attractive little biographies and that is it. Open *Graphis*, you'll find the same thing. Open any other design magazine. There is nothing, not one line of criticism. Do you think we can go on without criticism? Without criticism we will never have a profession.

We also need documentation. We need to document everything we do. We need to find out. We need to perceive ourselves as steps in a historical process. The need for documentation is not only for us; it is for the generations that will follow us. If the generations preceding ours would have documented themselves better, we would derive better conclusions of what we are and where we should go. So the need for documentation is extremely important and needs to be added to the other three areas of need we have discussed: history, theory, and criticism.

We also definitely need to know more about technology. We are getting into a future in which technology is going to play a great part. We need to know technology to take it out of the hands of the technicians who are using it now. When I see typefaces coming out as poor-looking as they are coming out now, I know that I need to know technology to get back to the technicians and tell them, 'You are killing typography by coming out with those phototypes.' Phototype is fine, but it needs a culture behind it. And the culture is not just a person who has been doing photo lettering for all of his or her life. We need Gutenbergs of our times. We need people who have cultural backgrounds, not only fine hands for slashing plastic around a letter.

One of our biggest tasks in doing graphic design history is to reassess the modern movement. Since we're all children of the modern movement, it's very had to do that. Nevertheless, other professions have been reassessing the modern movement. We have seen that it has been happening in architecture. Of course, the operation of reassessment is something which is very difficult. The high risk of miscarriage is always there. In graphic design the most we have seen lately is little dots and squares floating around the page like decorative tiles. I will not call this reassessment. That is neither communication nor development of graphic design beyond the post-modern movement. The issues and the structures of today are what make the post-modern movement; anything else is just a pretty fad. And when I say fad, I want to convey all the contempt that I have: typographic fads that arrange type on the side and big type here and there with a little dot and lines going all over the place. Would you believe that the Swiss, who have really understood the value of communication and have been doing fabulous graphics, were bound to come up with a new form of graphic design which means nothing beyond prettiness?

I think we have to reassess what the modern movement gave to us. We have to see if it's correct. I see a lot of things, for instance, that have taken years to come out from history. I can see how the beautiful inner structure of the Renaissance took a long time to disengage itself from the shapes in the bodies of the paintings to gradually begin to come out in the last century and finally emerge fully in this century as abstract forms. What we had in the intervening centuries was the structure of the Renaissance liberated from the past. That is one of the interesting things that happened in history. I think we need to look for the valid things the modern movement has given to us in order to develop them. And what was a fad of the moment, or was irrelevant, or merely transitory needs to be weeded out.

As designers we have to continuously sift the past and the present so that the things that remain on the top are the important ones, and the things that sift down are the gravel. We obviously want the golden nuggets at the top.

It seems to me that the most important thing that we have to do is improve the state of education in our schools. We've got to insert some level of culture, some level of history, some level of philosophy. Without that, we will have just a continuous stream of little designers and crafts persons, or paste-up people at best. We need to provide a cultural structure to our profession. That is the premier task of the 1980s for all of us. But we have to do it for ourselves. We all have to help each other. We are the leaders of awareness, and it's up to us really to put the systems and methods together. If we don't do this, we are condemned to a state of ignorance and we will perpetuate it.

As we go about increasing awareness of history, theory, criticism, documentation, technology, and culture, we can't lose sight the value of meaning over the value of form. It's not true that meaning is more important than form. It's not true that content is more important than form. Still, if for fifty years we have been trained and bombarded everyday with the idea that form is really the greatest thing around, then for the next fifty years we've got to say that meaning is more important than form. Perhaps then, fifty years from now, we might reach a state of balance between form and content.

We desperately need to establish journals where the issues of history, theory, criticism, documentation, technology are brought forward and where investigation is going to go on all the time. I know there is a group in Chicago that will publish the *Design Issues* journal. But where are the contributors? To find them is the most important thing. I'm sure there are people in Nebraska or people in Maine who are doing fantastic studies. We want to know where they are and we want to get in touch with them. We want to get together and investigate these issues. Let's make this step forward because there are no other alternatives. If we don't make this step forward, we are all culturally dead, and if that is the case, Amen.

Massimo Vignelli is President of Vignelli Associates, New York.
First published in *The First Symposium on the History of Graphic Design: Coming of Age*,
Rochester Institute of Technology, 1983.

GRAPHIC DESIGN HISTORY: DISCIPLINE OR ANARCHY?

PHILIP B. MEGGS
1985

A heady enthusiasm greeted the emergence, a decade ago, of an interest in graphic design history which sprouted across America like mushrooms after a Summer thunderstorm. The early stages of this movement were long on opinions and short on scholarship. Self-styled experts were suddenly available to deliver lectures to professional clubs and schools. Armed with reels of 35mm slides, their interpretations were loose and often highly opinionated. In art schools and universities, graphic design professors began to introduce design history as an informal part of studio courses, illustrated by images from such books as Herbert Spencer's *Pioneers of Modern Typography* and Dover Publications' *The Golden Age of the Poster* and *The First World War in Posters*, and so on. From this rather amateurish beginning, individuals around the country doggedly worked to bring substance to their research. A new field of inquiry – Graphic Design History – was coming of age. Symposia (notably the 1983 *Coming of Age, A First Symposium on the History of Graphic Design* at Rochester Institute of Technology and its 1985 sequel), books and articles, interest groups, and mailing lists have begun to create a network of passionately involved people.

What accounts for this growing interest in graphic design history? One factor is the shift in American society from an industrial to an information culture. Visual communications play a role in the emerging post-industrial society, which is similar to the role of automobile design during the 1950s, when America underwent the most rapid industrial expansion of any nation in the history of the world. The automobile was the tangible product and the visual icon of that era. Likewise, contemporary graphics are a major cultural manifestation of the information age. I am speaking of contemporary graphics in a comprehensive sense. Computer animation, video game iconography, and rock videos join more traditional graphics as expressions of this revolution. (The last ten years have seen a steady decline in sculpture and crafts enrollments in art schools and universities, accompanied by a steady growth in visual communications enrollments. This is an extension of the shift from industrial to information culture. The educational bureaucrats who believe these enrollment shifts are solely a reflection of a conservative generation's employment orientation miss the main point.)

Another factor is the graphic design discipline's quest for professional status and recognition as an important activity requiring specialized knowledge, skill, and even a measure of wisdom. If graphic design is to succeed in casting off the antiquated notion of 'commercial art' taking a rightful place beside architecture and painting as a major visual expression of our culture, the 'history void' must be overcome. A professional without a history is like a person without a country: a homeless refugee. The graphic design history movement bolsters the profession's quest for recognition.

Laymen develop an involvement in graphic design history through interest in its content. In its most populist forms, graphic design is history's hard copy; the documentation of revolutions and recording stars, politics and prosperity, real estate booms and Hollywood busts. On a more rarefied and aesthetic level, it can be an innovative, sometimes difficult art form. Its intrinsic value as design is one level of meaning; it also carries meaning as social message and historical artifact.

The design history experts are a lively and diverse group. But a unity of purpose and approach is lacking. Practitioners (notably those with a modernist, formal approach), design educators (who were trained as graphic designers and spend a significant amount of their professional week in teaching), and academicians (scholars trained in art history, philosophy or other academic disciplines) have all joined the movement. Each group has a different agenda and brings a unique viewpoint to graphic design history. While the result may appear to be zoo-like to some observers, each group brings special insights and knowledge to the dialogue.

There is not even agreement, for example, on the historical scope that should be studied. Some advocate the shortsighted view and believe that graphic design is a new activity, born of the industrial revolution. Others advocate a far-sighted view, believing the essence of graphic design is giving visual form to human communications, an activity that has a distinguished ancestry dating to the medieval manuscript and early printers of the Renaissance.

As yet, graphic design history is not a fully developed discipline in the sense that art history and architectural history are. The histories of other disciplines – science, medicine, architecture, and painting – have become important areas of human activity in themselves. Mixed in with the heroes and myths, the aspiring scientist or painter finds philosophy, values, and a sense of destiny. Formal, systematic opportunities to study graphic design history are not readily available. The University of Cincinnati is offering a master's degree in design history, and an increasing number of art schools and universities are offering courses. However, there is not yet a doctoral program for individuals who wish to make a lifetime commitment to researching and teaching design history.

Graphic design history must be studied in the complex context of its milieu. While we can speak of architectural history, painting history, product design history, graphic design history, etc., all of these are part of a larger *visual* history. Artists and artisans in each epoch freely borrow from one another. Ornaments in fifteenth-century French books echo architectural embellishment. The sinuous and organic lines of Art Nouveau lend unity to architecture, furniture, posters, jewelry, household objects, and fashions from the 1890s. The geometric stylizations of African masks and figurative sculpture, which were freely borrowed by Picasso and Braque as they pioneered Cubism, found their way into sculpture, architectural reliefs, book and fashion illustrations of the 1920s. While fashion and the excitement of the new shape this visual history, it may also be true that epochs embrace visual forms that relate to collective mythic needs born from historical circumstance.

The political and social circumstances of each time period have a significant impact upon graphic design history. The Depression and the rise of Nazism left an indelible stamp upon graphics of the 1930s. In posters from that decade which are housed in the squeaky drawers of the massive poster collection of the Library of Congress, we find that fantasy and escapism commingle with strident political messages. Faith in the multinational corporation and its ability to address and solve problems was prevalent during the 1950s. This faith was badly shaken during the social upheavals of the 1960s. Graphics from each decade must be understood and interpreted in light of these and other historical forces.

Another connection is technological. Advances in graphic arts processes are sometimes as important as creative insight or historical circumstance in shaping the visual communications vocabulary. An understanding of tools can lead to startling invention, with new forms and spatial configurations emerging from an engagement with advanced technology. During the mid-nineteenth century, the invention of color lithographic printing enabled imaginative visual artists to bring about a 'color revolution' that radically altered mass communications and made graphics 'every man's artform'.

An important part of Herb Lubalin's contribution to American graphic design was his sensitivity to the new phototypography of the 1960s. Lubalin understood its potential for extending the designer's creative potential and opening new communicative possibilities.

One problem that is yet to be resolved is the criteria to be used when making judgments about historical significance. This is a key philosophical issue for any area of aesthetics, criticism or history. At this point, the various experts do not agree. Logical criteria must be developed by those who make pronouncements about the value and importance of creative work. Two major, if unstated, approaches are the formalist approach and the socio-political approach.

Germanic in origin, the formalist approach sees design evolution in terms of its purity of form. Constructivism, de Stijl, and the Bauhaus are the genesis, the Swiss School is the realization, and the heirs of this tradition are seen as the significant designers of today. Graphic design, according to some advocates of this approach, is a new activity that did not exist until the twentieth-century visual revolutions. This view is myopic, for artistically trained individuals from Hans Holbein to hundreds of nineteenth-century artists of the chromolithography era were seriously involved in designing books, posters, broadsides, tins, and other printed matter from 1450 until 1900.

The socio-political approach sees this historical value of graphic design in terms of its political viewpoint and impact upon society. Political activists of several persuasions have embraced this approach. This dogma defines the value of graphic design in terms of its political correctness. The Solidarity logo becomes good; the logo of the multinational oil company becomes evil. This sociological approach is in direct conflict with the formalist approach. The logo or poster for the most worthy of causes might be graphically awkward, and work for the petrochemical monolith that creates the vilest of toxic waste dumps can be graphic invention of the highest order.

Graphic design is ill-served by a purely formal, or by a purely sociological approach. It is a pluralistic and complex activity. Responsible interpretation must consider form, content, chronological context, and social value. It must be viewed in relationship to what preceded and what followed it.

The importance of the late-nineteenth-century leader of the English Arts and Crafts movement, William Morris, offers a fascinating example of differing interpretations. Appalled with the mediocre quality of printed books of his time, Morris founded the Kelmscot Press in 1892 and attempted to recapture the quality of books from the early years of typographic printing. In *A History of Design from the Victorian Era to the Present*, Ann Ferebee writes that Morris' book designs had 'little to do with the impending twentieth century', while in *A History of Graphic Design*, I wrote of Morris' 'extraordinary influence... upon graphic design.' In *A History of Visual Communications*, Josef Müller-Brockmann reproduces a page from one of Morris' books, but does not mention him in the text. How can such different interpretations exist? Ferebee is operating from a vantage point of Victorian to Art Nouveau or Modern and is responding to Morris' lack of stylistic influence upon Modern design. *A History of Graphic Design's* reference is to the tremendous impact Morris had upon typography and the revitalization of book design through his influence upon Frederic Goudy, Bruce Rogers, and many others. Further, Morris had a strong philosophic impact upon the emergence of all forms of design in the early twentieth century through his call for workmanship, truth to materials, making the utilitarian beautiful, and the fitness of design to function. Possibly Müller-Brockmann did not feel that Morris was sufficiently important.

These different interpretations of design history are possible because, as mentioned above, a body of criticism and philosophy providing criteria and standards does not yet exist. Design historians take diverse vantage points based on their experience and interests. Although the design history movement is still in its infancy and suffers from growing pains, its emergence holds great promise for the future development of both graphic design and the study of history.

The design history movement should not lose sight of the fact that its subject is ephemera. Perhaps this is why the museum world has been so reticent to recognize the importance of graphic design, except for precious artifacts such as rare books and posters that relate to the twentieth century avant-garde. Graphic design exists of and for its time, but its value – both to elucidate methods for creating messages and demonstrate the evolution of a visual vocabulary – endures.

The ultimate goal of design history study should be more effective practice. Its contribution should go beyond the use of design history as a vast data bank of forms and solutions to problems that can be accessible to the contemporary designer, expanding his or her vocabulary of possibilities. Graphic design history is a history of ideas. Eric Gill's 1928 Gill Sans typeface was based on the idea of using the proportions of Roman inscriptional letter forms in a sans-serif type design. Its geometric contemporary, Paul Renner's 1927 Futura, was designed in enthusiastic embrace of industrialism, standardization, and scientific rationalism. Gill, however, sought to retain values from the humanist tradition. Understanding such divergent viewpoints leads to greater awareness of the nature of form and its meaning, and brings conceptual understanding to professional practice.

The study of design history can support the development of professional ethical and value systems. The sense of purpose found in the scholar-printers of the Renaissance, who were unlocking the lost knowledge of the ancient world; the urgency of John Heartfield, using photomontage in posters as a propaganda weapon in the struggle against Nazism, and the wholesome commitment to commerce (in the best sense of that word) by the pioneers of corporate visual identification – these examples represent graphic design practice motivated by a dedication to exemplary human values. This sense of purpose must be present, if graphic design aspires to the professional integrity that we associate with the best impulses of the medical, legal, and teaching professions. Otherwise, it's back to commercial art.

Philip B. Meggs, (1942–2002), Richmond, was an influential graphic designer, professor, historian and author. First published in *AIGA Journal of Graphic Design*, vol. 3, no. 4, 1985.

D E S I G N E R
NOVEMBER 1985 £1.75

Title ·   Durabeam (Standard).
Prov ·   M. Thatcher.
Attrib ·   B.I.B. (J. Drane Esq.) °1983
Insc ·   Duracell UK. Durabeam.
Exhib ·   Boots, Underwoods Etc.

DESIGN HISTORY: AN UNEASY NEW DISCIPLINE?

DESIGN HISTORY'S SEARCH FOR IDENTITY

ROBIN KINROSS
1985

It seemed a moment of liberation when the Design History Society was formed, at a conference in Brighton in September 1977: the decision to stop beating about the bush and just *do it* was urged on us by Tim Benton. (I remember him punching a fist into his other cupped hand.) The conference had been organised by members of the 'Design History Research Group' within the Association of Art Historians. But now we could be free from the burdens of art history: its doubtful methods, its stuffy Association, and the whole business of the sanctification and fetishisation of art objects. Design was different: part of ordinary life and to be *used* (not put in museums), and it needed to be studied not as a series of isolated objects but as an activity, in its whole social and material context. Turning away from art history, we looked towards social history, to the history of technology – and also, even, hoped to attract the interest of practising designers.

Now, nearly a decade later, that founding impetus has faded; the struggle to work out what design history might be, and to get recognition for it, is proving to be a long one. Although in the early days of the Design History Society efforts were made – with some success – to encourage contributions from the widest range of members (overtures were made to hobby enthusiasts), the active membership now consists of those teaching in further and higher education, with a scattering of museum people, librarians, publishers. So design history is in Britain being defined and developed as a component of design education in the schools, colleges and polytechnics. It is thus being considerably conditioned by the vicissitudes of the native educational scene. This brief consideration of the issue of design history will try to avoid much discussion of educational method (is there any more boring topic?), but some engagement with it is unavoidable. I should add that my discussion is directed towards the primary problem of teaching intending designers, and is less concerned with the education of design historians (as on the new MA courses).

The first large factor to be considered is the departmental set-up within which the subject is taught. The rubric is usually along the lines of 'General/Liberal/Related Studies', with 'History of Art' tagged on or subsumed. The suggestion is of a humanist portmanteau that will broaden and civilise otherwise visually or technically dominated minds. History of (fine) art has been there as a core, extending into our history of (usually high) culture. Following the emergence of specialised and increasingly vocational design courses – now, I under our present regime, given an emphatically political tone – the need for a correspondingly specialised historical component has been urged.

At this point in the argument, questions of subject matter are raised. What exactly is design history to consist of? At first glance the question may seem easy. Is it not just a matter of replacing 'art' by 'design' and keeping 'history'? Yes, but when does design start? With the cave-painters? The wheel? With capitalism? Industrialism? Morris? The Werkbund? Some skirmishes in the pages of the Design History Society Newsletter have brought the issue into sharper focus. The largely negative reception there of his Penguin *Dictionary of Design and Designers* forced Simon Jervis to reiterate his thesis that design history as conceived in the polytechnics (he did not altogether avoid the easy sneer that now accompanies the word) was narrow and partial. Against the DHS/Poly idea of design as a coordinating activity arising in response to the industrial division of labour and flourishing only in the last 60 years or so, Jervis – speaking for what one may call the South Kensington axis – affirmed a vision of design as decoration, with a time-scale 'from about 1450 to the present day'. Thus his *Dictionary* is peopled with engravers of patterns on guns, devisers of floral brooches, and so on, as well as its rather skimped representation of what we might think of as main-line design (say, Gottfried Semper to Dieter Rams). And, of course, the very idea of a dictionary of designers goes against the tendency in recent design history of an emphasis away from individual heroes and towards the study of anonymous production and economic and social factors.

This argument has brought more into the open the political drive of design history. Definition of the subject has come mainly from those with left sympathies or commitments. These people – I include myself among them – have grown up with and incorporated the assumptions of Modernism.

And, though recognizing the failures and perversions of Modernism, we do not want or think it possible to give up its aspirations: design in the service of a generously-tended public sphere, needed and long-lasting products, truthful communication.

At odds with this version is the eruption of free-for-all stylism and 'design for profit', fueled and given implicit sanction by historians. This movement against Modernism (usually described by the catch-all of 'Post-Modernism') can be seen most clearly in architecture, where a strange and sometimes embarrassed alliance of high-Tory classicists and trendy pace-setters (architects and their journalist lap-dogs) has been sloughing off the dirt of socialist Modernism. In this context it is more than ever clear that design history cannot be neutral.

Among possible responses to the request for history from those responsible for the training of designers, the easiest would be to provide a 'story of design' starting at whatever point was appropriate for the desired emphasis of the narrative. The story would be heavily illustrated with coloured pictures. For, at the crudest level, the function of design history seems to be the provision of images of designed objects as fodder for future production. Thus, in a self-fulfilling prophecy, historians could trace the influence of A, whose work was seen by B whose work was seen by C and so on. This is one of the legacies of bad art history, from which design history has a chance of breaking free. Apart from tending to deny individual initiative, in fixing on visual motifs it excludes the large set of special factors impinging on the particular act of design and the larger context in which the work is embedded.

If this essentially passive servicing role is rejected, what might other more active conceptions be? One influence has emerged under the name of 'cultural studies'. Unlike the frankly meaningless 'general (etc) studies' – within whose nest it has landed – cultural studies does have quite a precise character. Its object of study is mass culture, and it depends heavily for its method and assumptions on a large body of recent continental theory (political, psychoanalytic, semiotic). It breaks decisively with the English literary and moral critics (notably F.R. and Q.D. Leavis and also figures such as Richard Hoggart), for whom mass culture was a matter of concern and, to various degrees, of dismay. Cultural studies makes no such moral judgements and, while professing some variety of Marxism, gladly accepts every phenomenon that capitalism throws up and subjects it to critique with whatever methodological tools have recently been imported (in bad English translation) from Paris or Milan. This caricature is not wholly fair, though I think there is truth in it. But there have recently been some jargon-free and ethically conscious contributions from the cultural studies group, and the feminist presence – where it has emphasised individual and social reality – has been salutary.

The implications of cultural studies for design education are not yet clear, but one can make some preliminary observations. One simple fact is that theory at the high level of abstraction habitual in cultural studies – and especially ill-digested theory – will simply bore or confuse design students, the majority of whom are not politically-minded nor very literate. The more rarefied debate engendered by cultural studies will stay confined to discussions among teachers and post-graduate students, surfacing occasionally in journals such as *Block, Formations, Screen*. So far, cultural studies has seemed to pose a threat to design, and thus to some intending design history. For in its concern with mass culture, it not *only* accepts but inevitably connives at the world that lies outside the sphere of good design. While those who still hold to the faith of design (from Gottfried Semper to Dieter Rams, from Christopher Dresser to Kenneth Grange) avert their glance from the world of the *Sun,* James Bond and Tesco, to cultural studies, this world *and* that of Olivetti and 'good form' are all part of the same capitalism (though perhaps inhabiting different levels or moments), so that distinctions between good and bad in design are seen as trivial or false.

If cultural studies does not seem of much help, and may pose some threat to design education, it has the virtue of engaging with the major conditioning factors on design students. It is certainly easier and may be of more use to hold seminars on television advertising than it is to ask students to read and discuss a text by William Lethaby or Herbert Read. But both should be possible. I would only urge that a non-celebratory, critical and material-historical approach be applied to both the products of mass culture and those of design: holding on to certain values, which an a-moral cultural studies has often ignored.

What then might design history be? I am inclined to suggest that the term be discarded in favour of 'design criticism' ('design theory' sounds too forbiddingly remote in our pragmatic context). The point is that history happens anyway, as soon as one starts to ground something in its time and place. Within education, the urgent need is to escape from the deadly a-historical legacy (still rife on Foundation courses) of the Gombrichian 'story', 'day extraction', and slide lecturer in semi-darkness (what are slides if not illusions?).

One area of work to tackle is that of writing. Here a general studies tutor's pretension to literacy could be directed towards the writing not just of essays, but letters, reports, specifications, memos. The activity of finding out is common both to historical and to design activity, and experience drawn from doing academic research could usefully be brought to educating all inquisitive attitude in designing (finding out about available materials, and so on). Or these tutors could bring historically informed contributions to the progress of project work and to final critical evaluations. Experiments in integration along these and other lines are being tried, but they are isolated and under-nourished. One senses that some studio tutors would prefer to keep their day off and to have history uncritical and safely confined to the lecture theatre.

Where are these new design critics to come from? The answer must be that they will arrive by the same miscellaneous routes as the general studies tutors have travelled along. This would be appropriate, given the miscellaneous nature of design activity itself. And there is something to fear in a monolithic system whereby critic-historians are trained on specially devised courses in design studies. Here there are dangers of co-option into orthodoxy: that of the design establishment or of the cultural studies heresy. The best hope lies in the building up of a body of critical writings and discussions, which can, by a process of seepage, have its effect. The long-mooted *Design History Journal*, if it can get off the ground, should help. Though, remembering the Leavises – if not completely identifying with them – what is most needed is a *Design Scrutiny*.

Robin Kinross is a publisher at Hyphen Press, London.
First published in *Designer*, Society of Illustrators, Artists and Designers, 1985.

Design

HISTORY

a students' handbook

edited by Hazel Conway

GRAPHIC DESIGN

JEREMY AYNSLEY
1987

We live in a world in which we are kept informed by a mass-media. Newspapers, television, radio and advertising all help to keep us in touch with worldwide events, while at the same time they influence or form our attitudes. In other societies direct human contact still operates as a way of communication, although because of the power and appeal of industrialised communication, these constitute a diminishing proportion of the world. Inevitably, mass-communications involve many specialised activities. Journalists, writers, illustrators or photographers supply the media with information, while technicians, engineers and printers specialise in the most effective ways of transmitting those ideas. Somewhere, very often at an intermediate stage, there are people who are responsible for coding information and ideas, using patterns, styles and sequences that are at once conventional enough to be understood, but also sufficiently novel to attract our attention. It is at this intermediate stage that what we call graphic design happens.

It would seem sensible, if our world is made up of so much that has passed through the hands of the graphic designer, or been under the graphic designer's direction, that we should learn to understand its workings. This would help us to assess the quality of the design, and to test its effectiveness. A study of graphic design might also prevent us from becoming too passive or 'brainwashed', to use a popular word. As early as the 1920s, the writers Aldous Huxley, Bertrand Russell and F.R. Leavis suggested that schoolchildren should be taught how to 'read' advertisements, in order to defend themselves against their persuasion.[1]

In this chapter, I shall outline what a history of graphic design can involve. Of the stages outlined above, most design historians have concentrated on the second, that is, when the designer makes decisions that determine the visual aspect of the object, such as which typeface to use, or what sort of composition to employ. While I agree that analysis of particular images is important and will form a basis on which to develop an understanding of design principles and theory, the design only becomes part of a process if we ask questions about the other two stages. In other words, visual analysis is not sufficient as history. We also need to ask whose ideas were being conveyed by this design and for what context it was intended.

The Term 'Graphic Design'

As Raymond Williams has pointed out in his book *Keywords* (1976), words have their own histories and their use and meaning change with time. The term graphic design is no exception and we should first consider what it means. Graphic design has existed for a very long time, even if only relatively recently have these words been used to denote the activity. For example, we know that the Romans used advertising and that since pictographs on cave walls dating from c.15,000–10,000 BC there have been attempts at visual language.[2]

Other areas of design such as ceramics and textiles can be defined by their materials, but for graphic design there has been no cohesive factor about its medium since the invention of film. The suggestion that items with words and images printed by ink, registering on a surface form a distinct category, is still accepted by the Victoria and Albert Museum in London as a way of guiding its collection in the Department of Prints and Drawings. This department could be considered the major 'graphics' collection in the UK. Such a definition by medium can only be partial now that photography, audio-visual and filmic work are significant areas for graphic training and activity. Before the Second World War, graphic design was most often called 'commercial art'. The word 'commercial' as a prefix distinguished art for reproduction from 'fine' art, a distinction you may still hear today. Underlying this distinction was often the different training for these activities, the fine artist training at a school of art, the commercial artist very often training as an apprentice with a printer during the day, and at technical school at night.

Illustration and typography had long and interesting histories of their own, but in the nineteenth century these had been combined, in many instances prompted by the changing function of word and image within an industrialised society. The poster, combining word and image as a visual form, as well as mass-circulation magazines, newspapers and books all required new kinds of organization and 'design' for print. An introduction to these changes is given in Francis Klingender, *Art and the Industrial Revolution* (1972), and William M. Ivins, Jr, *Prints and Visual Communication* (1969). After 1945 graphic design courses evolved in art colleges, technical colleges and polytechnics, and the trained designers moved into the steadily expanding field of publication design, advertising and television, as well as corporate design for trade and industry. At its broadest, graphic design, and consequently its history, came to cover anything from the design of a bus ticket to sign systems for motorways, the packaging of cigarettes to the typographical organization of dictionaries, the design of the lead-in to nightly television news to art-directing a magazine. Recently, the term 'visual communication' has been adopted as one that allows film-based media to be subsumed under its heading. When we come to people, we still tend to define them as either 'illustrators' or 'graphic designers', even when the person does both. For instance, the well-known American illustrator Milton Glaser not only illustrates books and art-directs magazines, he also recently turned to work on the corporate design of a chain of food stores in the US.[3]

If we take communication as the characteristic of graphic design, then we should be aware that it is a social rather than a technical category. This means that advertising and book design, although carried out for different purposes and occupying distinct places within the economy, have something in common. Remaining at this very broad level, we can also say that graphic design is a *medium* for transferring an object or an idea. On the one hand, it is the medium by which you choose one type of product rather than another, and has a very clear purpose in material culture. On the other hand, it is often the material substance by which we reach ideas. For example, a book is important for the ideas assembled in its argument or narrative. We can be persuaded to like the ideas more because of their appearance and organization on the page, and in this way the designer, typographer, printer and publisher affect our understanding, but at some stage we dissociate a book's *form* from its *meaning*. It is this characteristic which makes graphic design so ambiguous in its status, but also so interesting. It is what distinguishes the design of a timetable, which I would place firmly within graphic design, and the design of wallpaper, which I would not, even though their materials, ink and paper, can sometimes be the same.

An enjoyable way to define your position, if you are interested in the ambivalent status graphic design holds as both transmitter and substance of the idea, would be to read Marshall McLuhan's work. In his book *The Gutenberg Galaxy* (1962), McLuhan discussed the relationship technology has with the potential content, and suggested that in advertising the two were in danger of becoming confused, a view he put succinctly in the phrase 'the medium is the message'.[4]

Range of Material

Clearly a tremendous amount of accessible material exists for the study of graphic design, but I would like to distinguish now between kinds of material available. It is also important to comment here on those historical periods that have already been well interpreted, with easily-found primary and secondary sources, and those periods that have still to be charted.

The scope of graphic design history is given in surveys, such as Josef Müller-Brockmann, *A History of Visual Communications* (1971), and Philip B. Meggs, *A History of Graphic Design* (1983). These are useful reference books, from which you can quickly find out who designed something and when. The limitations of such books, which are ambitious in scope, charting graphic art from Stone Age man to contemporary design, is that they produce a sequence of stylistic and technical change, linking designed objects with other designed objects. An assumption underlying this kind of history is that design has an autonomy. This encourages the view that designers only refer to previous design, whereas the real environment and public for design is in nearly all cases much broader than this.

Different periods have been researched to different stages, according to the sorts of questions they offer historians. For example, the Victorian era has proved popular, partly because the graphic art of that time was so central to the developing consumer society. Changes in the demand for a medium such as the newspaper or the poster were encouraged by the proliferation in printing developments and enormous growth in the types of design produced. This raises the question of the relationship design has to economic and social change and how design participates in that change.

Other periods that are well documented include the interwar years in Britain and the First and Second World Wars. Arriving in Britain in the interwar period, Modernism produced a wealth of designers' writings, giving explanations and definitions of theories and principles. In graphic design, Modernism can be identified by stylistic simplicity, a flatness of form, a taste for asymmetrical composition and the reduction of elements to a minimum. I would guard against the view, which you will find quite often expressed, that the success of the design depends on its approximation to the Modernist ideal. This ideal arose as a result of particular debates within design at a certain time, and the values held cannot be transposed across changing functions

Edward McKnight Kauffer's (1890–1946) poster for London Transport, *Spring in the Village*, 1936, shows how by the mid-1930s Modernist poster design was a possible solution to promote travel. This example acknowledged Cubism in the arrangement of lettering and shadow, and also Constructivism in the use of the photograph and its 'frame'. You might go on to ask why such a design was considered suitable in 1936, and what the alternatives might have been.

and contexts of design, in spite of a wish for graphic and stylistic homogeneity. A useful anthology of designers' and architects' writing from the period, which includes some specifically on graphic design, is Tim and Charlotte Benton with Dennis Sharp, *Form and Function: A Source Book for the History of Architecture and Design 1890–1930* (1975).

The enforced emigration of many exponents of Modernism in the 1930s in graphic design, from Germany to Switzerland, Britain and the US, and their impact on the indigenous design traditions in these countries, has been the subject of considerable investigation. In the patronage by certain British companies, such as Shell Mex and BP and the London Transport Passenger Board, in advertising agencies such as Crawfords or Highams, in commissions from government and other institutional bodies, such as the Empire Marketing Board and the GPO Film Unit, the impact of Modernism was felt. Also effective techniques of persuasion were necessary to mobilise a population at war under state control. During both World Wars, graphic techniques were developed which were to prove formative for subsequent design in peacetime. Other similar moments of social and political change are also interesting to examine, when often a prescribed set of demands operated. This can be said, for example, about the National Socialists' use of film in Germany between 1933 and 1945,[5] the recent tradition of poster design in Poland,[6] or the political graphics of May 1968 in Paris.[7]

The postwar period in graphic design has been relatively uncharted so far. This means that there are fewer secondary sources to approach. By contrast the proliferation of designers' writings continues throughout this period, and these form a good basis. Another advantage of working on a postwar subject is that most libraries will stock magazines and periodicals which can provide invaluable primary material. For example, by looking at a run of *Vogue* magazine from 1945 to 1965, you could make notes about many different aspects of the magazine. One obvious approach would be to trace the content of the magazine, to consider how the subjects of articles change and to evaluate the pattern of editorial work. You might then contrast this pattern with the kinds of advertising that went alongside it, to find how complementary or not both aspects of the content were. If you were pursuing this subject, a next step would be to place your observations against a reading of the position of women as a workforce and as consumers during the period in Britain. It might interest you, instead, to concentrate on the graphic style of the magazine. During this time in Britain, the American approach to magazine design infiltrated, whereby an 'art director' was responsible for commissioning and coordinating the different activities that go towards layout.[8] An analysis of the changing style in layout,

Cover of the British edition of *Vogue*, March 1951. Questions might concern the use of a photograph on the cover, the layout design, the content of the magazine, its readership or its production.

typography and photographic and line illustrations, leading to a comment on the pattern of their use in magazines, can be made. Most magazines list their staff on the frontispiece and you should decide whether to trace an individual's work, or whether it would be more interesting to ask thematic questions. Increasingly during this period, illustrators and photographers were acknowledged next to their work, which makes a search and identification easier. This also raises the significant point about the developing recognition of design and artwork by the public and industry.[9]

History of Art and History of Graphic Design

The notion of a separate discipline called the history of graphic design has its advantages and disadvantages. The history of art has developed a language and methodologies, now taught in schools, colleges and universities, which are often useful for a vocabulary to define characteristics of design. It is possible to transfer labels such as Constructivist and Art Nouveau and apply them to graphic design, and to realise that the graphic work of these movements was a central and integrated part of them. More significantly, perhaps, art and design can share a vocabulary because they are received by the same senses, and involve our visual sensibility.

Where a distinction enters is concerning the idea of uniqueness. As the German critic, Walter Benjamin, noticed in a series of important essays in the 1930s, whereas it is possible to speak of the unique object in painting and sculpture, this is not the case for design.[10] Although both objects of study, a painting and a poster, can be analysed in visual terms alone, the fact that the poster was made with reproduction specifically in mind should alter our approach to it.

Especially since the rise of Modernism, painting and sculpture have taken on areas of perception and experience that are extremely specialised and can depend on a public familiar with the ideas in the work. There is a complex apparatus that supports art, including aesthetic criteria, patronage, market value and the discourse of criticism, books and histories.[11] This is what is known as high culture. The intention of the graphic designer, on the other hand, is most often to render a message widely accessible with a systematic and public language. Whereas the art historian may address the subject of intention, and speak in terms of an artist's reaction as manifested in a unique object (although this is by no means all the art historian should do), the design historian, even when considering the object in its making, has to think in terms of a system, a group of people, and a process of manufacture. Although I have suggested that interpretative books will be less available for this recent period in contrast to earlier ones, this does not count them out entirely. To trace relevant books, as well as articles, you should use the art and design bibliographies. Articles from the design press are a major source of information and critical reviews and bibliographies usually list these by theme as well as by name. I include those most useful for graphic design at the end of this chapter.

Graphic Design Beyond Capitalism

Most of this chapter concerns approaches to design in the Western world, which has capitalism as its particular form of economic organization. Clearly graphic design exists in non-capitalist countries, as also in non-Western cultures. There has been considerable interest in the Soviet culture which followed the 1917 revolution, especially in the years of artistic experiment between 1917 and c.1928, known as 'Constructivism'. Forms of graphic communication played a tremendously significant part in the literacy campaigns during the revolution and posters were a central part of agitational propaganda. An artistic language that was not associated with the realism of Tsarist Russia, but was dependent on Parisian avant-garde ideas in painting, was preferred for a while. A detailed analysis of Constructivism, including a chapter on the events in publication and graphic design, is given in Christina Lodder, *Russian Constructivism* (1983), while for an anthology of manifestoes and artists' and designers' writings, I would recommend Stephen Bann, *The Tradition of Constructivism* (1974). The material is rich in questions concerning the place and form of mass-communications within a communist society. Many of these issues were formative for the debates that took place in the 1930s in Britain and the US. By studying how a system operated under a different economic organization, we can often distance and objectify our approach from the one with which we are familiar.

In the past, an interest in non-Western cultures has frequently started from an ethnocentric point of view. That is, other cultures are placed in relation to the West, and to their disadvantage. Too often the West was considered to be the dominant and more sophisticated culture, and used for establishing a set of comparisons by which other cultures were judged in a one-way relationship. This ideology informed artists and designers, who turned to oriental and tribal art and products to reinvigorate their work, finding attractive what they could not understand. Edward Said analyses the changes within this process in *Orientalism: Western Conceptions of the Orient* (1978).

The example of Japanese prints is illuminating with respect to graphic design. Japan's impact on the West was substantial once trade routes had been reopened after almost 200 years of isolation, in 1854.[12] In European capitals during the 1860s, a fashion for collecting Japanese artefacts for interiors was followed by painters, designers and architects adopting Japanese motifs and compositional devices and applying Japanese techniques. For graphic artists, Japanese woodblock prints were very different from the tradition of the European woodcut and the more recent wood-engraving. Their asymmetrical compositions, the unusual changes in scale in the depicted subjects, their concentration on silhouette, organic line and flattened patterns, were all borrowed. Painters such as Vincent van Gogh and Paul Gauguin started to integrate the effect of the woodcut in their paintings; other artists, including Édouard Manet, Henri de Toulouse-Lautrec and Édouard Vuillard, imitated woodblock effects in lithography, while Edvard Munch learnt how to cut woodblocks in the Japanese manner. For the historian of graphic design, there are many questions to be asked about the interaction between *fin-de-siècle* France and Japan. They might concern distinctions between what was borrowed directly and what was adapted stylistically and technically from Japanese prints. The contrasting markets for prints and their functions might be compared. For example, the print in France was partly developed as a commercial medium for advertising in the form of the poster, but also limited editions of lithographs and etchings were issued for private consumption. How does this compare with Japan? Were the Japanese woodcuts in Japan considered as art, or as a form of communication, or were these distinctions not made at that time?

To proceed, you would need to read about Japanese society, the patterns of work and leisure and find out what were the dominant moral and cultural attitudes. How the woodcut participated in forming these attitudes might be your focus. Whether you are considering Japanese or British graphic works, or the product of any other culture or period, it is always important that you recognise that your own background and attitudes will play their part in the sorts of questions that you ask.

Case Studies

I shall now give examples of three objects that have been chosen previously for design historical interpretation, in order to demonstrate which questions can be asked about graphic design.

Typographic Design
El Lissitzky, Pelikan Prospectus (1924), for Büro Bedarf (Office Equipment)

El Lissitzky's (1890–1941)
cover for the prospectus
for the stationery and office
equipment company Pelikan,
designed in 1924.

The basic structures of communication had been established by the turn of the century, as department stores, train stations, magazines, newspapers and all varieties of literature testified. The next stage was for many artists and designers to address this area, in the awareness that mass-reproduction needed aesthetic as well as technological criteria to govern it. Many of the principal theories underlying graphic communication were projected for the first time in the years following the First World War. In Holland, Germany and the Soviet Union especially, many design theories were formulated.[13] After several years of avant-garde activity, an embryonic language of abstraction could be said to have developed, which could be applied to design and architecture. In graphic design, this formal preparation was matched by technical advances, with improvements in photogravure printing for the reproduction of photography, followed by developments in colour printing and the sophistication of 16mm film techniques. El Lissitzky (1890–1941) had been trained as an engineer in Darmstadt prior to the war, and was conversant in debates concerning the role of the designer in the newly formed communist society of the Soviet Union. When approaching Lissitzky, you will find that there have been exhibitions devoted to him, and the definitive monograph by his wife, Sophie Lissitzky-Kuppers, *El Lissitzky – Life, Letters, Texts* (1980), assembles his writings and letters. Similarly, there is much written on debates within Constructivism, the movement in which Lissitzky's later work is placed. By pursuing these sources you find his statement on typography of 1923, one year before the Pelikan prospectus. Here, Lissitzky wrote of the importance of designing according to the visual quality of letters: 'optics instead of phonetics' was the phrase he used.[14] The way in which the whole page was used actively, with no sense of distinction between a foreground and background, and a concrete recognition of the weight of lettering was something he had developed from his abstract paintings and lithographs of earlier years, before moving to typographic design. Stylistically, we could connect this approach with de Stijl as well as with individual typographers such as Jan Tschichold and Herbert Bayer, who were also working on sans-serif typefaces based on geometry and simplification of form.[15]

We would be able to go a long way in talking about the work stylistically, and could also comment on how it fits into the sequence of Lissitzky's other designs. We could assume that this was bread-and-butter work, done when recovering from an illness while resident in Germany, by reading between the lines of the biography.

However from secondary sources there is apparently a limit to the kind of questions we can ask of an object, and because of this only a certain kind of history results. El Lissitzky is attributed as the 'designer', but we know little of the further circumstances of its production. For example, who did he work alongside, was there a design department or a publicity department at Pelikan, at that time? The monograph approach prevents other examples of Pelikan publicity from being shown in a book devoted to Lissitzky. By cross reference we can find that Herbert Spencer, *Pioneers of Modern Typography* (1984), illustrates examples of work by Kurt Schwitters for Pelikan, incorporating the same distinctive logo. El Lissitzky mentioned ideas about 'mobile and plastic advertising' also planned for the company.[16] Does this mean that someone at Pelikan was an enlightened patron of advanced design?

Our sources apparently produce material that make this design an isolated object. For although on earlier pages of the book we are shown posters also designed by Lissitzky for Pelikan, we know very little about how they related to one another. Where were they intended to be used? Was Lissitzky's choice of technique and colour expensive? The bronze on the lettering of 'Büro Bedarf' presumably was.

These types of questions are not restricted to this particular example, but can be applied to many of the reproductions of graphic work that you will encounter in the literature of graphic design. Quite often a piece of graphic design was destined for a specific context and had a currency that is subsequently lost. The original piece of design would be of a different size and texture and its general quality would most probably be unlike that of the clean page of a book. In order to find answers to this work by Lissitzky, the researcher would need to find out whether Pelikan has an archive. If not, then a search for references to the design in contemporary graphics journals would be useful. This example is a difficult one, as further research might require a reading knowledge of German and possibly Russian. I have chosen it as an example because it is a popular subject with students, and also because Constructivist design is a well-used reference within Post-Modern design. It would be appropriate now to outline the sort of questions that might be asked about a piece of graphic design. Before embarking on research, you could approach your example with such considerations as: Why was it designed? What is its technique? How should I characterise its style? Does the design imply that a set of principles or a design theory has been applied? In what context was it shown originally? Where am I seeing it now?

Cover for the Penguin Books edition of Vladimir Nabokov, *Laughter in the Dark*, 1963. The grid layout was the house style, overseen by the Penguin design department, which in this case incorporated an illustration by Morton Dimonstein.

Approaching Book Design:
Penguin Edition of Vladimir Nabokov, *Laughter in the Dark* (1963)

To understand the process of graphic design means more than simply placing a known designer in relation to his or her work. Once you leave the monograph approach behind, the sources of a history are diverse. The example of a paperback publishing company may help to show this.

The book illustrated is one that I happened to have on my shelf, and this shows how accessible the primary objects of graphic design history frequently are. On the cover are the book's title, the names of author and publisher, as well as the price. On the spine is a number – this is the company's number for the book and in more recent editions would be the ISBN (International Standard Book Number) – referring to the position of this title in the overall list. What is called the 'history' of the book is given on the verso of the frontispiece. Here we learn that the book was printed by Richard Clay of Bungay, and that it is set in Monotype Garamond typeface. The novel, we are told here, was first published in 1933, under the title *Kamera Obskura*, in Paris, and the author translated it for publication in 1938 in the US. Prior to Penguin's paperback edition, Weidenfeld & Nicolson had published it as a hardback in 1961 for distribution in the UK. We can analyse the cover, its colour, typography and layout. Familiar with other paperbacks, we know that this book is of conventional size and format, that there is a house style to which this volume conforms. Comment on the use of illustration, an engraving which is acknowledged on the inside cover to be by Morton Dimonstein, can also be made at this stage. Depicting a masked man, it is evocative rather than descriptive, a style of drawing that derives from the visual tradition of Expressionism.

At this stage the empirical or obvious evidence is exhausted. The next step is to pursue questions that take this object into the context of publication design in 1963, questions that assess how effective the design was and how it can be related to design issues of that period, and to consider the design, printing and marketing of paperback books.

To answer why the book looks as it does, a general sense of early 1960s design is important. By referring to surveys of graphic design and to the contemporary graphics press, especially *Graphis* and *Typographica* (first and second series), you can find comparative examples and also quite quickly find that Penguin Books occupied a place among seriously-considered design. Penguin has published its own history at different stages of its development, but apart from these publications you now need to move to secondary sources.[17]

Concerning the design of the book, you can consider the interior and exterior. The text was printed in a Monotype face. To read about the Monotype Corporation and how it made examples of historical typefaces available, at a time of hot-metal setting, refer to the writings of Stanley Morison.[18] Histories of printing and design are readily accessible in S.H. Steinberg, *Five Hundred Years of Printing* (1979), and John Lewis, *The Twentieth Century Book*, (1984), and one step is to place the typographic design of the book in a tradition. Again, if you are interested in the history of technology, you can investigate the technical considerations of paperback printing, those to do with paper, inks, size and binding. Cover design is the most controversial area of paperback design, and one that the historian needs to address. It is by the cover that the book is introduced to the public and the famous phrase, 'never judge a book by its cover' implies the potential conflict that might arise. In our example, the question of pictorial covers on a series that had become established and famous with typographical covers was a much-debated issue in the company and among the book-buying public. You need to ask who was responsible for the conception of the design. To speak of the 'designer' of the cover, you need to distinguish between the person responsible for the grid and house style of the book, and the illustrator or designer commissioned to provide the visual panel on the book. More difficult questions, but equally interesting ones, concern the cultural significance of such a design. What did it mean to put a commissioned illustration on a book cover, and what messages did it give? How did the illustration relate to the title? How did it help to sell the book, and to whom? Here questions of class and gender, age and interest can be raised. By this time in Britain, active marketing with front-forward display and self-service shops had changed patterns of book-buying, and Penguin Books were concerned to give a strong corporate identity in this competitive climate. To research the impact of this marketing change, you need to refer to trade journals, such as *The Bookseller* and *Publisher's Weekly*, rather than the design press. However, to assess the corporate solution made by the art director, Germano Facetti, for Penguin, you could refer to the design magazines of the period, to compare other publishers' design solutions and packaging. This need not be restricted to British examples, and an interesting comparison is with the French and German companies, Livres de Poche and Gallimard or DTV and Sührkamp.

To stray too far into editorial questions would take you into the social history of literature. Nevertheless, in order to assess whether the design was effective, you would need to understand the changes in editorial patterns. A familiarity with the subject of the books would also help. Why, for instance, should Nabokov be published in 1963? Was it at the first opportunity given, or did it reflect a positive campaign to introduce recent European and American writing? You may not be able to answer this directly, but to establish a sense of readership patterns you could refer to social histories of the period. One approach would be to relate publishing to changes in British society, the education system, the place of television and radio and changing patterns in leisure. *The Uses of Literacy* (1957) by Richard Hoggart, is an analysis of working-class life which attempts a broad cultural survey, giving invaluable background to the study of design of this period. I would also recommend Raymond Williams, *Communications* (1962), as a book which organises highly complex material about changes in the media in a useful way. Also at this introductory stage I would recommend Christopher Booker, *The Neophiliacs: A Study of the Revolution in English Life in the Fifties and Sixties* (1969), as a social history running parallel to Penguin Books' development.

Certain material or answers prove inaccessible during the process of historical investigation. You may find that the articles and books that you read do not provide information that you are looking for, or that the questions you think are important are not raised in the sources. This in itself is significant, if also frustrating. Occasionally your question may be inappropriate, but more often you may be pursuing a line of inquiry which connects things in new ways, for which the answers are not readily available.

With the example of the Penguin paperback book, I hope it becomes clear that graphic design history requires reference to many different fields. However the material which is the object of study is an important and accessible part of daily experience. A good visual analysis of an object, using the specific vocabulary that you will learn from other writers on design, is essential. To do this, it is a good idea to develop the habit of noticing the credits to designers at the end of television programmes, to check whether illustrators' or photographers' names are credited in magazines. Similarly, by looking carefully at the layout of the next book or magazine you read, consider: What was the role of the designer, typographer or illustrator? Can I place it in a stylistic category and, if not, how would it be best described? Are there any particularly noticeable features of the typography? By accumulating such references and training your eye, an approach to the history of graphic design can only be enhanced.

Analysis of a Magazine:
The Sunday Times Colour Supplement

The choice of magazine can reflect your own interests, and possibly the other areas of design you are studying. If you need some general ideas about the process of magazine layout, Jan V. White, *Magazine Design* (1982), is useful.[19] Most publication design is arranged according to a grid, which means that standardised and conforming column widths are applied throughout, and when illustrations are included, they are worked in as single, double or triple column widths, and so on.

Perhaps the most accessible kind of magazine for a first analysis is one of the Sunday supplements. The first of these in Britain, the *Sunday Times* colour supplement, was introduced in February 1962, and in spite of uncertainty about its potential in drawing advertisers, the magazine quickly became the model for many free supplements published by weekend and daily newspapers.

The supplement can be looked at as a designed product, in the way I have already suggested with the example of *Vogue* above. It also raises moral and political issues. In 1971, the writer and critic John Berger pointed out the impact of magazine advertising on the editorial content of a publication in his influential book, *Ways of Seeing*.[20] At the time, East Pakistani refugees were fleeing Bangladesh in the midst of civil war. Berger criticised the juxtaposition of a picture of refugees by the photojournalist Don McCullin with an advertisement for a bath oil. Consumerism and values of domestic comfort seemed badly out of place, but the two were connected, because advertising subsidised the publication, and because the position of the refugees was defined so acutely by this juxtaposition. Since *Ways of Seeing* was published, courses in Cultural Studies have extended this interest in the relationship of the media with political and ideological structures. For example, the Glasgow Media Group has studied television news programmes.[21] The Group's suggestion, an underlying principle of a sociological approach, is that language cannot be objective. In verbal language, factors such as the amount of time spent on the different sides of the debate, the adjectives used to describe news events and the tone of the newsreader's voice all construct an 'interested' point of view. The Group provides analysis and statistics to support this view.

An example of this approach applied to a historical study is Stuart Hall's *The Social Eye of Picture Post* (1972). Hall examined the position of the illustrated weekly magazine, *Picture Post*, which had begun in 1938 and continued during the Second World War. He was concerned to place *Picture Post* in the range of political options available to journalists and photographers during the war, and to evaluate the usual assumption that *Picture Post* represented a left-of-centre position. To do this, Hall analysed the 'construction' of messages through photographic and textual narrative. He concluded that the war had the impact of changing the subjects covered by the magazine: instead of the pressing social concerns of housing, education and a probing approach, the language and sequences of photographs went towards resolving problems and providing a positive vision of a Britain worth fighting for. If you are interested in ways to extend analysis to such questions of ideology and meaning, I would recommend this essay as a possible starting point.

Hall's essay is an early example of a historical analysis which is theorised. In this case he used Soviet and French theory about narrative construction. Since the early 1970s reference to texts that can clarify methods of approach has become more frequent, particularly in histories that attempt to explain the *meaning* of an object as well as its *production*.

Advertising

My final comments are on approaches to advertising design. Instead of a case study of one example, it is more useful to remain at the general level of methods of analysis, as the system is so large, and often similar approaches can be applied, with discrimination, to different examples.

Advertising is one of the most abundant forms of visual communication, occurring in diverse contexts, on street hoardings, in film and television, as well as in newspapers and magazines and collectively known as 'press advertisements'. Appropriately for such a vast system, there are many methods of approach and analysis to be taken by the commentator or historian. These can be broadly categorised into three types. First, there are the insiders' stories, explaining the intentions and techniques of particular campaigns, as well as tales of their success or failure. For an amusing early account, I would recommend Ernest Sackville Turner, *The Shocking History of Advertising* (1965), and for a more recent account, *Ogilvy on Advertising* (1983). The promotion of products, whether as a brand name or as a type, is another way insiders' stories about advertising are related. An interesting version of the former is Brian Sibley, *The Book of Guinness Advertising* (1985), whereas Michael Frostick, *Advertising and the Motorcar* (1970), compares advertising campaigns for different brands of the same product. Especially in the US, there has been a tradition of publishing tributes to successful campaigns or selecting examples from a company's work, as in Lawrence Dobrow, *When Advertising Tried Harder* (1984), which traces the highly successful work of Doyle Dane Bernbach. From such a source, a mixture of empirical evidence and private anecdote can be gained, but I would recommend that you assess critically any evaluation of the design's success.

The second category of writing on advertising is that which addresses the moral issues of consumer culture. Vance Packard, *The Hidden Persuaders* (1957), was an exposé of advertising techniques in the US, which condemned the use of market research and 'mass psychoanalysis to guide campaigns of persuasion'.[22] Packard's approach was new at the time, and formative for subsequent cultural criticism, especially as his attack was based on a knowledge of advertising in the US, where it was at its most sophisticated. For an analysis of British traditions in advertising and the special part played by the promises in the slogans and advertising copylines, Raymond Williams' essay, 'Advertising, the magic system', is instructive.[23] His point of view is an example of a moral, left-wing indictment of advertising. He argues that the structures of advertising turn people from 'users' to 'consumers', and that the practice of finding words and images to persuade someone to believe that their lives will be transformed 'if they do this' is dishonest and hides real needs behind a language of magic.

Thirdly, for the historian or designer, a system of analysis that provides a specialist language that can be applied to a diverse set of examples from advertising has its appeal. Such an approach is offered by 'semiology'. This can be defined as 'the science of signs'. The term semiology derives from the work of the linguist Ferdinand de Saussure and its possible applications are taken up by advertising agencies and universities alike, although by no means all agencies consider de Saussure or practise semiotics. De Saussure's *A Course in General Linguistics* (1974) was concerned to study the way language produces meaning. He distinguished between what an object is and how it is depicted linguistically or visually. For example, we know the difference between a picture of a cow, the word 'cow' and the animal in the field, but accept the conventions by which we call that animal (and all other animals in the species) 'cow'. De Saussure suggested that the word 'cow' be called a 'sign': it is used to label an object. For the purposes of analysis, the sign is broken down to the 'signified', which is the meaning of the object, and the 'signifier', which is the object itself. In the case of the cow, it becomes a particular cow by the process of signification; colour, texture, size and associative values are added to the animal, to make it a real cow with qualities that we can refer to, whether they are 'holy', 'frightening' or 'brown'. De Saussure believed that in daily experience we do not distinguish between the signifier and signified, but he also argued that it was at this abstract level of signification that so much of our knowledge and meaning is given to representation.

Advertising is not referred to in De Saussure's work, but it is an appropriate area for such analysis, because it depends on an immediate and efficient system of references, which can be understood by a wide audience. More than anyone else, the French sociologist Roland Barthes extended the application of semiology to visual language. During the modern period, art historians have developed ways of studying past paintings by iconography and iconology, suggesting meanings for depicted figures and subjects that are no longer readily apparent or available to the contemporary viewer. Semiology provided a similar method of looking at contemporary images from popular culture, which depended on an equally elaborate system as painting. In the compilation of his short essays, *Mythologies* (1973), Barthes tested his opinion that a viewer reads associative meanings into advertisements and other photographic imagery. Among subjects he discussed were the face of Greta Garbo, the new Citroën (the DS 19), and cooking articles from *Elle* magazine. For Barthes, popular visual images were made up of signs, often understood unconsciously by the public. He applied the idea from social anthropology, that as long as a system is consistent, it need not be logical or relate to a real world; instead it can develop what he called a mythical structure. In advertising, this meant that the possible contradictions of life are avoided by constructing an ideal world. Barthes explained his theory in the essays 'The photographic message' and 'The rhetoric of the image', which are in the anthology *Image Music Text* (1977). For a commentary on semiology, I would recommend Terence Hawkes, *Structuralism and Semiotics* (1979).

In the case of advertising, values can be given to consumer objects, status can be given to film actors and properties given to consumer durables, which are fictional. For example, a woman in a cosmetic advertisement is presented as having 'perfect' skin. If we read the caption we are given information that persuades us, giving an explanation of how she has achieved it, with references to science as well as a promise of transformation. Barthes' approach would be to consider the language of the copy for the hidden associative values in the writing. Semiology would also suggest that we could 'decode' the photograph here, black and white, clinical, and with light used as an active element in the composition, to reinforce the authority of the text. Although we may agree that the idea of pure skin is physiologically impossible, as we look at the advertisement we make the imaginative leap to believe that by using that product our skin could be similar.

An advertisement for Lancôme, from *Vogue* magazine, November, 1986. A semiological analysis might question the use of words or the interaction of word and image.

Judith Williamson, *Decoding Advertisements* (1978), is an example of this approach applied to a range of commonplace press advertisements. Like Barthes', her language is specific and theoretical, using recent French philosophical ideas. If you are interested in extending this approach to advertising in which a narrative is implied, Erving Goffman, *Gender Advertisements* (1979), shows how advertising uses the language of the theatre to suggest relationships between the sexes which can be understood at a glance.

As you might have guessed from the use of the word 'structure' in explaining Barthes' work. The semiological approach to an object should be distinguished from the historical. Barthes assumed the existence of the image or object he is interested in. Instead of asking how has this object been *made*, and considering the range of possible determinants and conditions that surrounded its making, the semiologist asks how this object *gives* meaning. In this case the *consumption* of design is the focus. The designer is no different from a member of the public, and is not the 'author' of the work, with a privileged understanding of its entirety. The emphasis tends to be on the contemporary reading – Barthes does not ask whether it was different to look at the same image at other times, a question that should interest the historian.

As a way of analysing graphic imagery, there is much that can be learnt from such sources. When you read them, you should test whether they are guilty of 'reading in' meaning that might not have been present at the time of the making or the original reception of the advertisement. The advantage of the semiological approach for a history of graphic design is that it takes the subject from the particular to the general, to place single images within a system of representation, a process which in turn questions cultural values.

Graphic design is a rich and complex subject and the possible approaches to the study of its history reflect that richness and complexity. In this chapter I have indicated some possible approaches to its study with examples of book, poster and advertising design. The semiological approach to advertising design can provide rewarding insights although initially it may seem rather daunting. It is however a technique that is being applied to an increasing range of two- and three-dimensional designs, particularly under the influence of Post-Modernism.

Jeremy Aynsley is Director of Research at the Royal College of Art, London.
First published in *Design History: A Student's Handbook*, Allen & Unwin, 1987.

1 As quoted in Raymond Williams, 'Advertising, the magic system', in *Problems in Materialism and Culture* (London: Verso, 1979), p.181.

2 For such early examples of visual language, see Josef Müller-Brockmann, *A History of Visual Communications* (1971).

3 Milton Glaser resists being labelled, as the article in *Design and Art Direction* (12 July 1985), showed. For Glaser's earlier work, see *Milton Glaser Designer* (London: Secker & Warburg, 1973).

4 For a commentary on Marshall McLuhan's ideas, see Jonathan Miller, *McLuhan* (London: Fontana, 1971).

5 See Julian Petley, *Capital and Culture: German Cinema, 1933–45* (London: British Film Institute, 1979) and David Welch, ed., *Nazi Propaganda* (London: Barnes and Noble, 1983).

6 For the work of Polish poster design there are several magazine articles, but fewer books in English. The range of visual styles can be seen in *Das Polnische Plakat von 1892 bis Heute* (The Polish Poster from 1892 until Today) (Berlin: Hochschule der Kunste, 1980). John Barnicoat, *A Concise History of Posters* (London: Thames & Hudson, 1972), outlines the general tradition of poster design.

7 See Atelier Populaire, *Posters from the Revolution* (London: Dobson, 1969).

8 See William Schneider, 'What is an Art Director?' in *Art Director's Eighteenth Annual* (New York: Longmans Green, 1939).

9 For an introduction to *Vogue*, see William Packer, *The Art of Vogue Covers, 1909–40* (London: Octopus, 1980).

10 Walter Benjamin, member of the Frankfurt School of Social Research, was interested in photography as it changed the status of the art object. See his essays, 'The Work of Art in the Age of Mechanical Reproduction', in Stanley Mitchell, ed., *Understanding Brecht* (London: New Left Books, 1977) and 'The Author as Producer', in Hannah Arendt, ed., *Illuminations* (London: Fontana, 1973). For a commentary on Benjamin and other members of the Frankfurt School see Perry Anderson, *Considerations on Western Marxism* (London: Verso, 1979) and Janet Wolff, *The Social Production of Art* (London: Macmillan, 1985).

11 Marcia Pointon, *History of Art: A Students' Handbook* (London: Allen & Unwin (revised edn 1986)).

12 See Frank Whitford, *Japanese Prints and Western Painters* (London: Studio Vista, 1977). For the French prints affected by the Japanese prints refer to the British Museum catalogue, *From Manet to Toulouse-Lautrec: French Lithographs 1860–1900* (London: British Museum Publications, 1978), and for Japanese prints see *Japanese Prints: 300 Years of Albums and Books* (London: British Museum Publications, 1980).

13 For an introduction to the period, see Reyner Banham, *Theory and Design in the First Machine Age* (London: Architectural Press, 1960).

14 Sophie Lissitzky-Kuppers, *El Lissitzky – Life, Letters, Texts* (London: Thames & Hudson (revised edn, 1980)), p.359.

15 For this work, see Herbert Spencer, *Pioneers of Modern Typography* (revised edn, 1984) and *Bauhaus Typographie* (Düsseldorf: Edition Marzona, 1985).

16 Lissitzky-Kuppers, op.cit., p.57.

17 See William Emrys Williams, *The Penguin Story* (Harmondsworth: Penguin, 1956), and *Fifty Penguin Years* (Harmondsworth: Penguin, 1985).

18 Stanley Morison, *A Tally of Types* (Cambridge: Cambridge University Press, 1973), and *The Typographic Book, 1450–1935* (London: Benn, 1963).

19 Also extremely useful, Harold Evans, *Editing and Design, Books I–V* (London: Heinemann, 1973), considers the stages of newspaper production. Volume IV is on *Picture Editing* and Volume V is on *Newspaper Design*.

20 John Berger, *Ways of Seeing* (London: BBC and Penguin Books, 1972) was also produced as a BBC television series in that year.

21 Glasgow Media Group, *Bad News* (London: Routledge & Kegan Paul, 1976). This was followed by *More Bad News* (London: Routledge & Kegan Paul, 1980) and *Really Bad News* (London: Writers and Readers Press, 1982).

22 Vance Packard, *The Hidden Persuaders* (Harmondsworth: Penguin 1961), p.11.

23 Williams, op.cit., p.2.

DESIGN
& CULTURE

AN ANTHOLOGY OF
WRITING FROM THE
AIGA JOURNAL OF
GRAPHIC DESIGN

EDITED BY STEVEN HELLER AND MARIE FINAMORE

IS THERE A CANON
OF GRAPHIC DESIGN HISTORY?

MARTHA SCOTFORD
1991

A *canon*, defined by the *American Heritage Dictionary* as it might relate to graphic design, is a basis for judgment; a standard; a criterion; an authoritative list (as of the works of an author or designer). The word was originally used to designate the books of the Bible officially recognized by the Church. The concept of *canon* is under debate right now in literary/educational circles, as its existence is alleged to produce a culturally narrow and elitist university curriculum, among other cultural problems.

Having followed the discussion about the problems arising from the study of literature produced mainly by Western white males, it occurred to me that the study of graphic design history, coming out of its infancy, may be producing its own canon, perhaps unintentionally and unconsciously. What would such a canon consist of? Are there designers and works that are used to represent whole periods, styles, and theories in graphic design history? Are some designers' works more revered than others? Why? Judgments are implied when certain designers and works become better known than others; is this process wholly legitimate and deserved? What is it based on? What problems will it cause for the future study of graphic design history?

Premise

I wane to make it very clear at the outset chat in suggesting a canon here, I do not wish to perpetuate one; only to show one may exist for the purpose of discussion. Given what I believe is its unintentional nature, it may be that there are 'mistakes': this could be *a* canon, but not *the* canon of graphic design. It could very well be that some designers and their work do not belong here or that others have been overlooked.

If a canon of graphic design exists, or is developing, how can this be proved? The specific period I am discussing here, modern graphic design, is broadly dated as beginning in 1850. Given the visual nature of the subject, it is most strongly established and communicated in a visual way, i.e., by reproduction, especially in books. Exhibitions and poster reproductions could also be studied, but books seem the most widely available and least ephemeral source at present to explore the presence of a canon.

Method

Five books were chosen for the study; these represent the best known general historical surveys of the past twenty years. The following is a description, alphabetical by author, of each volume and explains the criteria cited by the authors (with page reference noted) used for the inclusion of design works in each of the volumes. It also includes the limitations, if any, of each for the purposes of this study.

1. James Craig and Bruce Barton, *Thirty Centuries of Graphic Design* (New York: Watson-Guptill Publications, 1987), 224 pages; 10 pages for study period; 400 black-and-white illustrations. The subtitle, 'An Illustrated Survey,' accurately describes the prolific use of reproductions over text. The text is more in outline form than prose, and is often in the form of timelines, lists, and technical sidebars. The book starts with prehistory and includes more discussion and reproductions of the fine art concurrent with graphic design than do the other books in this study. 'Designers and illustrators have been carefully selected to show diversity and to create a feel for a specific period.' (p.9.)

2. Alan Fern and Mildred Constantine, *Word and Image* (New York: Museum of Modern Art, 1968), 160 pages; 138 pages devoted to study period; 211 illustrations, 30 in full color. The most limited resource, in subject matter, for this study because it is restricted to posters and to those in the MoMA collection. However, it is critical because posters, collected and saved, have always been one of the most prominent and important media in graphic design and its history. In addition, this particular collection is large and well regarded. It must be accepted that there have been judgments at all levels: what was selected for the collection and then what was chosen for inclusion in the book (about ten percent of the collection). Critical selection is what makes a canon. The preface to the books states that works for the collection have been 'selected primarily for their aesthetic quality, but also include work of mainly historical or social significance'. (Constantine, p.6.)

In his essay's introduction, Fern states that the book 'is a brief history of the modern poster (and its close typographical relatives) as an arc form. I have limited my investigations to those designers who have approached the poster as a means of expression as well as communication, and have explored graphic design and typography as serious creative media'. (p.11.)

3. Steven Heller and Seymour Chwast, *Graphic Style: From Victorian to Postmodern* (New York: Harry N. Abrams, 1988), 238 pages; 233 for study period; over 700 illustrations, 225 in color. This is the most recent publication and covers exactly the period under discussion. The book is a survey like the others, but makes no attempt at scholarly analysis. Rather, it 'is primarily concerned with the images, not the image maker... we consistently emphasize the formal, emblematic visual characteristics of a design period ... we are tracing nothing less than the evolution of the popular tastes of the period'. (p.12.)

This is the only volume among the five to concentrate on visual form. It is notable for its many anonymous pieces and for the breadth of its visual offerings.

4. Philip B. Meggs, *A History of Graphic Design* (New York: Van Nostrand Reinhold, 1983), 511 pages; 335 pages on study period; over 1,000 illustrations, all black-and-white. The first survey published in the United States, this book appeared just as many design programs were incorporating graphic design history into their curricula. It has become the textbook for such courses and the standard reference for design professionals. The author expresses the necessity for the understanding of the past so 'we will be better able to continue a cultural legacy of beautiful form and effective communication'. (p.xi.) The survey begins with the invention of writing after the pictograph and petroglyphs of prehistoric times.

5. Josef Müller-Brockmann, *A History of Visual Communication* (Niggli/Teufen, Switzerland, 1971), 334 pages; 214 for study period; 570 illustrations, 6 in color. The only European publication among the five, this was the first historical survey of the subject to be published. It explores the wide scope of the field that its well-known author/designer considers more accurately termed *visual communication* than *graphic design*. He states that the survey is not complete, but he has 'concentrated on those aspects of particular interest to me: factual advertising, experiments which influence our thinking, and artistic works which set the stylistic trend'. (p.6.) The book begins its discussion with prehistoric cave paintings and early writing forms.

Criteria for Analysis

Having selected these books for study, what are the criteria for tabulating what is published in them? One, of course, is the visual imprint – how certain works and designers are made more memorable than others by differences controlled by size, color, and repetition. A caveat is in order: I have no pretensions to being a social scientist and have developed the tabulation system here as a way to prove relative rather than absolute presence of designers and works. I have been as accurate as possible with the tabulation, and the numerical interpretation (using the median and setting the categories) is governed by my desire to be inclusive. It is hoped that no one will waste time recounting the numbers. That is not the point.

The study began with the creation of a list (alphabetical by author), tabulating each reproduction of a design work and noting whether that reproduction is black-and-white or color, and its relative size to other work in the book. In general, small is any size up to one-quarter page; medium is one third to two thirds of a page; large is two thirds to full page. Once this list of 286 designers/partners was compiled for each book, and the information from all books was combined, the list was edited to cull a list of all the designers (205) who were represented at least twice among the five books: either a single work reproduced in two different books, or two different works shown in one or two books. The list was then studied to discover what patterns of appearance might exist among the designers and the works that could prove a canon existed. It could then describe what it contained. Once this tabulation was complete, these findings were broken down even further, to study other criteria for each designer:

1. Total number of individual works reproduced.
2. Total number of all works reproduced.
3. Number of repeats (#2 minus #1).
4. Total number of large reproductions.
5. Total number of medium reproductions.
6. Number of large and medium reproductions (#4 plus #5).
7. Total number of color reproductions.
8. Total number of large reproductions in color.
9. Total number of single works reproduced four times (four books).
10. Total number of single works reproduced three times.
11. Total number of single works reproduced twice in color.
12. Country of birth/significant practice.
13. Gender.
14. Born before 1900.
15. Born 1900–1919.
16. Born 1920–1929.
17. Born 1930–1939.
18. Born after 1940.
19. Deceased.

From the edited list of 205 designers, a smaller list (63) was made of designers/partners who had a significant appearance in at least one category of the first eleven. *Significant* was defined as having a number two-below the median for that category or higher. The results of this operation were studied and the absolute lack of women was duly noted. I decided to include on the list those women designers (6 out of 14) having the highest frequency of reproduced works. As well, a very few other well-known designers were allowed, whose numbers were just below the cutoff point and were interesting in relation to the others. I fully realize this might be a

DESIGNER	Total # individual works reproduced	Total # works reproduced	Total # repeats	Total # large	Total # medium	Large & Medium	Total # in color	Total # large & in color	Total # × 4	Total # × 3	Total # × 2 and in color	Born before 1900	Born between 1900–1919	Born between 1920–1929	Born between 1930–1939	Born between 1940	Deceased	Country of birth / significant practice
MEDIAN	*18*	*23*	*5*	*3*	*8*	*11*	*3*	*1*	*1*	*2*	*1*							
Baumberger	4	4	0	3	1	4	1	*1*	0	0	0	•	•	•	•	•	•	Switzerland
Bayer	**30**	**40**	**10**	**4**	**17**	**21**	**0**	**0**	**2**	**1**	**0**		•				•	**Austria/Germany**
Beardsley	16	16	0	1	3	4	1	0	0	0	0	•					•	Great Britain
Beggarstaff	5	8	*3*	*3*	2	5	0	0	0	1	0	•					•	Great Britain
Behrens	11	17	6	1	6	7	0	0	*1*	0	0	•					•	Germany
Bernhard	9	12	3	2	2	4	3	*1*	0	1	*1*	•					•	Germany
Bill	15	19	4	3	9	12	0	0	0	1	0		•				?	Switzerland
Binder	5	9	4	0	2	2	0	0	*1*	0	0	•					•	Austria
Bonnard	3	6	3	1	4	5	1	0	0	1	0	•					•	France
Bradley	*18*	19	1	0	6	6	1	0	0	0	0	•					•	United States
Brodovitch	14	15	1	0	5	5	1	0	0	0	0	•					•	Russia/France/US
Carlu	5	9	4	2	3	5	2	*1*	*1*	0	0		•				•	France
Casey*	4	4	0	0	2	2	0	0	0	0	0			•				United States
Cassandre	**19**	**27**	**8**	**6**	**12**	**18**	**7**	**2**	**0**	**3**	**1**		•				•	**Russia/France**
Cheret	11	15	4	1	7	8	2	0	0	2	0	•					•	France
Chermayeff & Geismar	15	15	0	0	5	5	0	0	0	0	0			•				Great Britain/US
Erdt	2	4	2	1	1	2	1	0	0	1	0	•					•	Germany
Glaser	11	12	1	1	1	2	0	0	0	0	0			•				United States
Golden	5	7	2	0	2	2	0	0	0	1	0		•				•	United States
Grasset	8	10	2	0	3	3	0	0	0	1	0	•					•	France
Greiman*	8	9	1	1	2	3	0	0	0	0	0				•			United States
Heartfield	*19*	19	0	0	5	5	2	0	0	0	0	•					•	Germany
Hofmann	11	12	1	1	3	4	2	0	0	0	0			•				Switzerland
Hohlwein	12	17	5	2	*10*	*12*	3	0	0	1	0	•					•	Germany
Huber	7	1	2	2	4	0	0	0	0	0	0		•					Switerland/Italy
Huszar	7	10	3	0	4	4	1	0	0	1	0	•					•	Netherlands
Kamekura	10	12	2	1	2	3	0	0	0	1	0		•				•	Japan
Kauffer	16	20	4	*4*	4	8	5	*2*	0	0	0	•					•	US/Great Britain
Lissitzky	**39**	**49**	**10**	**6**	**17**	**23**	**4**	**3**	**1**	**4**	**1**	•					•	**Russia/Germany**
Lubalin	*21*	21	0	0	5	5	0	0	0	0	0		•				•	United States
Macintosh	5	9	4	0	8	8	2	0	0	1	0	•					•	Great Britain
Marinetti	6	10	4	0	2	2	0	0	0	1	0	•					•	Italy
Matter	**16**	**25**	**9**	**4**	**9**	**13**	**3**	**1**	**1**	**1**	**0**	•					•	**Switzerland/US**
Moholy-Nagy	**18**	**23**	**5**	**1**	**11**	**12**	**2**	**1**	**0**	**1**	**0**	•					•	**Hungary/Germany/US**
Morris	9	13	4	*3*	3	6	0	0	0	0	0	•					•	Great Britain
Moscoso	5	6	1	0	3	3	4	0	0	0	0				•		•	United States
Moser	16	7	0	7	7	2	0	*1*	*1*	0	0	•					•	Austria
Mucha	12	12	0	1	5	6	2	0	0	0	0	•					•	Czechoslovakia/France
Müller-Brockmann	**14**	**23**	**9**	**3**	**12**	**15**	**4**	**1**	**0**	**3**	**1**		•				•	**Switzerland**
Neuberg	7	7	0	2	2	4	1	*1*	0	0	0		•				?	Switzerland
Philips	5	5	0	1	0	1	5	*1*	0	0	0	•					•	United States
Rand	*24*	28	4	2	7	9	0	0	0	0	0		•				•	United States
Ray	5	3	2	0	4	4	0	0	0	1	0	•					•	US/France
Rodchenko	*18*	18	0	1	7	8	5	0	0	0	0	•					•	Russia
Roller	6	8	2	0	3	3	1	0	0	1	0	•					•	Austria
Rudin*	5	5	0	2	4	5	0	0	0	0	0			•				Switzerland
Schelmmer	3	5	2	0	2	2	0	0	0	1	0	•					•	Germany
Schuitema	7	7	0	2	3	5	0	0	0	0	0	•					•	Netherlands
Schmidt	8	13	5	0	7	7	0	0	*1*	0	0	•					•	Germany
Schultz-Neu	1	3	2	0	2	2	1	0	0	1	0	•					•	Germany
Schwitters	11	13	2	2	2	4	3	*1*	0	0	0	•					•	Germany
Sutnar	*23*	25	2	0	7	7	0	0	0	0	0	•					•	Czechoslovakia/US
Thompson	10	10	0	0	5	5	1	0	0	0	0		•					United States
Tissi*	5	6	1	0	0	0	1	0	0	0	0				•			Switzerland
Toulouse-Lautrec	**11**	**17**	**6**	**2**	**12**	**14**	**5**	**2**	**0**	**0**	**1**	•					•	**France**
Tschichold	*20*	20	4	2	8	10	1	*1*	0	1	0		•				•	Germany/Switzerland
Van de Velde	6	9	3	0	5	5	1	0	*1*	0	0	•					•	Belgium
Van Doesberg	9	12	3	1	3	4	*4*	*1*	0	1	0	•					•	Netherlands
Vivarelli	7	10	3	1	6	7	0	0	*1*	0	0		•				?	Switzerland
Weingart	14	14	0	0	3	3	2	0	0	0	0					•		Switzerland
Wyman & Terr	7	8	1	*3*	5	8	0	0	0	0	0				•			United States
Yokoo	7	8	1	1	2	3	*4*	*1*	0	0	0				•			Japan
Zwart	**21**	**29**	**8**	**1**	**14**	**15**	**0**	**0**	**0**	**1**	**0**	•					•	**Netherlands**

Boldface = Canon   * *Female*   *(Median) numbers in italic* canon trap in itself; my reasoning is that one instinctively looks for certain designers and would want to see these numbers for comparison. I think these inclusions strengthen the example.

Discovering the Canon

The table gives the corresponding numbers for the sixty-three designers/partners and each criterion. These are not scores or ratings; this is not a contest. These numbers reveal the relative weight/importance that these specific five books have placed on certain designers and works.

The numbers in bold are those that are considered significant for the final cut of the list; these fall at or above the median for each category. This again seems the broadest way to include individuals. You will notice a range in the amount of bold numbers among the designers. There are eleven categories; it was decided that if a designer had bold numbers in five or more categories (that is, a significant showing in eleven criteria), that designer had been consistently 'featured' by the majority of the books and could be considered part of the canon of graphic design. The table here produces a canon of eight designers (in alphabetical order): Herbert Bayer, Afonse Mouron Cassandre, El Lissitzky, Herbert Matter, Laszlo Moholy-Nagy, Josef Müller-Brockmann, Henri de Toulouse Lautrec and Piet Zwart.

Interpreting the Canon

What do we notice about this group? First, and more about this later, the canon is all male. They were all born before 1920, several before 1900, and all but one (Müller-Brockmann) are deceased. They are all native Europeans: two are from Eastern Europe (Lissitzky and Moholy-Nagy; Cassandre was born in Russia to French parents, but left Russia to attend school); two are French (Cassandre and Toulouse-Lautrec); two are Swiss (Müller-Brockmann and Matter); one is Austrian (Bayer); and one is Dutch (Zwart).

Are there surprises here? Perhaps the only surprise is Toulouse-Lautrec, who, though considering him important to poster history, most would not expect to make the graphic design canon. One should question the inclusion of Müller-Brockmann because he is the author of one of the books; however, records seem to indicate he has been approximately as generous to himself as was Meggs.

More surprises in the inclusion area: chauvinistically, we might murmur, 'What, no Americans?' And there are several poster 'masters' – you can fill in your favorites – who might be expected on the list. Each period/style has its heroes, but, across the broad survey period, it is difficult for these individuals to stand out consistently. There are also several designers who have very respectable showings in the category of 'number of reproductions,' but who have not been set apart by size or color of such.

A possible explanation for some of these exclusions may be the nature of the work. For instance, Armin Hofmann's revered posters are originally in black and white, so featuring him by a color category is difficult. (This is one example of the possible disservice to individual designers by the criteria used for this list.) Another designer in a similar situation is William Morris. He worked as a graphic designer primarily in book design; books are mostly printed in black and white.

Other designers, working mainly with typography, are using smaller formats that are seldom reproduced in a large format.

One case struck me as a serious misrepresentation of the designer's work, not in the number of reproductions, but the nature of them. Cheret's posters were and are important for their pioneering use of color, both technically in historical terms and aesthetically for the richness of the effects he achieved in lithography. Yet, these five books present only two of his works in color.

Interestingly, after the initial curiosity of discovering the canon's identity, the rest of the list shows how different designers are represented in the books, and brings to mind those designers who have not made the edited (and amended) list of 63. Here, in my opinion, are the more intriguing cases of inclusion and exclusion.

The most obvious distinction, about which I do not intend to get polemical, is that of gender. There are no women in this canon. There are six women represented on the edited/ amended list, four of them independent designers. (Margaret and Frances McDonald were part of the Mackintosh group and had less to do with graphics than other design formats.) The numbers for the independent four indicate they are poorly represented in all categories. There may be explanations, but not many excuses: the women are all younger than the men (two of the women born in the 1920s, one in the 1930s, one in the 1940s) and therefore have had shorter careers (less production is not always a correlation). But even comparing the two oldest, Casey and Rudin, with male designers of their generation, Glaser and Hofmann, produces a serious discrepancy. And the youngest woman, Greiman, is reproduced more frequently than the rest, but not featured as well as the second youngest, Tissi. Once we have passed into the post Second World War generation, there are many more female designers from which to choose, but this option has not been exercised. Possibly, there are problems with critical distance, yet the contributions of Muriel Cooper, Barbara Stauffacher Soloman and Sheila Levrant de Bretteville (among others) have been recognized elsewhere.

As stated before, I believe the canon that exists was unintentionally created. That is, each book in the study is an individual set of decisions. But what were all those decisions based on? Aesthetics? Economics? And who made the decisions? Authors? Publishers? Book designers? Clive Dilnot pointed to (his problem in 1984, before several of the books used for this study were published:

'At present, there is no real discipline of design criticism, but a canonical list of "important" design and designers is rapidly being established, despite that the critical arguments for their inclusion in such a list remain almost unstated. We are seeing this sharp differentiation into "important" and "unimportant" design works, which is tending to exclude the unimportant works from the definition of design and to restrict the material we actually discuss.'[1]

Each book is a different and separate case, and no specific research has been done by me on this aspect. But one anecdotal piece of evidence leads me to suspect the general logic I would otherwise credit to the authors: the relative and real sizes of the reproductions in each book are related to the design format of that book. One assumes the authors of each are selecting the pieces to be reproduced, and that they have some reasonable idea of what they consider more or less important for their particular presentation – and would seek to express this by size and color. However, Philip B. Meggs has told me that the publisher's designer did the layouts for his book and, as that particular inexperienced designer was not a historian, the design works were used to fill six pages as needed. For purposes of the canon, this is the reality that the reader finds, assuming there are few other resources for the beginning graphic design student.

There may be some other practical issues affecting the canon. The availability of works for reproduction is affected by several factors. Some works that a conscientious author would want to show are not available due to collection restrictions, or the cost of permission is prohibitive. There may be copyright restrictions. In many cases, where no source is given for the work, it is from a private collection that may also be that of the author. How does this affect selection? In only one area might it be salutary: the increased inclusion of anonymous work.

What about color? Two of the five books have no color reproductions at all; one (Müller-Brockmann) has very few. The decision is mainly about economics, the trade-off being the ability to print more black-and-white illustrations rather than fewer in black and white plus a few in full color. A cursory inspection of *Word and Image* shows that the appearance of a poster in color may have more to do with its location relative to page imposition than with aesthetics or critical importance. Looking through *Graphic Style* also reveals that specific pages in each signature are available for color; it is hard to assess how much this dictates to the authors and how much they will work within this production limitation. *The History of Visual Communication*, with so few reproductions in color (only six), may be the only book to express an accurate opinion with color.

Does this dismiss color as a criteria? Yes and no. Since it is my belief that this canon and the list it generates are unconsciously created, we need not be concerned with the lack of control on the author's part over color, but we do need to deal with the reality of the reader. Not knowing and/or not concerned about bookmaking, the reader may naturally assume color has significance and will pay more attention to and remember works shown in color. If we consider color a non-category, given this discussion, what happens to the canon if color is removed as a criterion? Left with eight criteria (the median then becomes four), are there significant changes? No, the eight designers remain and no one is added. The color categories remain.

As I have mentioned, many designers' works have been reproduced in healthy numbers; that is, the books have provided a reasonably broad presentation of the possible designer pool (exceptions as noted). Some designers you might have expected in the canon have a strong presence in the books, based on frequency of appearance: Beardsley, Bill, Bradley, Brodovitch, Chermayeff & Geismar, Heartfield, Hohlwein, Kauffer, Lubalin, Rand, Rodchenko, Sutnar, Tschichold and Weingart. If this group is added to the Canon Eight, we get a much broader selection by geography/nationality and by generation (but still no women).

You will undoubtedly have thought of some designers you consider important and will have attempted to find them on the list here. Lustig and Danziger are two that come to mind. They both have considerable western US connections. Is there bias for the East Coast in this list? De Harak and Vignelli are two others who do not appear on the final list. It is true that it takes time for judgments of historical and contemporary importance of individual designers to be made. This is the most obvious reason we see so few postwar generation designers represented: careers are not long enough yet; the time-distance is not sufficient, and there are so many more to choose among than in the case of earlier generation designers. The same cannot be said for the generation born in the twenties and thirties; they are quite sparse on the list here and have certainly developed their work/careers sufficiently for us to assess it.

The canon and the list are Western biased (First and Second worlds). Some of the books have sought to partially redress the imbalance with some work from the Far East and Third World nations. Japan, as the Eastern nation with (he most highly developed (in a Western sense) graphic design, is represented by two designers: Kamakura, of the first generation to adapt Western/Swiss design, and Yokoo, much younger and influential here in the early 1970s. They are better represented than any of the women.

Other questions and comparisons will occur to you. Feel free to use the table to satisfy your curiosity. There are even some silly discoveries: accounting for variations among languages, the most popular name for a designer is William (eight); the second most popular is John, and the third is a tie between Herbert and Henry. For national chauvinists, looking at geographical distribution and birthplace, we find the US with 13, Switzerland with 11, and Germany with 10. Consider population size.

Problems for the Future

Is the existence of a canon a problem? Is this canon a problem? A canon creates heroes, super-stars, and iconographies. In singling out individual designers and works, we may lose sight of the range of communication, expression, concepts, techniques, and formats that make up the wealth of graphic design history. As we attempt to become more objective and critical, it will also be harder to assess the 'stars'.

The existence of a graphic design canon, so early in the development of graphic design history and criticism, may focus too much attention and research in certain areas, to the exclusion of others equally significant. A canon reduces a lot of material (designers, works, facts, biographies, influences, etc.) to a smaller and perhaps more manageable package. Fewer names and works may make it easier to teach and learn and even to imitate, but reduces the rich, complex, and interrelated history that truly exists. If we narrow the field now, it will take much longer and be much more difficult to properly study and understand our cultural and professional heritage. For students new to the study of graphic design, a canon creates the impression that they need go no further; the best is known, the rest is not worth knowing. This is unfair, dangerous, and shortsighted.

The existence of a canon is the result of a natural reliance on art history (and on the example of architectural history) as a model for studying graphic design history. There are other ways of looking at, and exploring, graphic design history. These may well result in other ways of understanding and categorizing design works: by explicit and/or implicit content, by communication intent, by communication concept, by audience, by visual/verbal language, etc. The master/masterpiece approach also dismisses the existence (and possible importance) of anonymous works. How can the study of ephemera ignore the significance and influence of this category of works? Graphic design work will always, and finally, reveal its cultural origins. These origins need not be a particular person to be appreciated and understood; the origins can well be a specific time and place and people. With a perspective closer to *cultural* history than to *art* history (with its implied elitist flavor), we might come closer to a realistic and meaningful evaluation of our design cultural heritage.

Whether we agree that there should be a canon or not, I submit one exists and is being created, and that this process will continue at an increased pace as graphic design history develops further through publications, exhibitions, scholarship, and collections. We need to evaluate and control the process; if we need a canon, if we really need to label and separate, we need to assess better what canon exists and to amend it to make it intentional, conscious, responsible, and truly meaningful for all.

Martha Scotford is Professor Emeritus of Graphic Design at the College of Design,
North Carolina State University, Raleigh.
First published in *Visible Language*, vol. 28, no. 4, 1994.

1   Clive Dilnot, 'The State of
Design History, Part II: Problem
and Possibilities', *Design Issues*
vol. 1, no. 2 (Fall 1984).

Journal of
Design
History

Volume 5   Number 1   1992

OXFORD UNIVERSITY PRESS

CONVERSATION WITH RICHARD HOLLIS
ON GRAPHIC DESIGN HISTORY

ROBIN KINROSS
1992

The following informal conversation took place in London in July 1991. The transcript was edited by both parties. Some minor amendments or omissions have been made for this publication, and a few illustrations added. The dialogue was an attempt to raise issues of graphic design history that were sometimes discussed informally, but that had, at that time, hardly found their way into print: this must be the excuse for its indirections, imprecisions and occasional repetitions. Sometimes the topic changed abruptly as Hollis' attention was diverted by the view from the window. But we have decided to keep these detours.

The immediate pretext for the conversation, and its chief subject, was the short history of graphic design that Hollis was engaged in writing for the World of Art series, published by Thames & Hudson. The book appeared three years later, in 1994, as *Graphic Design: A Concise History*. Hollis was a practising designer, and relations between history and practice form one of the themes of the discussion.

'Graphic design' receives some definition in the course of the conversation, particularly towards the end. By way of introduction, one might say that 'graphic design' is here understood as the activity that evolved out of what had been known as 'commercial art'. Where the latter had been intimately linked to advertising and, in its methods, to drawn or painted illustration, graphic designers saw themselves as professional designers able to work across a wide range of fields and with different media: for companies and corporate bodies, in book or magazine publishing, exhibition design, signing and architectural graphics, television graphics and so on. Typically, as in Hollis' case, British graphic designers of his generation (born in the 1930s) studied in one of the London art schools and then – perhaps with the interruption of 'national service' – began to work in group practices or freelance, supplementing this with part-time teaching.

As the conversation suggests, for young British graphic designers at that time it was important to look abroad for inspiration. While there were a few older designers working in Britain who had made the transition from 'commercial art' to 'graphic design' (such as F.H.K. Henrion and Hans Schleger), it was work done in the USA and on the European Continent that interested them. As this testimony confirms – from quite a typical member of this 'first generation' – as a young designer, Hollis was already engaged with the subject of 'graphic design' and its history.

Early in his practice, Hollis' commitments were – crudely and broadly – to 'Swiss' Modernism. This came through his interest in 'concrete art', and in 1958 he visited Swiss artist-designers such as Richard Paul Lohse. (Unusually for a British designer, he had a working knowledge of German.) As some index of interests and allegiances, it is interesting to note that when Hollis was teaching at the West of England College of Art in Bristol (1964–66), Emil Ruder and Paul Schuitema were among the designers whom he invited there on short teaching engagements.[1] Hollis' work as a designer has been especially interesting for the ways in which it has worked with and through the Modern tradition, and – though this is not the place for an examination of it – it may be that his consciousness of the history of design has played a part in this development.

Origins of the Project

Kinross: You are a practising designer. What are you doing writing about the history of graphic design?

Hollis: I often ask myself that, if only because it's very difficult to do both designing and writing together. They're such different activities. How did I start to do it? It had in fact been begun by a colleague, Philip Thompson, who had co-written a book for Thames & Hudson called *Art without Boundaries*, which overlapped designers and people who were really artists. One of the things I've found is that most of the interesting designers in Europe up until the Second World War, and a bit beyond, were primarily artists: nearly all painters or sculptors. Kurt Schwitters, Willi Baumeister, Friedrich Vordemberge-Gildewart – these are among the most obvious. It is the sort of thing you don't immediately realise. It raises the most tricky problems about how you talk about their activity, and raises all kinds of ideas about the place of art in society and whether they could actually place art in society: insert art into everyday life by the design of functional items. Anyway, that's another issue, which we'll get on to.

Thompson was commissioned by Thames & Hudson to do a book on graphic design history. He started around 1985, worked away for two years and eventually gave up. When I rang to ask if he'd finished it, he said he had just found it completely impossible, that he had lost two stone – he's a thin man – and was just in total despair. Eventually I offered to do it, and he recommended me.

You weren't frightened by this story – that someone had been made ill by the project?

No. It's a story of vanity, really: you just think that you can do it. It then becomes a kind of challenge, but you don't realise how extraordinarily difficult it is. It's all very well to do lectures in an art school, because you can just take completely independent topics, or designers whose work you think is important and talk about them. You show images on screen, usually in a chronological order; maybe you make comparisons between one designer and another, or work from one period and another. But really you're talking about your enthusiasms and you're always showing pictures. Projected images always look much more impressive than the work itself, because of the scale. And everybody is concentrating in the dark on this brilliant screen: it's an extreme distortion. So that – to digress a bit – when you have a tiny illustration in a magazine, it's a closer approximation to what the actual work is like.

There's nothing more extraordinary than going to auction sale rooms, where posters appear now, and seeing the actual thing. It's often produced by a technique which you don't imagine it to have been produced by, or, for example, it's printed by letterpress and litho together. It's both technically different and transformed by the scale. So as soon as you reproduce anything, it's a very great distortion of what the original was like. It's interesting that when the magazine *Octavo* [no.7, 1990] reproduced pieces by the Ring neuer Werbegestalter designers, the work was shown so that it looked more like things as you handle them: in full colour, out of square, with shadows and so on. It was an attempt to give a better idea of material presence. But it somehow isn't more satisfactory, in that it also makes things look embalmed, even chic, rather than what they were – part of everyday life. It was curious, because they were so beautifully presented. But it was good to see things that hadn't been seen before.

As soon as something is reproduced, it becomes the stereotype to represent work that was done at that period, and then it is constantly re-reproduced. And that's one of the problems about most of the histories of the 'Twenty Centuries of Graphic Design' kind. They tend to be constantly regurgitating the same works, which are presented as the key works. Often they are, if they were recognised at the time as key works. But now a huge amount of material which isn't dross is beginning to surface. Of course a great deal was thrown away or lost, in the Wars and so on.

Can I tell you a story about reproductions? John Lewis in his Typography: Basic Principles *reproduces a booklet about Dessau, from the collection in the Museum of Modern Art in New York, which he says is by Jan Tschichold (the script typeface perhaps suggests this). In fact it was designed by Joost Schmidt. I told this to James Sutton, who with Alan Bartram was doing a specimen book (*Typefaces for Books*), and they wanted to reproduce that image.*

We looked very carefully at the photograph of it: it seems to have a fold down the middle, and I argued that it was probably a folded leaflet, though fortunately he didn't put this in the caption. Last month in an archive I saw the leaflet itself – which credits Schmidt with the design – and realised that it was never designed to be folded. It just has a heavy crease from the impression of a halftone block on the other side of the paper. So this was a complete misreading of the photograph.

It's typical. I'm sure I'll make the same sort of mistake. It's awful, having to rely on photographs.

And photocopies are even worse, of course. But back to your book.

Yes, so I got a contract from Thames & Hudson – that must be three years ago now – which I kept for a year before eventually signing it, because I thought the terms were so miserable.

Did you do a sample chapter?

I wrote an introduction, which was supposed to say what graphic design was – and which they found completely unsatisfactory. But they approved a synopsis: a formality, because I've changed it a great deal. I think I probably then started writing. I should say that I did start a book years ago. But that was on the whole of graphic design: a practical book.

It included a historical chapter, which was much more theoretical than I expect anything in this book will be. I'd just discovered Claude Lévi-Strauss and I thought he was the key to communication in society and so on. That was when I was in Bristol, and teaching at the art school there. But I found it was impossible to go on, because I was working, as a designer.

The Present Context for Writing History

So how can you do this now? I suspect that it must fit into your development as a…

It fits into the recession! Clients are going bust all around…

But there wasn't a recession when you started.

No, you mustn't take that too seriously. In a way that was chance. So it didn't connect with my work at all. Although this is a more penetrating question than I might acknowledge. Because I was as aware as anyone that there was a kind of crisis in design. The computerised designers were going off in one direction, led first of all by Basel – Wolfgang Weingart, particularly – and developed commercially by April Greiman and the 'New Wave' Americans. This influence coincided with an expansion in retail business, so that things like the Next catalogue (in Britain) were able to reflect this. It was something to do with graphic and typographic freedom and with making new images, presenting information as a decorative style. This emerged from the new technology of the computer. Maybe I can explain this better when we talk about general notions of what graphic design is.

The graphic designer doesn't actually control the content of what he or she is designing. For that reason I have been inclined more recently to work for art galleries – where I am interested in the information – that's to say, the content. Here there is a problem about the form which the information can take. If you are dealing with paintings from up to and including the nineteenth century, you feel that perhaps it is proper to use symmetrical layouts and to caption symmetrically. In Britain, the extraordinary Thatcherite Conservatism had as a side effect – the mannered use of spaced capital letters and 'small capitals'. I've recently noticed that the Swiss really laughed at this in publications, saying 'How is it possible for designers in 1988 (as it was then) to use centred caps and small caps. Surely we have gone beyond that?' But in England it was bound up with notions of heritage. It wasn't really tradition, but a bogus notion of history. And I suppose for me there was – maybe unconsciously – a need to go back and find out what we were, as designers.

I should add that I had actually met many of the figures I'm now writing about, or certainly seen their work first hand. For example, I got to know the Dutch designer Schuitema, who showed me the original sheets of the exhibition of the Ring neuer Werbegestalter (Circle of New Advertising Designers) designers in Amsterdam in 1931. I visited the design studios and schools in Switzerland, went to Ulm, met Vordeberge-Gildewart, saw Chermayeff & Geismar's work at the 1958 Brussels exhibition, saw Saul Bass's work at the 1968 Milan Triennale, met him later, and so on. That helps in understanding and interpreting the material now.

Of course there was also Post-Modernism, of which a large element is eclecticism, in other words borrowing past styles and applying them. You begin to wonder, as you get a historical grasp on it, whether there aren't perhaps conventions of modern design, as there are orders in classical architecture; and to wonder whether these orders can be exploited, very much as Bruno Monguzzi has done. He is a classic modern typographer, I think, and he has depended on his understanding of history. While he is an intelligent designer, he isn't highly original. That is the Miesian notion of 'I don't want to be interesting, I want to be good'.

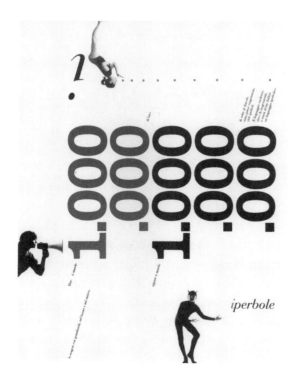

Page from publicity booklet designed by Bruno Monguzzi for Milanese printers, 1982. The typographic freedom recalls the work of the Dutch typographer Piet Zwart, about whom Monguzzi had written.

Modernism, Technique and Graphic Design

There's a big contradiction within the Modern Movement. On the one hand, always trying to be modern and new; but then saying that it's going to be timeless, eternal and also something you don't notice anyway. Like the Braun philosophy of the dumb object, which is just there to service your life, but not to get in the way.

There's a very clear connection between that kind of Ulm-ish attitude and Ulm-ish typography. I suppose I've adopted the Billian notion that art is pure aesthetic information. It's easiest to see graphics as information, and that inevitably some of that information is going to be aesthetic. And that it's quite easy to separate them out. I suppose the Ulm-ish view would be that the amount of aesthetic information is extremely limited. But of course, with somebody like Mies van der Rohe, the actual richness of material – bronzed girders, marble, that sort of thing – gave a sense of luxury to spareness. The typographer hasn't had that. You don't normally use handmade paper. Such things are antipathetic to notions of spareness, of economy. Unlike marble, a textured paper like Whatman paper can't be made smooth. Well it can be, but then you wouldn't notice its quality. Marble is much more obviously rich.

You can see this richness in very good printing nowadays. But that didn't exist when Modernism was new.

Yes, the technology didn't lend itself to this idea then. In the book, I've drawn a parallel between the way in which Herbert Matter used vignetted halftone letterpress blocks as though it was offset litho, where you could feather away the edges of the halftone image, and the way Le Corbusier might build with cement blocks, then render the surface to make it look like concrete: that kind of disjunction between appearance and technical reality.

Letterpress gives the impression of offset litho when the airbrushed artwork, the process-engraver's vignetting and the printing are technically impeccable. Pages of a colour tourist brochure designed by Herbert Matter, 1934.

Similarly, I was astounded to see some Swiss posters produced by hand chalking. When you see them reproduced, you think it's just photo-lithography or photogravure, or sometimes photomontage, when it isn't at all. This is true of many Russian posters too, particularly those by the Stenberg brothers. One astounding example of craft skill is Ruder's poster for the 'Abstract Photography' exhibition. The image on the catalogue cover was enlarged, dot for dot, and a halftone block was cut by hand out of lino: incredible. There's often such a distortion, but also enjoyment of this extraordinary skill.

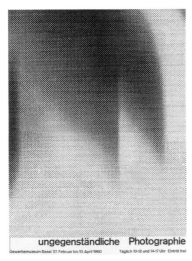

Poster by Emil Ruder, for
the exhibition 'Abstract Photography',
Basel, 1960. The halftone image
is printed from a lino block cut
by the designer.

Can I pick up this idea that Modernism now forms a body of knowledge about how to do things, or maybe that it has a pedagogic application: that this is a way of learning how to do graphic design? One thing that gives me trouble is this coincidence between graphic design and Modernism. I always think that, in a sense, they are the same phenomenon. Graphic design is Modernism in the graphic field. So that 'typophoto' – or, more generally, the conjunction of image and text – is really what graphic design is all about. And this only comes with the Modern Movement. Does this make sense?

Yes. The crucial thing is the relationship between image and text. But you can say that before the Modern Movement image and text were separated by the technology of letterpress printing, movable type and engraved blocks. With lithography (from 1800) illustration and text could be joined on the same printing surface, drawn by hand.

Apart from the conjunction of text and image, there is also the conjunction of image and image. Photography changed this both by providing raw material for montage (as in John Heartfield) and by making Surrealism more possible, since it depended on images that appeared to be machine-made. Dreams are thought to have an imagery which is closer to photography than to handmade or confected surfaces. This is very clear in the wartime posters of Abram Games, who painted his 'photographs' with an airbrush.

Drawn in photographic style, a wartime
poster warning of the dangers of finding
unexploded munitions. Lithographic poster
by Abram Games, 1943.

52

But you're right, photography was the central generator of graphic design, especially when it's considered as part of the Modern Movement. Photography made it much more possible to integrate words and images. But the separation of words and images continued, with photographs used as illustrations, with a clear separation, but interaction of image and text, as in American advertising in general, and the Volkswagen advertisements in particular.

Is Volkswagen contemplating a change?

Photography as illustration, typical of the New Advertising. Art directed by Helmut Krone at Doyle Dane Bernbach, 1959.

The US and the Art Director

That raises another big question: America and Europe. Is America a special case in all this?

This is where the poor design historian gets into terrible trouble! Because you have the 'art director', who directs 'Art'. Usually the art they were directing was illustration. But they also came to direct the whole make-up of, for example, an advertisement. This is a thread which is terribly difficult to follow, because it clearly has nothing to do with the Modern Movement, but is an important element in design, particularly in the US.

So the presence of the art director seems to be intangible…

The awful thing is that it probably is tangible, if you actually go… looking out of the window: Look at that! Somebody's over-painted a British Telecom van, a new one. We ought to photograph that… Oh it's just a new Telecom van… So that is it: it's kind of subliminal. [Noticing a BT van in the old colours] Look, you've got the two together. How extraordinary. That says everything about why you need graphic design history. It is this odd notion of marketing. I've just been writing about it. Did you see that correspondence describing the symbol as the 'prancing ponce'? There's a very funny letter in one of the magazines…

From graphic design to marketing: successive liveries and symbols for British Telecom. Left, blue on yellow, designed by Banks & Miles, 1981. Right, the piper, designed by Wolff Olins, replaced it in 1991.

It's such a pathetic, wispy image – pipe-dreams.

It needs so many excuses. It's so badly drawn. But it is interesting. As far as I can tell, Wolff Olins were the first to reintroduce images as identifying signs that were not obviously connected to the product or service. Like the fox on the Hadfields paint pots, which at the time puzzled designers, but came to be accepted as a possible way of doing it.

Teamwork: paint firm identity, art direction at Wolff Olins by Michael Wolff; illustration by Maurice Wilson (a Royal Academician); design by Kit Cooper, 1969.

Can you identify the individuals responsible for this?

Oh, Michael Wolff: it was just after he joined the practice, before then he had been with Main Wolff. But I suppose we ought to get back?

To the art director?

I don't know. I'm so confused about that, I think it may be unwise. But I think it will be a perpetual confusion. Because some of the most brilliant Americans are difficult to describe. For example, Bob Gage, who worked for Doyle Dane Bernbach, was obviously brilliant at organizing persuasive communication. And I have to think: well, is he someone you include in the history of graphic design? There is an enormous number of very good people, whose position and importance you simply can't assess. So you tend to take people who are paradigms, in your view.

Can you fit advertising into this? Does it have a clear place?

I think it must. Partly because a lot of the medium for design (not of course 'Good Design') – in magazines – was dependent on advertising. So the relationship is significant. Design was very affected by advertising, and advertising by design. They overlapped, in a rather curious way, in the 1960s. They almost came together in the Sunday newspaper colour supplement magazines. The same photographers were used for taking editorial photographs as were used for taking studio photographs that expressed some marketing idea. Then company reports began to look like colour magazines. So there is a terrific interplay. And when the Americans, like Bob Gill, came to Britain in the early 1960s, they had worked in American advertising. I remember when the White Horse campaign started, with the level of the whisky tilted in the bottle. The Americans came with the idea that you had to have a 'concept'. When they taught in art schools here they were ramming home the idea of a concept – 'you've got to have a concept'. It was totally anti-design, really, because it was anti-form. Students were reduced to tears because they had no 'concept', although they might have very good typography, with a decent headline and properly chosen type.

But that won the day here – if you think of Fletcher/Forbes/Gill, now Pentagram.

The content of much of their communication was excitement, and excitement isn't exciting thirty years later. They were good, particularly Alan Fletcher, but there were a lot of designers and small design groups doing very good work then in Britain (or London). It is interesting how one says 'good work'. You have this awkward business of what the criteria of judgement are. Reputations were built, which when one examines them – big reputations in their day – one finds that what they have deposited is really very limited. And there is the accretion of interesting work by people who weren't apparently so important, but which can build into a much greater 'reputation'.

Evaluation and the Processes of Design

So what are the criteria?

One criterion is simply what was thought good at the time and therefore reproduced, so it's easy to find. And then with some important things that have been kept, the historian has to consider whether to pay £250 for a booklet designed by Piet Zwart, because that is the only way one is going to be able to reproduce it. But the only reason something like this has survived is because somebody recognised its quality.

Because you know how design work gets done you must look at these finished items and wonder how they really got to be like that. My suspicion about some historians is that they just accept the finished thing, without questioning it.

Yes, I think that's right. It's not just a question of technique, of 'letterpress or litho', but of what could be done in the circumstances, and in the time. There is a different mentality in the person who is actually making something. The person writing about it probably doesn't recognise the way things are improvised. With metal typography, for example, the particular forms could be determined by the technology. But, as the Futurists showed, the technology need not be inhibiting – though of course it is easier to work with metal typesetting's rectangular modules.

The Americans seemed to behave in a much freer way; there was more variety. But the difference between the masters who were then working in what you can call the manner of the Modern Movement, and people who were going through the motions some time later, is that the people who were innovating somehow have a particular finesse, a particular conviction. I think that is what is interesting about Anthony Froshaug's work, and one or two of his students, is its finesse. But most of that sort of work wasn't produced under pressure, and it didn't have art directors and all kinds of other people involved. And the difference between designing and advertising – and between designing as it has changed – is that there is much more teamwork in the latter. So there can be much more compromise, not only about what is acceptable to the client, but what is also acceptable to the other designers involved. This is one of the great changes. Whereas up to 1965, say, you tended to be talking about individual designers, you begin then to talk about design groups, and you don't know who in particular was involved.

If you are asking how the two things, history and practice, relate, I don't think they do very much. Except very badly. I'm not passionately interested in any particular period. I'm interested in all of them. I can't pretend that I'm very interested in the use of graphic design in marketing, because I can't separate the graphics from the marketing. And there is this complicated question about who graphic design is for. It seems to me that graphic design is for the middle classes. It's a distinctly bourgeois activity, which has occasionally, probably through pop music, had connections with some sort of mass culture. On a less evidently cultural level, in road signs, forms design and that sort of area, it has been part of the social services. But I think that design is connected with middle-class culture.

That sounds like a Cultural Studies explanation of the matter: you are locating it very clearly as the pursuit of this class. It is done by middle-class people for middle-class people.

Do you think that's true? I haven't talked about this in what I've written so far. And I don't know whether it's going to become the – [distracted by a radio in the street, looks at the British Telecom vans again, now preparing to move off]. It's incredible: the old van and the new van. You see: there is 'graphic design' moving away, followed by 'marketing'. That was a rather useful intervention, or confrontation. You didn't respond to my question.

To be very provocative, I think that the answer in your case, if you are designing a catalogue for Fischer Fine Art, is that it is clearly a middle-class or upper-middle-class activity.

I wasn't really thinking of my own activity... But, apart from pop music, I can't think of any area – and that's very much on the borders.

It's refreshing to hear this uttered, but it denies the dreams about mass communication, and also the earlier Socialist dreams of design for the masses: the dreams of the early Modern Movement.

Politically, the problem with that is that it has somehow become associated with notions of social engineering. Plainly, my own view of design is that it is inevitably part of the social servicing, and that is why bad or incoherent design is offensive.

What about British Telecom? Lots of people think the new identity is bad design.

I suppose it was the middle class assuming they were satisfying the 'man in the street'. It is a horrible patronising attitude – that design can't be understood by everybody. Whereas I think that everybody has said, in the face of British Telecom, that it is, in any way of looking at it, bad design. People don't like it. To what extent that's an aesthetic reaction, I don't know. Of course it also involves the fact that a lot of money was spent. But almost everything they touched seems so...

Telephone boxes in the identity designed
by Wolff Olins, London, October 1991.
The label 'Telephone' has a strong
pink background; the 'Phonecard' panel
is lime green.

The use of one of the nicest text typefaces, the Century italic, as a single word on the telephone boxes, white out of black, with a cerise stripe: it doesn't look like a piece of information. It doesn't look as though it is saying 'Telephone'. It looks descriptive, adjectival. It is those kinds of judgement that seem to be inept. The quality of the decision making appears to be so poor.

And then there's an illogicality in the call boxes labelled 'phonecard', as if they are not 'telephone'. But these are rather sophisticated criticisms: that this identity is not working in the terms in which it might be discussed in a design office discussion; that it fails at the concept level, and in using the wrong visual language.

Then you have to bring in the symbol. But we'd better not go into this.

I don't know. I think that the ideal in writing about design is that you can actually have a completely detailed description of a symbol, which also brings in some sort of evaluation, both formally and in other ways, particularly socially. This would be my ideal: that you could talk about the way the hands were drawn on the symbol, and connect that with the boardroom ambitions for the company, the value of the stocks and everything else. It all goes together.

It does. I suppose I have only talked about that kind of thing in one case. With Matter's design – because it's famous – for the New Haven Railroad. I have mentioned that the scheme couldn't be fully carried out, partly because of the protests about the service from commuters who used the trains. So that Matter was in a sense camouflaging the bad service, by giving it an image of cleanness and efficiency.

New Haven Railroad symbol,
designed by Herbert Matter, 1954.

How do you know that story?

One piece that I found in *Print* magazine of the time, the late 1950s. There was another source in an American magazine, a trade magazine.

It is perhaps one level removed from talking with the people concerned, to read a contemporary report in a magazine. What I'm getting at is that behind every bit of graphics there is a story like this, if only you could get to it.

I don't really want to talk too much about the context in which something is done. Even if you talk to the designers involved, they have a very partial view of what happened. Unless you can find reports of meetings – rather in the way that you found the letters of Herbert Bayer, Stanley Morison and Herbert Read about *Art and Industry*.[2] But the amount of actual work needed to find out this kind of thing is enormous. There simply isn't the time. Design history is very much dependent on people who do exactly that kind of work, which the very generalist person like myself can use. Even to write a superficial view is appallingly difficult. It is curious, starting to write about something that one thinks is deeply boring: more and more things crawl out of the woodwork and present themselves as being far more interesting than you thought they were. Things that you thought were important are far away in the perspective of the picture.

The Scope of Coverage

What have the discoveries been, things that you have become more interested in?

One develops passionate admirations. For example, the Italians after the Second World War, whom I'd always thought interesting: because they were connected with rebuilding the country and there was an optimism, together with a tremendous political activity, which preceded economic recovery. And the number of Italian designers – whose work often isn't easy to distinguish one from another. I've left out designers here, whose work would seem, in another country, of extraordinary brilliance.

Then there were people who were so deeply committed to design that they would suddenly set off for another part of the world, to involve themselves in a literacy programme. They were a kind of *graphistes sans frontières*, and have been overlooked. I'm very aware of this ignorance, and that I'm not dealing with it. Indeed, the whole of the African continent is completely ignored. It's not practically possible to deal with it. But it is crazy to excuse oneself, when one also leaves out Latin America – and Australia, which has extremely interesting designers. And, for example, I can only mention Canada, when in fact it had the most thorough-going corporate design for Canadian National railways.

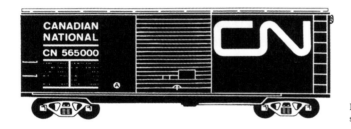

Identity for the Canadian National railway
system, designed by Allan Fleming, 1959.

Eastern Europe gets a very raw deal, when in fact it's quite important. China, too, is ignored. So my work will be extremely superficial, partial. I can only hope it won't be quite as inadequate as what has preceded it. But then when you look at the difficulties, you begin to have considerable respect for people who attempted to do anything at all. I just hope that the sources I use will be a bit less secondary. But not many of them will actually be primary.

To get back to your list of questions. I think we've dealt with the business of my sympathies being wider than they were twenty years ago?

It sounds as if they've always been wide.

I think they have. My generation of designers certainly had heroes. I get the impression that students don't so much now. But because graphic design hardly existed then, one did look at the people who were working at the time, not those in history. Certainly in the first few years of my awareness of graphic design, they were then American. People who are now almost unheard of, like Roy Kuhlman. People like Alvin Lustig, who now seem to be more important as personalities than for their work, except the work they did before the Second World War. If you look at Lustig's postwar work, it's not actually terribly interesting, apart from one or two book jackets. And it was really quite a long time before someone like Tschichold was mediated, mainly through Froshaug. And certainly there was very little awareness of the Russians, whom I've never been deeply interested in, partly because of the language. But from about 1960, the big influence was really the Swiss, and that was pervasive.

You obviously weren't limited by that. Presumably, if you had followed the theory, you would still be doing Swiss things now. For example, someone like Derek Birdsall seems to me still a lot more fixed in that period. This is not a criticism; in a way it's a strength, that he somehow manages to stick with that Swiss-and-American thing.

Yes, he found his influences, if you like – his way of working – young. Though it was what all of us were interested in then. He was actually a proper student of Froshaug. And of course he was grounded in metal setting. He was very typical of that period. People had a terrific involvement with this new profession. There was an intensity, which I don't believe exists now, simply because there isn't that notion of cutting new paths. With a job that Birdsall had worked on, say until two in the morning, he would pin it up at the bottom of the bed, so that when he opened his eyes, first thing in the morning, he'd get a fresh, critical view of it, before he'd had the distraction of anything else. And you wouldn't call Derek particularly...

Critical?

No, certainly critical, but not in that way. There was a climate of tremendous intensity then. He is somebody that I think is far more interesting than I had remembered. Maybe partly because I've seen him intermittently over the years, and perhaps it is only when you look at the work again... He did some extremely interesting things for Pirelli – advertising – I suppose in the early 1960s. He's a kind of craftsman-designer. He would never take risks, and always had to have mad obsessions about reproducing bits of paintings in the same size as the original. But in a way they were the obsessions that an artist might have. And while he is not innovative, what he does has to do with design. And he has been extremely consistent. Whereas some people who were much more aggressively or flamboyantly excellent, and who got involved in being part of a design group and in management, have become figures of fun. Which is very sad. But they haven't kept up that kind of craftsmanship. They are like imitation Paul Rands. So they then revert to being bad artists. You cannot get away with being arty and call it design.

I think things have got beyond that. I'm deeply antagonistic to the uncritical interest in Shell advertising of the 1930s, under Colonel Jack Beddington. That was the worst kind of middle classism: forcing rather parochial art down people's throats. I suppose I'd assumed – if we are talking about reputations – that Edward McKnight Kauffer was interesting. He's basically a pretty awful designer, who occasionally went beyond that. But because of his personality he somehow overcame his limitations. Unfortunately the clients didn't overcome his limitations. It's mysterious. There were no criteria then, whereas now there are. And I think that's why somebody who was obviously intelligent could get away with being so woolly.

The influence of American advertising:
a design by Derek Birdsall, early 1960s.

59

'Woolly' sounds more precise as a criticism than 'awful'. But what really is the criticism?

'Woolly' is better, of course. But what happened was that in the 1960s you got this notion that design was something to do with solving problems. So you get The Graphic Artist and his Design Problems (the English title of Josef Müller-Brockmann's book). And people got interested in the idea that you could treat graphic design as industrial design.

And, by techniques such as algorithms, you could do your work by solving problems.

But where does this book stop?

Well, there is going to be a kind of epilogue. It will arrive at 1968, with technological and political upheavals, with the change to a lot of different ways of looking at things, which will then elide into Post-Modernism, and that will sum up where we've got to. It may have something more, with photography particularly, as a way of generating words – then of course you get computers.

All that's in an epilogue?

I think it might be. And that's where the Japanese come in, which I'm just sorting out. Because of the West Coast they are very influential. And also they are extremely interesting, because of the uninhibited way in which they would just use graphic imagery, irrespective of whether it could be read, because the references would be to things that were entirely Western. I suspect there's a lot of designing for other designers. But then there are so many designers: quite a big audience! We ought to move on. You were going to ask?

I was just going to commiserate with you. Whatever you do, people will pick holes with what you've left out. It seems a necessary thing to do, but also a thankless one. It seems like some slow leapfrog process, one book after another, which just has to go very slowly.

In fact, what's been left out is almost as important as what's been put in. There is a sifting process, through stuff you have to consider and instinctively reject as not being interesting. So inevitably one is imposing a view that is dependent on taste one had, or people had, some time ago. So you could say that the most important historians are people like Walter Herdeg or Charles Rosner: editors who were sifting through the stuff at the time.

Illustration and Description

Will you take pictures from those magazines and annuals?

Sometimes I'll have to. But the reproductions will be very small. Fortunately it's not all that long ago, and I'm hoping I'll be able to reproduce from originals. The ideal is always from the original.

But it's illustration as reminder or as snapshot, rather than as 'this is a substitute for the real thing'.

Quite. As reminder, or 'it was something like this'. That sort of thing. What I want to avoid is taking the things that are very known. Because that prevents people thinking; it just refers people to the other books. I want to have colour at the beginning and the end, to discuss in some depth things produced in colour. Like that Tschichold poster Der Berufsphotograph, which I've talked about at length in the text – to take some of these things, simply so that they can be properly looked at. Steven Heller, for example, in his books, never talks about the actual thing. The people who write about it don't look at what they are talking about. Partly because they don't understand how it was produced. They assume that just reproducing it helps people to see it, which it doesn't at all. So I hope that I can make people look at things.

So with the Tschichold, you've seen the original poster?

Yes. There are so many things that you don't realise otherwise. But also it is just the way that something like that is so carefully constructed: controlled intellectually and formally. It's a masterpiece, that work! It is interesting that I use this term. I mean that it is a key work, which you can use to talk about other works.

It sounds like you're just talking about formal values.

Oh no, no! If you're showing the idea of 'the professional photographer', what image do you use? As a designer you might be talking to the curator of the exhibition. Though nowadays you'd be talking to the marketing people, too. This is what is different: on anyone job, the clients have multiplied – which probably accounts for British Telecom. But to get back to the Tschichold poster… Well, what have I said about it? [quotes from the manuscript]:

> For an exhibition, *Der Berufsphotograph* (The Professional Photographer), at the Gewerbe-museum Basel in 1938, the exiled Jan Tschichold produced the last work which followed his precepts of asymmetric typography. This is a small poster of extreme economy and precision. The image is a photograph in negative, its left-hand edge on the centre of the sheet. The word-element 'photograph' starts at the edge of the image. This is overprinted on the image, and so forms a unit of meaning with it, and is the first part of a subtitle 'sein Werkzeug' (his apparatus). The second half of the subtitle, 'seine Arbeiten' (his works) is placed after a dash. The dash bridges between the image area and the white paper of the sheet, so that the works are literally the outcome of the process. The rest of the textual information is related by size and position according to its importance. 'Where' (the museum) is aligned horizontally with 'what' (Ausstellung: exhibition). This is related vertically to 'who' (the name of the collaborating organization) at the top, and

Poster printed in black and with 'rainbow' inking, designed by Jan Tschichold, 1938.

the start of the main title below. 'When' (the dates and opening times) is related with less coherent logic, by the device of reversing the dates in white out of black, making a further negative. The days and times are presented in tabular form, which emphasizes the Sunday morning and Wednesday evening openings. In a vertical line of text on the right are listed the designer, photographer, photo-engraver and printer. All the type, except the main title, is printed in black, with the photograph. In a single separate run through the press, with yellow on the inking rollers on the left, blue in the middle, and red on the right, the horizontal rules of the main title and subtitle are printed. Tschichold's and Matter's knowledge of the processes of the printing industry freed them to use the medium to extend the designer's expressive range. Overprinting was used not merely to create the effect of space, but by allowing the image and the colours to exist in the same space without cancelling...

And so on. So my editor is going to say: 'what are you doing describing something which you're illustrating?', but I'll insist. Unless you describe it, people won't read this image, they will just see an image, and won't understand the terrific concentrated intelligence that has produced it.

'Heroic' is a better term than 'masterpiece'. It's just that somebody took the trouble. That is what is so impressive. Nowadays people don't take the trouble. The BT visual identity seems so badly done! Where is the intelligence or the craft? I do feel that in a sense it is a missionary thing. A few of these people were just so good. 'Oh they are just images, they are just designers.' But look at Matter's travel posters, produced in five, six, seven, eight languages, and he's got to allow for all of them. People see the image just with one text in one language, not realizing that maybe it had also to allow for all these other contingencies.

Colour photogravure posters designed by Herbert Matter, 1934 The changing text, here German and Dutch, was overprinted by litho.

A masterpiece, a pioneering work or whatever you take it to be – it makes a lot of art look just self-indulgent. That's why graphic design in those days was important. And why now it's lost the kind of wonder it had for people like Birdsall.

When Birdsall did his Pirelli work, it was a question of his asking, 'How can this be done?'. For example, showing ice on a windscreen, he put salt on photographic paper.

There wasn't a language to express something. There weren't all the routine things that theatre managers have for making special effects. These designers were innovating, making. Of course this is still being done on Apple Macintoshes today – 'how do you do this?' – but there was much less of an inherited know-how. With so many things, it was innovation, innovation. They were real breakthroughs of human intelligence. Comparable with some scientific discoveries. I think it matched the Modern Movement in architecture. It did less damage! – with paper – when it wasn't making propaganda for something dire. But it was the imagination.

De-icer pack designed
by Derek Birdsalll, 1960.

There are many things that Max Bill did – or Anton Stankowski – that leave you just astounded. How did they do something so original, with such confidence? They didn't say 'Erm, oh well, what do you think?' There it was. It is extraordinary. Ruedi Ruegg in Switzerland told me that Americans haven't heard of Stankowski. Yet there was somebody whose whole life is this consistent trail of activity – and he wrote a great deal, too. In his case it happily didn't particularly connect with politics, so it can be seen as a traditional adjunct to business, really. It is an extraordinary career.

He stayed in Germany through the war?

I'm not sure – I haven't got there yet – but I've dealt with him prewar, and there the information came from Japanese magazines, which say he was a prisoner in Russia. He then became editor of the Stuttgarter Illustrierte. As far as I know he is alive, well, and living in Stuttgart. I should ask him!

To go back a bit, I'm inclined to say that your description of that poster is heroic, too. It matches the endeavour of the poster, because you do talk about the thing in an internal way...

They will probably cut it!

It is the advantage you have, understanding how these things get produced. If you just see it as an image, you're terribly limited in the language you can use.

And also for students. They see these images and think, 'That's a good idea'. It's so removed from the way it was produced. It may not matter that it's seen as style, but it's not interesting – when a piece of paper is able to yield so much information about so many things. It is much more interesting than a lot of art. It is more interesting than a lot of Bill's painting, in my view...

You're muddling up Bill and Tschichold.

Yes, because I go on to talk about Bill's *Negerkunst* poster. With Bill, you have a key, and once you've got the key, you can unlock something pretty instantly.

What are the other kinds of language you've found yourself using, in describing work? This example you've quoted is the language of production and also of ordering information.

That's of course where this overlaps with my own interest in exploiting process and, as a designer for art galleries, in making people, with luck, arrive at the museum when it's open.

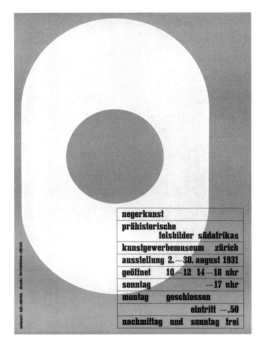

Poster designed by Max Bill – 'Negro Art and Prehistoric Rock Paintings of South Africa' – printed in black and buff from type and a linocut block, 1931. The geometrical design follows the form of a sculpture by the artist.

But, for example, your mention of Lévi-Strauss reminds me of other ways of describing images – as systems of meaning.

I think in this kind of book, it would be good to write as simply as possible. It is directed at students and lay people, who will inevitably be switched off by anything that smacks of theory. Information and communication theory, Ulm-school ideas of visual rhetoric, semiology, are all useful, but not here. I somehow have to find a way of talking about bits of paper without using words that are semi-technical. If you use words that you would use in painting, like 'support', it gets muddled: it's associated with something that is physically supported. But how do you talk about that plane (or plain) surface, without saying 'sheet of paper'?

You want it to be more abstract. There's no word. You have to get round problems like this when you're talking to a lay audience. I suppose somebody has to invent some terms that become acceptable. Or do we all talk about 'sheet', even if it's a piece of metal?

'Sheet' also means the whole sheet, from which smaller pieces are then cut. It has that problem too.

Yes. It is something that carries the signs, the words and images. But we have no word to say what that is. It is difficult to have theoretical notions when you are still not sure what to call the specific object.

It sounds like a very pragmatic approach.

Absolutely. Not being a professional writer, one spends a lot of time struggling to find a way of saying something. It is all very well for the publishers to say 'Don't worry, just get the facts down!'

Is that what they said?

Yes... There aren't too many facts in the book. I think there will be a serious lack of mentions of when particular people went to particular places, and when there were exhibitions of work. I may be able to introduce these, now that I know more. One's constantly finding out little bits more of that sort of information.

Will you acknowledge your constraints in doing the book? It seems that you are clearly constrained by what's available to you for illustration and for discussion, especially the constraint of what was reproduced in magazines.

A Definition of Graphic Design

It is interesting that when you go beyond that, you seem to go beyond what is traditionally considered to be graphic design. Magazines, like *Graphis*, or the annuals, like Modern Publicity, seem to define what graphic design is. So that graphic design is not just 'visual communication', it is 'visual communication seen by graphic designers to be graphic design'. It's like the difference between architecture and building. The division is somehow to do with – what? is it to do with class? It has certainly to do with what is accepted to be a profession. There are all kinds of interesting distinctions between commercial art and graphic design, and where boundaries are drawn.

To take a clear example, something like a Mars bar wrapper...

... is not Graphic Design, although it uses every aspect of graphic design. And (unless it's changed) it seems to me to be entirely suitable.[3] It's like art: 'art' is what is done by artists, and 'graphic design' is what is done by graphic designers. It's an odd phenomenon.

Sometimes, in the company of Cultural Studies people, I feel a bit guilty that I'm interested in Graphic Design (capital letters), and I'm not much interested in Mars bars wrappers, or even in something less disreputable than that.

It is a strange convention, that something is 'graphic design'. But commercial art still exists: it calls itself 'packaging' or marketing, which, like advertising, may contain graphic design or may not. It may be done by graphic designers, but it seems it can well not be. Graphic design is somehow adding some kind of cultural weight. Although it's all got very much more confused. And this is why I've asked myself whether graphic design hasn't finished. Quite seriously. Because if you look at things that inevitably had a heavy cultural component, like book covers, they now have a very low cultural component, apparently, in terms of graphic design. In fact they are packaged.

One can ask if there are any graphic designers left. There are typographers who design books. People do company reports, which look like commercial art. Are people who do road signs graphic designers? But then you wonder about Wolff Olins: they employ graphic designers, but they probably wouldn't call themselves a graphic design consultancy.

Yes, they seem bigger than that. It sounds as if you do have a picture of the graphic designer: someone whose name you can find out, who sits and controls where everything goes in this image which is on something we call a sheet or image area. It sounds like this is the phenomenon that happened when artists entered this field, and that it still has this basis in – to go right back – the artist at the easel.

When you asked if my views had changed, I suppose I hadn't realised before that artists had made graphic design. It was a profession constructed by the social and political aspirations of Dadaist artists. It's a very odd conclusion to come to – obviously it's not entirely true. Maybe writing this book is part of the same direction: a sort of social zeal. And it is that social zeal that has collapsed. The end of ideologies, maybe.

Except that we know that ideologies reappear in some other form.

Maybe graphic design was an ideology.

And then tied in with the Modern Movement in some deep way. Could it be that graphic design is coming to an end because the Modern Movement has got into this terrible trauma?

I'd have thought that what the Modern Movement has left – if we are talking about graphic design – is very good, useful designers, like Monguzzi and Birdsall, with a way of working that you could say is perpetually valid. You could also consider many of the ideas of the Modern Movement, particularly in domestic design: planning in terms of spatial organization, for every kind of activity. It's totally transformed this. Of course, it could not cope with market forces, because it was a social movement, it assumed a benevolent socialist state, or the patronage of a German grand duke, or patronage of one kind or another. In England, graphic designers had the excuse that they were working with under-educated clients, whom they didn't bother to educate. Where the state has employed it, graphic design has had some extraordinary successes. For example, in Switzerland, or with the Canadian National railways, or indeed with bits of British Rail or British road signs, it has contributed a great deal. And with some enlightened local authorities – not much in England – a lot has been done. People like Grapus have produced more interesting images than any recent French painters. So I think, within visual culture, graphic design has made a huge contribution.

Robin Kinross is a publisher at Hyphen Press, London.
First published in *Journal of Design History*, vol. 5, no. 1, Oxford University Press, 1992.

1   Schuitema came twice in that period; Ruder was ill and could not come. For some description of the school at Bristol, see Norman Potter, *What is a Designer* (London: Hyphen Press, 1989), p.204–7.

2   Robin Kinross, 'Herbert Read's Art and Industry: A History', *Journal of Design History*, vol.1, no.1 (1988), p.35–50.

3   For a short argument for the importance of investigating the consumer and consumption, which concludes 'The Mars bar, rightly understood, has more to teach us than Baudrillard', see James Obelkevich, 'Myths and realities of the post-war Consumer Revolution', *Issue*, no.7 (1991), p.4–5.

eye

THE INTERNATIONAL REVIEW OF GRAPHIC DESIGN 6 92 DIE INTERNATIONALE FACHZEITSCHRIFT FÜR GRAFIK-DESIGN

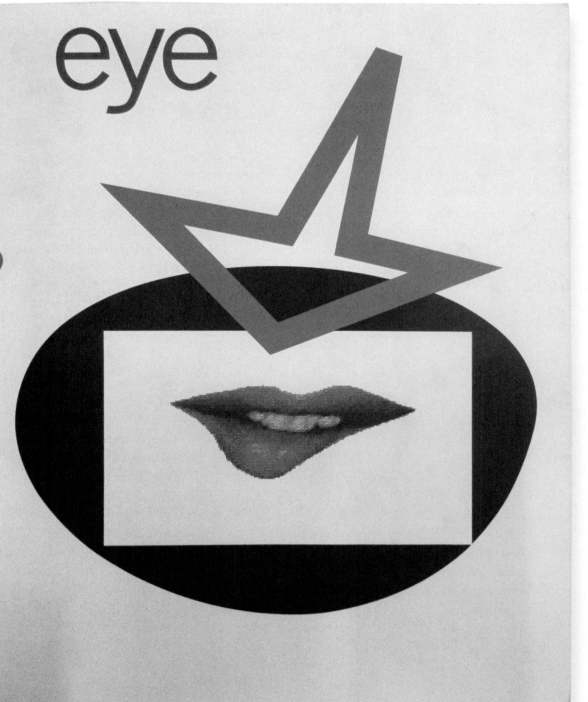

WHY IS DESIGN HISTORY SO OBSESSED BY APPEARANCE?

BRIDGET WILKINS
1992

No More Heroes

It is taken for granted that graphic designers will be familiar with the history of the discipline and that they will know what Milton Glaser's posters or Herbert Bayer's typography look like. But how does this 'look' inform or help us, apart from functioning as a 'naming of the parts', or as a store of outdated visual clichés? Why do we need it, and do we even need it? Is it time to question what kind of history is actually being fed to us?

Old-Fashioned Approaches

At present, graphic design history is modelled on the earliest approaches to art history. On the one hand there is the 'hero' approach, which singles out individuals and emphasises the designer not as a communicator but as a personality. Life stories and anecdotes predominate; presented in a linear way, from birth to education to eventual maturity. On the other hand, there are the stylistic and thematic approaches. These treat categories such as 'corporate identity' or 'New Wave' in a similarly linear fashion, progressing from the earliest examples to the most recent, and encouraging us to classify objects and images as though they were universal and indefinitely fixed.

These linear concepts of history are ignoring some of the central issues in graphic design. The discipline is defined by the technological limits of the time in which the design is made, as well as the motives and ambitions of the commissioning agent – and these factors need a much closer analysis. But, above all, it is to do with communication. The strangest aspect of graphic design history as it is presently written about, taught and discussed is the almost total absence of discussion about the way in which these communications are received by their audiences. Did grandma find the geographical distortions of the London Underground map (1931) confusing because they were so modern and unfamiliar? Such questions are rarely asked. But it is only with the inclusion of this normally absent context that there can be meaningful and constructive comprehension of history.

Contextual Criticism

Compared with other areas of design, graphic design has been given short shrift by historians. In recent years much attention has been devoted to consumer and household designs and the circumstances surrounding their production and consumption, with a spate of books and exhibitions on the subjects of chairs, cars, hoovers and living-room decor. These studies are less concerned with the analysis of visual style than with the consideration of the context in which the design was produced. One such book, Adrian Forty's *Objects of Desire: Design and Society 1750–1980*, analyses the ways in which patterns of consumption dictated the form of transport, typewriters and appliances.

How far could such an approach be applied to graphic design history? On the whole, graphic design does not fit the same categories of consumption as fridges, hoovers, and so on. Most graphic design – shopping bags, bank leaflets, company logos – is not an 'object of desire', although some might put such things as album covers and style magazines in this class. Most of it is ephemeral. Much of it is locked into a particular time and place and loses its relevance once the moment has passed. Often it is not purchased or consumed in an active sense so much as received – like a telephone directory, street poster or stamp. The graphics, if they are consciously noticed at all, have only secondary significance.

Material Values

For these reasons, the status of graphic design (and graphic designers) is quite low in the hierarchy of design. The objects do not have the same material value, are not as collectable and do not have the same display potential as three-dimensional forms of design. Of course, books, posters and album covers are collected, displayed in the home and treasured for their nostalgic qualities, but in the museums they are not big crowd-pullers compared to the other applied arts. Those items that are regarded as display-worthy are selected not by consumers but by self-appointed arbiters of taste, such as exhibition curators, collectors and historians. What criteria have they used in this selection? I suspect that it is those that look punchiest, or will come across well when reduced and reproduced in the pages of books and magazines, where the same old chestnuts appear again and again.

But the fact that so much has already been discarded could work to the advantage of graphic design history. It means that the still emerging discipline is not wholly saturated with the superficial coverage some areas of art and design have received. And it creates a space in which a new, more meaningful approach to history could be developed. This still begs the question: what is the most appropriate approach?

On the occasions when two-dimensional design is displayed in museums – as, for instance, at the Bodoni Museum in Parma, Italy – history is presented in terms of objects (books, punches and matrices) in isolation, as exotic specimens caught under glass. This allows us to admire them as artefacts, but it tells us nothing of the way in which they came to be created, or how people received and evaluated them at the time of production (or later).

Designed for Life

Graphic design remains arguably the most immediate and instantaneously arresting of the design disciplines. We need to capitalise on this and use it to relate the objects to their context in a meaningful way. If most graphic design is seen, used and owned by the public, why should it not have a lively history that constructively explores and communicates its qualities? Everyone uses letters, words and imagery. Everyone has a view of the redesign of their daily newspaper, or the appropriateness of using a newborn baby, or someone suffering from HIV/ AIDS, in a billboard ad.

We need to explain not 'what it looks like' but 'why it looks the way it does', how a piece of graphic design communicated and to whom. We should not allow a preoccupation with financial and aesthetic value to blind us to the historical value of all graphic ephemera. A wartime ration book has as much to tell us about communication design, people's daily experience and society in the Second World War – in other words, graphic design history – as a poster by Abram Games. The danger of graphic design hierarchies, museum collections of acknowledged 'classics', and the hero approach is that they prevent us from seeing this. An excessive concentration on the look of a piece of graphics also ignores the fact that we live in multicultural societies and that visual images are understood by different cultures in different ways.

If graphic designs are to communicate effectively in the future, it is essential to examine issues deeper and wider than the purely visual. What better way to start than by addressing your own history in this way?

Bridget Wilkins is a Research Fellow (retired) at Central Saint Martins College of Art and Design, The University of the Arts, London.
First published in *Eye* 6, 1992.

eye

THE INTERNATIONAL REVIEW OF GRAPHIC DESIGN   No13   VOL. 4 SUMMER 1994

PRINTED IN GREAT BRITAIN

HAVE YOU EVER REALLY LOOKED
AT THIS POSTER?

RICHARD HOLLIS
1994

In 1961, the Swiss magazine *New Graphic Design* published an account of pioneering Dutch work of the 1920s and 1930s. For me and some of my colleagues in the Design department of what was then the London School of Printing and Graphic Arts, the article provided an insight into what graphic design is and what it might be. In 1964, at the Icograda conference in Zurich, I was introduced to the author of the article, Paul Schuitema. He found our interest in work done 30 years earlier perverse and disturbing. The past was over. There had been a world war. Now we lived in an atomic age, in a different world, with different problems. To Schuitema, being seen as a pioneer of the early days of graphic design was an embarrassment. Yet in his studio he kept the complete exhibition, mounted on boards, of the 1931 Amsterdam show Ring neuer Werbegestalter.

If Schuitema belonged to the first generation of graphic designers, then he must be at the beginning of a history. Yet in Philip B. Meggs' 500-page *A History of Graphic Design* (1983) he appears on page 356, while in the best-known history of the subject before Meggs, the Swiss designer Josef Müller-Brockmann's *A History of Visual Communication* (1971), his work is discussed more than two-thirds of the way through. Of course, both books have an elaborate pre-history. Müller-Brockmann's subtitle is frank about its scope: 'From the Dawn of Barter in the Ancient World to the Visualized Conception of Today'. But a history of visual communication is not a history of design, even if the story is presented as an inexorable development towards graphic design. A glance at histories by non-designers, such as Lancelot Hogben's *From Cave painting to Comic Strip* (1949), exposes the problem. It is like saying that building is architecture; that a history of one is a history of the other.

My own *Graphic Design: A Concise History* tries to separate graphics from design. Graphic design becomes 'what a graphic designer does'. The result is a specific form of visual communication: not only is the activity called design, but design is the outcome and expression of what a designer does. Graphics before graphic design – the forms of the alphabet, symbols and signs with understood meanings like the arrow – become part of a general pre-history. And this raw material in turn has its own pre-history which it shares with the fine arts: two-dimensional, formal techniques (tone, line and perspective) and such graphic devices as silhouette and positive-negative reversal.

Before graphic designers there were craftsmen who made printing in the way they thought printing should look. Technology has transformed the way we make and see images and the way they are reproduced: first through photography and then through computers. The history of graphic design is the history of the designer taking control of the craftsman's process – a trend that has continued until, with the Macintosh, it is almost total.

If our concern is with the control of the process, then the pre-history of graphic design can begin at the end of the nineteenth century, with the colour poster. This is convenient because it is an instance in which we cannot avoid discussing the connections between the social circumstances in which the works were produced, the prevailing aesthetic and stylistic influences, and the means and techniques of their production. These, and later the relationship of text and image in a structure to convey an idea, are the underlying concerns of *A Concise History*, which uses these considerations as a basis for criticism of individual works. As with a coat that fits and hangs well, we may recognise and admire the choice of cloth, but only by unpicking the stitches can we see how its form depends on the way it has been cut, sewn, lined and interfaced. This unpicking assumes that the process of design involves a series of more or less conscious decisions, and that these can be identified by a scrutiny of the work.

What work? First and most obviously, that which has survived. Often this is not as original artefacts, but as what was reproduced – particularly in professional journals and yearbooks – soon after its appearance. Such survivals are often fortuitous, dependent on the designers' energy in self-promotion and their contacts with design journalism. Once reproduced, works survive, design histories give them a third life, and familiarity breeds acceptance into a canon.

Conspicuous as an example of this process is the work of the expatriate American poster artist and illustrator Edward McKnight Kauffer. In England his status was assured by his authorship of *The Art of the Poster* (1924). His career in the 1920s and 1930s was recorded in the pages of the monthly *Commercial Art*, which acclaimed each new design. A retrospective of his work was held at the Museum of Modern Art in 1937; another, a year after his death in America in 1954, at the Victoria & Albert Museum. A full biographical study was published in 1974.

A look at Kauffer's career takes us to the central issue of graphic design history. In a critical torpor, a vacuum, such work has an assured place. But the subject of critical discussion of a design is the relationship the message has to the formal content and its organisation, and of these to the means of their production. To compare Kauffer with Cassandre in this light reveals that in Kauffer's designs there is little effective connection between the elements of the message and their graphic expression. We are left with the style, the crass adaptations of cubistic mannerisms, customising the message with a snobbish vulgarity. The reader may infer that this flattered his clients' conceit in their modern outlook, aesthetically and socially. Cassandre had similar clients, employed a graphic language with the same roots in Cubism, yet his posters are formal concepts, derived from the name of the product or slogan, that fuse the image, lettering and technique into a geometric construction.

Cassandre's 'Étoile du Nord' railway poster has become a paradigm of the Good Design to which we all aspire. But do we ever really look at this poster? If designing is about deciding, and good design about good decisions, then critical history can illuminate its exemplary character: the concentrated intelligence in its expression of the north star in word and image; in its mathematical structure; in its use of colour and the construction of its lettering. It is also a work of its time: demonstrably pre-photographic in its cubistic technique, its tonal gradation achieved by splatter and its colour by selected, not process, colours.

The detailed discussion of individual graphic artefacts is the simplest way to help us understand how graphic design was carried out in a particular period. The criterion for the choice of work should be the importance of what it can be made to reveal. This does not allow for some of the many shortcomings of graphic design history recited by Bridget Wilkins (*Eye* 6): its failure to include 'the motives and ambitions of the commissioning agent' and 'the way these communications are received by their audiences'. But this is not the central aim of design history. Where facts can be found, they should be brought to bear on the discussion of a work, particularly those that shed light on the designer's intentions. But as designers know, post hoc analyses (case studies) of individual jobs are not necessarily intended to present a factual account, but are part of a public relations initiative; they are as useful as the general staffs report on a battle is to military historians. Discussing work with the designers who made it is productive when it focuses on the work itself. The rest is conjecture.

By contrast with architecture, whose ideological development in the Modern movement it has paralleled, graphic design history has attracted little academic or even journalistic interest. Gestalt psychology, mathematical theories of communication and information, semiology, the Postmodern concept of a building as a conglomerate of signs, Structuralist interest in images – all might have shed more light on visual communication. Architects have been important polemicists, while film-makers, particularly those of the French Nouvelle Vague, have helped to establish an intellectual foundation for their work. Many graphic designers have written too, but we have paid them less attention. Important texts that lie hidden in trade magazines need to be collected. Will Burtin's and Ladislav Sutnar's arguments for information design should be reprinted. Texts of European authors should be translated into English; as has been shown in the case of Jan Tschichold, they have lasting relevance.

In writing history there is a sense of paying our debts to our predecessors, of celebrating their achievements by following their example. As a young radical typographer, Tschichold was a constant student of the past. Towards the end of his life, when his own work had returned to traditional forms, he was doing research for an article on El Lissitzky. Designers should not feel that an interest in the past will inhibit their working practice. The study of history teaches us that what has survived as pioneering work is work that has been searching for and finding a way to communicate. 'It is a mistake', wrote Schuitema, 'to think that the work we did then was a new style. Today they call us pioneers, but... our pioneering struggle was in making our work show things clearly.'

Richard Hollis is a freelance designer and writer based in London.
First published in *Eye* 13, 1994.

Visible Language 28.3

New Perspectives

**Critical Histories
of Graphic Design**

Part 1: **Critiques**

THE PARTICULAR PROBLEM
OF GRAPHIC DESIGN (HISTORY)

ANDREW BLAUVELT
1994

'Solutions are not to be found in history. But one can always diagnose that the only possible way is the exasperation of the antitheses, the frontal clash of positions, and the accentuation of contradictions.'
— Manfredo Tafuri[1]

It is helpful at the outset to distinguish the disciplinary aspirations from the field of inquiry, or paraphrasing historian John A. Walker, graphic design history from the history of graphic design.[2] Many events could be cited to demonstrate the existence of what could be best labelled a proto-discipline of graphic design history: books and journals published, conferences organized, papers written, archives established, exhibitions presented, 'courses of study formed and persons claiming the status of "historian"'.[3] I use the term 'proto-discipline' to describe graphic design history because, despite these numerous activities, a coherent body of autonomous knowledge has not formed, which would be a prerequisite for any disciplinary status. The reasons for this seem quite numerous, but probably lie in the activity and social status of graphic design itself.

Most discussions of graphic design history are subsumed under the rubric of design history, a field that potentially comprises all design activities but that eschews certain design practices, namely architecture (which it sees as somehow distinct) and, more specifically, graphic design, in favor of the study of industrially-produced consumer products and certain (mostly pre-industrial) decorative art forms. While all forms of design activity must, by definition, conform to some shared traits, their historical specificity would reveal differences and demand certain approaches. It is these conditions or situations that, for better or worse, established the bracketing of art history, then design history from the larger field of historical studies. An umbrella approach of design history under which would fall the history of graphic design (among others) strives for a problematical unifying philosophy of design which undermines the significance of graphic design as a distinct field of inquiry, with specific historical contexts which demand particular attention.

If graphic design history has as its field of study the thing we have come to call 'graphic design', then it is this term and its changing definitions that constitute a fundamental problem for sketching the limits of the discipline. While Philip B. Meggs ascribes the origins of graphic design to the cave paintings of Lascaux, others trace its development from the invention of movable type (Western with Gutenberg, rather than Eastern with Pi-Shêng). The current definitions of graphic design, however, come from the middle of this century and have as their objective the consolidation of certain activities and the exclusion of others for the benefit of professional autonomy (i.e., specialization of the designer and the segregation of production). Even the most general definitions regarding its status as printed matter have been rendered problematic by advances in electronic technologies and the often predicted demise of printed materials. As Victor Margolin noted in an essay about a decade of design history in the US, the impetus for graphic design history as a field of study comes largely from those persons affiliated with educational institutions – teachers of the professional practice of graphic design.[4] This scenario has helped to shape the constitution of this proto-discipline. The ambiguity of definitions is reflected in the shifting terminology of the academy as educational programs have changed titles from 'commercial and applied art' to 'visual communication' and eventually 'graphic design'. To compensate for this, graphic design history has absorbed discrete histories of relevant areas such as those of technologies like printing and photography as well as the aesthetic models and approaches of art history. The ad-hoc nature of graphic design history creates its share of disadvantages since its incorporation of other disciplines' histories and methods has been undertaken with a characteristically unproblematic critical assessment. Ironically, many graphic design historians have treated the importation of 'theory' (as somehow distinct from history) from other disciplines with prejudicial scorn, particularly if it emanates through graphic designers or, if it emanates through those individuals outside of graphic design, with resistance to academic 'carpetbagging'.[5]

The shortcomings associated with the developments of a graphic design history have been reflected more recently in a series of articles written by both design historians and practitioners. I will attempt to reprise some of the major problems associated with the history of graphic design as a field of study and graphic design history as an emerging discipline.

The distinguishing characteristic of graphic design from both architecture and product design lies in its inherent ephemeral state. The ephemeral nature of most graphic design simply means that many of the objects of study no longer exist and are not normally collected or archived. The transitory nature of graphic design creates a condition of 'presentness' which, in turn, creates an ahistorical sensibility about the objects and the conditions of their formation and reception. Design historian Bridget Wilkins has commented that '[m]ost graphic design ... is not an "object of desire,"' ... 'and, therefore, does not afford the attention and the significance attributed to certain product designs.'[6] Paradoxically, this lack of objects has nevertheless contributed to the object-oriented nature of most, if not all, histories of graphic design. This orientation developed as an inheritance of art history, which itself developed out of the connoisseurship, historical attribution and classification of objects. For graphic design this has meant the selection of objects that testify to the value of design, or more appropriately the cultural capital of 'good design'. This selection process, its nebulous criteria and its accompanying rejection of certain objects of graphic design as somehow unworthy have been recently challenged.[7] Similarly, the focus accorded designers in the various accounts of graphic design history can be linked to the need for an emerging profession's legitimization, including the desires of teachers to offer historical 'role models' for students studying the contemporary practice of graphic design. The combined effects of both of these orientations (understood as the subjects and objects of heroicism) has been to underplay the significance of the complex processes that allow for the production of both designers and design artifacts. What is also lost is the complexity surrounding the circumstances in which such artifacts are distributed, received and/or consumed in and through various segments of society, and increasingly, societies.[8] As it is currently most often taught, at least in the US, the history of graphic design has been organized around the notion of contemporary professional practice wherein all previous subjects and objects ('history') are traced back and unfold in a linear, chronological fashion segmented through a series of stylistic successions – a procession that takes its cue from the avant-garde movements of the early twentieth century. The unfolding story is a *progression*, both technological and professional, from its past to its teleological present. The professional benefits of this type of history are, as Victor Burgin has related, 'to legitimate careers and commodities – history writing as underwriting'.[9] Clive Dilnot has noted the consequences of this myth-making process:

How is myth manifested in design history? Most obviously by the reduction of its subject matter to an unproblematic, self-evident entity (Design) in a form that also reduces its historical specificity and variety to as near zero as possible. This reduction also restructures the history of design to a repetition of designers' careers and to the past as simply anticipating and legitimating the present.[10]

As Dilnot has noted, the legitimizing function of a history in service to its profession denies the historical specificity, and thus understanding, of the professionalization of graphic design as a condition of its *current* state as well as its relative position to the vast amount of graphic design produced as a vernacular activity with anonymous contributors.[11] More importantly, the social significance of the activity of graphic design (i.e., the process of designing) is rendered absent as it is taken for granted, this at a time when the profession of graphic design tries to demonstrate its efficacy to both clients and society at large by relating its abilities against those of untrained professionals. Thus, the mythologizing of graphic design as a story related through its history and told to its future practitioners confronts the technological demystification of its production through the advent of personal computers, software programs and desk-top publishing.

The overall effect is a lack of critical positioning and contextual understanding surrounding the practices of graphic design and its historical antecedents. The lack of critical dimension and theoretical application was noted as early as 1983,[12] again in 1988 by Victor Margolin[13] and who, in 1992, commented on the continuing failure to provide an adequate set of limits with which to organize a coherent body of knowledge that could be considered 'Design History'.[14] In response, Margolin's proposal called for a reappraisal of the notion of design history for a more inclusive concept of *design studies* which he described as:

> ... that field of inquiry which addresses questions of how we make and use products in our daily lives and how we have done so in the past. These products comprise the domain of the artificial. Design studies encompasses issues of product conception and planning, production, form, distribution, and use. It considers these topics in the present as well as in the past. Along with products, it also embraces the web of discourse in which production and use are embedded.[15]

In a similar gesture, Walker offered an alternative model for understanding the social context of design that describes its production, distribution and consumption.[16] Again disciplinary coherence, or rather the lack of it, precipitates his proposal:

> The bulk of the literature on design consists of 'partial' studies in the sense that there are books on designers, products, styles, design education, etc., but what is lacking is a general account of how all of these specific studies interrelate and, taken together, constitute a coherent totality.[17]

Both Margolin's and Walker's models share a common concern for the social context of design and could be compared with similar events occurring in art history which fostered the development of the social history of art out of the same kind of criticisms that have been levelled at the history of graphic design. The social history approach seeks an understanding of art and design outside of the objects and their creators – the transcendence of aesthetics and the artist/designer genius.[18] It provides a context for the objects insofar as they could be understood to manifest class struggle, and thus is indebted to a Marxist approach to interpretation. While Margolin's and Walker's models develop out of a Marxist understanding of production and consumption as reciprocal moments in an economic cycle, the type of context offered in both propositions goes beyond a traditional Marxist approach and has yet to be applied in most analyses of graphic design. What graphic design history has applied is not an understanding of class struggle or even the economic forces that serve to constrain design practices, but rather context as a background of world events or the filler of biographical anecdotes. As with the social history of art, the effect has been to simply reproduce the canon (with more 'details' or 'context'), albeit without the economic determinism of a Marxist analysis. Graphic design history has yet to undertake the task of understanding its social context, understood as a range of effects: from the reproduction of cultural values through the work of graphic design to the shifting nature of consumption and reception, both conspicuous and symbolic, by audiences.[19]

Instead it is the canon of graphic design history which has served as the site for most contestation. The first inroads made were from feminist theories which challenged the operation of patriarchy in design (mainly architecture, product design and advertising). Not surprisingly, feminist theories have provided design history with its most developed critique for understanding design's social effects.[20] The specific response of graphic design history to the critiques provided by feminism has been the recuperation of the roles of certain women graphic designers who are 'lost' to history. [21] Similarly, the canon is being challenged as individuals endeavor to understand the role race has played not only in terms of the existence and achievements of designers of color but also in the understanding of how racism is socially reproduced in the practices of design. Again, graphic design history has responded by seeking the recuperation of individual practitioners and by an examination of the representations of 'others' in the work of graphic design.[22] Additionally, the impetus provided by the heightened awareness of cultural relativity (i.e., multiculturalism) has served to challenge the centrality of the canon with its focus on graphic design from the US and Western Europe.[23] The response has been a call for the expansion of the canon to accommodate work from outside these boundaries, but little attention has been paid to a critical assessment of what the canon actually allows as examples of graphic design or of the seemingly operative definition of graphic design as an exclusive product of industrialized, late-capitalist democracies.

New Perspectives: Critical Histories of Graphic Design

Historical perspective therefore authorizes the operation which, from the same place and within the same text, substitutes conjunction for disjunction, holds contrary statements together, and, more broadly, overcomes the difference between an order and what it leaves aside.
— Michel de Certeau[24]

What all of the aforementioned arguments suggest is an understanding of the cultural activity of graphic design as one rooted in particular social practices. The activity of graphic design would be understood as historically relative and therefore changing, contributing to the notion of multiple *histories* of graphic design. The subjects and objects of graphic design history would move beyond the artifacts and designers to encompass the complexity of the forces that allow for their very existence. This *critical* positioning would include an awareness of the limits of any historical project as revealed through the historian's particular *perspective*. Incumbent in such a heightened awareness would be the acknowledgement of the disciplinary forces at work that serve to constrain the roles of not only graphic design and graphic designers but also of historians and history writing, including the constitution and uses of knowledge. This concept of historically specific constraints was theorized by Michel Foucault,[25] whose work, as outlined by Mark Poster, suggests that:

[t]he emancipatory interests promoted by historical materialism are sustained only with a detotalized theoretical stance such as that proposed by Foucault, a theoretical asceticism that severely restricts the truth claims of texts. There are two constraints of particular importance: 1) that the historian acknowledge his or her political orientation and 2) that the historian's text not claim to exhaust the meaning of the field to be investigated. [26]

Bearing these constraints in mind, the collection of essays contained in three consecutive issues of this journal have been positioned by the editor in order to facilitate certain ideas presupposed by the project itself and those suggested by common themes among the essays. The first collection of essays, contained in this issue, has been arranged with an emphasis on a critical appraisal of current approaches undertaken in the name of graphic design history. These essays address both general problems of historiography and history writing as well as specific problems arising from current narrative accounts of graphic design history and the particular problem of typographic histories. The second collection of essays, found in *Visible Language*, volume 28, issue 4, has been grouped under the rubric of practice. They speak to a conception of graphic design as a variety of theoretically informed and socially engaged practices. Eschewing many current operative definitions of (mainly professional) practice, they address the role that graphic design does and could play when understood in its greater social context and the plurality of its activities. The diverse range of concerns shown in these essays moves us to an understanding of the cultural context of the practice of graphic design, from issues of social activism and the making of history to the methodological problems of examining the historically specific roles that women practitioners have played in patriarchy. The third collection of essays, found in *Visible Language*, volume 29, issue 1, offers specific case studies of graphic design. They represent a critical position in relationship to their object of study, focusing on the roles of historical interpretation, from the assignment of meaning(s) to the understanding of performative effect(s). The subject matter of these case studies ranges from a reassessment of historical icons from graphic design history's canon to the inclusion of previously ignored products of the vernacular practice of graphic design. These essays strive for an understanding of their subject matter as a product of greater cultural forces while acknowledging the active role designers and society play in their construction.

An Opening: Graphic Design's Discursive Spaces

Acknowledging the homogenizing tendency of the editorial process of ordering wherein differences are effaced, the texts represented in these volumes are in service to the project at hand. They have been arranged in three issues, each issue with a particular focus (critiques, practices and interpretations) and each essay serves this ordering purpose and simultaneously defies it. The act of ordering texts only serves to undermine the editorial purpose as each focus overflows the boundaries of its imposed limits. The artificial nature of these foci is exposed in the overlapping themes of the essays across all three issues. In this way, we can detect, for example, critical assessments of graphic design history either explicitly or implicitly in all essays. While the ordering of texts has been determined and the foci fixed, the connections between essays are indeterminate and unfixed. History is thus understood as a production, one which is completed fully only when it has been engaged – and its meanings negotiated – as it passes from an (un)fixed writing to an (un)fixed reading. The accentuation of the boundaries and the play between the three foci determine the limits of this project. As such, this historical project is simply another work on the margins as it defines itself against some contiguous 'other'. In turn, the marginal limits of historical projects form the field of investigations. The historian Michel de Certeau relates:

Whatever the author's own position, his work both describes and engenders the movement which leads history to become a *work on the margins*: to situate itself through its relation to other discourses, to place discursivity in its relation to an eliminated other, to measure results in relation to the objects that escape its grasp; but also to establish continuities by isolating series, to analyze methods closely by distinguishing distinct objects which they grasp at once in a single fact, to revise and to compare the different periodizations that various types of analysis bring forth, and so forth. Hereafter the 'problem is no longer of tradition and trace, but of delimitation and margins.' [27]

Consequently, the boundaries of each study and the project as a whole begin to create a set of limits to the field of inquiry, both through their presence – their positive formations with discernible edges – and through their absence – their negative ground by which they are rendered visible. This project creates a group of present or visible points (the essays) as well as a field of absences, what de Certeau refers to as the 'eliminated other'. Thus, I would contend that this project defines as much by what it leaves aside as by what it includes. This opening in the field of graphic design history creates a discursive space for investigation insofar as we are able to conceive of the absences that are generated by history itself. These absences could be understood as those elements which are effaced in conventional historical accounts that favor the transparency of objects, the assignment of meanings, the attribution and classification of objects, the centrality of the designer and (usually) his or her intentions, the evolution and refinement (development) from past to present, the logical succession of events and styles, etc. In contrast, discursive accounts would emphasize the opacity and complexity of relationships that allow for the production of graphic design and graphic designers, the understanding of the performative effects of such production, a critical understanding of the role of the subject (designer and audience) neither solely as a free, autonomous agent nor as an individual completely dominated or determined by the prevailing hegemony, the examination of the exclusions of graphic design history's canon and a move away from history as a chain of events to history as a space of critical positions. [28]

Perhaps we should be pleased with the proto-disciplinary nature of graphic design history, in the sense that it has not achieved full disciplinary status. After all, it is the instrumental uses of knowledge and its segregation into discrete units that has been rendered so problematical in the last few decades by the blurring of boundaries between disciplines. The complex nature of the design process necessitates an understanding of it that integrates knowledge from many different disciplines and in the process develops its own particular account. For the discursive spaces of graphic design to be opened for investigation requires that the defensive posturing and the shoring-up of the walls of graphic design history be exchanged for the active examination of the 'limits' of graphic design. [29]

Andrew Blauvelt is Curator of Architecture and Design and Chief of Communications and Audience Engagement at the Walker Art Center, Minneapolis.
First published in *Visible Language*, vol. 28, no. 3, 1994.

1   Manfredo Tafuri, *Theories and History of Architecture* (New York: Harper & Row Publishers. Inc., 1980), p.237.

2   See John A. Walker, *Design History and the History of Design* (London: Pluto Press, 1989).

3   See Victor Margolin, 'A Decade of Design History in the United States 1977–87', *Journal of Design History*, 1:1 (1988), p.51–72.

4   Margolin, op.cit., p.56.

5   Victor Margolin, ed., *Design Discourse* (Chicago and London: University of Chicago Press, 1989), p.158. The term and concept are borrowed from an essay by Frances Butler, 'Eating the Image: The Graphic Designer and the Starving Audience', Clive Dilnot addresses the 'resistance to theory' encountered in design history in his essay 'The State of Design History, Part II: Problems and Possibilities', in the same collection.

6   Bridget Wilkins, 'No more heroes', *Eye* 2 (1992), p.6.

7   For one account see: Frascara, Jorge, 'Graphic Design History: Its Purpose and Relevance', *Design Statements* (Winter 1993) p.13–16. The types of graphic design shown in history classes and reproduced in books tends to cater to an art historical tendency in which the things closest to paintings, like posters, get shown and where entire areas of graphic design produced for society are ignored, like the products of 'information design', product packaging and even print advertising.

8   I am attempting to describe two effects. One is the circulation of design in and through socially defined audiences (as opposed to a 'mass' audience) and the other is the circulation of design across national boundaries mostly in the form of multinational corporate capitalism.

9   Victor Burgin, 'Something About Photography Theory', reprinted in *The New Art History*. A.L. Rees and F. Bonello, eds. (Atlantic Highlands, New Jersey: Humanities Press International, 1988), p.45.

10 Clive Dilnot, 'The State of Design History, Part II, Problems and Possibilities', reprinted in *Design Discourse*, Victor Margolin, ed. (Chicago and London: University of Chicago Press, 1989), p.237.

11 Here I would distinguish the role of vernacular design, which Dilnot suggests has passed in relationship to disciplines such as architecture and industrial design, with the increase of non-professional graphic design practice which has surfaced with the advent of the personal computer. See Dilnot, op.cit., p.245.

12 See Massimo Vignelli, 'Keynote Address', *The First Symposium on the History of Graphic Design: Coming of Age* (Rochester, New York: Rochester Institute of Technology, 1983), p.8–11.

13 Margolin, 'A Decade of Design History in the United States 1977–87', op.cit., p.58.

14 Margolin, 'Design History or Design Studies, Subject Matter and Methods', *Design Studies*, 13:2 (1992), p.105–6.

15 Margolin, 'Design History or Design Studies, Subject Matter and Methods', op.cit., p.115.

16 See John A. Walker, 'Production-consumption Model', in *Design History and the History of Design*, p.68–73.

17 Walker, 'Production-consumption Model', op.cit., p.68.

18 For the incorporation of a post-structuralist account of authorship and intentionality in the social history of art see: Janet Wolff, *The Social Production of Art*, second edition (New York: New York University Press, 1993). For an account of the development of the social history of art, particularly in the UK, see: A.L. Rees and Frances Borzello, eds., *The New Art History* (1988).

19 For an argument of the conventional call for context understood as a set of social influences on graphic design see: Douglass Scott, 'Graphic Design History – In Context', in *Spirals Book Six* (Providence, Rhode Island: Rhode Island School of Design, Department of Graphic Design, 1991), p.217–225.

20 See Cheryl Buckley, 'Made in Patriarchy: Toward a Feminist Analysis of Women and Design', in ed. Margolin, *Design Discourse*, op.cit., p.251–262 and Judy Attfield, 'FORM/female FOLLOWS FUNCTION/male: Feminist Critiques of Design', in John A. Walker, *Design History and the History of Design*, op.cit., p.199–225.

21 The direct reference is to a lecture by design critic Karrie Jacobs entitled 'Lost Women in Design', presented at the 1992 Modernism and Eclecticism Conference (School of Visual Arts, New York).

22 Although sparse, the recuperation of graphic designers of color has been carried forward by several individuals through various forums such as lectures and articles. In particular see: Cheryl Miller, 'Black Designers Missing in Action', *Print*, 41:5 (1987), p.56–65, 138. Fath Davis Ruffins of the Smithsonian Institution in Washington, D.C. provided a historical account of ethnic representations in her lecture at the 1994 *Modernism and Eclecticism Conference* (School of Visual Arts, New York) entitled, 'Race and Representation: Ethnic Imagery in American Advertising 1800–1960'.

23 Works of graphic design have been allowed into the canon from outside the US and Western Europe when they conform to the expectations of what constitutes graphic design in 'first world' terms, such as posters that show the influence of European Modernism.

24 Michel de Certeau, *The Writing of History* (New York: Columbia University Press, 1988), p.89.

25 See Michel Foucault, *The Archeology of Knowledge and the Discourse on Language* (New York: Pantheon Books, 1972).

26 Mark Poster, 'Foucault, the Present, and History', in *Critical Theory and Poststructuralism* (Ithaca, New York: Cornell University Press, 1989), p.73.

27 de Certeau, op.cit., p.40.

28 The history of graphic design as a history of positions is put forward by Frascara in his essay, op.cit., p.16.

29 I use the term 'limits' here instead of Foucault's 'discontinuities', because, as de Certeau observes, it is too suggestive of a rupture in reality. I do not intend to set definable or defendable limits for the field of graphic design.

Visible Language 28.3

New Perspectives

**Critical Histories
of Graphic Design**

*Part 1: **Critiques***

A POETICS OF GRAPHIC DESIGN?

STEVE BAKER
1994

There is a continuing dissonance between the history and practice of graphic design. In particular, the stylistic experimentation and political engagement that characterized some of the most influential developments in twentieth-century graphic design practice have not found an equivalent in the ways in which the subject's history has been written. Even when the restrictiveness and bogus neutrality of design history's conventional linear narratives have been recognized and criticized, little has been done to develop a more 'spatial' writing, a writing which moves – at least at a poetic or metaphorical level – closer to the image. This article proposes that the work of the French feminist writers Hélène Cixous and Luce Irigaray could serve as the basis for devising a more imaginative form of critical writing that might help to draw the history and practice of graphic design into a closer and more purposeful relation.

'I am only interested in the texts that escape.'
— Hélène Cixous[1]

'I notice that my characters, my animals, my insects, my fish,
look as if they are escaping from the paper.'
— Hokusai [2]

It would be quite wrong to assume at the outset that graphic design history – any graphic design history – should necessarily have a close structural relation to the broader (and itself much disputed) field of design history. Nevertheless, some of the complaints against contemporary design history may be equally applicable to graphic design history as it is currently conceived. This is certainly the case, I would suggest, when it comes to considering how questions of gender are to be addressed in design writing. The significance of feminist design history's exploration of such questions is now not only acknowledged but also emphasized by some male writers. Victor Margolin, for instance, has recently proposed that 'feminism is the most powerful critique of design history thus far', and John A. Walker has argued that 'if men were to take the lessons of feminism seriously, then the predominantly masculine discourse of design history would be transformed.'[3] What neither these writers nor the feminist historians they praise have addressed in any sustained manner, however, are the *ways* in which the discourses of design history might be transformed by attending more closely to gender's implication in and for history. What, in other words, might an alternative and more gender-conscious design writing look like? What form might its visible language take? The argument of the present essay is that this question is particularly pertinent in relation to graphic design's possible histories. Let there be no doubt: a graphic design history is above all *a way of writing*, and the question here is the form that writing is to take – is able to take, inclined to take or even imaginable to take.

It is certainly not simply a matter of heeding calls, such as that made by Cheryl Buckley in *Design Issues* some years ago, for a design history that would 'acknowledge the governance of patriarchy and its operation historically.'[4] The problem may be with history itself as a mode of writing. This idea is presented with particular force in the work of the French feminist writers

Luce Irigaray and Hélène Cixous, where each of them addresses – at a rhetorical rather than a simplistic biological level – the gendered character of power relations in the discourses of history.

Irigaray's *An Ethics of Sexual Difference* explores Western culture's hierarchical association of men with time, and of women with space or place. She writes that 'man has been the subject of discourse, whether in theory, morality or politics.' Philosophy's historical privileging of time over space, she proposes, puts the masculine subject in a position in which it comes to be understood that 'time becomes the *interiority* of the subject itself', and in which 'the subject, the master of time, becomes the axis of the world's ordering.' She observes that 'this leads, on the social and cultural level, to important empirical and transcendental effects: with *discourse* and *thought* being the privileges of a *male* producer.'[5] This positing of the operation of a gendered division of time (as masculine) and space (as feminine) in Western philosophy might suggest that the writing of any 'history' will itself be structurally oriented to the masculine.

Cixous', earlier classic text, 'Sorties', is more forthright on this matter. Writing in the mid-1970s, Cixous sites received notions of history firmly in 'L'empire du propre' (usually translated as 'The Realm of the Proper'), a Hegelian realm defined by its concern to mark and to defend the boundaries of established power, privilege and self-certainty. Of this rhetorically masculine conception or history, she remarks:

> A commonplace gesture of History: there have to be two races – the masters and the slaves... The same masters dominate history from the beginning, inscribing on it the marks of their appropriating economy: history, as a story of phallocentricism, hasn't moved except to repeat itself... History, history of phallocentricism, history of propriation: a single history... History has never produced or recorded anything else... And it is time to change. To invent the other history.[6]

The space in which this 'other history' is to be invented is for the most part that of the *écriture féminine* which Cixous has continued to explore across the range of her writings, and which she makes clear is not, in principle, restricted to women's writing. She has stated plainly in an interview that 'I do not equate *feminine* with woman and *masculine* with man.' The challenge to 'the masculine future', she suggests in 'Sorties', will come (regardless of their sex) from 'thinkers, artists, those who create new values, "philosophers" in the mad Nietzschean manner, inventors and wreckers of concepts and forms, those who change life.'[7] In their feminine manifestation, at least, Cixous calls them *les désordonnantes*.[8]

In terms of the possibility of a new attitude to writing history, including graphic design history, there are good reasons to focus on Cixous and Irigaray, who are generally taken to represent the 'deconstructive-psychoanalytic' wing of French feminist theory. One reason, to which I will return, is their underlying 'political optimism', their insistence on the possibility of change.[9] Another is the light their work might cast on the current status of deconstruction and related aspects of French theory in debates on graphic design's history and practice.

When Cixous' work came up for consideration in a previous issue of *Visible Language* – the much discussed 1978 special issue 'French currents or the letter' – the article's layout, like that of the others in that issue, was given a self-consciously 'deconstructive' treatment by graduate students of the Cranbrook Academy of Art.[10] Katherine McCoy, co-chair of the Design Department there, has described Cranbrook graphic design of the late 1970s and 1980s as consciously drawing on French post-structuralist theory, and a recent review of this work named Cranbrook 'the academy of deconstructed design' and its *Visible Language* layout as 'still the academy's most uncompromising assault on typographic convention as a transmitter of meaning.'[11] But at a time when the adoption of this post-structuralist 'attitude' is widely seen as a progressive move in discussions of design practice, it is precisely the focus of criticism for those with a more conservative concern for the history of that practice. Adrian Forty's response to Margolin's comments on the shortcomings of much contemporary design history argued that the discipline had in fact been 'over-willing' to embrace 'new lines of thought', and what Forty considered specifically 'unhelpful to design is the post-structuralist view that all judgments are as good or as bad as each other.' He cited Robin Kinross' *Modern Typography: An Essay in Critical History* as a good example of the defense of traditional values in current graphic design history, and it is perhaps significant that a few years earlier Kinross had himself proposed that 'post-structuralism promises no benefits for design theory.'[12]

My concern is not, for the moment, the extent to which any of these writers may or may not be thought to misrepresent post-structuralism, and I certainly want to work towards a view of graphic design history writing which could draw back from the unproductively polarized positions implied in the previous paragraph. It is clear, however, that in the Anglo-American debate on graphic design's histories, much still hinges on various aspects of French theory. Rather surprisingly, and notwithstanding the *Visible Language* article on Cixous, that debate continues to focus overwhelmingly on writers such as Roland Barthes and Jacques Derrida and not at all on *écriture féminine* and the critique of the 'masculinization of thought' which is found in the works of Cixous and Irigaray. Once I have briefly enlarged on a specific problem concerning the methods adopted in writing graphic design history, I shall suggest that Cixous and Irigaray offer some especially productive ways forward.

Against a 'Masculine' Linearity

One of the principal complaints of feminist historians concerning the 'masculine' orientation of design history has been a very simple one, and is at least superficially similar to one which is also frequently found both in male and female historians' critiques of conventional histories of design. It is the complaint that these histories are unduly linear and Pevsnerian in their accounts of a 'pioneers'-based sequence of stylistic developments. Two nice examples will suffice. Buckley, reviewing a history of women in design (written by a female historian), objects to its reproduction of a model of history 'which is linear, progressive and peopled by female "pioneers"', since it fails to see that the method itself perpetuates the legitimization of a particular view of design that results in 'much of women's design', which is 'often anonymous, traditional and made in a domestic sphere', continuing to be 'left out of the history books'. More recently Bridget Wilkins, writing about graphic design history (though not specifically from a feminist perspective), has argued that its overriding concern with the 'look' of things is 'modelled on the earliest approaches to art history' and emphasizes either the linear career development of the individual 'hero' or a linear progression of styles. In either case, she suggests, 'these linear concepts of history are ignoring some of the central issues in graphic design', as they tend to distort the ephemeral nature of much graphic design and to ignore the question of how these communications were received and understood by the largely non-professional audience they addressed.[13] In the present context my concern will be to address not how design history in general might deal with the avoidance of linearity, but specifically to speculate on how a way of writing about graphic design might do so.

The Gendering of Word and Image

One of the most obvious characteristics to distinguish graphic design from other fields of design is its concern with the conjunction of word and image. I shall propose here (and it may be viewed either as a rhetorical conceit or as a move with entirely practical implications) that a form of a writing appropriate to the study of graphic design might itself attempt to bring the visual and the verbal into a closer relation.

The challenge facing graphic design writing, to put it in terms of Irigaray's gendered distinction, might thus be said to be the production of a move from the linear history writing of the masculine word to the spatial inscription of the feminine image. Such a project corresponds in certain specific respects to matters alluded to all too briefly in Joseph Hillis Miller's recent book, *Illustration*. In seeking to isolate a possible 'mode of meaning specific to the graphic image', Miller includes a glancing reference to a 'traditional gendering of acts' in which the process of writing's linearity, 'engraving a furrow, the art of scratch, is seen as male', while drawing's conceptual proximity to the embroidering of a surface, the weaving of a cover, 'is seen as female.' He suggests that in a sense the 'double act of engraving and embroidering' is already present in all forms of graphic activity, since both word and image have their origin in 'the primordial act of scratching a surface to make it a sign.'[14]

My suggestion here is that it may nevertheless be instructive to *reopen* this sign, the better to examine and understand it, and to take more seriously the possibility that words, somehow, continue to be regarded as having a masculine orientation, and images a feminine one. What would such a distinction say about the relative power of word and image? Would it be a reflection of, or at any rate seem to run parallel to, the widespread cultural privileging of the verbal over the visual (even in much of the graphic design literature)?[15] By what means might it be challenged and undone? Might a form of graphic design history writing be imagined which was consonant with the practice of graphic design, and which would challenge this sign's gendered priorities by weaving a way of writing from (or around) one of the particular characteristics of its subject: the endlessly changing and infinitely complex relation of word and image? This would be writing of a heightened visibility, an imagistic writing, a writing which, by whatever means, sought to minimize the 'remoteness' of academic writing by replenishing it with those things, such as dreams, of which Cixous complains that one finds less and less in contemporary narratives and histories:

less and less poetry
less and less angels
less and less birds
less and less women
less and less courage [16]

Hardly Recognizable as History

It goes without saying that such a writing may be hardly recognizable as history. Its concern is primarily with what's going on *in the writing* of graphic design's histories (and where power lies in that writing), and rather less with the historical matters that are being written about. In this respect its focus on questions of gender will be distinct from that of Michael Rock and Susan Sellers, for instance, who argue that 'while most design history and criticism claims to be non-ideological and value neutral, it is a fact that design has been controlled and produced by men.' It is not a case simply of attending to historical circumstances overlooked by conventional histories, important as those matters may undoubtedly be, but of grasping Irigaray's point (which might apply equally to graphic design's history and to its practice) that 'the generation of messages is not neutral, but sexuate.' [17]

When Irigaray asserts that 'sexual difference is probably the issue in our time which could be our "salvation" if we thought it through', the point is not to assume from this that questions of gender will *themselves* always be central, but to see their acknowledgement as at present constituting a most effective way of *rhetorically opening up history* to a more inquiring attitude. Irigaray's ethics of sexual difference is not only a matter of sexual politics. It extends to contesting 'religiosity, slogans, publicity, terror, etc. All forms of passively experienced passions in which the subject is enclosed, constrained.'[18] Like Cixous' call for the invention of another history, Irigaray wants 'the creation of a new *poetics*'. One of the things such a poetics would make manifest is what she calls 'the sexuation of discourse', even at the level of syntax. 'To say that discourse has a sex, especially in its syntax, is to question the last bastion of semantic order' – an order that grimly and blindly clings to the presumption of its own 'neuter, universal, unchanging' validity and transparency.[19]

What Irigaray imagines, in other words, is a poetics that would render history, history's procedures, history's 'syntax', history's effects, opaque. A thick and treacly stuff. Like reading one's way through Velcro™ – the words conscious of their pull on each other. Graphic design history (like much of design history, as it happens) isn't yet sufficiently historically self-conscious, opaque to itself, and is often still deluded into thinking that the writing of a history is essentially straightforward and unproblematic and needs simply to be done 'well'.[20] What is needed, on the contrary, and what can only hesitantly be worked towards, is an appropriate *form* of self-consciousness and unfamiliarity. The historian here might aspire to something like the condition of the unfamiliar philosopher of Irigaray's new poetics:

> Philosophy is not a formal learning, fixed and rigid, abstracted from all feeling. It is a quest for love, love of beauty, love of wisdom, which is one of the most beautiful things.... the philosopher would be someone poor, dirty, rather down-and-out, always unhoused, sleeping beneath the stars, but very curious, skilled in ruses and tricks of all kinds, constantly reflecting, a sorcerer, a sophist, sometimes exuberant, sometimes close to death. This is nothing like the way we usually represent the philosopher: a learned person who is well dressed, has good manners, knows everything, and pedantically instructs us in the corpus of things already coded. The philosopher is nothing like that.[21]

Cixous, in a more recent essay on painting, similarly characterizes that activity as an ongoing quest and argues that 'the painter, the true painter, doesn't know how to paint.'[22] It might equally be true that the kind of historian envisaged here would not know 'how' to write history.

Finding the Right Metaphors

In Cixous' earlier and more obviously feminist theoretical writings, which stress the imperative of women's taking up writing for themselves ('Why don't you write? Write! Writing is for you'),[23] the *écriture féminine* she has in mind is itself seen as part of the 'work to be done' against the fixed, coded, institutionalized and in many respects masculine hold on meaning, on discourse, on history: 'There's work to be done against *class*, against categorization, against classification...against the pervasive masculine urge to judge, diagnose, digest, name...'.[24] In certain of her recent writings, however, and especially in an extraordinary essay entitled 'Without End/no/State of Drawingness/no, rather:/The Executioner's Taking off', she suggests that visual imagery, and drawing in particular, might in a certain sense better allow us to get 'between the lines' of the artificially complete, 'finished' and orderly discourse of the *propre*.[25]

In the present context the particular interest of this work is that the metaphors with which it is packed are essentially the same as those she now uses to characterize the forms of writing she most admires. Writing and drawing, word and image, are presented as undertaking similar work and having a similar sense of purpose. The principle metaphor is that of the cut or the blow, *le coup*, which can also be the word for the stroke both of the brush and of the pen, as well as the one describing the more violent effects of the axe or the dagger. In *Three Steps on the Ladder of Writing* Cixous quotes Kafka: 'If the book we are reading doesn't wake us up with a blow on the head, what are we reading it for?... A book must be the axe for the frozen sea inside us.' The writers Cixous admires, she claims, have all written '*by the light of the axe:* they all dared to write the worst' – the urgency of their writing metaphorically illuminated by the glint of the executioner's axe at the instant before it falls.[26]

In the 'State of Drawingness' essay, the drawing's blow is inflicted both on us and by us – no distinction is drawn between producer and consumer of the image. 'This morning in the museum, I was passing in front of the drawings, in the slight alarm of the reading which doesn't know from where the blow will come...' A moment earlier she was writing of drawing as though it were indistinguishable from our active involvement in writing: '*What do we want to draw?* What are we trying to grasp between the lines, in between the strokes, in the net that we're weaving, that we throw, and the dagger blows [*les coups de stylet*]?'[27]

The proposal that *le coup* may also be a productive metaphor for characterizing a possible graphic design history – that such a history may be thought of (though clearly not too literally) as being written by the light of Cixous' axe, or under the aegis of this axe – will not necessarily take us as far from familiar territory as it might seem. Her active and purposeful conception of the bonding of word and image – 'the to-be-in-the-process-of writing or drawing' – finds echoes both in Margolin's emphasis not on design but on 'designing' as 'an activity that is constantly changing', and also in Kinross' proposal that design should be 'understood not as a noun but as a verb: an activity and a process'.[28] What is more, if the metaphor of *le coup* serves as a means of proposing a *reading* of graphic design history, such a reading may be regarded as part of the 'work to be done against' less critical histories, since as Cixous herself suggests, 'reading is a wonderful metaphor for all kinds of joy that are called vicious.' Miller's *Illustration* offers a similar account of the work of reading: 'Even in the case of visual ... signs, the word *read*, in its emphasis on an interventionist and productive activity of interpretation that takes nothing for granted, is still the best word available.' He argues that 'only an active and interventionist reading... will *work*, that is, effect changes in the real institutional and social worlds.'[29]

Voice

The question remains as to how to get the work of that reading into writing, into a non-linear and more visual form of history writing, which we should perhaps not balk at calling a poetics of graphic design.[30] Ironically, the apparently more verbal notion of *giving voice* may be of particular importance here. Sheila Levrant de Bretteville, the head of graphic design at Yale, defines her own conception of feminist graphic design practice in terms of establishing 'the equality of all voices', and looking for 'graphic strategies that will enable us to listen to people who have not been heard before.' Anne Burdick, similarly, argues that the much needed shift in perspective which would enable graphic designers to 'consider themselves authors, not facilitators' is one which 'implies responsibility, voice, action'.[31] From the historical perspective, while the discourse of history is seen both by Cixous and Irigaray as being ordered by and oriented to the 'masculine', Irigaray observes that it paradoxically ensures 'the extinction of voice in discourse'. 'The text of the law, the codes, no longer has a voice.' It 'holds sway in silence.' It may therefore be supposed that this authoritative discourse will be positively fearful of the 'feminine' or of the unauthorized gaining access to speech and to history, 'access to sharing, exchanging, or coining symbols', access to the production of meaning – or to the means of disrupting meaning.[32] This is the basis of the urgency of Cixous' *écriture féminine*; it gives access, it gives voice, it allows 'work to be done'.

Interruption, Ekphrasis and the Axe

There are obvious problems with any attempt to be prescriptive about effective strategies for a modified form of history writing, but here at least is one modest proposal. It stems, among other things, from de Bretteville's account of the gendered experience of designing:

> There is a prevalent notion in the professional world that only if you have eight or more uninterrupted hours per day can you do significant work. But if you respond to other human beings... you never really have eight uninterrupted hours in a row. Relational existence is only attached to gender by history – not by genes, not by biology, not by some essential 'femaleness'. ... A relational person allows notions about other people to interrupt the trajectory of thinking or designing...[33]

Might the linear trajectory of a graphic design history similarly find the form of its writing somehow *marked* by interruption, struck through with interruptions, in recognition of the complexity and fragmentation of its project (to say nothing of the of the lives of its writers)?

The form of this interruptive marking will need to be something more substantial than a typographic effect such as the famous 'fault line' running through the McCoys' essay 'The New Discourse' – an essay which one reviewer described as 'maddening to read, because of the application of their ideas to the page layout, in which two columns of text are purposely and dramatically out of alignment.'[34] Applying a deconstructive 'look' to ordinary historico-critical writing is missing the point. If this writing is to be hard to read on occasion, it should be because of the unfamiliarity or outlandishness of the ideas and not just the novelty of the typography.

The poetic device of *ekphrasis* will be more useful in elaborating the idea of a strategic and, in certain respects, gendered form of interruption. Ekphrasis, defined by W.J.T. Mitchell as 'the verbal representation of a visual representation', is more fully explored in an invaluable article by Grant Scott. In literature the ekphrastic description, Scott explains, might be a 'featured inset' which 'digresses from the primary narrative line.' Although generally intended as 'a sidelight', 'it often threatens to upstage the dominant narrative, Ekphrasis frustrates linear progression and offers an alternative poetics of space and plenitude.'[35] In this connection the device has been characterized by some commentators as representing a 'florid effeminacy' of style. Scott suggests that for such writers:

> The mistrust of finery and ornament at least in part... stems from a fear of its origins in the feminine unconscious. To embellish is to do women's work; to declare plainly and straightforwardly to further the 'manly' cause. The dichotomy derives from a debate between clarity and sophistry deeply embedded in Western thought. It belongs to a long tradition of suspicion towards artist...[36]

– toward exactly those who Cixous defines as threatening 'the masculine future', that is.

This is not to suggest, of course, that in graphic design history writing the ekphrastic description would necessarily stick out like a sore thumb, or like a dazzling and elaborate subversion of the text. Its effect may be more discreet, but just as purposeful. A clear example is given in a discussion between Kinross and the designer Richard Hollis concerning Hollis' book *Graphic Design: A Concise History*, prior to its publication.[37] Hollis complains to Kinross that too many historians fail to draw back from the flow of their narratives in order to 'look at what they're talking about.' It is not enough, he proposes, simply to reproduce a piece of graphic design as an illustration in order to get the reader to understand it. Hollis quotes from his own lengthy description of a Jan Tschichold poster, *Der Berufsphotograph*, in order to make the point that it is often the writer's carefully crafted description of the thing itself, rather than of its historical context or circumstances, which creates understanding. He goes on:

> So my editor is going to say 'what are you doing describing something which you're illustrating?', but I'm going to insist. Unless you describe it, people will not read this image, they will just see an image, and won't understand the terrific concentrated intelligence that has produced the image.[38]

The *work* of the reading, the reading of the image, occurs outside of the history's linearity, in the more 'spatial' plenitude of the ekphrastic description. In the space, in other words, of an alternative and interruptive poetics.

Cixous' own extraordinary ekphrases in the 'State of Drawingness' essay do something similar, structurally if not stylistically. Openly ahistorical, they are imaginative attempts to enter *into the time*, into the instant, of the drawings they describe. They want to explore what happens '*during* the drawing', in the interiority of our experience (or of our imaginative reconstruction) of the drawing. As viewers we are once again also the image producers, and our concern is with 'what escapes: we want to draw the instant. That instant which strikes between two instants, that instant which flies into bits under its own blow [*sous son propre coup*].' We want 'to see everything in a flash, and at least once shatter the spine of time with only one pencil stroke [*d'un seul coup de crayon*].'[39] *Le coup* is, here, the all-purpose figure of this multivalent interior turmoil. Its violence is very different from that of an externally imposed 'History, which is always a History of borders' – these borders being defined by Cixous as 'invisible lines that stir up war.'[40]

The poetics of graphic design, which has been very provisionally gestured towards here, takes its lead from Cixous' demonstration that the visual and the verbal need not always be kept strictly apart, but can escape into each other's territories and beyond. The glint of her metaphorical axe might fancifully be thought of as lighting the way towards a critical writing on graphic design which could itself be distinctive, but without borders; characteristic of (and enacting) its own concerns, without ever troubling with anything so banal as the 'boundaries' of the discipline. Heedless of received ideas of its 'proper' limits or 'proper' concerns, it would always be exceeding its own body, multiplying its instants, its instances, proliferating, profligate, fecund. This would be a forward-looking critical writing which took the form of a pushing out towards, a working for, rather than a backward-looking gathering up of its significant moments. As Cixous rather enigmatically puts it, 'you will recognize the true drawing, the live one: it's still running.'[41]

Steve Baker is Emeritus Professor of Art History at the University of Central Lancashire, Preston.
First published in *Visible Language*, vol. 28, no. 3, 1994.

1 Hélène Cixous, *Three Steps on the Ladder of Writing*, trans. Sarah Cornell and Susan Sellers (New York: Columbia University Press, 1993), p.98.

2 Quoted in Cixous, *'Coming to Writing' and Other Essays*, ed. Deborah Jenson, trans. Sarah Cornell et al. (Cambridge, Massachusetts: Harvard University Press, 1991), p.117.

3 Victor Margolin, 'Design History or Design Studies: Subject Matter and Methods', *Design Studies*, 13:2 (1992), p.113 and John A. Walker, *Design History and the History of Design* (London: Pluto Press, 1989), p.199.

4 Cheryl Buckley, 'Made in Patriarchy: Toward a Feminist Analysis of Women and Design', *Design Issues*, 3:2 (1986), p.6.

5 Luce Irigaray, *An Ethics of Sexual Difference*, trans. Carolyn Burke and Gillian G. Gill (London: Athlone Press, 1993), p.6, 7, 87.

6 Cixous, 'Sorties', in Cixous and Catherine Clément, *The Newly Born Woman*, trans. Betsy Wing (Manchester: Manchester University Press, 1986), p.70, 79, 83.

7 Cixous, 'Sorties', op.cit., p.84. The interview with Cixous is in Verena Andermatt Conley, *Hélène Cixous: Writing the Feminine*, Expanded edition (Lincoln & London: University of Nebraska Press, 1991), p.129–61.

8 Cixous' phrase, 'nous, les désordonnantes', has been translated both as 'we women, the derangers' and as 'we, the sowers of disorder'. Neither version really conveys the full resonance of the term in her work. For a fuller discussion, see Steve Baker, 'Flying, Stealing: The Gift in the View of Cixous', in Pat Kirkham, ed., *The Gendered Object* (Manchester & New York: Manchester University Press 1995).

9 Nancy Fraser, 'Introduction', in Nancy Fraser and Sandra Lee Bartky, eds., *Revaluing French Feminism: Critical Essays on Difference, Agency and Culture* (Bloomington and Indianapolis: Indiana University Press, 1992), p.5, 12.

10 Verena Andermatt, 'Writing the Letter: The Lower-case of *hélène cixous*', *Visible Language*, 12:3 (1978), p.305–18.

11 Ellen Lupton, 'The Academy of Deconstructed Design', *Eye* 1 (1991) p.44.

12 Adrian Forty, 'A Reply to Victor Margolin', *Journal of Design History*, 6:2 (1993), p.131 and Robin Kinross, 'Semiotics and Designing', *Information Design Journal*, 4:3 (1986), p.196.

13 Cheryl Buckley, 'Designed by Women', *Art History*, 9:3 (1986), p.403 and Bridget Wilkins, 'No More Heroes', *Eye* 6 (1992), p.4.

14 J. Hillis Miller, *Illustration* (London: Reaktion Books, 1992), p.66, 78, 75.

15 See for example Steve Baker, 'Re-reading the Corporate Personality', *Journal of Design History*, 2:4 (1989), p.275–92, in which I suggest that the work of Wally Olins, the foremost British writer on corporate identity design, betrays a thoroughgoing 'mistrust of the visual'.

16 Cixous, *Three Steps on the Ladder of Writing*, op.cit., p.108.

17 Michael Rock and Susan Sellers, 'This is Not a Cigar', *Eye* 8 (1993), p.45 and Luce Irigaray, 'The Three *Genres*', in Margaret Whitford, ed., *The Irigaray Reader* (Oxford & Cambridge: Basil Blackwell, 1991), p.143.

18 Irigaray, *An Ethics of Sexual Difference*, op.cit., p.5, 72.

19 Irigaray, *An Ethics of Sexual Difference*, op.cit., p.5, 112, 124.

20 Forty, 'A Reply to Victor Margolin', op.cit., p.132, instructs that 'the aims of design history should be to write good history.'

21 Irigaray, *An Ethics of Sexual Difference*, op.cit., p.24.

22 Cixous, 'The Last Painting or the Portrait of God', in *'Coming to Writing' and Other Essays*, op.cit., p.110.

23 Cixous, 'The Laugh of the Medusa', trans. Keith Cohen and Paula Cohen, *Signs*, 1:4 (1976), p.876.

24 Cixous, 'Castration or Decapitation?', trans. Annette Kuhn, *Signs*, 7:1 (1981), p.51.

25 Cixous, 'Without End/no/State of Drawingness/no, rather:/ The Executioner's Taking off', trans. Catherine A.F. MacGillivray, *New Literary History*, 24:1 (1993), p.96, 93. The essay was originally published as 'Sans Arrêt, non, État de Dessination, non, plutôt: Le Décollage du Bourreau', in the Louvre exhibition catalogue *Repentirs* (Paris: Éditions de la Réunion des musées nationaux, 1991), p.55–64. In notes 27 and 39 below, page numbers refer first to the translation, then (in parenthesis) to the original.

26 Cixous, *Three Steps on the Ladder of Writing*, op.cit., p.17, 63. Cixous explained the metaphor in terms of the glint of the executioner's axe during a conversation with Nicole Ward Jouve entitled 'Writing for the Theatre and Other Stages', Institute of Contemporary Arts, London, 7 July 1993.

27 Cixous, 'State of Drawingness', op.cit., p.96 (59).

28 Cixous, 'State of Drawingness', op.cit., p.91 and Margolin, 'Design History or Design Studies', op.cit., p.110 and Robin Kinross, *Modern Typography: An Essay in Critical History* (London: Hyphen Press: 1992), p.12.

29 Cixous, *Three Steps on the Ladder of Writing*, op.cit., p.119 and Miller, *Illustration*, op.cit., p.58, 17, 18.

30 For a comparable use of the term *poetics* in relation to the conjunction of word and image, see, for example, the 1988 special issue of *Style*, 22:2, on 'Visual Poetics'.

31 Sheila Levrant de Bretteville, 'Feminist Design is Caring, Inclusive, Relational', interview by Ellen Lupton, *Eye* 8 (1993), p.13 and Anne Burdick 'Parameters and Perimeters', *Emigre*, 21 (1992), unpaginated.

32 Irigaray, *An Ethics of Sexual Difference*, op.cit., p.140, 169, 141, 114.

33 Levrant de Bretteville, op.cit., p.14.

34 Katherine McCoy and Michael McCoy, 'The New Discourse', in *Cranbrook Design: The New Discourse* (New York: Rizzoli, 1991), p.14–19. Judith S. Hull, book review, *Design Issues*, 9:2 (1993), p.86. See also Katherine McCoy, 'Book Format Design Concept', *Emigre*, 19 (1991), unpaginated.

35 Grant F. Scott, 'The Rhetoric of Dilation: Ekphrasis and Ideology', *Word & Image*, 7:4 (1991), p.301–302.

36 Scott, op.cit., p.303, 305.

37 Richard Hollis, *Graphic Design: A Concise History* (London & New York: Thames and Hudson, 1994).

38 Robin Kinross, 'Conversation with Richard Hollis on Graphic Design History', *Journal of Design History*, 5:1 (1992), p.83–84.

39 Cixous, 'State of Drawingness', op.cit., p.97, 101 (63), 102–103 (64).

40 Cixous, *Three Steps on the Ladder of Writing*, op.cit., p.131.

41 Cixous, 'State of Drawingness', op.cit., p.93.

THE
POLITICS
OF
THE
ARTIFICIAL

VICTOR
MARGOLIN

Essays
on
Design
and
Design
Studies

NARRATIVE PROBLEMS OF GRAPHIC DESIGN HISTORY

VICTOR MARGOLIN
1994

'Narrativity becomes a problem only when wish to give real events the form of a story.'
— Hayden White, 'The Value of Narrativity in the reproduction of reality'

Introduction

In recent years, scholars have devoted considerable attention to the study of narrative structures in history and fiction.[1] Central to their concerns are several key questions, notably, what constitutes a narrative as opposed to other forms of temporal sequencing of actions and events and how does a narrative make claims to being true or fictive. Regarding the first question, Hayden White has identified three kinds of historical representation: the annals, the chronicle and history itself. Of these, he argues, only history has the potential to achieve narrative closure.[2] By organizing our accounts of the past into stories, we attempt to 'have real events display the coherence, integrity, fullness and closure of an image of life that is and can only be imaginary.'[3] While some theorists like White regard history as a narrative that refers to events outside itself, others, particularly those who define themselves as Post-modernists, refuse to make a distinction between fact and fiction and, in effect, treat all history as fiction.[4] That is not the position I will take in this essay, but I mention it to acknowledge a climate in which the idea of history as objective reality is heavily contested.

The distinction that White makes between the messiness of events and the order that historians seek to impose on them is important because it denaturalizes the narrative itself and obliges us to interpret the historian's strategy as a *particular* attempt to order events rather than present the historical work as an objective account of the past. This brings to the fore the necessity of including an analysis of the historian's method in the discussion of a work of history, whether or not that method has been made explicit by the historian.

The problem of method in the construction of narratives is particularly acute in the field of design history, which, since Nikolaus Pevsner's *Pioneers of the Modern Movement* was first published in 1936, has been highly charged with moral and aesthetic judgments that have conditioned the choices of subject matter and the narrative strategies that historians have employed.[5] Adrian Forty, a prominent architecture and design historian, has claimed that the judgment of quality in design is central to the enterprise of design history.[6]

I do not believe that design quality is the primary concern of the design historian, although it raises necessary questions about how different people give value to products. In truth, the question of what design history is about has rarely been thoroughly addressed or debated. This has resulted in considerable confusion in the field, a situation that the move to establish graphic design as a separate subject area of design history has been unable to escape despite its singular focus.[7]

Issues in Graphic Design History

The first graphic design history to gain widespread attention was Philip B. Meggs' *A History of Graphic Design* of 1983.[8] It encompasses a wide range of material and has been used extensively as a text in design history courses. In 1988, Enric Satué, a graphic designer in Barcelona, published *El Diseño Gráfico: Desde los Orígenes hasta Nuestos Dias* (Graphic Design: From its Origins until Today), which originally appeared as a series articles in the Spanish design magazine *On*. The most recent books on the topic are Richard Hollis' *Graphic Design: A Concise History* and Paul Jobling and David Crowley's *Graphic Design: Reproduction and Representation since 1800*.[9] In addition, there have been supplementary works such as *Thirty Centuries of Graphic Design: An Illustrated Survey* by James Craig and Bruce Barton, which appeared in 1987, and *The Thames & Hudson Encyclopaedia of Graphic Design + Designers* by Alan and Isabella Livingston, published in 1992.[10] Varying numbers of entries on graphic designers and firms have also been included in reference works such as *Contemporary Designers*, *The Conran Directory of Design*, and *The Thames & Hudson Encyclopaedia of 20th Century Design and Designers*. There are as well chronicles and histories of graphic design in particular, countries such as *Visual Design: 50 Anni di Produzione in Italia*, by Giancarlo Iliprandi, Alberto Marangoni, Franco Origoni and Anty Pansera and *La Grafica in Italia* by Giorgio Fioravanti, Leonardo Passarelli and Silvia Sfligiotti; *The Graphic Spirit of Japan* by Richard S. Thornton; *Chinese Graphic Design in the Twentieth Century* by Scott Minick and Jiao Ping; *El Diseño Gráfico en España: Historia de una Forma Comunicativa Nueva* (Graphic Design in Spain: History of a New Form of Communication) by Satué; *A Fine Line: A History of Australian Commercial Art* by Geoffrey Caban; *Dutch Graphic Design, 1918–45* by Alston W. Purvis and *Dutch Graphic Design: A Century* by Kees Broos and Paul Hefting; *The Origins of Graphic Design in America 1810–1920* by Ellen Mazur Thomson, and *Graphic Design in America: A Visual Language History*, the catalog of an exhibition curated by Mildred Friedman at the Walker Art Center in 1989.[11]

While this plethora of publications is commendable for the attention it brings to the subject of graphic design, it has not led to any clarification of how graphic design has been constituted by the respective authors, nor has it marked a satisfactory course for the fuller development of a narrative structure that can begin to explain graphic design as a practice. The term 'graphic design' itself as it is applied in most books on the subject remains problematic. William Addison Dwiggins was the first to use it in an essay he wrote for the *Boston Evening Transcript* in 1922.[12] It was subsequently adopted, beginning sometime after the Second World War, to replace such appellations as 'graphic art', 'commercial art' and 'typographic art'.[13]

Some authors have used 'graphic design' to account for all attempts since the beginning of human settlements to communicate with graphic devices. Writing in 1985 in a special issue of the *AIGA Journal of Graphic Design* on the topic of graphic design history, Philip B. Meggs noted the disagreement among experts on the historical scope of the subject:

> Some advocate the short-sighted view and believe that graphic design is a new activity, born of the industrial revolution. Others advocate a far-sighted view, believing the essence of graphic design is giving visual form to human communications, an activity which has a distinguished ancestry dating to the medieval manuscript and early printers of the Renaissance.[14]

When one considers Meggs' own book, it is clear that he has chosen the 'far-sighted view' in that he identifies the cave paintings of Lascaux as the beginning of a sequence that ultimately connects with the contemporary posters of April Greiman. Likewise, as Craig and Barton argue in the introduction to their illustrated survey,

Graphic design – or visual communication – began in prehistoric times and has been practiced over the centuries by artisans, scribes, printers, commercial artists and even fine artists.[15]

Satué takes a similar long view, beginning his own narrative with a chapter entitled 'Graphic Design in Antiquity'.

The problem with the comprehensive accounts of graphic design history that Meggs, Craig and Barton and Satué propose is that they assert a continuity among objects and actions that are in reality discontinuous. Corporate identity programs did not grow out of Renaissance emblem design, nor was the design of books a direct precedent for advertising art direction. Suggesting such connections by locating these different practices in a linear narrative makes it difficult, if not impossible, to disentangle their separate strands and write a more complex account of their relations to one another.

To do so is to begin from a different position than those in the above mentioned texts. It means looking far more closely at the activity of designing as a way of understanding the specific moves by which designers expand the boundaries of practice. This strategy is addressed by Hollis in the introduction to *Graphic Design: A Concise History*:

Visual communication in its widest sense has a long history… As a profession, graphic design has existed only since the middle of the twentieth century; until then, advertisers and their agents used the services provided by 'commercial artists'. These specialists were visualizers (layout artists); typographers who did the detailed planning of the headline and text, and gave instructions for typesetting; illustrators of all kinds, producing anything from mechanical diagrams to fashion sketches; retouchers; lettering artists and others who prepared finished designs for reproduction. Many commercial artists – such as poster designers – combined several of these skills.[16]

Hollis' distinction between the different specialists who produce 'commercial art' is helpful because it facilitates the tracing of distinct strands of practice such as typography, illustration and art direction that sometimes interwine within a particular professional category. By maintaining the separation between these strands, we can then look more deeply at the particular discourses within each one and understand better how their histories are contextualized and recontextualized into new narratives.[17]

For example, the graphic projects of the poets and artists of the early twentieth-century avant-garde are usually incorporated within the history of graphic design even though they were frequently produced outside the client-practitioner relationship that normally characterizes professional design activity. The innovations of syntax and mixtures of typefaces such as those we see in the Futurist poet Filippo Tommaso Marinetti's *Parole in Libertà* (Words in Liberty) were integral components of specific poetic texts that he wrote, just as the visual forms of concrete poems written by others in later years were to be. Similarly, El Lissitzky's small book *Of Two Squares* originated as an argument for a new reading strategy that had implications in Lissitzky's thinking that went far beyond the formal order of the book page.

When Lissitzky's book was assimilated into the discourse of the 'new typography' by Jan Tschichold in 1925, it was recontextualized and its original meaning was altered from a new way of thinking about reading to an argument for a modern design formalism. These shifts of intention and context tend to be suppressed when diverse graphic products are drawn together within an assimilationist narrative based on a theme such as modernity or innovation.

Meggs, looking farther into the past than the moment of the modernist avant-garde, describes the visual practices of the Renaissance and Rococo as 'graphic design', thus suggesting a continuity between the design activity during those periods and that of contemporary practice. While later designers have engaged in typography, book design and related forms of visual production that were practiced in much earlier periods, most do so within a significantly different type of professional setting that is not so continuous with earlier activities as Meggs' use of terminology suggests.

Another problem is the conflation of graphic design and visual communication as we see in the introduction by Craig and Barton. Graphic design is a specific professional practice, while the term 'visual communication' denotes a fundamental activity of visual representation (I would include here coded body language and gestures as well as artifacts) in which everyone engages.[18] Visual communication is a considerably larger category than graphic design, which it includes. A history of visual communication also suggests a completely different narrative strategy from that of a history of graphic design. The former rightly extends back to the cave paintings of Lascaux and Altamira and continues up to the present examples of urban graffiti. The emphasis in a history of visual communication is inherently sociological and does not exclude anyone on professional grounds. While such a history may focus as well on the semantic issues of how words and images visually transmit communicative intentions, its principal subject matter is the act of communication itself.[19]

Conversely, if we are to adhere more strictly to the meaning of 'graphic design' as a description of professional practice that arose at a particular historic moment, we are obliged to consider the way such a practice has been institutionalized in order to include some practitioners and exclude others. This would certainly explain the absence of vernacular material done by non-professionals.[20] We would also have to address the ways in which different forms of practice have been professionalized. Are typographers, calligraphers, art directors and illustrators to be considered graphic designers, even when they have their own organizations, exhibitions, publications and the like?[21] Unless a history of graphic design honors the distinctions among these practices, there is no way to delineate how the profession has developed socially. Ironically, the cultural identity of the graphic designer will be strengthened more through such an approach than by conflating graphic design with all the other activities that produce visual communication.

Following the latter strategy, the texts by Meggs and Craig and Barton, in particular, result neither in a history of graphic design as a professional activity nor in a history of visual communication as an explanation of human communicative acts. Instead, they minimize the differences between the two and ignore the distinctions among the images they incorporate, which range from Egyptian hieroglyphs to Ohrbach's advertisements.

Narrative Strategies of Graphic Design History Texts

We can now turn to the three major texts by Meggs, Satué and Hollis to better understand how they tell the story of graphic design.[22] We should first note the different emphases that the authors give to the preindustrial, industrial and postindustrial periods. Meggs makes the strongest argument for a continuity between these, providing the lengthiest account of the preindustrial era. He establishes analogies between works in earlier and later periods on the basis of characteristics such as formal arrangement, and he unifies communicative activities in different periods by attributing common qualities to them such as 'genius' and 'expressivity'.[23] Satué moves in three brief chapters to the beginning of the nineteenth century while Hollis begins his history in the 1890s with a discussion of the illustrated poster.[24] Regarding the material included for the nineteenth and twentieth centuries, the three authors have much in common, particularly in the sections that begin with the arts and crafts movement and then continue through turn-of-the-century posters, the European avant-gardes, the 'new typography' in Germany, wartime propaganda, the émigré designers in America and the subsequent emergence of an American mass communications style, corporate identity, Swiss typography and its revisions, European pictorial posters and protest design of the 1960s.

All the authors were trained as graphic designers and share similar values about the canon of their profession. This canon has neither developed randomly nor been institutionalized in the manner of an academic literary canon. Rather, it resulted from a selection process that has celebrated noteworthy designs in professional magazines such as *Novum Gebrauchsgraphik*, *Graphis* and *Print*, as well as in numerous picture books and occasional museum exhibitions.[25] An important factor in the canonization of graphic design pieces is the visual satisfaction they give to the trained graphic designer. As the three books under discussion show, there is a considerable consensus among the authors regarding the visual quality of the work they include. What is generally missing, however, are accounts of work by lesser known designers who played important roles in the development of the profession – for example, Fritz Ehmke in Germany or Oswald Cooper in the US. Ehmke was important because he wanted to preserve design traditions at a moment when Tschichold and others were promoting the new typography. In Chicago, Cooper was the best of the lettering and layout men who preceded the emergence of graphic design in the city as we now know it.

One significant difference between Meggs, Satué and Hollis is the varying amount of attention they give to geographic areas outside the European and American mainstream.[26] Satué, who is from Spain, is considerably more aware than either of the other two authors of how graphic design developed in the Spanish-speaking countries, as well as in Brazil. He devotes almost one hundred pages to this material while Meggs dedicates three pages to 'The Third World Poster', a section that mainly refers to Cuban posters of the 1960s with a brief mention of posters in Nicaragua, South Africa and the Middle East. Hollis, by contrast, devotes a little less than two pages to Cuban posters in a section entitled 'Psychedelia, Protest and New Techniques of the Late 1960s'. In the texts of Meggs and Hollis, Japanese graphic design is discussed briefly, but the authors refer mainly to postwar activity. When Meggs makes reference to prior work, he mentions early printing in Japan and then later talks about the nineteenth-century ukiyo-e woodblock prints and their influence on Western designers. Satué does not include Japan at all. None of the authors make any reference to modern design in China or other Asian countries nor do they mention graphic design in Africa.[27]

Although Meggs presents typographers such as John Baskerville, Henri Fournier and Giambattista Bodoni, who worked in the eighteenth century, as geniuses, he merges typography as a practice with other design activities when he reaches the twentieth century, where he neglects, as do the other two authors, some of the most eminent modern typographers such as Victor Hammer, Jan van Krimpen, Giovanni Mardersteig and Robert Hunter Middleton.[28]

The three authors' relation to other visual practices such as advertising vary somewhat. According to Hollis,

> However effective, such work [i.e., early twentieth-century German posters of Lucian Bernhard, Hans Rudi Erdt, Julius Gipkins and Ludwig Hohlwein] belongs to a history of advertising. Only when advertising has a single visual concept, as it developed in the US in the 1950s... does it have a significant place in the history of graphic design.[29]

Meggs, by contrast, does not even identify these posters as advertising artifacts. He accounts for them in terms of a formal style, which he calls 'pictorial modernism'. Satué too treats this work as exemplary of a modern visual style.

Of the three authors, Hollis is most attentive to the differences among visual practices, making reference, for example, to the calligraphic training of Edward Johnston, who designed an alphabet for the London Underground in 1916. He also mentions the contribution that art directors in America made to the emergence of graphic design as a profession. At the same time he removes noteworthy practitioners, firms and work from the discourses in which their practices were embedded – such as the discourse of advertising – and inserts them into a different narrative. Hence, we encounter the 'new advertising' not as a response to the constraints of earlier advertising, but as a contribution to the development of a sophisticated visual sensibility within the graphic design profession.

While none of the authors writes an exclusively connoisseurist history, each is particularly attentive to visual quality. This plays an important role in the construction of their stories, which are propelled along by changes in the look and form of designs as well as by other factors. I make this observation not to espouse instead a social history of graphic design that subordinates discussions of form to arguments about social meaning but to stress that describing how artifacts look does not sufficiently address the question of *why* they look as they do.[30]

The latter can only be answered by extracting artifacts from narratives that draw them together for the purpose of creating a tradition of innovation that never existed. The artifacts must be reinserted in the various discourses within which they originated – whether those are related to art, advertising, typography or printing – and then they need to be related in new ways.

Conclusion

What then might a history of graphic design that respected the varied discursive locations of visual design activity be like? It would preserve many elements of the narrative sequences established by Meggs, Satué and Hollis but would be more attentive to a close reading of visual practices in order to discriminate between the different types of work. As a result, we would understand better how graphic design has been shaped by borrowings and appropriations from other practices instead of seeing it as a single strand of activity. By recognizing the many routes into graphic design, we can learn to see it as more differentiated than we have previously acknowledged it to be. This will enable us to better relate emerging fields of endeavor such as information design, interaction design and environmental graphics to what has come before.

Clearly, the history of graphic design does not follow a neat linear path that can be characterized by unifying themes such as innovation, excellence, modernity or post modernity, Because there have been no shared standards that define professional development nor has there been a common knowledge base to ground a definition of what graphic design is, its development has been largely intuitive and does not conform to a common set of principles shared by all designers![31] While the scope of what we call graphic design today has considerably expanded from what it once was, it has not done so in any singular way. Frequently individual designers have simply moved into new areas of practice and have then been followed by others.

Not all graphic designers work on the same kinds of projects. Some specialize in posters and function like artists. Others are involved with strategic planning and make use of management skills. And some designers specialize in information graphics, which requires a strong knowledge of social science.[32] A history of graphic design should explain the differentiations between the various activities that fall within the rubric of graphic design. It should acknowledge the tension that arises from the attempt to hold these activities together through a discourse of professional unity while designers continue to move in new directions. A recognition of this tension will ultimately teach us much more about graphic design and its development than would the attempt to create a falsely concordant narrative of graphic design history.

Victor Margolin is Professor Emeritus of Design History at the University of Illinois, Chicago.
First published in *Visible Language*, vol. 28, no. 3, 1994, and then in *The Politics of the Artificial*, The University of Chicago Press, 2002.

1 The study of narrative forms is a distinct field of research called narratology. A useful introduction to the subject is David Carrier, 'On Narratology' in *Philosophy and Literature* 8, no.1 (April 1984), p.32–42. For a full account of the subject, see Mieke Bal, *Narratology: Introduction to the Theory of Narrative*, trans. Christine van Boheemen (Toronto: University of Toronto Press, 1985).

2 Hayden White, 'The Value of Narrativity in the Representation of Reality', *Critical Inquiry* 7, no.1 (Fall 1980), p.9.

3 Ibid., p.27.

4 Linda Hutcheon provides an account of this position in *The Politics of Postmodernism* (London and New York: Routledge, 1989). See particularly the chapter 'Re-presenting the Past'.

5 Nikolaus Pevsner, *Pioneers of the Modern Movement from William Morris to Walter Gropius* (London: Faber & Faber, 1936). The book was subsequently republished in several revised editions as *Pioneers of Modern Design from William Morris to Walter Gropius*.

6 Adrian Forty, 'A Reply to Victor Margolin', *Journal of Design History* 6, no.2 (1993), p.131–132. Forty's comment was part of a response to my article, 'Design History or Design Studies: Subject Matter and Methods', which originally appeared in *Design Studies* 13, no. 2 (April 1992), p.104–116 and was republished in *Design Issues* II, no.1 (Spring 1995), p.4–15.

7 Arguments for a separate history of graphic design have been voiced for a number of years now. See Steven Heller, 'Towards an Historical Perspective', *AIGA Journal of Graphic Design* 2, no.4 (1984), p.5 and the special issue of the same publication entitled 'The History of Graphic Design: Charting a Course' edited by Sleven Heller, *AIGA Journal of Graphic Design* 3, no.4 (1985); and Steven Heller, 'Yes, Virginia, There Is a Graphic Design History', *AIGA Journal of Graphic Design* 10, no.1 (1992), p.4.

8 Philip B. Meggs, *A History of Graphic Design*, 3d ed. (1983; New York: John Wiley & Sons, 1998).

9 Enric Satué, *El Diseño Gráfico: Desde los Origenes hasta Nuestros Días* (Madrid: Alianza Editorial, 1988); Richard Hollis, *Graphic Design: A Concise History* (London and New York: Thames & Hudson, 1994); and Paul Jobling and David Crowley, *Graphic Design: Reproduction and Representation since 1800* (Manchester and New York: Manchester University Press, 1996). The books by Meggs, Satué, Hollis and Jobling and Crowley were preceded by several volumes that were essentially visual chronicles such as Karl Gerstner and Marcus Kutter, *Die Neue Grafik* (Teufen: Arthur Niggli, 1959), and Josef Müller-Brockmann, *A History of Visual Communication* (Teufen: Arthur Niggli, 1971). A brief illustrated survey of postwar graphic design is Keith Murgatroyd's *Modern Graphics* (London and New York: Vista/Dutton, 1969).

10 James Craig and Bruce Barton, *Thirty Centuries of Graphic Design: An Illustrated Survey* (New York: Watson-Guptill, 1987), and Alan and Isabella Livingston, *The Thames & Hudson Encyclopedia of Graphic Design + Designers* (London: Thames & Hudson, 1992).

11 Giancarlo Iliprandi, Alberto Marangoni, Franco Origoni and Anty Panser, *Visual Design: 50 Anni di Produzione in Italia* (Milan: Idealibri, 1984); Giorgio Fioravanti, Leonardo Passarelli and Silvia Sfligiotti, *La Grafica in Italia* (Milan: Leonardo Arte 1997); Richard S. Thornton, *The Graphic Spirit of Japan* (New York: Van Nostrand, 1991); Scott Minick and Jiao Ping, *Chinese Graphic Design in the Twentieth Century* (London: Thames & Hudson, 1990): Satué, *El Diseño Gráfico en España: Historia de una Forma Comunicativa Nueva* (Madrid: Alianza Editorial, 1997); Geoffrey Caban, *A Fine Line: A History of Australian Commercial Art* (Sydney: Hale & Iremonger, 1983); Alston W. Purvis, *Dutch Graphic Design, 1918–45* (New York: Van Nostrand Reinhold, 1992); Kees Broos and Paul Hefting, *Dutch Graphic Design: A Century* (Cambridge: MIT Press, 1993); Ellen Mazur Thomson, *The Origins of Graphic Design in America, 1870–1920* (New Haven and London: Yale University Press, 1997); and *Graphic Design in America: A Visual Language History* (Minneapolis: Walker Art Center and New York: Harry N. Abrams, 1989). Shorter accounts of American graphic design history can be found in the fiftieth anniversary issue of *Print* (November–December 1989), edited by Steven Heller with articles on each decade from the 1940s to the 1980s by different authors, and the special issue of *Communication Arts* (March/April 1999), 'Forty Years of Creative Excellence'.

12 Dwiggins' essay, 'New Kind of Printing Calls for New Design', is reprinted in *Looking Closer 3; Classic Writings on Graphic Design*, eds. Michael Bierut, Jessica Helfand, Steven Heller and Rick Poynor, with introductions by Steven Heller and Rick Poynor (New York: Allworth Press, 1999), p.14–18.

13 The first American associations of graphic designers were called, respectively, the American Institute of Graphic Arts, founded in New York in 1914 and the Society of Typographic Art, established in Chicago in 1927.

14 Philip B. Meggs, 'Design History: Discipline or Anarchy?' *AIGA journal of Graphic Design* 3, no. 4 (1985), p.2.

15 Craig and Barton, *Thirty Centuries of Graphic Design: An Illustrated Survey*, p.9.

16 Hollis, *Graphic Design: A Concise History*, p.7–8.

17 Howard Lethalin provides an excellent model for how separate strands of design practice might be researched in his article 'The Archeology of the Art Director? Some Examples of Art Direction in Mid-Nineteenth-Century British Publishing', *Journal of Design History* 6, no. 4 (1993): p.229–246.

18 Hollis recognizes this when he includes 'the imprint of an animal in the mud' as a form of visual communication in the introduction to *Graphic Design: A Concise History*.

19 An excellent example of a sociological approach to the history of communication is J. L. Aranguren, *Human Communication* (New York and Toronto: McGraw-Hill, 1967). Aranguren discusses both linguistic and visual communication as well as transmission media.

20 This does not preclude designs that adhere to institutional standards of quality being considered within the canon even if their makers are not trained professionals, nor does it prevent designers from appropriating vernacular forms for professional use as Charles Spencer Anderson has done with his 'bonehead' design. But it does exclude designs that can be easily defined as vernacular because of their difference

from work by professionals. In fact, graphic design is not a profession with a body of technical knowledge that can easily exclude non-professionals. If anything, the proliferation of desktop publishing software makes it more and more possible for non-professionals to approximate, or at least appear to approximate, professional standards. There has been, however, some debate within the profession about the place of vernacular graphics in design history. The late Tibor Kalman, Abbott Miller and Karrie Jacobs argued in their 1991 manifesto 'Good History/Bad History' that graphic design was a medium rather than a profession and therefore its history should include vernacular forms as well. 'Graphic design', they wrote, 'is the use of words and images on more or less everything, more or less everywhere.' *Tibor Kalman: Perverse Optimist*, eds. Peter Hall and Michael Bierut (London: Booth-Clibborn Editions and New York: Princeton Architectural Press, 1998), p.77.

21 Specialized histories of these practices were among the building blocks that preceded Meggs' own more comprehensive history. Books by those engaged with typography such as Frederic Goudy's *Typologia*, Daniel Berkeley Updike's *Printing Types: Their History, Forms, and Use*, or Stanley Morison's *A Tally of Types* provide coherent accounts of how typographic design developed and also assert standards of quality. Frank Presbrey's pioneering work, *The History and Development of Advertising*, is a history of professional advertising practice that describes the changes that led from selling space to comprehensive campaigns.

22 I have not included Jobling and Crowley's *Graphic Design: Reproduction and Representation since 1800* in this discussion because it does not purport to be a comprehensive history of graphic design.

23 Thus Meggs applies the term 'Spanish pictorial expressionism' to Spanish manuscripts of the tenth century that feature letterforms as pictoral objects, while 'American typographic expressionism' refers to New York graphic design of the 1950s and 1960s.

24 The problem with Hollis' strategy of writing a progressive narrative that identifies illustrated posters as precursors for more conceptual

design work is that it then makes the posters less accessible for other histories such as a history of illustration, which does not have a similarly progressive character. For a discussion of Hollis' thoughts on graphic design and how they influenced the writing of his book, see Robin Kinross, 'Conversation with Richard Hollis on Graphic Design History', *Journal of Design History* 5, no. 1 (1992), p.73–90.

25 Martha Scotford discusses the problems of canonization in graphic design history in her article 'Is There a Canon of Graphic Design History?' *AIGA Journal of Graphic Design* 9, no. 2 (1991), p.3–5, 13. Among the points she makes is that women are noticeably lacking in the canon. Scotford took steps to rectify this situation with her book *Cipe Pineles: A Life of Design* (New York and London: Norton, 1999).

26 I refer specifically to the US rather than North America. Although Canada has a rich history of graphic design, including some outstanding designers in the postwar era, none of the authors mention it as a distinct site of graphic design practice. An excellent presentation on the history of graphic design in Canada was made by Peter Bartl at the International Council of Graphic Design Associations (ICOGRADA) congress in Dublin in 1983. For further information on Canadian graphic design, see Michael Large, 'The Corporate Identity of the Canadian Government', *Journal of Design History* 4, no. 1 (1991): p.31–42, and 'Communication Among All People, Everywhere: Paul Arthur and the Maturing of Design', *Design Issues* 17, no. 2 (Spring 2001); and Brian Donnelly, 'Mass Modernism: Graphic Design in Central Canada, 1955–65 and the Changing Role of Modernism' (MA thesis, Carleton University, 1997),

27 See *Dialogue on Graphic Design Problems in Africa*, ed. Haig David-West (London: ICOGRADA, 1983). This publication reports on a 1982 conference held in Port Harcourt, Nigeria, under the sponsorship of ICOGRADA. One of the few Africans to enter the ranks of internationally recognized graphic designers is Chaz Maviyane-Davies of Zimbabwe. See Carol Stevens, 'A Designer from Zimbabwe', *Print* 47, no. 5

(September–October 1993): p.84–91, 233. Since the end of apartheid, there has also been an upsurge of work by black graphic designers in South Africa.

28 This obscuring of the typographic tradition and the lack of sufficient recognition for twentieth-century typographers was ameliorated to some degree by the publication of Sebastian Carter's *Twentieth Century Type Designers* (London: Trefoil, 1987) and Robin Kinross' excellent *Modern Typography: An Essay in Critical History* (London: Hyphen Press, 1992).

29 Hollis, *Graphic Design: A Concise History*, p.31.

30 This is the aim of Jobling and Crowley in *Graphic Design: Reproduction and Representation*, op.cit. They succeed far better than Meggs, Hollis or Satué in creating a social context for the work they discuss but, as I noted in a review of their book, 'at times the authors appear to be writing social history rather than the history of design in its social context.' The review was published in *Eye* 25, no. 7 (Summer 1997), p.83–84.

31 Some designers and design educators now prefer the term *communication design*.

32 For a critique of graphic design as an art-based profession, see Jorge Frascara, 'Graphic Design: Fine Art or Social Science?' in *The Idea of Design*, eds. Victor Margolin and Richard Buchanan (Cambridge: MIT Press, 1995), p.44–55. The article first appeared in *Design Issues* 5, no. 1 (Fall 1988), p.18–29. Frascara proposes to shift the definition of design quality from the way things look to their effect on the intended audience.

Visible Language 28.3

New Perspectives

**Critical Histories
of Graphic Design**

Part 1: *Critiques*

MASKS ON HIRE:
IN SEARCH OF TYPOGRAPHIC HISTORIES

GÉRARD MERMOZ
1994

Aims and Objectives

The aim of this paper is not to take graphic design studies one step closer towards a definitive history of typography but, more realistically, to offer some preliminary remarks and guidelines for a critical examination of existing histories and for writing alternative typographic histories, on an renewed theoretical basis. By opening up the field of typographic history beyond its traditional boundaries – displacing its focus from a dominant concern with technological factors to one concerned with design and related issues – I hope to extend the scope of historical and theoretical research about typography.

Although this paper is critical of recent attempts at dealing with the history of typography, the suggestions that follow do not claim to make previous histories obsolete. The fact that, for centuries, typographic histories have legitimized a restricted range of typographic values and practices should not be overlooked nor dismissed as ideological. Since historical writings cannot transcend the historical conditions and ideological preoccupations through which they come into being, the forms of history writing I envisage will need to acknowledge the effects of these contingencies on its own claims to truth and face the epistemological implications.

Finally, the challenge, for contemporary historians of typography is to write histories capable of *presenting typographic pluralism with appropriate theoretical tools*. A direct consequence of this methodological shift will be the opening up of the *typographic scene* – to accommodate a wider range of works and preoccupations – and the redefinition of key terms through which it is to be rearticulated: text, legibility, reading, typographic reference, interpretation.

Dualism One:
(Mis)representing Typographic Differences

The present essay was written out of a personal dissatisfaction with the way typographic differences are (mis)represented in typographic histories, and how they have been obscured in the recent debate around the 'new' typography.[1] As a survey of twentieth-century typographical literature testifies, experimental deviations from typographic forms have often been dismissed for an alleged lack or failure to comply with rational, objective or universal criteria (the 'fundamental principles of typography' invoked by Stanley Morison). Ironically, classic typefaces such as Baskerville and Bodoni have, at various times, been the target of dogmatic criticism, impervious to the argument that the legibility of letterforms and graphic layouts is relative and culture-bound. Karl Gerstner put it succinctly when he remarked: 'even with the best of methods, it is not possible to determine which is the most legible face of all, and for one simple reason: the function of reading is based on subjective habits rather than on objective conditions.'[2] The new bibliography reinforces this point when it states: 'there is no inherent physical display of text and apparatus that is more natural to a specific work than any other.'[3]

The reluctance, or incapacity, of historians to evaluate typographic differences in term of their cultural, aesthetic and semiological *specificity*, across the full range of typographic practice (from continuous text to display typography, from Modernism to Post-Modernism) continues to be a major obstacle towards writing typographic histories. Regretfully, this incapacity is not the prerogative of a few polemicists, but is characteristic of the typographic scene which – from Morison to Paul Rand, Ken Garland, Steven Heller and others – has displayed a singular dogmatism when confronted with works conceived outside its ideological frame of reference. Unable to acknowledge these ideological differences as productive and significant – constitutive of a legitimate cultural pluralism – these authors too readily take up the role of defenders of typography against the threat of corruption from the outside. In this, they echo early critiques of Modernism which deplored that 'many of its early exponents violated both traditional customs and good taste', and that 'there was for a time a danger that the more simple and beautiful forms of typography would become submerged beneath a flood of freak type-faces arranged in most bewildering and unorthodox styles.'[4] These remarks, combined with the assertion that 'the new typography in England has infused no vitalizing spirit into current typography' sadly represent the main strand of typographic thinking in eccentric Britain between the wars.[5]

From the margins came a different voice which acknowledged the relation of typography to painting and architecture, and regretted that the new typography 'has been almost unknown in this country, and has found here not more than one or two disciples.'[6] In Britain, the anti-Modernist view prevailed, amidst a display of telling metaphors:

> There is a possibility, noted William Atkins, of some of these freak types finding a temporary lodgment in this country, but the inherent good taste of British typographers, allied to their instinctive love for the practical and the beautiful, will enable them to weed out any 'alien undesirable' and 'nationalize' only those forms of letters which can conform to our national sense of fitness.[7]

By 1938, the 'danger that the new functional materials, the mechanistic typefaces that originated in Germany, would be used with a ruthless logic' seemed averted, as John Gloag looked forward to 'a glorious restoration of fun and games with shapes and colours, and an end to the nervous trifling with "off-white", and "off-pink", and angles and straight lines and vast, unrelieved surfaces.'[8] The Festival of Britain was on its way...

From 1949 to 1967, under the editorialship of Herbert Spencer, *Typographica* published a extensive range of articles about 'major typographic experiments of this century' which, together with his *Pioneers of Modern Typography* (1969) and John Lewis' *Typography: Basic Principles* (1963) contributed to expand the typographic horizon of designers. Lewis' *Anatomy of Printing* (1970) and Josef Müller-Brockmann's *A History of Visual Communication* (1971) followed on, confirming the relevance of Modernism to contemporary typographic practice.[9]

Although pitched at a general, introductory level, the works of Lewis are significant in their attempt to present typographic differences in terms of their respective concerns and overall significance in typographic history. In contrast with Walter Tracy, who excluded Whistler and other artists from the *Typographic Scene* – for reasons that could be described as corporate and technical[10] – Lewis' acceptance of 'Whistler as a typographer' denotes a willingness to extend the field of typography to accommodate significant contributions from outside the profession.[11] Tracy's insistence, in Morisonian tone, that, 'typography is a professional activity directed towards a practical, and usually commercial, result', warrants his exclusion of major experimental works and closes the field to outside influences, precludes major transforma-tions.[12] It is regrettable and somewhat surprising that, in 1988, one should retain such a restric-tive view of the subject; a view that – against the efforts of Spencer, Lewis, Müller-Brockmann and others – insists so categorically on excluding the contributions of artists to typography.

The widespread dogmatism found in writings on typography may be imputed to their authors' lack of knowledge about those disciplines that bear upon the theory and practice of communication, namely: linguistics, semiotics, cultural theory, bibliography, anthropology, psychoanalysis, etc. It may also be a direct consequence of a restrictive interpretation of infor-mation design, and of a tendency to use criticism as a platform for the illustration and defense of corporate views and personal opinions.[13] This is most apparent in the recent polemic around the 'new' typography, where lack of insights have been volunteered by designers as serious, responsible criticism and typographic truth.

It could be argued that academic historians do not proceed very differently; however, it is a requisite of academic criticism to address different objects and positions in terms of their own specificity, to consider the interaction and the effect of different factors on any given situ-ation, and, finally, to reach a conclusion on the basis of a reasoned argument. This is not so in typographic writings, where – whether in manuals, manifestos or design journalism – ideas are often presented in *normative* forms, usually set up against existing positions and practices, past or present. Furthermore, the low level of theorizing found in writings about typography is manifest in oversimplified views about the functional relation between typography and lan-guage, the role of typography as a public service and the place and function of style in graphic communication. Let's note, finally, that one chief obstacle towards accommodating typographic diversity springs from the insistence, among writers, to view the typographic scene through a stifling dualism.

Dualism Two:
Assessing Typographic Literature

In addition to classic surveys such as Updike's *Printing Types*, the most useful texts currently available are those that set out to document specific aspects of typographic history.[14] Allan Stevenson's *The Problem of the Missale Speciale* (1967), for instance, typifies a genre of applied research which brings together, in a scholarly way, a considerable body of documentary evi-dence concerning technical aspects of print production for the purpose of dating and making attributions. This form of scholarship is extremely valuable, as it provides an essential basis for history writing.

Extending this methodology into the field of social and cultural history, Robert Darnton's studies of the production and distribution of books in eighteenth-century France not only extends the scope of typographic histories, but also dispels a few myths about the role of authors, publishers, printers and book sellers in the dissemination of knowledge.[15] In *The Coming of the Book*, first published in 1958, Lucien Febvre had begun to redirect the aims of typographic history from its previous focus on the history of techniques to a critical examina-tion of their social, political and cultural implications:

> ... the story is about something other than the history of a technique. It has to do with
> the effect on European culture of a new means of communicating ideas within a society
> that was essentially aristocratic, a society that accepted and was long to accept a culture
> and a tradition of learning which was restricted to certain social groups.[16]

Measured against Febvre's methodological concerns, recent histories of typography and graphic design display a marked theoretical naiveté in their assumption that the facts of typographic history can speak for themselves, when allowed to unfold along a chronological path unhindered by theory or ideology.

The least theoretically developed aspect of typographic histories is that of typographic analyses, where the methodology remains disappointingly pedestrian. This is a direct consequence of the insufficient theorizing of typography as a discursive practice; for, in spite of Gérard Blanchard's attempt in *Pour une Sémiologie de la Typographie*, the project of a semiology of typography still awaits theoretical formulation as a discrete field of enquiry, characterized by a specific object (typographic design), its conditions of possibility/existence, structural determinants, the modes and contexts of its production, distribution and uses.[17] In the absence of a developed critical methodology and language, writings on the subject remain superficially descriptive and bound by a *problématique* centered around technical factors and parameters.

Among recent histories, Robin Kinross' *Modern Typography*, subtitled 'an essay in critical history', announced itself as a critique of 'the existing model of the genre'. Kinross' objections concerning 'books about "the pioneers of modern typography" or "Bauhaus typography" [that] situate their subjects in a vacuum, without historical precedent and without relation to the unmentioned but implied contemporary traditional norm', are justified and welcome; as is his intention to focus 'away from products… towards the ideas that inform production.'[18]

However, the omission of Futurism and Dada from his account of modern typography, the dismissal of the 'new' typography and of the problems it poses seriously undermine its claims. The exclusion of two of the most radical typographic experiments of the twentieth century, directed simultaneously at language and its typographic presentation, is somewhat problematic in a book (cl)aiming to be 'an essay in critical history'.

It is symptomatic, however, of the closure which prevents historians of typography and graphic design to address design issues outside the binary structures which set up established values (whether classicist, functionalist or modernist) against alternative new styles. This can be verified by charting the negative response to *die neue Typographie* in Britain during the 1920s and 1930s and, today, to the new trends associated with Neville Brody, the Cranbrook Academy of Art, Emigre graphics and, more generally, all forms of experimental typography. Kinross' omission of two key moments in the history of typographic design could also be read as demonstrating, by default, the enduring challenge raised by those two movements – from their museum grave – to the impoverished ('one size only') view of Modernism perduring in official circles.

What I hope to make clear in the ensuing pages is that reference to universal typographic criteria is not likely to produce *critical* histories of typography, but, more likely, to consolidate typographic *orthodoxies*. One central argument running through this paper is that the writing of critical histories of typography requires a higher level of theorizing than is currently brought to bear on the subject. Failing this, typographic histories will continue legitimating entrenched dogmas, tracing their genealogy from a mythical origin – along a Vasarian path – oscillating between grandeur and decadence towards an ever-deferred promise of perfection.

Definitions

Since ontologies and teleologies crystallize in definitions, I shall begin with a critical examination of the concepts of 'typography' and 'typographer', their definitions and semantic transformations, pointing out structural correlations between definitions and typographic theories and practices. The plural form used in the title signals the intention to avert essentialism by acknowledging that, whatever our aspirations and claims to truth, typographic histories are primarily discursive objects, functionally linked with material and ideological preoccupations, and that their references to historical events, problematic as they stand, need to be subjected to a rigorous epistemological critique. The outcome is not likely to be an objective account, free from ideological constraints, but a narrative that acknowledges the effect of interests and ideologies without attempting to clothe them in a veil of universality.

The Object/s of Typographic Histories

The 1986 edition of the *Encyclopaedia Britannica* acknowledges that 'some confusion and "some lack of uniformity"' is 'involved in talking about typographers and typography.' This view is echoed in Alan Marshall's remark that typography is characterized by 'conflicting schools of thought' and, 'despite its conviviality... has never been free of dissension', but 'thrived on it'. [19] This is to be expected for, as Georges Gusdorf remarked in his *Introduction aux Sciences Humaines*: 'the meaning of words is established in relation to time and events; meaning changes with the times, in such a way that the same word may be used to pose and resolve essentially different problems.' [20]

Modes of production, distribution and consumption, combined with a concern to establish functional relations between the form and function of printed matter have informed definitions of typography, from the time of the second invention of printing from movable types in Europe. It should be noted, however, that the nature of the Chinese script, the higher cultural status of calligraphy over printing and other historical and cultural factors prevented the first invention of printing from movable types – by Pi Shêng in China – to achieve the worldwide impact the second invention by Gutenberg et al. had; a reminder that the historical impact of a technological 'break through' is determined, above all, by its socio-economic, political and ideological relevance at the time and in the context(s) in which it occurs. In this instance, linguistic factors played a decisive part in shelving a potentially revolutionary invention; revolutionary, that is, for those societies that had adopted alphabetic writing. [21]

In English, the interchangeability between the terms 'typography' and 'printing', on the one hand, and 'typographer' and 'printer', on the other, dates back to the beginnings of printing. Today, in spite of the considerable changes that have affected modes and relations of print production, this semantic overlap continues to prevail in modern dictionaries – not only in sections dealing with the history of the terms, but also in those that list their current usage.

After pointing out its derivation from the Latin 'typographia' (1493), via the French form 'typographie' (1577), the *OED* defines typography as: '1. the art or practice of printing', and by extension: 'a printing establishment, a press', '2. the action or process of printing; esp. the setting and arrangement of types and printing from them; typographical execution; hence, the arrangement and appearance of printed matter'. From a contemporary perspective, the formulation is somewhat problematic, since what we would call today typographic *design* (the *semiological* dimension of printing) is subsumed and appears conditioned by technological factors. Put differently, this emphasis on the material aspects of typography marks the acceptance of technological determinism over design, not only in the 'setting and arrangement of type' and in the corresponding 'arrangement and appearance of printed matter', but also in the historical accounts that ensued.

Anchored in the technological constraints inherent in the modes of print production in the early printing office, and reinforced by the adoption of a restricted range of (typo)graphic conventions from manuscript books, this determinism retained its validity throughout the history of printing and lasted well into the twentieth century, when new historical conditions brought about the rise of the *designer* and, with it, the possibility of free individual interventions and radical transgressions.

Two early examples given by the *OED* – one from an eighteenth-century advertisement stating: 'The typography of both editions does honour to the press' (1793), another from 1900, stating: 'The typography is clear' – suggest that, before the rise of the designer, typography (defined as a specific set of rules) could only be good or bad. In that context discourses on typography could either lay out typographic norms to be followed and emulated, or issue warnings against negligence or failure to comply with the rules. These texts, from Hieronymus Hornschuch's *Orthotypographia* (1608) to John Southward's *Modern Printing* (1898) – subtitled: *A Handbook of the Principles and Practice of Typography and the Auxiliary Arts* – emphasize, by their names and in their content, the prescriptive nature of typographic literature. Characteristically, Martin-Dominique Fertel's *Science Pratique de l'Imprimerie* (1723), John Smith's and Caleb Stower's *Grammars* (1755 and 1808), Antoine-François Momoro's and Pierre Fournier's *Traités* (1793 and 1825) and Charles Henry Timperley's *Manual* (1838) follow a didactic rather than a reflexive approach to their subject.

Typographer ancillus Typographiae

With characteristic symmetry, the *OED* defines 'typographer' as 'one skilled in typography; a printer'. By the time Joseph Moxon wrote his *Mechanick Exercises* (1683–84), the division of labor between letter cutter, caster and dresser, compositor, corrector, press-man, ink-maker, smith and joiner (for the making and repairs of the presses) was already well established: 'For the more easie managing of Typographie, the Operators have found it necessary to devide it into several Trades, each of which (in the strictest sence) stand no nearer related to Typographie, than Carpentry and Masonry, & are to Architecture', noted Moxon. The effects of this fragmentation, deplored by Moxon and others before him, called for a central figure capable of coordinating work in and around the printing office. It is from this context that Moxon's definition of the Typographer acquires its full significance. For Moxon, the Typographer was the unifying agent who could 'either perform, or direct others to perform... all the handy works and physical operations relating to typographie.'[22]

In retrospect, it should not come as a surprise that Moxon linked the quality of printed matter with the technical and material aspects of print production. Since the Middle Ages, the scholastic theory of the *artes mechanicae* had defined 'art' as a fixed set of rules for the correct execution of any given task. In the words of Thomas Aquinas: art is nothing but the correct deduction of things to be done (*ars nihil aliud est, quam ratio recta alliquorum operum faciendorum* or, more concisely, *recta ratio factibilium*).[23] According to this view, the correct application of the principles of the 'art' of printing could only produce good typography; imperfection arising not from the rules of the art, but from a failure by the artisan to implement them. Conversely, individual interventions in the mechanical arts did not affect the rules of the art, but merely removed the obstacles that prevented their implementation: 'art does not add to what is, but removes the obstacles towards it manifestation' (*'non generat novam artem'*, noted John of Saint Thomas, *'sed tollit impedimentum exercitii ejus'*).[24] In this context, the modern concept of the designer as initiator of new practices was absolutely irrelevant.

Although the notion of the 'designer' as a free, autonomous agent, capable of initiating change was incompatible with this episteme, the division and organization of labor within the printing office called for an individual capable of ensuring that the *rules* and the *fundamental principles* were followed scrupulously, at all stages of the process. Moxon's allegorical representation of the 'Master Printer' as 'the soul of Printing' and of 'all the Work-men' as 'members of the body governed by that Soul, subservient to him', who 'would not carry out their art... but by Orders from the Master-Printer',[25] emphasizes the importance of coordination. The picture of a printing office (*figure 1*) illustrating 'the Master's duties, the correctors' chores, the work of readers and compositors' as well as the harder labor of press-men and apprentices (present in the image, but absent from the caption), highlights the managerial role alongside the crafts-men's diligence and application. What the picture does not show, however, is the system of rules, prohibitions and fines which ensured order in the *chapel*.[26] Contrasting with this emphasis on the material aspects of printing, a contemporary allegory (*figure 2*) reminds us that the aspiring typographer was expected to acquire mastery over six aspects of language – represented by six concentric levels: from reading, writing, understanding to grammar – before he was deemed worthy of serving typography (*sic dignus es intrare*). The allegory implied that competence was to be acquired through a guided ascent, at the term of which the typographer could *serve, but in no way substitute himself for Typography.*

Left (Figure 1): Picture of a printing office.
This cut, the work of Thymius' accurate hand
Shows all at once how printing shops are manned:
The masters' duties, the correctors' chores,
The work of readers and compositors.
To this small book then you'll apply your mind
Good reader, if you're not the vulgar kind,
So that a picture in your mind may rise
To match this picture that's before your eyes.

Right (Figure 2): 'Typographia' allegory of typography from Gessner's *Buchdrukerkunst* (Leipzig, 1743).

Design-led and Profit-led Typographies in the Eighteenth Century

In 1608, in a text described by its modern editor as 'the first in a long line of technical manual written for members of the printing trade', the German corrector Hornschuch urged master printers to take greater care over all aspects of their work. After deploring that too many print-ers 'do everything solely for the sake of money and whatever is given to them to be printed they send back ever worse, with types often so worn down and blunt that their feable impres-sion on almost crumbling, dirt-coloured paper can scarcely be detected by the keenest eye', he concluded: 'they debase their material whatever it is with so many shameful mistakes, with the result that one cannot find ever one page completely free of errors.'[27] Departing from idealized textbook stereotypes, Hornschuch's account is valuable as it highlights, in very specific ways, the negative consequences of commercialism in the early seventeenth century.

In the light of these examples, it should be clear that the distinction we draw today between typographic design and printing, as two discrete branches of graphic communication, was incompatible with a system of knowledge in which causality operated through the *system* rather than through the individuals working within it. In that context, the 'art' of printing stood out as the determining factor in the production of good typography, individual merit measuring the ability to excel *through* the parameters and *within* the boundaries of the art.

The Author as Typographer

Before *design issues* could emerge in typographic literature, technological determinism first had to be *relativized* and the design process conceptualized as an activity capable of challenging – as Filippo Marinetti did – technological norms and their design implications. Conversely, not before a functional distinction and a relative autonomy between the material and design aspects of printing were granted, could the figure of the typographer emerge as the person capable of *redefining* typographic practice on the basis of innovation.

Given the corporate organization of printing as a trade, and the tight regulations used to preserve order in the *chapels*, it is not surprising that, in the area of book design, deviations from typographic norms were first instigated by authors seeking more appropriate typographic forms for the presentation of their texts, From the historical precedents of Laurence Sterne in *The Life and Opinions of Tristam Shandy* (1759–67) and Rétif de la Bretonne's setting of *Monsieur Nicolas* (1796–97) to James McNeill Whistler's *Gentle Art of Making Enemies* (1876), Stéphane Mallarmé's *Un Coup de Dé* (1897), Guillaume Apollinaire's *Calligrammes* (1917) and Marinetti's *Mots en Liberté Futuriste* (1919), the expressive use of type and deviations from typographical norms were motivated by authorial decisions. What was new in these and other experiments was the deliberate exploration of the relation between typography and language. Instead of accepting the standard typographic conventions set by the industry, these authors – in collaboration with sympathetic printers – took up the initiative to experiment with new typographic forms.

The significance of these experiments should not be regarded as marginal or peripheral – as Walter Tracy intimated – but as an essential part of the typographic scene, like the long neglected mass of Victorian display typography, now available for study thanks to the pioneering work of Nicolete Gray, Michael Twyman and Lewis.[28] The object of these experiments was not, as is often imputed, to engage in gratuitous games (form/decoration for its own sake) or shout louder than their neighbor in the frenzy of self-expression or economic competition, but to consider how the limits of typographic conventions may be extended *purposefully*.

Today, the insertion of these experiments in a *general* history of typography calls for an examination of the issue of *typographic reference*; that is to say of the referential function of typography in relation to the texts it presents. Too long obscured by claims and counter-claims about legibility, the transparency or invisibility of the text and other related issues, the question of typographic reference has been effaced from typographic writings. This needs to be remedied if typographic differences are to become intelligible within an enlarged typographic scene, enriched by more sophisticated theoretical tools.

On Futurism's Birthday

'Writers like James Joyce were giving new form to the English language,
but our typographers were not doing much about it.'
— J. Lewis (1978:50)

In spite of the growing consensus around the historical significance of Modernism, historians of graphic design and typography tend to signal the existence of such experiments with a surprising brevity and lack of attention to typographic language. Although both Edward Gottschall's *Typographic Communication Today* (1989) and Philip B. Meggs' *A History of Graphic Design* (1992) acknowledge the historical significance of Futurism, both, in my view, fail to provide an adequate account of Futurist typography and an assessment of its contemporary relevance.[29]

Gottschall starts with a predictable quotation from Herbert Spencer's *Pioneers of Modern Typography*: 'The heroic period of modern typography may be said to have begun with Marinetti's *Figaro* manifesto of 1909', and follows by reiterating the usual art historical clichés about the beauty of speed. His observation that 'in Futurism, social protest, new ideas, and new ways of expressing them came together explosively', that 'Futurist typographers scream with large black type waving in all directions' and that consequently 'the world of typography was blown on to a new course', shows an unfortunate vulnerability to the power of the most predictable Futurist metaphor. The author's lack of ease and familiarity with the subject may explain the cursory treatment of Futurism with respect to other movements. Let's note how, in this form of external characterization, Futurism is construed as an eccentric form of deviance, and the reader *confronted* with a collection of images rather than *engaged* in a productive dialogue with Futurist principles and their implications for the *production of texts* and their *typographic presentation*.

Meggs' characterization follows a similar line, encapsulated by his remark that 'Marinetti and his followers produced an explosive and emotionally charged poetry that defied correct syntax and grammar.' Although Meggs is more specific in his account of Futurist achievements, he never discusses the implications of Futurism on typographic history.

It may come as a surprise to find two classic texts attempting to deal with Futurist typography without referring specifically to those manifestos that spell out Futurist intentions in detail. In Meggs' case, it is somewhat paradoxical as his bibliography lists the very source in which they were reprinted, in translation.[30] The consequences of this oversight are serious, for not only do these authors fail to provide an adequate description of Futurist intentions and achievements, but also, more importantly in a historical account, their treatment of Futurism precludes any assessment by the reader of its *historical significance* and *contemporary relevance*.

Several things are lost in these accounts: the fact that behind and through the aggressive rhetoric of Futurist typography (its most easily spotted 'noisy' side), comes a specific, extensive and coherent critique of typographic orthodoxy, and the realization that addressing the *problématique* opened up by Futurism is important for a contemporary practice, especially in the wake of the debate around Post-Modernism. Put differently, addressing Futurism at its face value – rather than at the level of its theoretical preoccupations – has generated different forms of *estrangement* leading either to marginalization or dismissal, or to superficial admiration, inspiring stylistic 'rip-offs' and fashionable pastiches.

Against typophilia and 'belle-lettrisme' Marinetti argued that 'the so-called typographical harmony of the page' is 'contrary to the flux and reflux, the leaps and burst of style that run through the page.' This observation, printed in a section entitled 'typographical revolution', was followed by a set of recommendations that situates Marinetti in the tradition of expressive typography traced by Robert Massin, in *Letter and Image*, from François Rabelais to Guillaume Apollinaire.[31] Let's note, however, that Marinetti's personal contribution to typography extended beyond its literary precedents, in that it advocated a radical intervention on language, at the level of seven grammatical parameters: noun, adjective, verb, onomatopoeia, syntax, modes of reference and orthography.

The theorizing of the 'semaphoric adjective', for instance, provides some useful insights into the relation between typography and language. After remarking that 'one should treat adjectives like railway signals of style, employ them to mark tempo, the retards and pauses along the way', Marinetti notes: 'What I call a semaphoric adjective, lighthouse-adjective, or atmosphere-adjective is the adjective apart from nouns, isolated in parentheses. This makes it a kind of absolute noun, broader and more powerful than the noun proper.' Marinetti's concern to liberate images and analogies and to express them with 'unhampered words and with no connecting strings of syntax and with no punctuation' aimed to produce more than a few burst of energy onto the page, as current characterizations tend to imply. Marinetti summarized his objectives in a manifesto published in *Lacerba* on 15 June 1913:

With words-in-freedom we will have: CONDENSED METAPHORS. TELEGRAPHIC IMAGES. MAXIMUM VARIATIONS. NODES OF THOUGHT. CLOSED OR OPEN FANS OF MOVEMENT. COMPRESSED ANALOGIES. COLOUR BALANCES. DIMENSIONS, WEIGHTS, MEASURES, AND THE SPEED OF SENSATIONS. THE PLUNGE OF THE ESSENTIAL WORD INTO THE WATER

OF SENSIBILITY, MINUS THE CONCENTRIC CIRCLES THAT THE WORD
PRODUCES. RESTFUL MOMENTS OF INTUITION. MOVEMENTS IN TWO,
THREE, FOUR, FIVE DIFFERENT RHYTHMS. THE ANALYTIC, EXPLORATORY
POLES THAT SUSTAIN THE BUNDLE OF INTUITIVE STRINGS.

To an attentive reader informed about linguistic and literary theory, Marinetti's experiments deserve more than the cursory mention or stereotypical treatment they receive in typographic and graphic design histories. A preliminary line of research could involve a comparative study of the tools and modalities of *reference* in typography, starting with a definition of typographic reference and a discussion of typograhic *denotation* and *connotation* in relation to theories of writing, editing and reading. This would have the advantage of extending the scope of typographic writing beyond closed dualisms (between traditionalisms and avant-gardes) and superficial formalist descriptions.

Since John Lewis mapped out 'the influence of art and history' on typographic design in his *Anatomy of Printing* (1970), typographic histories have reiterated, with minor variations, the same themes and motifs, without substantially extending the analytical tools necessary for a better description of typographic texts. Unfolding from a mythical origin (the controversial context of the invention of printing and the laying out of its foundations by its founding fathers), along a Vasarian path, typographic histories do not question the assumptions upon which they rest. Paradoxically, the systematic *taming* of the literary text brought about by the invention of printing, and its consequences on typographic design, have never been examined as a subject in its own right. Twenty four years after its first publication, the impressive body of visual material anthologized by Massin in *Letter and Image* is still awaiting adequate theoretical and historical contextualization. Thus, the impoverishment and closure (through standardization) brought about by the invention of printing from movable types – with respect to the variety of approaches found in the manuscript presentations of text in the pre-Gutenberg age – has been obscured by the more optimistic themes of the advancement of learning and democratization of knowledge arising from the diffusion of books. In conclusion, I would like to suggest that attention to Marinetti's critique of language and its conventional typographic presentations, could, if related to other areas of typographic history, renew the problématique of typographic histories by inducing a closer examination of the effects of typography on the presentation and interpretation of texts. This would extend the debate on legibility beyond the retinal/optical dimension stressed by traditionalists to the much neglected *cultural and semiological implications of typographic structures*.

One conclusion I shall draw from this discussion is that, *in the 1990s, one should not attempt to write typographic histories without a sound knowledge of those disciplines which bear upon typography and language, namely linguistics, semiotics, literary theory, art history, bibliography, philosophy, etc. Failing this, chronicles will continue to assume the role and claim the status of history writing.*

The Function of Typographic Histories

A close examination of the historiography of printing shows that the writing of typographic histories has always been functionally related to typographic practice. James Watson's stated objectives in translating and printing Jean de La Caille's *History of the Art of Printing*, in 1713 – 'to know to whom we are oblig'd for so fine an Art, and how it began' – reminds us that one important function of typographic history was to anchor typographic practice in an exemplary past which provided models for those training in the 'typographic art'. Experiencing typographic history in narrative form became a significant part of the *rite de passage* through which the apprentice was admitted into the trade.

The relevance of typographic history to practice was acknowledged by Martin-Dominique Fertel who, in his *Science Pratique de l'Imprimerie* (1723) refers his readers to two 'traités d'histoires de l'imprimerie': La Caille's, from 1689, and an anonymous *De Germaniae...*, published in Leipzig. For a functional integration of history and practice, we need to turn to John Smith's plan to follow his *Printer's Grammar* of 1755 with a separate volume on *The History and Present State of Printing* and to Philip Luckombe's *History and Art of Printing* (1771), which offers a 'Historical Account', outlining 'a concise history of the art from its invention to the present time', and an 'Instructive and Practical Part', dealing with technical aspects of printing: materials, presses, paper, composition, corrections, casting-off copy, alphabets and warehouse management, followed by a glossary of technical terms used in printing.

Although Antoine-François Momoro's *Traité Elémentaire de l'Imprimerie* (1793) only included a brief sketch of 'the birth of printing and the propagation of this art', Caleb Stower's *Printer's Grammar* (1808), John Johnson's *Typographia or the Printer's Instructor* (1824) and Thomas Curson Hansard's *Typographia* (1825) provided substantial accounts of typographic history, which, in Johnson's and Hansard's case, represented one half of the entire treatise. The first Dutch manual published by Pieter Marius van Cleef in 1844 contains a brief survey as does Henri Fournier's *Traité de la Typographie* (1825).

The absence of any historical account from Timperley's *The Printer's Manual* (1838) was explained by the author's intention to 'concentrate all that is useful and requisite to the inexperienced apprentice or journeyman.' Similarly, Jon Savage's *Dictionary of the Art of Printing* (1841) and A. Frey's *Nouveau Manuel Complet de Typographie* (1857) both focus on technical aspects of printing without delving into its history. Timperley's *Dictionary of Printers and Printing* (1839), reissued in two volumes in 1842, under the title of *Encyclopedia of Literary and Typographical Anecdotes*, provided a 'Chronological Digest of the Most Interesting Fact Illustrative of the History of Literature and Printing from the Earliest Period to the Present Time', a clear indication of the persisting relevance of typographic history. Timperley's publication of technical and historical material in separate form, however, signals a functional differentiation in the readership of books on typography, and an acknowledgment by the author that the appeal of typographic histories extended to a wider public of non-professionals, incorporating those Momoro called *'les curieux de l'historique.'*

A close look at the ways in which early typographic manuals dealt with historical information reveals significant differences in conceptions and attitudes. As Harry Carter noted, Pierre Fournier 'was determined to be the historian as well as the practitioner of his art' and many of 'his notes on the old letter-cutter were often simply reprinted in biographical dictionaries until the middle of the nineteenth century.' By contrast, Momoro's reasons for not dwelling on typographic history were determined by considerations about his intended readership, 'the inexperienced apprentice, or journeyman', whose preoccupations he distinguished from the *'les curieux de l'historique.'* Furthermore, we know from his *Avertissement* that the lack of comprehensive and up-to-date books on the subject – since Fertel's *Science Pratique* (1723) – combined with the extent of technological progress, informed his decision to focus on technical and practical aspects (*'ce qui a rapport absolument à son but'*).

Hansard's intended readership, however, was broader; it embraced two categories: 'the young practitioner' and 'the amateur.' This may explain the balance between the sections dealing with the history and the practice of typography. Momoro's decision to provide an update on recent technological developments – rather than to reiterate the well established facts of typographic history – was understandable; since one feature of history writing was the incestuous practice among authors to liberally borrow their material from each other. Thus, Hansard remarked that 'upon a close comparison much of Luckombe will be found to be plagiarized from Smith, altered a little in arrangement and phraseology and that in his turn Stower copied from Luckombe.' Luckombe, however, had acknowledged that the historical part of his book was derived from

Ames, Moxon and others. It is somewhat paradoxical, therefore, to see Hansard praise Luckombe's account of *The Introduction of the Art into England*, as 'the most satisfactory of any to be met with; in proof of which, it may be seen that every subsequent writer on the subject has either copied his work, or quoted, by his means, the same authorities which he had consulted', when Luckombe had clearly stated that his account was 'extracted' from 'a curious dissertation concerning the *Origin of Printing in England*' written by 'Dr. Congers Middleton, Principal Librarian of Cambridge', and 'printed in 1735.' In 1841, Savage summarized the situation rather well when he noted: 'There has... hitherto been but little said on the History or Practice of Printing, the numerous books on the subject being chiefly copies from one or two of the earliest writers.'

Envoi

To this day, educators have reasserted the relevance of typographic history to typographic practice: whereas for Lewis it represents a useful set of references for finding one's own style,[32] Ruari McLean emphasizes the role of history in ensuring quality by providing a basis for the reinterpretation of tradition.[33] Today, however, the desire to preserve continuity between past and present is less of an issue among the exponents of the new typography. Free from the rules and technical constraints of letterpress, designers who developed an interest in typography through the Macintosh, in a do-it-yourself art school environment – 'on a crash course to typo-hell', as a student put it recently – many exponents of the new typography experiment with a blissful disrespect of rules they never learnt.[34] It is not surprising, therefore, that a long-standing way of inducing conformism within typographic practice has come to be regarded with suspicion by the new vanguard.

It is interesting to note that in Britain, during the late seventies and throughout the eighties, the formalist account presented by Herbert Spencer in *Pioneers of Modern Typography* inspired young designers dissatisfied with the conservatism of art school training. As Savage pointed out at the time, this led to a shameless plunder of Modernist forms;[35] on a more positive level, however, it gave a new impetus to typographic design which, through the work of Neville Brody for *The Face*, Peter Saville and Malcolm Garrett in record sleeve design and that of many others, contributed to draw typography out of the rarefied atmosphere of the workshop, to a new, younger audience, eager to consume it without any preconceptions.

Whatever we may think about the results, they are undoubtedly significant and, like the explosion of display typography that occurred in the Victorian age, are an integral part of typographic history. To insert these developments into a comprehensive history of typography is no easy task, as it requires a number of epistemological and ideological decenterings which are not easily achieved by a single person.

Another difficulty about writing typographic histories in the 1990s is the unilinear format of the academic paper. This unilinearity encourages authors to oversimplify and cut corners. In light of recent developments in multimedia technology, and given the long-standing claims of 'hypertexts' to deliver more than traditional printed texts, it may be opportune that typographic histories should consider the possibilities of developing multilinear accounts of typographic pluralism. Combined with the epistemological and ideological decenterings such moves would imply, the histories I have in mind would delete the ambition of restoring the past to its pristine glory, and settle for an exploration of the possibilities opened up by the dimension of the work. At that point, typographic histories and criticism would assume the role of a hermeneutic of interpretation, in collaboration with other disciplines, generating meanings without intimation of transcendence.

Gérard Mermoz is a freelance artist, designer, curator and writer based in Coventry and Prats de Mollo.
First published in *Visible Language*, vol. 28, no. 3.

1 'Massimo Vignelli vs Ed Benguiat', *Print* XLV:V (1991), p.88–95, 142–144 and 148.
– Ken Garland, 'Stop Footling Around', *Design* 527 (1992), p.11–13.
– Steven Heller, 'Changing of the Guard', *Eye* 8 (1993), p.4–5, and 'Cult of the Ugly', *Eye* 9, p.52–59.
– Various, 'Letters', *Eye* 10 (1993), p.3–5.
– Michael Bierut, 'Playing the Game by Rand's Rules', *Eye* 10 (1993), p.77–79.
– Various, 'Letters', *Eye* 11 (1993), p.3.
– Paul Stiff, 'Stop Sitting Around and Start Reading', *Eye* 11 (1993), p.4–5.
– Jeffery Keedy, 'The Rules of Typography According to Crackpots Experts', *Eye* 11 (1993), p.48–55.
2 Karl Gerstner, *Compendium for Literates* (Cambridge, MA: The MIT Press, 1974), p.132.
3 D.C. Greetham, 'Editorial and Critical Theory: From Modernism to Postmodernism', in: George Bornstein and Ralph G. Williams, *Palimpsest* (Ann Arbor: The University of Michigan Press, 1993), p.14.
4 William Atkins, ed. *The Art and Practice of Printing*, vol. 1–6 (London: Pitman and Sons, 1932) vol. 1, chapter XIV, 'Typographic Display', p.198–246.
5 John C. Tarr, 'What Are the Fruits of the New Typography' (1936), reprinted in *Printing in the Twentieth Century: A Penrose Anthology* (London: Northwood Publishers, 1974), p.151.
6 Bertram Evans, 'Typography in England, 1933: Frustration or Function', *Penrose Annual* (1934), p.58.
7 Atkins, op.cit, 1.
8 John Gloag, 'Design Marches On', *Penrose Annual* (1938), p.19–20.
9 Aaron Burns, foreword to *The Liberated Page*, ed. Herbert Spencer, (London: Lund Humphries, 1987), p.7.
10 Walter Tracy, *The Typographic Scene* (London: Gordon Fraser, 1988), p.11.
11 John Lewis, *Typography: Design and Practice* (London: Barrie and Jenkins, 1978), p.16–19.
12 Tracy, op.cit., p.11.
13 Robin Kinross, 'The Rhetoric of Neutrality', *Design Discourse*, Victor Margolin, ed. (Chicago: Chicago University Press 1989), p.131–143.
14 Daniel Berkeley Updike, *Printing Types: Their History, Forms and Use* (Cambridge, Mass: Harvard University Press, 1922; 2nd ed. 1937).
15 Robert Darnton, *Gens de Lettres, Gens du Livre* (Paris: Editions Odile Jacob, 1992).
16 Lucien Febvre, *The Coming of the Book* (1st ed: *L'Apparition du Livre*, Paris: Albin Michel, 1958; London: Verso, 1993), p.12.
17 Gérard Blanchard, *Pour une Sémiologie de la Typographie* (Andenne: Rémy Magermans, 1979).
18 Robin Kinross, *Modern Typography: An Essay in Critical History* (London: Hyphen Press, 1992), p.11–12.
19 Alan Marshall, 'Type Review' (Review of Kinross' *Modern Typography*), *Bulletin of the Printing Historical Society* 35:16 (1993).
20 Georges Gusdorf, *Introduction aux Sciences Humaines* (Strasbourg: Publications de la Faculté de Lettres, 1960).
21 Thomas Francis Carter, *The Invention of Printing in China* (New York: The Ronald Press, (rev. by Luther Carrington Goodrich, 1955)).
– See also: Tsien Tsuen-Hsuin, 'Paper and Printing', in *Science and Civilisation in China*, vol.5, part 1, ed. John Needham (Cambridge: Cambridge University Press, 1985).
22 Joseph Moxon, *Mechanick Exercises on the Whole Art of Printing* (1683–84); reprinted, eds. Herbert Davies and Harry Carter (London: Oxford University Press, 1962), p.11–12.
23 Quoted from: Jacques Maritain, *Art et Scholastique* (Paris: Librairie de l'Art Catholique, 1920), p.10, 28.
24 Jacques Maritain, *Art et Scholastique*, 17 and 122 no.15.
25 Joseph Moxon, *Mechanick Exercises...*, p.12.
26 On the organization of printing workshops or 'chapels': Frederick Compton Avis, *The Early Printers' Chapel in England* (London: FC Avis, 1971).
27 Hieronymus Hornschuch, *Orthotypographia* (Leipzig: M. Lantzenberge, 1608), p.5. Reprinted with an English translation by Cambridge University Library, (1972).
28 Nicolete Gray, *Nineteenth Century Ornamented Types and Title Pages* (London: Faber and Faber, 1938; 2nd rev ed. 1976).
– John Lewis, 'Printed Ephemera: The Changing Uses of Type and Letterform', *English and American Printing* (London: Antique Collector's Club, 1962; 2nd rev ed. 1990).
– John Lewis, *Collecting Printed Ephemera* (London: Studio Vista, 1976).
– Michael Twyman, *Printing 1770–1970* (London: Eyre and Spottiswoode, 1970).
29 Edward M. Gottschall, *Typographic Communications Today* (Cambridge, Massachusetts: The MIT Press, 1989), p.2, 18.
– Philip B. Meggs, *A History of Graphic Design* (New York: Van Nostrand Reinhold, 1992), p.241, 485.
30 Umbro Apollonio, *Futurist Manifestos* (London: Thames & Hudsons, 1973), p.95–106.
31 Robert Massin, *Letter and Image* (London: Studio Vista, 1970) p.155–244.
32 John Lewis, *Typography, Design and Practice* (London: Barrie and Jenkins, 1978), p.13.
33 Ruari Mclean, *Manual of Typography* (London: Thames and Hudson, 1980), p.12.
34 Simon Manchipp, 'Typo mystique', *Typographic News*, 68 (1993), p.13.
35 Jon Savage, 'The Age of Plunder', *The Face*, January (1983), p.44–49.

ELLEN MAZUR THOMSON

The Origins of
Graphic Design
in America
1870–1920

ALMS FOR OBLIVION:
THE HISTORY OF WOMEN IN
EARLY AMERICAN GRAPHIC DESIGN

ELLEN MAZUR THOMSON
1994

'Wage-earning women stressed the contradiction between social ideas
about women and the actual reality of their own lives.'
— Sarah Eisenstein, *Give Us Bread But Give Us Roses*

When Linda Nochlin's article 'Why Have There Been No Great Women Artists?' appeared in
1971, it generated enormous interest in neglected work by women artists. Nochlin challenged
art historians to analyze the institutional and ideological structures that distort what women
have accomplished or have been unable to accomplish. She warned that women must 'face up
to the reality of their history and of their present situation, without making excuses or puffing
mediocrity. Disadvantage may indeed be an excuse; it is not, however, an intellectual position.'
Since then feminist historians have explored the limitations placed on women who pursued
careers in the arts and on the representation of those women who did succeed in the literature
of art history. Only recently, however, have historians of graphic design faced the biases in
their own field and begun to identify individual women and document their position in graphic
design history.[1]

Martha Scotford began this process by showing that the major texts used to teach graphic
design concentrate on the work of a limited number of 'great men' and that, consciously or
unconsciously, graphic design historians have created an unacknowledged canon that excludes
women. She suggested that cultural history, rather than art history, would provide a better
model for historians to follow.[2]

A reading of the basic texts of graphic design history leads one to assume that women
were marginal if not absent in the transformation of the field. Even feminist art historians,
when they include illustrators in their histories, are inclined to ignore the commercial aspects
of the artists' work. Art historical models are often based on the great artists and their masterpieces and so fail to go beyond narrations of lives, assessments of influence, and progressions
of styles.[3] In describing women's experiences in the printing industry, the advertising industry,
and commercial illustration, one can show, however briefly, not only where women participated in graphic design but how their experience reveals the profession's ties to other aspects
of American culture.

In a pioneering article, Cheryl Buckley argued that women's role in all fields of design has
been defined by 'the sexual division of labor, assumptions about femininity, and the hierarchy
that exists in design.' Preliminary research confirms that this is true in graphic design. During
the second half of the nineteenth century many women worked in the printing industry, but
in limited, gender-based capacities. Women were gradually forced out of the printing trades
because male-dominated unions argued that the work was too physically demanding even as
it became less so. Women worked in the advertising industry but are absent from the histories
because they were unable to reach the higher levels of management, where their names would
be associated with particular campaigns. At the same time, the women's movement, identified

with the fight for voting rights, grew in power and forced the nation to confront 'the woman question.' The number of schools and colleges, including schools of fine and applied art open to women, increased dramatically. This was in part a result of the Aesthetic and Arts and Crafts movements. Changing attitudes toward the applied arts and women's education gave female illustrators new opportunities, but it encouraged them to work on domestic subjects and in a decorative style.[4]

The changing definition of gender-appropriate work is an important aspect of this story. In her encyclopedia on *The Employments of Women* (1863), Virginia Perry listed career options for women to consider. Like her contemporaries, Perry defined some work as masculine and some as feminine, but she argued that many male-dominated professions were essentially 'feminine' and that women should be able to pursue these vocations. For example, Perry considered copperplate engraving (the production of business cards, calling cards and invitations) to be a feminine occupation that was dominated by men. 'The patience and careful attention to details requisite, and the sedentary nature of engraving, render it a more suitable occupation for women than men', she wrote.[5]

This attitude was shared by John Durand, editor of the *Crayon*. In an editorial of 1861 entitled 'Woman's Position in Art', he declared that lithography and wood engraving were, or ought to be, feminine occupations.

Man is not made for sedentary life; woman, on the contrary, conforms to it without inconvenience; she better maintains that close, unceasing attention, that motionless activity which the engraver's pursuit demands. Her nimble fingers, accustomed to wield the needle, lend themselves more easily to minute operations, to the use of small instruments, to the almost imperceptible shades of manipulation that wood-engraving exact. Cutting on copper and steel demands also a patience and minutia much more compatible with the nature of woman than with that of man. It is only in *womanizing* himself, in some degree, that man succeeds in obtaining the development of these faculties so contrary to his physical constitution, and always at the expense of his natural force.[6]

Fanny Palmer, *The Rocky Mountains: Emigrants Crossing the Plains* (1866).
Prints and Photographs Division, Library of Congress.

At the same time, real working women were ignored in the literature. A good example of this is the case of Frances Flora Bond Palmer, known as Fanny Palmer. Palmer was one of two full-time lithographers at Currier and Ives. Although Palmer was all but forgotten after her death, modern feminist art historians have revived her memory. Born and trained in England, she emigrated to New York in the 1840s. At Currier and Ives, Palmer was responsible for more than two hundred lithographs, making the original drawings and transferring them to the stone. She worked in a tremendous range of subjects: landscapes, cityscapes, hunting scenes and still-lifes, as well as prints of trains, steamships and buildings, and dramatic Civil War scenes. These were not defined as 'feminine' subjects (ironically, Palmer was thought to be weakest in rendering the human figure). Her 'Rocky Mountains, Emigrants Crossing the Plains' (1866) was one of the company's most popular prints and could be found in homes throughout the country. Palmer also contributed to the technical aspects of commercial lithography: she developed a method of printing a background tone and, with Charles Currier, improved lithographic crayons. Although she was unusually gifted and productive, her historical fate was nonetheless typical. Palmer was an employee, so her work was not recognized as that of an individual in her own right, but subsumed under the Currier and Ives imprint. She supported an alcoholic husband and their children, yet her obituary identifies her only as her husband's wife, in the less than felicitous terms of that day: 'a relict of Edmund S. Palmer of Leicester, England'. Palmer was mentioned only in passing, as a part of Currier and Ives history, until feminist art historians became interested in her work.[7]

Documentation

To understand the positions women found in graphic design, we must turn to documentary sources that provide a broader picture of the profession and the era when it began. The relation between the struggling printers' unions and women who worked in the printing trade was discussed in union journals and the popular press of the period. Workers in the printing industry regarded themselves as a highly skilled and close fraternity, and their trade unionism developed early. The ambivalence union members felt toward female workers explains as much about the situation women faced in entering the design profession as it does about the precarious situation of trade unionism itself.[8]

Histories of the women's movement, whether by participants or by modern feminist writers, are excellent sources because many suffragettes published and edited newspapers and magazines as part of their activities. Susan B. Anthony and Amelia Jenks Bloomer were allied with women trying to find jobs in the printing trades, and their confrontations with local and national printing unions are well documented.[9]

Many of the art and design schools that opened throughout the country in the second half of the nineteenth century accepted women students. The published histories, original charters, and early annual reports of these institutions describe the ideological basis for education in the applied arts and explain why women were encouraged to pursue careers in design.

If women's presence in the workplace generated heated arguments about trade unionism and women's rights, it also attracted the attention of statisticians and economists. Statistical studies describe the position of female workers in the larger picture of economic development.[10]

Trade magazines for printers, typographers, and advertisers reflect the prevailing attitudes of their professions toward women and only unintentionally reveal women's participation. Unfortunately, as we shall see, these journals often preferred to ignore women and so are eloquent, if not informative, by their silence.

Histories of art, particularly of American graphics and illustration, and biographies of American women artists contain information on women who worked as illustrators for magazines, books, and posters. They continue to emphasize painters, sculptors, and 'fine' print-makers untainted by commercialism, although women art historians have written about individual female illustrators. By concentrating on broader cultural issues rather than individual artists, a few art historians have shown how particular artistic movements have influenced educational and professional opportunities for women. Roger B. Stein argued that promoters of the Aesthetic theory encouraged upper-class women to pursue artistic interests, thereby diverting them from radical political activity. Even the Arts and Crafts movement, as Anthea Callen has demonstrated, reinforced patriarchal ideology as it opened opportunities for women in the arts.[11]

Women in the Printing Trades

A number of men associated with the beginnings of graphic design began their careers in printing establishments, and so it is logical to look for women there as well. Indeed, from the colonial period on, women were well represented in the American printing industry. Several presses, including the first press in North America, were run by women. It is often argued that women became printers only when it was their family's trade, but to the extent that this was true, it held equally for male printers. Girls, however, were generally trained in the printshop at home, in contrast to boys, who often learned their craft during an apprenticeship. The issue of apprenticeship, as we shall see, became a critical one for women.[12]

There is no doubt that some female printers attained the respect of their profession. The *Typographic Advertiser* carried an obituary for Lydia R. Bailey, a widow, who took over her husband's printing establishment. It noted that from 1808 to 1861 'her office was one of the largest in Philadelphia. She instructed forty-two boys into the mysteries of typography; and some of our present prosperous master-printers served their apprenticeship under her. For a considerable period she was elected City Printer by the Councils; and her imprint was well known. She had great energy and decision of character.' Bailey's achievement, moreover, was placed in the wider context of political and economic rights: 'Of late days we hear much talk about women's rights. Something may probably come of it to women's advantage: how we may not forecast. There is certainly room enough for improvement in the condition of many women; but will the privilege of suffrage bring it about?'[13]

Women not linked by family ties to printing were nevertheless interested in the printing trades because they were relatively open to them and offered higher wages than the other industries where they found employment, notably in textiles, clothing, tobacco, and papermaking.

Composing Room, Riverside Press
Paper World (December 1880)
General Collection, Library
of Congress.

Yet women who worked in printshops earned considerably less than their male counterparts. In Boston in 1831, for example, men were paid three times as much as women and boys: the 687 men in printing earned $1.50 a day, whereas the 395 women and 215 boys in printing earned just 50¢ a day. In 1860, women in the printing trades earned on average $18.65 a month, more than women in any other branch of manufacturing. By 1880 in Boston the average weekly earnings for women in all trades was $6.03, whereas women in printing and publishing earned $6.61, an additional 9 percent.[14]

In 1853 the suffragette and social reformer Amelia Jenks Bloomer began publication of the *Lily: A Ladies' Journal Devoted to Temperance and Literature*. When, a year later, she tried to hire a woman apprentice, the printers refused to work and went on strike against both her publication and one produced by her husband. Bloomer persisted and finally found three women and three men to publish both papers; she paid them equal wages, although at less than union rates.

By the end of the Civil War, more women had entered the profession. In 1868, for example, there were two hundred women typesetters in New York City, approximately 15–20 percent of printing trade workers. And the printing trades attracted an increasingly larger percentage of women workers (see table 4). In 1870, 3.7 percent of compositors were women, in 1880, 4.7 percent, in 1890, 9.9 percent, and in 1900, 10.3 percent. Despite the introduction of new technology that raised worker productivity, an increase in demand for printed matter allowed the total number of workers in printing to expand.[15]

Number and Percentage Distribution of Female Gainful Workers
in Printing and Allied Industries, 1870–1930

	1870	1880	1890	1900	1910	1920
Printing and allied industries	4,233	8,947	23,771	31,613	45,090	45,274
Women workers (%)	40.8	39.1	51.6	53.8	59.4	55.8
Engravers	29	103	303	453	538	561
Women workers (%)	0.3	0.4	0.7	0.8	0.7	0.7

Adapted from H. Dewey Anderson and Percy E. Davidson, *Occupational Trends in the United States*
(Palo Alto: Stanford University Press, 1940), p.300–301.

Composition sometimes required a high degree of skill and a strong sense of design. On 'straight matter' the compositor might simply be required to follow a standard format with a limited number of fonts; other material demanded considerably more judgment. Advertisements, for example, appeared in a variety of media: trade cards, posters, and stationery, as well as newspapers and periodicals. In general, men underwent an extended apprenticeship and became skilled at a variety of work. Women, in contrast, were taught for six weeks without pay and then put to work setting plain matter and redistributing type.[16]

As noted, printing professions were practiced in two very different environments: newspaper and periodical printers and the book and job trades. Few women were employed at large city newspapers, and even in smaller cities, where they often did set straight matter, they did not design layouts or advertisements. In 1900 newspapers and periodicals employed 73,653 men earning $45 million ($610 per month) and 14,815 women earning $4.6 million ($310 per month). There are no comparable figures for women in book and job offices, but they represented, respectively, two-thirds and half the total number of workers. Of 9,045 linotype machine workers, just 520 were women.[17]

Local printing unions, which had existed in a variety of forms during the first half of the century, formed a national organization, the United Typographical Union, in 1852. In contrast to their progressive tradition, these all-male organizations were highly ambivalent about unionizing female workers. Many printers hired women at lower wages under the guise of giving them an opportunity to learn the trade, and women often worked as scab labor during strikes. The unions had two options: either fight for equal wages and unionize women or ban them from the industry. They tried both tactics. The editorial positions of the *Inland Printer* reflected the contradictions. In 1884, the editor wrote:

> The printers employed on the *Evening Wisconsin*, of Milwaukee, twenty-three in number, are on a strike because the manager of that sheet insisted, after several remonstrances, on paying the female compositors, members of the Cream City Typographical Union, twenty-eight cents instead of thirty-three cents per thousand ems – the union scale – as paid to the male compositors; and this, too, in the face of the admission that the women did better work than a majority of the men.
>
> The action of the union in making the cause of the girls its own is worthy of all commendation. Of course, no protective organization could tolerate, for a moment, a *sliding scale* arrangement, all its members, irrespective of sex, age or nationality, being required to observe the minimum rate of wages. Any other policy would be suicidal. The standard raised – 'equal pay for equal work' – is one which will command the sympathy of every right-minded citizen; and it is needless to add that those now engaged in this struggle have our warmest wishes for their success.[18]

In spite of these sentiments, this same editor advocated barring female students from trade schools and accused any woman who wanted such training – or indeed worked in the trades – of selfishly taking jobs away from men with families to support. Although they did not all subscribe to the idea that women were incapable of performing the tasks or less hard-working, contributors to the journal argued that the printing trades required a greater amount of time to develop skills and that many female workers left as soon as they married. Some arguments appeared in the form of patriarchal sermons on the need to protect women from the dangers of the work: their exposure to materials dangerous to health, their supposed frailty and inability to carry heavy type forms, and their potential contact with 'unsuitable' printed matter. Others argued that women lacked training, that they were incapable of doing anything but the most straightforward jobs because few had served an apprenticeship. Women, indeed, accounted for only 9.7 percent of all apprentice typesetters. But the most troubling issue, and the primary focus of the opposition, was that women worked for lower wages and were used by employers to fight unionization. And it was on this issue that the suffragette leader Susan B. Anthony entered the fray.[19]

Anthony encouraged women to learn typesetting by taking jobs they were offered by printers, even during strikes. It is unclear if she really lacked an understanding of the need for worker solidarity, as some writers charge, or if she, unlike female unionists, considered male workers so unsympathetic that they would never voluntarily integrate their shops. In a report of her fight for admittance to a union convention, printed in the *Workingman's Advocate* in August 1869, Anthony said she represented:

> a class of women that had no husbands, and who were on the street penniless, homeless and without shelter. Now, I ask you what we are to do with these girls? Shall we tell them to starve in the garrets because the printers, by their own necessities, open their doors and give a slight training to a few girls for a few weeks? Shall I say to the girls, 'Do not

go in, but starve?' or shall I say, 'Go in, and get a little skill into your hands, and fit your-selves to work side by side with men?' I want to ask the Co-operative Union of New York how many girls they have taken to learn the typesetting business? How many women have you ordered each department or establishment to take as apprentices, and to train in the art of typesetting?[20]

Union leader Augusta Lewis clashed with Anthony over these tactics. Lewis (c.1848–1920), a journalist and typesetter, believed that by preserving union solidarity, by foregoing the immediate advantage of work, women would eventually find an equal place in union shops. Lewis had founded the Women's Typographical Union no.1 (WTU) in October 8, 1868, and she urged women members not to accept nonunion work. A year later, in 1869, the United Typographical Union became the first national union in the country to admit women, and in 1870 Lewis herself was elected corresponding secretary of the national organization.

Yet Lewis was soon disillusioned by the union's treatment of its female members. '[We] have never obtained a situation that we could not have obtained had we never heard of a union. We refuse to take the men's situations when they are on strike, and when there is no strike if we ask for work in union offices we are told by union foremen 'that there are no conveniences for us.' We are ostracized in many offices because we are members of the union; and although the principle is right, disadvantages are so many that we cannot much longer hold together.'[21]

When women did succeed, they were derided as unfeminine and grotesque. In describing an itinerant printer he had met in western Ohio, one writer claimed: 'She was dressed plainly but neatly in what might be called a cross between a traveling and office suit of brown color. The toughened expression on her face indicated that she was familiar with the tricks of the profession, versed in the study of vulgarity. No tender, trusting female was she, but a hardened, suspicious, masculine woman.'[22] When they were not questioning women's abilities, the jour-nals ignored them. They were quick to take umbrage at similar treatment from women, how-ever. The *Inland Printer* reprinted an article from a British trade journal reporting that women compositors in Boston published a journal called *Elle*: 'This paper is a veritable man-hater; not the slightest mention of man in any shape or form is to be found in its columns, neither is the *genus homo* allowed to hawk it!' The notice is doubly significant. *Elle* does not appear in any of the standard sources on magazine literature, and it is possible that no copies have survived. We know of its existence now only because it irritated the editors of a mainstream journal.[23]

The introduction of new technology, particularly the Mergenthaler Linotype begin-ning in the 1880s, might have increased opportunities for women. The typographer's union admitted that women learned to work with the system more quickly but also charged that they lacked endurance. In the end the union insisted that only fully qualified – that is, male – print-ers should be allowed to operate the machines. In typesetting, the one printing profession in which women significantly competed for work, they had lost ground. By 1900 only 8 percent of women belonged to unions, compared with 32 percent of men, and that number decreased rapidly. Only 10 percent of compositors were women, while only approximately 700 of 12,000, or just 5.8 percent, operated typesetting machines. Barred from the apprentice system and trade schools and betrayed by the trade unions that ostensibly represented them, working-class women rarely followed men who made the transition from the printshop into the design of printed material.[24]

The private press movement inspired American printers and designers from Boston to San Francisco, but women are excluded almost completely from its history. Fragmentary records indicate, however, that these presses existed and that some women took part in the movement. In 1873 two sisters, trained designers and wood engravers, founded the Crane and Curtis Company in San Francisco. Women ran the Chemith Press in 1902 in Minneapolis and the Butterfly Press from 1907 to 1909 in Philadelphia. Bertha Sprinks Goudy, who operated the Village Press with her husband, Frederic Goudy, is fulsomely praised for her work, but only in studies of her husband's life and career.[25]

Artist-designed bookbinding was a significant field before the advent of the book jacket both in the private press movement and in commercial publishing during the 1890s. Most of the women book designers who gained recognition for their work came from upper-class backgrounds; Margaret Neilson Armstrong (1867–1944) was one of the first and one of the most prolific. Armstrong was born into a socially prominent, wealthy New York family, and both she and her sister, Helen, made their careers out of choice rather than economic necessity. By 1913 she had designed more than 250 book covers, working as a freelance artist, although Scribners was her most important client. Sarah Wyman Whitman, an important member of Boston society, was a leader of the Arts and Crafts Society as well as a successful designer. Ellen Gates Starr (1860–1940), a colleague of Jane Addams, was also a disciple of William Morris; she shared his beliefs on art and his commitment to socialism and studied book design in England with Thomas J. Cobden-Sanderson at the Doves Press. Starr returned to Chicago to establish a bookbindery in the 1890s. Unlike others in the movement, Starr recognized the contradiction between fundamental social reform and the handicraft tradition. She eventually abandoned design for political activism, writing, 'If I had thought it through, I would have realized that I would be using my hands to create books that only the rich could buy.'[26]

Modern historians may explain the relatively large number of successful women in book design and binding in terms of the receptivity of the Arts and Crafts movement to their participation. Contemporary observers and participants, however, ascribed it to gender-specific skills. Cobden-Sanderson, Starr's teacher, is quoted as having said, 'Women ought to do the best work in bookbinding, for they possess all the essential qualifications of success: patience for detail, lightness of touch, and dexterous fingers.' These views were not held by men alone. Alice C. Morse, herself an accomplished book-cover designer, claimed that women had an inherent ability: 'Women seem to have a remarkable faculty for designing. Their intuitive sense of decoration, their feeling for beauty of line and harmony of color, insures them a high degree of success.'[27]

It is no coincidence that the Arts and Crafts societies begun in 1897 were among the few clubs to include women or that when the prestigious Society of Printers was founded in 1905 in Boston, no women were admitted. In fact, women were not admitted until 1974, after a prolonged and acrimonious battle. Women were not allowed to become members of the Grolier Club until 1976, although the club exhibited their work much earlier. The Art Directors Club also showed women's work but refused women membership until 1948, admitting Cipe Pineles (1908–75) only because her husband, William Golden, refused to join without her. Fifteen years passed before the second female member was admitted. The Graphic Group was exclusively male, as was the American Institute of Graphic Arts in its early years. In 1926, after a change in its charter, the Newsletter proudly announced that Frances Atwater, a typographer at the New York Times, and Florence N. Levy, director of the Baltimore Museum of Art, 'share the distinction of being the first women members.'[28]

Advertising Artists

Although women were immediately recognized as important targets for advertisers' messages, they were rarely mentioned in the early advertising journals as practitioners and are absent from advertising histories until the 1920s. Information about women in the advertising industry appears fortuitously in advertising trade journals, which were unsympathetic to them in general but which intermittently championed the work of individual women. More frustrating are the published reports of design contests in which women's names appear regularly as winners, suggesting that there must have been a significant number of trained and employed women in the field.

With its first issue in 1891, *Profitable Advertising* sounded the derisive note that it sustained throughout its years of publication. The ridicule and warning, though somewhat incoherent, were impossible to ignore:

> The Boston *Globe* is encouraging women to become 'writers on business', female 'Powers', as it were; scientific experts, etc. O, General Taylor, this is too much. And offering prizes for advertisements, too, written by women! Great guns! There are about 6,946 male scientific advertising experts in the US who will soon with Othello raise the very devil about their flown occupation. The result will be more disastrous than the female typewriter craze. Of course the women will cut rates. Boys, get together, formulate a union and boycott *The Globe*. Or start the women off on writing advertisements for pants. Would they succeed? Well, *would* they? They would find virtues in pants us poor males never dreamt of.[29]

Women's participation on the editorial staff of any trade journal was extremely rare and, given prevailing attitudes, even when they were present, editorial policy was not enlightened. Kate E. Griswold began at *Profitable Advertising* as manager and became editor in October 1893. Earlier that year, in June, an article appeared that she may have written. Signed 'Miss Progress', it was a diatribe against uniform wage scales. The writer acknowledged that women have been limited in their professional opportunities in the past 'but that day has gone. Oh, no, we are not ranting 'women's righters' in the common acceptance of the term. We have no fondness for women who disgust men, as well as members of their own sex, by their arbitrary methods of attempting to secure what they are pleased to sum up as their 'rights'.[30]

Even when their work was noticed, women's achievements were attributed to their femininity. *Advertising Experience*'s issue of February 1898 featured advertising photographers Beatrice Tonnesen and her sister, Clara Tonnesen Kirkpatrick. In praising their work, the editors claimed that 'the fact that the Tonnesens are women photographers has no doubt made it possible for them to secure a better class and a larger selection of models than could be secured by a male photographer.' Years later, *Printers' Ink* acknowledged that Beatrice Tonnesen was the first photographer to use 'live models'. She had organized a register of models from which to draw so that 'when she received an advertising order, she first created an idea and then selected a model best suited for its expression.' Evidently, the 'Tonnesen Models' were nationally known.[31]

Photography may have provided an entry for some women into advertising, although little research has been done in this area. Women participated in the photography fad in the 1890s, but many preferred to remain 'amateurs' devoted to personal artistic expression. We know of some who did become professionals and worked in portraiture and photojournalism. In an study from a feminist perspective, C. Jane Gover shows that from 1890 to 1920 photography was a profession adopted by economically secure women who found in it a measure of personal freedom and yet remained firmly tied to Victorian gender definitions by upholding 'the domestic ideal and woman's place as nurturer' in their work. Unfortunately, Gover, like most historians of photography, does not include advertising photographers in her study, although she does mention Beatrice Tonnesen in other contexts.[32]

Advertising posters provided work for many illustrators, including a significant number of women. Jacquelyn Server argues that because poster design was a new field, without the usual prejudices, women were relatively successful. The numbers of women involved, however, should be put in perspective. In an exhibition of work by prominent poster designers held in 1896, of the eighty-three designers whose works were shown, just seven were women. Some women poster designers continued in graphic design. Blanche McManus (Mrs. Francis Milton Mansfield) (b. 1870) designed posters and illustrations for books and magazines and in 1911 became art editor of *American Motorist*. Helen Dryden (b. 1887) designed posters and stage scenery, illustrated for magazines, and worked as an industrial designer. (She was involved in designing the 1937 *Studebaker*.)[33]

Ethel Reed (b. 1876) was the most famous female poster artist of her day. For a short period she designed book posters for the publisher Lamson, Wolffe and Company of Boston, and she was the only women profiled in the *Poster*. The author began with a lengthy dissertation on womens' limited abilities in general and women artists' lack of artistry in particular. He then praised Reed, because she 'knows well the marvelous secret of design and colours, and while she executes pictures with clever hands, she sees with her own and not masculine eyes; her work has feminine qualities, one sees in it a woman, full of sweetness and delicacy, and this is the greatest praise one can bestow upon a woman.'[34]

Will Bradley also profiled Reed in 'The Womans' Number' of *Bradley: His Book*. He tackled the issue of nature versus nurture directly: 'The so-called 'poster movement' has brought into first prominence but one woman designer. Whether this is due to a defect in the ordinary course of training for artistic purposes, from which young women students too seldom have the courage to break away, or is owing altogether to the lack of original inventiveness which women themselves evince, it would be hard to say. Probably both conventional training and inherent incapacity that mar making ventures into new fields of work are to blame for the undeniable fact that thus far men hold the honors in this new branch of art production, with the single exception, it may be, of Miss Ethel Reed of Boston.'[35]

Ethel Reed, *Folly or Saintliness* (1895)
Prints and Photographs Division, Library
of Congress.

Advertising art was rarely signed, and it is unusual to be able to identify the artist. Jessie Wilcox Smith was an exception; Smith's name appeared prominently on all her work. She produced advertisements throughout her career for Campbell's Soup, Eastman Kodak, and Ivory Soap. Very popular male artists, such as J. Leyendecker and Charles Dana Gibson, also signed their advertising work.

In 1913, Elizabeth Colwell (b. 1881) became the only woman ever featured in *Graphic Arts* (1911–15), a magazine that regularly profiled leading printers, designers, and advertising artists. A Chicago designer, Colwell did publicity for Marshall Field and for Cowan Company. She designed bookplates and was known for her lettering and book designs. The editor of *Graphic Arts*, Henry Lewis Johnson, acknowledged in a note preceding this article that 'it has been an axiom among designers, although just why it is hard to say, that women cannot do good lettering. Miss Colwell with many other women designers, offers direct proof to the contrary.' [36]

The Work of Elizabeth Colwell
Graphic Arts (March 1913)
General Collection, Library
of Congress.

An Art Directors Club exhibition held in 1921 at the National Arts Club in New York included the work of a significant number of women. Reviewing the exhibition, *Arts and Decoration* reported that women 'have attained real distinction in the field' and were responsible for 'some of the most interesting and arresting exhibits on the walls.' Yet women faced overt sexism that cut both ways. The author of an article in the *American Advertiser* criticized one agency director who refused to hire a female assistant because he doubted she would be as capable as a man. The author argued, however, that because so much advertising was directed at the female consumer, female advertisers, with their unique 'insight', would create more persuasive campaigns. Like their male advertising counterparts, only women in executive positions earned substantial salaries, and in 1905 just a dozen women had reached this level.[37]

In her autobiography, *Through Many Windows*, Helen Rosen Woodward, a pioneer in advertising, describes advertising practices as well as the atmosphere of the workplace: the sexism and anti-Semitism encountered by workers at the turn of the century. When Woodward began in New York in 1903, agents were expected not only to plan campaigns but to design advertisements, write copy, and hire and direct illustrators. At that time female agents earned eighteen dollars a week, men twenty-five dollars. In 1926, Woodward reported, 'The difference between the pay of men and women for the same work has largely disappeared in the advertising business but it is still hard for women to get positions where the bigger money lies.'[38]

This was corroborated by Taylor Adams, who began his advertising career in the 1920s. According to Adams, 'Women began flowering in the creative departments of agencies in the 1920s, but you could hardly have said they were prevalent. With a single outstanding exception, they were either temporary tokenists hired for specific tasks (such as 'influencing' decision makers of client or prospect) or more often anonymous foot-sloggers who rarely made it to title or stockholder.'[39]

Of course, the work of most advertising artists, male and female, was unsigned and ephemeral. The heads of advertising agencies took credit for successful campaigns, and women remained part of anonymous teams. And although trade magazines encouraged higher standards of composition, drawing, and typography, little was written about the people who designed advertising.

Illustrators

To the degree that the proponents of the Aesthetic and Arts and Crafts movements broke down barriers between fine and applied art, they gave many of the crafts traditionally associated with women a new legitimacy. They also encouraged the establishment of schools to train women in the arts, although their motives here were not straightforward. Walter Smith, the English Arts and Crafts advocate who became director of art education for Massachusetts, saw the arts as a way to divert women from their struggle to gain political power. 'We have a fancy', he wrote, 'that our lack of art schools and other institutions where women can learn to employ themselves usefully and profitably at work which is in itself interesting and beautiful, is one of the causes which drives them to so unsex themselves as to seek to engage in men's affairs. Give our American women the same art facilities as their European sisters, and they will flock to the studios and let the ballot-box alone.'[40]

In the US the first applied art school for women began in Philadelphia at the behest of Sarah Peter, a wealthy philanthropist, under the auspices of the Franklin Institute. The School of Design for Women opened on December 3, 1850, with a class of ninety-four students and expanded rapidly. The arguments for its establishment, found in the Franklin Institute proceedings, reflect the ideology of the Aesthetic movement: the legitimacy of the applied arts and women's contribution to them, the development of women's 'natural' ability as it related to their domestic life, and the non-threatening nature of women's work. Peter was explicit; she wanted 'to enlarge the sphere of female occupation' without endangering male employment or upsetting women's tradition sphere: 'I selected this department of industry, not only because

Frank Holme, *Miss B. Ostertag*
Brush and Pen (December 1897) General
Collection, Library of Congress.

Blanche Ostertag was acclaimed as a
young and talented designer at the turn of
the century. Little is known of her life or
career, only that she was born in St. Louis
and studied in Europe before coming to
Chicago, where she designed posters and
advertisements for leading businesses.

it presents a wide field, as yet unoccupied by our countrymen, but also because these arts can be practiced at home, without materially interfering with the routine of domestic duty, which is the peculiar province of women.' The chairman of the Franklin Institute expanded Peter's argument: 'Women are especially adept at decoration and this would not cause an economic problem: their quick perceptions of form and their delicacy of hand very especially fit them; while even should they, in these and similar branches of labor, finally supplant men entirely, no evil could occur, especially in a country like ours, where such broad fields for male labor lie entirely unoccupied.'[41]

The number of art schools for women or open to them increased in the 1870s. The earliest, begun in the East, separated the sexes; Western schools were generally coeducational. The Lowell Institute in Boston, begun in 1850, followed the Eastern pattern. During the 1871–72 academic year the school enrolled 124 male and 127 female students; classes for women were held in the afternoon, those for men in the evening. Similarly, in 1856, when Peter Cooper endowed an Academy of Design for Women, 'in which the art of engraving and designing will constantly be taught', women studied during the day and men at night.[42]

Most women and men who trained in design schools found careers in textile design, mechanical drawing (including drawing for the US Patent Office), architectural drawing, and wood engraving. New York, with its publishing businesses, was, the center of wood engraving but women also worked in Chicago, Boston, Saint Louis, and Cleveland. Apparently pay equity varied considerably: female wood engravers earned half the rate of their male counterparts in engraving offices, although they could earn the same rate as men by freelancing. The few women who engaged in mechanical drawing were also paid at the same rate as men.[43]

Many of the early women cartoonists began their careers in the suffrage movement. Taking advantage of new educational opportunities, they trained as illustrators and then used their skills in the battle for the vote. Edwina Dumm, Rose O'Neill, May Wilson Preston, and Lou Rogers were among them. Often they combined cartooning with illustration for books and magazines and advertising work.[44]

Although women were allowed greater access to an art education, they were still blocked from membership in artist clubs. As we have seen, many clubs began as informal sessions for sharing work and evolved into social occasions for editors, printers, publishers, and other potential employers to meet with artists; they provided opportunities for professional advancement. But as one writer noted, without a trace of cynicism: 'When a woman steps boldly beyond pretty copying and does work that is strong and imaginative, she is admitted to comparison with and the companionship of brother artists; she may not be elected to active membership in the Water Color Society, but she may hope for honorary membership in that august organization, and more than content herself with being an officer of high degree in the Water Color Club.'[45]

The Society of Illustrators, founded in 1901, had ninety-six members by 1911, all male, and four associate members. The associate members were four of the most successful women illustrators of the time: Elizabeth Shippen Green, Violet Oakley, Wilson Preston, and Jessie Wilcox Smith. When the society incorporated in 1920, however, these women became full members. One of the few clubs for professional female artists was founded in 1897 in Philadelphia. Led by Alice Barber Stephens, an illustrator and teacher at the School of Design, and by Emily Sartain, an artist and director of the school, the Plastic Club provided the same kind of community and publicity that male illustrators had found so useful.[46]

In the 1880s and 1890s the need for illustrations for magazine covers and stories, outdoor advertisements, and popular fiction swelled as the number of periodicals, newspapers, and advertising posters grew. Three notable chroniclers of the Golden Age of Illustration, Francis Hopkinson Smith, Frank Weitenkampf, and Henry Pitz, mentioned women illustrators in their discussions but always grouped them apart from men and singled out just two or three for praise.

Smith was himself an illustrator and contemporary of his subjects, and his *American Illustrators* (1892) was a dramatized account of the activities in the New York illustrators' clubs he frequented. He reviewed and praised American male illustrators and showed their work in beautiful reproductions, but because women were not members of the clubs, Smith mentioned them only in a review of the annual Water Color Society exhibition. Although he made fun of most female exhibitors, in 'their devotion to the mild-eyed daisy and the familiar goldenrod standing erect in a ginger jar of Chinese blue', he allowed exceptions: Rosina Emmett, Mary Hallock Foote, and Alice Barber Stephens. These women are praised but their work is neither discussed or shown.[47]

Jessie Wilcox Smith, *Kodak Advertisement*
Colliers (26 November 1904)
General Research Division, New York
Public Library, Astor, Lenox and
Tilden Foundations.

In *American Graphic Art* (1912), Frank Weitenkampf also considered women illustrators in a separate division. Indeed, he remarked that the disruption of his chronological organization was 'brought about by the convenient classification by sex.' And he, too, commended the work of Foote and Stephens. Weitenkampf maintained that the illustrations of Howard Pyle's women students 'exemplify various possibilities resulting from the application of the female temperament to illustration.'[48]

Many female illustrators did specialize in domestic subjects, and some, though not all, worked in a decidedly decorative style. Pyle was not only a famous illustrator but equally important as a teacher, at the Drexel Institute in Philadelphia and at his own school for professional illustrators at Chadds Ford, Pennsylvania. A third of Pyle's students at Chadds Ford were women. Pyle himself used a dramatic, realistic approach to illustrating, as did many of his male students. In *The Brandywine Tradition* (1968), Henry Pitz concluded that the women were naturally drawn to another style and subject matter: 'The women artists, with a few exceptions, give the impression that they formed a consistent school somewhat different from the men. ... Their almost un-failing sense of the decorative, a shared technique and their natural inclination toward feminine, homely, re-poseful subjects are there in almost every picture.'[49]

To what degree was Pyle responsible for the style and interests of his students? All were highly accomplished before they studied with Pyle, and many had some professional experience. One can also imagine that art directors encouraged a specific subject matter; illustrators then as now were classed as specialists in a particular genre. Nonetheless, this did not necessarily force women to concentrate on domestic subjects. In an autobiographical sketch, Jessie Wilcox Smith recalled that her first illustrating assignment was for a book about American Indians. Having successfully completed the first assignment, she was offered a second book on the same subject, and then a third. 'I felt I must speak or forever after be condemned to paint Indians. So I wrote to the publishers that I did not know much about Indians and that if they had just an everyday book about children, I thought I could do it better. I was immediately rewarded with one of Louisa M. Alcott's stories, and a letter saying they were glad to know I did other things, as they had supposed Indians were my specialty!' [50]

Women illustrators in the decade before and after the turn of the century were successful by any standard. Their work was published widely, they supported themselves and their families, and some were known by name to the public in an age when popular illustrators were celebrities. But in a newspaper article of 1912, 'Qualities that Make for Success in Women Illustrators', the author was clear about what aspects of women's illustrations gained them adherents: 'The field of illustration has been steadily widening for women since those days in the early 1970s when Addie Ledyard's pictures of ideally pretty children with sweeping eyelashes won our young hearts and Mary Hallock Foote, whose quality of exquisite tenderness, rather than the strength of her drawing, brought her ardent admirers, was illustrating her own and other people's stories.' [51]

Women graphic designers were allowed to work at jobs that took advantage of their culturally defined sex-specific skills. They were thought to be able typesetters because women generally have smaller hands than men. Their supposed affinity with decoration and domesticity made them illustrators of women and children. They were encouraged to participate in those careers in which they did not threaten male economic advantage. When they ventured beyond those limits, they were belittled or vilified or 'disappeared' from history.

It is clear that women participated in significant though not overwhelming numbers in all aspects of work that would – by the first decade of the twentieth century – be recognized as the province of graphic design: in the printing industry, in advertising, and in illustration. Artistic theories during this period elevated the status of applied arts, including the decorative and domestic arts, and allowed women to participate more fully in them. Art and design schools were either open to women or established specifically to train women. Nonetheless, women were still seen as having specific abilities associated with their gender. The exceptions proved the rule; historians who praised a chosen few felt justified in ignoring the majority.

The graphic design process is a collective effort, and because women rarely headed art departments in advertising agencies, publishing houses or magazines, their contributions are difficult to document. The record of women's participation in early graphic design is meager unless the researcher goes beyond standard design histories to statistical studies, to suffragist histories and histories of minorities, to documents and institutional histories of advertising agencies, publishing firms, art and design schools, and artists' clubs, to union histories, and to the trade journals. A comprehensive history of women in graphic design would right the old imbalance. It would also provide a more realistic view of the context in which graphic design began.

Ellen Mazur Thomson is an independent scholar based in Boston.
First published in *Design Issues*, vol. 10, no. 2, 1994 and then in *The Origins of Graphic Design in America 1870–1920*, Yale University Press, 1997.

1   Linda Nochlin, 'Why Have There Been No Great Women Artists?' *Art News* 69, 9 (January 1971), p.22–39, 67–71. This article also appeared as 'Why Are There No Great Women Artists?' *Women in Sexist Society: Studies in Power and Powerless,* ed. Vivian Gornick and Barbara Moran (New York: Basic Books, 1971), and *Art and Sexual Politics,* ed. Thomas B. Hess and Elizabeth C. Baker (New York: Colliers, 1971). Feminist art historians have expanded Nochlin's agenda considerably. For an overview of feminist art criticism and art history in the 1970s and 1980s, see Thalia Gouma-Peterson and Patricia Mathews, 'The Feminist Critique of Art History', *Art Bulletin* 69, 3 (September 1987), p.326–57.

2   Martha Scotford, 'Is There a Canon of Graphic Design History?' *AIGA Journal of Graphic Design* 9, 2 (1991), p.3–5, 9.

3   See Lange's article, cited above, for the omission of women designers from major graphic design texts. The two most useful biographical references for women in graphic design are concerned with women artists: Chris Petteys, *Dictionary of Women Artists: An International Dictionary of Women Artists Born before 1900* (Boston: G. K. Hall, 1985), and Charlotte Steifer Rubinstein, *American Women Artists from Early Indian Times to the Present* (Boston: G. K. Hall, 1982). One of the problems encountered in any attempt to track women is that of multiple surnames. Cross-references are not always used. In addition, many women and men signed their work with initials instead of first names and some first names are gender neutral – a problem in identifying signatures in published work in cases when it is signed. Most advertisements and magazine illustrations were not signed.

4   Cheryl Buckley, 'Made in Patriarchy: Toward a Feminist Analysis of Women and Design', *Design Discourse: History Theory Criticism,* ed. Victor Margolin (Chicago: University of Chicago Press, 1989), p.262.

5   Virginia Penny, *The Employments of Women: A Cyclopaedia of Woman's Work* (Boston: Walker, Wise, 1863), vii, p.53.

6   'Woman's Position in Art', *Crayon* 8, 2 (February 1861), p.28.

7   Basic information on Fanny Palmer can be found in Henry T. Peters' *Currier and Ives: Printmakers to the American People* (Garden City, N.Y.: Doubleday, 1942), p.26–29. Peters summarizes her life and identifies the prints known to be hers. Otherwise she is absent from graphic history until Mary Bartlett Cowdrey's 'Fanny Palmer, An American Lithographer', in *Prints: Thirteen Illustrated Essays on the Art of the Print,* ed. Carl Zigrosser (New York: Holt, Rinehart and Winston, 1962), p.219–34, and her entry in *Notable American Women,* ed. Edward T. James, 3 vols. (Cambridge: Belknap Press of Harvard University Press, 1971), 3:10–11. Charlotte Steifer Rubinstein included Palmer in *American Women Artists* (Boston: G. K. Hall, 1982), p.68–70, and wrote in depth about her in 'The Early Career of Frances Flora Bond Palmer (1812–1876)', *American Art Journal* 17, 4 (Autumn 1985), p.71–88. Penny, in an obvious reference to Palmer ('Mrs. P. Brooklyn, an English lady') writes that 'she is probably the only lady professionally engaged in this business in the US.' *Employments of Women,* p.69.

8   For bibliographical information, see Martha Jane Soltow and Mary K. Wery, *American Women and the Labor Movement, 1825–1974* (Metuchen, N.J.: Scarecrow, 1976). Especially useful histories on women in the printers' union include Elizabeth F. Baker, *Technology and Women's Work* (New York: Columbia University Press, 1964); Mary Biggs, 'Neither Printer's Wife Nor Widow', *Library Quarterly* 50, 4 (1980), p.431–52; Eleanor Flexner, *Century of Struggle* (Cambridge: Belknap Press of Harvard University Press, 1959), especially 'Women in Trade Unions, 1860–1975', p.131–41; Belva Mary Herron, 'Labor Organization Among Women', *University Studies* 1, 10 (May 1905), and *University of Illinois Bulletin* 2, 12 (July 1, 1905), p.15–25; Philip Sheldon Foner, *Women and the American Labor Movement,* vol.1 (New York: Free Press, 1979); George A. Stevens, *New York Typographical Union no.6* (Albany: J. B. Lyon, 1913), p.421–40; and Barbara Mayer Wertheimer, *We Were There* (New York: Pantheon Books, 1977). Roger Levenson's *Women in Printing: Northern California, 1857–1890* (Santa Barbara, Calif.: Capra Press, 1994) not only restored the Women's Cooperative Printing Union (1868–80) in San Francisco to American type history but greatly increased our knowledge of a significant number of women typographers and printers in the West.

9   For guides to women's periodicals, see Maureen E. Hady, *Women's Periodicals and Newspapers from the Eighteenth Century to 1981* (Boston: G. K. Hall, 1982); Nancy K. Humphreys, *American Women's Magazines* (New York: Garland, 1989); Mary Ellen Zuckerman, *Sources on the History of Women's Magazines, 1792–1960* (New York: Greenwood Press, 1991). See also Lynne Masel-Walters, 'To Hustle with the Rowdies', *Journal of American Culture* 3, 1 (Spring 1980), on the history of the suffragette press. A study of women cartoonists who worked for pro-suffrage publications is the subject of Alice Sheppard's *Cartooning for Suffrage* (Albuquerque: University of New Mexico Press, 1994).

10   A fine example is the work of Carroll D. Wright, then chief of the Bureau of Statistics of Labor, whose study appeared in 1889 as *The Working Girls of Boston* (Boston: Wright and Potter, 1889; New York: Arno Press, 1969). It was undertaken 'to ascertain the moral, sanitary, physical and economic conditions of the working girls of Boston', including those in the printing trades (1). Wright concluded that, 'the working girls are as respectable, as moral, and as virtuous as any class of women in our community; that they are making as heroic a struggle for existence as any class is a fact which all the statistics prove' (120). And in case anyone missed the point, he spelled it out: 'girls cannot work hard all day and be prostitutes too' (121).

See also Edith Abbott and Sophonisba P. Breckinridge, 'Employment of Women in Industries', *Journal of Political Economy* 14 (January 1906), p.14–40; Joseph A. Hill, *Women in Gainful Occupations 1870 to 1920,* Department of Commerce, Bureau of the Census, Census Monographs, 9 (Washington, D.C.: Government Printing Office, 1929; Westport, Conn.: Greenwood Press, 1978); Helen L. Sumner, *Report on Condition of Woman and Child Wage-Earners in the United States: History of Women in Industry in the United States,* vol. 9 (Washington, D.C.:

Government Printing Office, 1910), p.212–21; *Women at Work: A Century of Change*, no. 161 (Washington, D.C.: Government Printing Office, 1933).

11 Roger B. Stein, 'Artifact as Ideology: The Aesthetic Movement in Its American Cultural Context', in *In Pursuit of Beauty*, exhib. cat. (New York: Metropolitan Museum of Art, 1986), p.22–51; Anthea Callen, *Women Artists of the Arts and Crafts Movement, 1870–1914* (New York: Pantheon, 1979), and 'Sexual Division of Labor in the Arts and Crafts Movement', *Woman's Art Journal* 5 (Fall–Winter 1984–85), p.1–6.

12 Leona M. Hudak, *Early American Women Printers and Publishers, 1639–1820* (Metuchen, N.J.: Scarecrow Press, 1978), p.2. Elizabeth Harris Glover established the Cambridge Press, the first press in North America, in 1639. Her husband, Jose Glover, wishing to set up a printing business, boarded a ship from England with his family, a press, and printing supplies. He died en route. See Hudak, p.9–19. See also Ava Baron, 'An 'Other' Side of Gender Antagonism at Work: Men, Boys, and the Remasculinization of Printers' Work, 1830–1920', in *Work Engendered* (Ithaca, N.Y.: Cornell University Press, 1991), p.47–69.

Mary Biggs notes that the percentage of female apprentices in printing was high compared to women in other skilled trades and that there is some reason to believe the percentage of men who actually underwent a six-year apprenticeship was relatively small. Certainly the trade journals complained of this and supported technical education for boys to make up the deficiency. Biggs, 'Neither Printer's Wife Nor Widow', p.438.

13 *Typographic Advertiser* 14, 3 (April 1869), p.1.

14 Edith Abbott, 'Harriet Martineau and the Employment of Women in 1836', *Journal of Political Economy* 14 (1906), p.615; Penny, *Employments of Woman*, 490. This average is for New York and New England; Wertheimer, *We Were There*, p.92; Wright, *Working Girls of Boston*, p.82–83.

15 Foner, *Women and the American Labor Movement*, p.145; H. Dewey Anderson and Percy E. Davidson, *Occupational Trends in the United States* (Palo Alto, Calif.: Stanford University Press, 1940), p.300–301. The authors note

that although printing material increased by more than 760 percent from 1899 to 1929, only 120 percent more workers were employed (309). Lois Rather, *Women As Printers* (Oakland, Calif.: Rather Press, 1970), p.25.

16 Herron, 'Labor Organization Among Women', p.16.

17 Ibid., p.15–16.

18 *Inland Printer* 1, 6 (March 1884), p.10.

19 In the 1880s and 1890s, the *Inland Printer* regularly attacked women in the printshop. See *Inland Printer* 1, 1 (October 1883), p.1; 2, 12 (September 1885), p.534; 7, 1 (October 1889), p.108–9; 7, 9 (June 1890), p.819–20; 9, 10 (July 1892), p.875–76; 10, 5 (February 1893), p.195; and 10, 6 (March 1893), p.501. Charles J. Dumar, president of the New York Typographical Union, argued that union women were given preferential treatment: see 8, 10 (July 1891), p.1001–2. F. M. Cole, 'Lady Compositors', *Inland Printer* 7, 2 (November 1889), p.109. *Inland Printer* 1, 6 (March 1884), p.10.

The rhetoric used by both sides is instructive. A printshop owner recommended hiring women as typesetters and wood-engravers because they were more obedient, did not use foul language, and cost considerably less. He concluded, 'At least let women have a fair opportunity to do something else besides get married. What man is there who would not resent being told that his chief ambition in life should be to be a father? Yet women are told daily that they should devote twenty years of a lifetime in the preparing for motherhood, at least ten years in bearing children, and the rest of their lives in recovering from the effects. If they prefer to think that the world is populated sufficiently, or that to bear a child does not call for the sacrifice of a lifetime, they are snubbed, and especially so when they show any inclination to compete with men in trades.' 'Male Versus Female Labor', *Art Age* 3, 25 (August 1885), p.14.

20 'Proceedings, National Labor Union, August 1869', *Workingman's Advocate* 6, 5 (September 4, 1869), reprinted in *America's Working Women*, ed. R. Baxandall, L. Gordan, and S. Reverdy (New York: Random House, 1976), p.112–13.

21 From a report given by Lewis at the International Typographers

convention in 1871 and cited by Stevens, *New York Typographical Union*, p.437.

22 Cole, 'Lady Compositors', p.109.

23 'Woman as Compositors', *Inland Printer* 7, 8 (May 1890), p.820.

24 Baker, *Technology and Women's Work*, p.45. The experience of women printers in the territories and states in the West was somewhat different. In a pictorial study of frontier journalism, numerous photographs from state archives show women working as editors, printers, and compositors. See Robert F. Karolevitz, *Newspapering in the Old West* (Seattle: Superior, 1965), especially 'Printers in Petticoats', p.173–80. Karolevitz also includes photographs of women in printing classes in state universities as well as in a special school for American Indians. Sherilyn Cox Bennion, *Equal to the Occasion: Women Editors of the Nineteenth-Century West* (Reno: University of Nevada Press, 1990), estimates that in western regions there were 344 women printers (5 percent of the total) in 1890 and 959 women (10 percent) in 1900 (10). Levenson's *Women in Printing*, though ostensibly limited to northern California, is an invaluable source of information on all women in American printing with extensive documentation on women who worked in California.

25 Edna Martin Parratt, 'Women Printers', *Bulletin of the New York Public Library* 56, 1 (January 1952), p.42–43. Often cited, this was only a brief reply to an item on women printers. The names of other women printers can be found in Rather, *Women as Printers*. See also Susan Otis Thompson, *American Book Design and William Morris* (New York: R. R. Bowker, 1977), p.206. The exception is a profile in an exhibition catalog published by Women in Design, Chicago, *Ten Years: Women in Design Chicago Anniversary Exhibition*, 1988. It is clear, however, that the authors were unable to determine the extent of Bertha Goudy's contribution to the design of books issued by the press.

26 For information on Armstrong, see Charles B. Gullans, *A Checklist of Trade Bindings Designed by Margaret Armstrong*, UCLA Library Occasional Papers, no. 16 (Los Angeles: University of California Library, 1968), and her obituary, *New York Times* (19 July 1944). Whitman

is one among several women in Nancy Findlay's *Artists of the Book in Boston* (Cambridge: Harvard College Library, Houghton Library, Department of Printing and Graphic Arts, 1985). Starr is quoted in *Notable American Women*, p.352.

27 *The Craftsman* 2, 1 (April 1902), p.33–34; Alice C. Morse, 'Women Illustrators', in *Art and Handicrafts in the Woman's Building of the World's Columbian Exposition*, ed. Maud Howe Elliot (Paris: Goupil, 1893), p.75. There are several examples of work by women in Susan Otis Thompson's 'Arts and Crafts Book', in *The Arts and Crafts Movement in America, 1876–1916*, ed. Robert Judson Clark (Princeton, N.J.: Princeton University Press, 1972), p.93–116, and her *American Book Design*. See also Wendy Kaplan, *'The Art That Is Life': The Arts and Crafts Movement in America, 1875–1920* (Boston: Little, Brown for the Museum of Fine Arts, 1987), for reproductions of work by women with extensive captions by Thompson.

28 *The Society of Arts and Crafts, 1897–1924* (Boston: The Society, 1924), p.7, 8; Charles Rheault, Jr., *S. P. at Seventy-Five: The Society of Printers, 1955–1980* (Boston: The Society, 1981), unpaginated; Martha Scotford, 'The Tenth Pioneer', *Eye* 18 (Autumn 1995), p.56–57; 'Newly Admitted Members', *News-letter of the American Institute of Graphic Arts* 19 (10 July 1926), p.2.

29 'Editorial Squibs', *Profitable Advertising* 1, 1 (June 1891), p.9.

30 In addition to Kate Griswold, who eventually became publisher of *Advertising Experience*, several other women gained prominence in journalism at the turn of the century. See 'No Sex in Success?' *The Ad-School: A Practical Advertiser* 1, 7 (July 1901), p.11. See also *Inland Printer* 8, 7 (April 1891), p.680, for profiles of Mrs. Frank Leslie, who edited her father and her husband's publications, and Mary Louise Booth, who worked at *Harper's Bazaar*. Quotation from 'Women in the Business World', *Profitable Advertising* 3, 1 (June 15, 1893), p.37.

31 'Photography in Advertising', *Advertising Experience* 6, 4 (February 1898), p.24; *Printers' Ink, a Journal for Advertisers: Fifty Years, 1888–1938* (New York: Printers' Ink, 1938), p.118.

32 Clarence Bloomfield Moore, 'Women Experts in Photography', *Cosmopolitan* 14, 5 (March 1893), p.580–90; C. Jane Gover, *The Positive Image: Women Photographers in Turn of the Century America* (Albany: State University of New York Press, 1988), xvii. See also Naomi Rosenblum, 'Not Just for Fun: Women Become Professionals, 1880–1915', in her *A History of Women Photographers* (New York: Abbeville Press, 1994), p.55–70.

33 Jacquelyn Days Server, 'The American Artistic Poster of the 1890s' (Ph.D. diss., City University of New York, 1980), p.92; *Poster Show*, exhib. cat. (Richmond, Va.: n.p., 1896).

34 S. C. de Soissons, 'Ethel Reed and Her Art', *Poster* (November 1898), p.199–202.

35 'Ethel Reed, Artist', *Bradley: His Book* 1, 3 (July 1896), p.74. (Reed went to England and has disappeared from subsequent histories.)

36 Alice Rouillier, 'The Work of Elizabeth Colwell', *Graphic Arts* 4, 4 (March 1913), p.237–48; Petteys, *Dictionary of Women Artists*.

37 'A Declaration of Art in Advertising', *Arts and Decoration* 14, 6 (April 1921), p.464–65, 498; M. R. Edmondson, 'Where Woman Fits in the Advertising World', *American Advertiser* 21, 3 (March 1905), p.56–57.

38 Helen Woodward, *Through Many Windows* (New York: Harper and Brothers, 1926; New York: Garland, 1986), p.147.

39 Taylor Adams, 'Early Women in Advertising – All Uphill', in *How It Was in Advertising, 1776–1976*, comp. editors of *Advertising Age* (Chicago: Cain, 1976), p.30.

40 Walter Smith, *Industrial Art*, vol. 2 of *The Masterpieces of the Centennial International Exhibition Illustrated* (Philadelphia: Gebbie and Barrie, 1877), p.95–96. In this catalog of works appearing in the Philadelphia Centennial, Smith praised Englishwomen for their expertise in needlework, a skill learned at new schools of applied design.

41 *First Annual Report of the Committee on the School of Design for Women* (Philadelphia: The School, 1852), p.2–4; *Proceedings of the Franklin Institute of the State of Pennsylvania, for the Promotion of the Mechanic Arts, Relative to the Establishment of a School of Design for Women* (Philadelphia: The Institute, 1850), p.1, 5. The school's history can be found in T. C. Knauff, *An Experiment in Training for the Useful and Beautiful* (Philadelphia: The School, 1922), and Nina de Angeli Walls, 'Art and Industry in Philadelphia: Origins of the Philadelphia School of Design for Women, 1848 to 1875', *Pennsylvania Magazine of History and Biography* 117, 3 (July 1993), p.177–99. The curriculum was divided into three departments: drawing (a basic course for all students), industrial design (including textile, wallpaper, oil cloth, carpet, and furniture design), and wood engraving and lithography (illustration for the arts, sciences, and natural history). From its first year in existence, students obtained patents and sold their work to manufacturers and publishers.

42 Walter Smith, *Art Education*, p.110–19 and appendixes with detailed description of curricula, p.370–80; Peter Cooper, *To the Legislature of the State of New-York, in Senate and Assembly Convened* (New York: n.p., 1856). The importance of many of these institutions in graphic design education remains to be explored. The best sources I have found on early design education are Isaac Edwards Clarke, *Art and Industry*, 6 vols. (Washington, D.C.: US Office of Education, 1885–98), and Arthur D. Efland, *A History of Art Education: Intellectual and Social Currents in Teaching the Visual Arts* (New York: Teachers College Press, 1990); Penny, *Employments of Women*, p.55–58; Thomas Woody, *A History of Women's Education in the United States*, 2 vols. (New York: Science Press, 1919), 2, p.75–80.

43 Penny, *Employments of Women*, p.57–58, 104.

44 See Alice Sheppard, *Cartooning for Suffrage* (Albuquerque: University of New Mexico Press, 1994), and Trina Robbins, *A Century of Women Cartoonists* (Northampton, Mass.: Kitchen Sink Press, 1993). For a rare personal note on the strength it took for a woman to enter the profession, see 'Fay King, Cartoonist', *Federal Illustrator* 2, 2 (Midwinter 1917–18), p.12–13.

45 Frances M. Benson, 'Five Women Artists of New York', *Quarterly Illustrator* 1, 1 (January–March 1893), p.34.

46 James J. Best, *American Popular Illustration: A Reference Guide* (Westport, Conn.: Greenwood Press, 1984), p.120; 'About the Society of Illustrators' (New

York: The Society, n.d.), single sheet; Ann Barton Brown, *Alice Barber Stephens: A Pioneer Woman Illustrator* (Chadds Ford, Pa.: Brandywine River Museum, 1984), p.24–25.

47 Francis Hopkinson Smith, *American Illustrators* (New York: Scribners, 1892), p.54.

48 Frank Weitenkampf, *American Graphic Art* (New York: Holt, 1912; Johnson Reprint, 1970), p.189–90.

49 Rubinstein, *American Women Artists*, 159. For a comprehensive list of students and references, see *'A Small School of Art': The Students of Howard Pyle*, ed. Rowland Elzea and Elizabeth H. Hawkes (Wilmington: Delaware Art Museum, 1980); Henry Pitz, *The Brandywine Tradition* (Boston: Houghton Mifflin, 1969), p.178.

50 'An Autobiographical Sketch' was published in *Good Housekeeping* in October 1917 and reprinted in Gene Mitchell, *The Subject Was Children* (New York: E. P. Dutton, 1979), p.4–5.

51 Frances R. Marshall, 'Qualities That Make for Success in Women Illustrators', *Public Ledger* [Philadelphia] (December 15, 1912), p.1.

Visible Language 28.4

New Perspectives:
Critical Histories
of Graphic Design

Part 2: Practices

MESSY HISTORY VS. NEAT HISTORY: TOWARD AN EXPANDED VIEW OF WOMEN IN GRAPHIC DESIGN

MARTHA SCOTFORD
1994

For the contributions of women in graphic design to be discovered and understood, their different experiences and roles within the patriarchal and capitalist framework they share with men, and their choices and experiences within a female framework, must be acknowledged and explored. Neat history is conventional history: a focus on the mainstream activities and work of individual, usually male, designers. Messy history seeks to discover, study and include the variety of alternative approaches and activities that are often part of women designers' professional lives. To start the expansion, a typology of roles played by women in graphic design is proposed for further research.

In contemporary graphic design practice, women and men designers participate in the same business and institutional structures; previously they have been part of the same educational systems. However, the experiences for each group within these structures has been different, in large part due to gender and the way it has been socially constructed through identity, roles and expectations. In the past, such gendered experiences were even more divergent, as these began earlier in life and were more tradition-bound and pervasive in professional life. For the study of women and men in graphic design, remaining cognizant of the double truth that women and men in graphic design are the same and that women and men in graphic design are different will result in a more inclusive understanding of past and contemporary graphic design production.

The focus of this paper is on women graphic designers. I do not forget the other axes of race and class by which to study historical players. The problematic areas discussed will often be shared by designers of color and other marginalized designers of both genders; however, attempting to avoid the extremes of essentialism, may I suggest that the problems will more frequently be those of women in graphic design. The historiographical methods used to recover their participation and accomplishments will be beneficial to all previously unacknowledged designers.[1]

Cheryl Buckley has brought feminist theory and feminist history to design history, though she does not discuss graphic design history specifically.[2] Buckley allows that women have filled a variety of roles in design (practitioner, theorist, consumer, historian, object of representation), but asserts that each of these is circumscribed by patriarchy. Buckley discusses patriarchy within the capitalist economic system of industrialized societies. Her working definition of patriarchy comes from Griselda Pollock: 'patriarchy does not refer to the static, oppressive domination of one sex over another, but a web of psycho-social relationships which institute a socially significant difference on the axis of sex, which is so deeply located in our very sense of lived, sexual identity that it appears to us as natural and unalterable.'[3] This paper is an attempt to extend some of Buckley's ideas into graphic design history.

Buckley posits that the silence of history about women designers is a 'direct consequence of specific historiographical methods. These methods which involve the selection, classification and prioritization of types of design, categories of designers, distinct styles and movements, and different modes of production, are inherently biased against women and, in effect, serve to exclude them from history.'[4] In her review of design literature she discovers that when women do make it into the literature they are too often limited by their association with products for women or by their association with male designers who are family members. In many ways, the case of women in design history parallels the discussion of Linda Nochlin on women artists in her article 'Why Have There Been No Great Women Artists?'[5]

Graphic design history has proceeded, for the most part, along well-established art historical lines. Canons of designers and design works have been established and accepted through publication and exhibition. The prevailing approach has concentrated on individuals and individual effort, institutions and business, the active client/reactive designer relationship, the synchronic analysis establishing stylistic 'periods', and the diachronic presentation of innovation and influence. This approach is problematic for reasons of exclusion. While it purports to be the responsible application of established standards, it turns out to be arbitrary as well as unfair.[6]

The conventional graphic design history literature of the past decade has had a difficult time with women designers. Take, for example, the most widely distributed book, Philip B. Meggs' *A History of Graphic Design*, used as the textbook in most college courses.[7] First published in 1983 and substantially revised in 1992, the author still finds the inclusion of women graphic designers problematic. The first edition mentioned fifteen women and reproduced the work of nine; the second edition mentions thirty-one women designers and photographers, and illustrates and reproduces the work of twenty-three, to be compared with the discussion and work of hundreds of male designers. Meggs never addresses the issue of women designers (or designers of color) directly. In the index, the entry 'women' directs the reader to four very brief discussions of women as representational subject matter. In his preface to the new addition, Meggs states the intent of the book is 'to identify and document innovation in semantic and syntactic aspects of visual communications. The graphic designs of each period discussed have been investigated and assessed in an attempt to distinguish works and their creators that influenced the ongoing evolution of the discipline.'[8] Meggs goes on to obliquely counteract criticism by preferring the bias of 'pivotal individuals' to the bias of a more collective approach, though he claims to attempt to credit all collaborators when appropriate. In the end, 'a line of descendancy toward contemporary graphic design in post-industrial culture was a primary determinant.'[9] He also points out that reproduction criteria include practical limits of quality and availability. The pluralism of content and voice found in contemporary graphic design is not sufficiently described or assessed by this method. When, to be included in this history, work must 'come from somewhere in history', the chances for inclusion of wholly new ideas and new players are few. And are the margins forever fixed? Even 'pivotal' social changes like the women's movement are barely mentioned: there is no discussion of new imagery or of the influx or new 'voices' of women designers into the profession.[10]

Feminist historians have argued against the primacy of individual agency in creativity. While the study of individual creativity is occasionally required and useful (there are pivotal women in design), and the loss of individual women to history is an example of patriarchy at work, much design is a collaborative and collective effort. It is this process, the dynamics and sets of relationships within and among design groups and between designer and client, that needs to be more fully understood. Research on women in design has been focused on women as objects of representation[11] and on women as audiences or consumers (in the broadest sense) of graphic design artifacts;[12] to this should be added the breadth of the design activities in which women engage.

Neat history (conventional history) involves the simple packaging of one designer, explicit organizational context, one client, simple statements of intent, one design solution, a clearly defined audience, expected response (in other words, the old Shannon and Weaver communication model of sender, message, channel, receiver, no noise). For a long time such a model involved a white, male, middle-class designer working for a design studio or advertising agency with a client in government or private business requiring a visual message to be sent through one of several discrete and traditional (printed) formats to communicate with a mass audience assumed to resemble, or aspire to resemble, the designer and client. It was easy to answer the questions: Who? What? Why? From whom? For whom? This simplistic history has served the establishment (white, male, business, design and academic worlds) well.

Contrast this with messy history: designers who do not work alone but in changing collaborations; design works that are not produced for national or large institutions but for small enterprises or local causes; design works that are not produced in great numbers and may even be at the scale of a 'cottage industry;' design works that may use cultural codes not part of mainstream culture; design work for small and specialized audiences; design work in forms more personal and expressive; design practices organized around family life and personal issues; design that turns its back on mainstream design, etc. I do not mean to suggest that this wholly or exclusively describes women's design activity (much of which is mainstream), only that it describes alternative conditions, many of which are more true of women's practice and conditions than men's.

As one way to conceptualize the inclusion and significance of women in graphic design, I propose a typology of women's involvement. I will define some of the types, give some concrete examples and suggest some questions about them to encourage further study and discussion. Looking at women in graphic design by this method is one example of the effect of women's inclusion on graphic design history; the roles, in their diversity, reveal a more complex interaction with design activity on the part of women than was thought to exist when the (male) focus was on men designers. While there are roles that women and men both play, there are some that seem solely available to women. It must be noted that examples from past and contemporary practice are used to make these types more concrete, but do not in any way exhaust the pool of possible example, I have chosen examples among better known designers, mostly American, mostly women. The examples range among historical periods; comparisons over time, studying the contextual variables that explain differences will be valuable. Whereas study of broad historiographical methods has prompted much of what I propose, often a specific individual and her particular place in American design history has suggested questions. Current practice and examples also raise issues. While it is a mistake of 'presentism' to use the present to interpret the past, the present is a useful model for comparison with the past; through comparison the differences and similarities are discovered and questions raised.[13]

A Typology of Women in Graphic Design

The reconceptualization of historical study through the different and shifting alignments of groups of people has been of primary importance to the study of women in history. For women in design this suggests that while it is important to add individual names and achievements to the historical record, it is also critical to look at group characteristics and group dynamics. Because men, in their public/professional spheres, have defined most of the 'roles' of the graphic designer, it is necessary to study how women graphic designers have accepted, adapted or rejected these roles, and under what conditions. The study of women designers' experience shows that 'design experience', as described by design literature and assumed to be universal, has actually been the male experience. Study of women shows that there is more than one experience. In studying women designers, it is important to compare their experience with male designers' experience of the same period, as well as to understand the private and public roles available to women at each particular time.

Women Practitioners

Beliefs in women's capabilities have changed over time. The primary vocational route of graphic designers in the earlier days was from typesetting and printing, both highly skilled and mechanical trades. Other, lesser, routes were through sign painting (often itinerant) and the fine arts. Typesetting and printing skills were acquired by hard work through the ranks from apprenticeship. The patriarchal construction of roles for women did not allow them business or vocational training. Even more recently when women have had access to practical training (as well as formal education), they were kept out of the typesetting and printing trades because these are mechanical, dirty and physically strenuous and, therefore, 'not suitable'. [14] With desktop publishing making typesetting electronic and functionally opaque, and as clean and as easy as typing, women (as former typists) are filling the ranks. Are the skills once valued in male typographers equally valued in female computer typesetters? It may be significant that the professional title of 'typographer' is no longer used and the general activity less respected because 'anyone (read women) can do it.'

Design and pre-press production have been partly reunited in current practice but the distinction between them blurred. Design and pre-press production have experienced a changing relationship since Gutenberg. As design/production configurations change, are women more likely to be involved in roles of technical ('hand-skills') or conceptual ('head-skills') aspects of design? Study cannot continue to concentrate only on the dominant sites of production (i.e., those of the designers' idea-generation), but must investigate the full range of interrelated processes and services. The whole topic could be studied from Johannes and Frau Gutenberg to the husband and wife team at *Emigre*, Rudy VanderLans and Zuzana Licko. [15]

Earlier in the century, most graphic designers emerged from a background of fine art or training in the trades. Within the fine art route, men studied to become artists, while many women studied to become 'accomplished'. Study would discover if these two routes coincide with different class origins. If the trades (except some forms of 'commercial art' such as illustration) were not open to women, what were the routes into design for women? And what difference did class make for them?

Hierarchy, and its corollary of ghettoizing, exists among design sectors (publishing, advertising, corporate design, non-profits, government, institutions, etc.). Within the sectors, women designers have been represented in changing proportions. Where were the 'velvet ghettos' of the 1930s, 1940s, 1950s? What is the meaning of the preponderence of women in publishing: books, magazines especially, fewer in newspapers? Research on the organizational structures of any of these sectors would discover where women would most likely be found, during what historical time periods. What was their significance for design in these sectors? For example, there were many women who worked with Dr. Mehemed Fehmy Agha at Condé Nast. Cipe Pineles went on to art direct several influential magazines. What happened to the other women?

Ghettoizing in design can also be within the practice of design itself. Most design offices, of whatever size, have tended toward the corporate organizational model of pyramidal hierarchy, with power (ideas and money) concentrated at the narrow top. When women are owners or partners, has this been conceived differently? Recently there have been increasing reports of women-derived alternatives that are less structured, non-hierarchical and more collaborative. In business, some examples have described more open and cooperative production groups in factories. In design, female principles are less supervisory and more collaborative, giving equal credit to associates for design projects. As interaction with staff can be defined alternatively, so can that with clients. Reports from both side of the interaction indicate that women designers are more likely to work with clients toward a solution, rather than decreeing a solution as their male counterparts do. This distinction shows up in studies of other design disciplines, such as architecture and industrial design.

Questions about the organization of the workplace and the division of labor in graphic design must be more probing. In addition to studying the presence of women in mainstream design practice, and understanding their roles as influenced by patriarchy's sexual division labor, where else are women active? Women, or any marginalized group, will fill in the empty spaces in a labor market. For example, 'artists books' sit in an overlapping area between graphic design and fine art. This is an area of varied production methods and approaches, largely dismissed by professional graphic design. It is also a marginal area inhabited by many women, including Frances Butler and Judy Anderson. Is 'marginal' work a strategic choice or a default position? As a choice it may be interpreted as a mode of resistance to the demands and definitions of mainstream graphic design practice. To include these book arts in graphic design, the definition must be enlarged since acceptable methods of reproduction cannot be solely those of mass production. Access to mass production is another limitation imposed by patriarchy.

For graphic design, professional organizations developed out of trade organizations. Have women benefited from the support of professional organizations? For a long time women were not welcome in the trades nor were they acknowledged by the organizations. The New York Art Directors Club only admitted its first woman member, Cipe Pineles, to its Hall of Fame in 1975. Leadership positions in these organizations were held by men until recently; jurors for competitions were all male, and professional awards of merit were seldom bestowed upon women. What has been the impact on professional organizations of the increasing presence of women in graphic design? Slowly, in the last decade, women are becoming officers, jurors and award winners. They are writing increasingly for professional publications. Less often they are speakers for and to the profession.[16]

Independent Designers and Owners

Women practice alone as independent designers or as freelance designers; they practice as owner/designers of small design businesses. Currently, women are more likely to be freelance designers (and, therefore, part-time designers) than men. In a 1992 survey of AIGA members, 33 percent of the women respondents were owners/designers, as compared to 42 percent of the men, with the women tending to have smaller staffs.[17] In the distant past, independent business operation was not an option for women, except for those who came to it through widowhood. A common route to printing and publishing for women was helping their husbands in the shop and taking over at their death. (Not a felicitous career path, nor one to actively pursue.)[18]

Design Employees and Workers

Women are more likely found as employees of design studios, agencies, publishing houses, corporate design office and other organizations and institutions. We could see them as cultural workers in the trenches. They may be at all levels of these organizations: art and creative directors, staff designers, production managers and freelance artists. How are women involved in the decisions made about design: the concepts, images, audiences? This is the largest group of women practicing; how have technical developments in design changed women's roles and design work? As an antidote to the conventional focus on 'heroes', an important addition to our knowledge of women in design would be attention to the not-so-famous, the non-name designers, their conditions, their experience, their impact on their clients and communities if not on the 'design world'.

Designer' Partners, Spouses and Significant Others

One of the primary points of feminist theory has been the intersection of private roles and public roles for women. Working women (especially those with families) have been unwilling and unable to keep their domestic and professional lives as separate as working men have sought to do. Mary Catherine Bateson[19] and Carolyn Gold Heilbrun[20] have provided examples of famous and/or public women 'composing' and creating their productive lives around private necessity. They have discovered that many women do not follow the (male) linear career path, and do not consider women's accretion model aberrant but responsive to different experience. Study incorporating the stage of women's lives, their physical and psychological development, the expectations of society, with women's professional design practice, choice of professional roles and achievement will show differences with male paradigms for achievement. This connection of private and public affects all the decisions they make and, for many women designers, impacts the work they do, how they do it and what it means. There are generational differences in this area as well; the pure increase in the number of women designers in the last twenty years is the result of changes in women's roles and affects the practice of design as well. Study should be made of the impact in many areas of the influx of women into design.[21]

Women raise interesting questions for biography or any writing about them beyond the strictest focus on design artifacts. In any historical period, society has constructed roles for women which include a set of constraints and expectations. In the past there was a clear distinction between the public or male sphere and the private or female sphere. Increasingly the line has become less clear.

In writing about women designers historically, it is obvious that they must and do interact with male designers and other men in business; this communication, cooperation, collaboration and changes within these relationships are worth study. There is a twist on these professional relationships that has not been researched: those professional relationships that are also intimate ones. (Gasp; even I have labeled this 'tacky biography' to myself.) Why this response? The response is as interesting as the question. Men and women have been involved in design together for a long time; when the research focus is male the model is 'unique, independent, creative genius' and all others involved, especially women and especially in private life, are assumed to have no effect on the designer, the production or the work. Sometimes this is so. When the focus changes to women designers, with their intertwined lives, other people are often involved. So questions need to be asked; they needed to be asked of the male designers too, now perhaps they will be. Part of the reticence on this topic undoubtedly relates to a possible double standard; it is acceptable for men to engage in a variety of personal relationships; this has not been considered true for women. Standards change; there have always been exceptions. Another problem is that the imputation of influence has previously been harmful to women, though not to men. Does influence go only one way? The issue of 'significant others' has recently been addressed, in the fine arts, in an eponymous book.[22] Critics considered the results mixed and some too close to gossip, but the door is opened on what is, theoretically, a useful area.

The original spouse/partners in design business were the women (and children) who helped out in the shops and learned the businesses: punch-cutting, typesetting, printing, publishing. More recently, Bertha Goudy and Edna Beilenson helped their husbands with typesetting and presswork. Beilenson was also part of a women printers' organization, The Distaff Staff.[23] Ray Eames was an equal partner in name and credit, though the exact nature of her contributions is unclear.[24] In our well-intentioned eagerness to have 'women designers in history', Ray Eames may have been swept up and set up in a role she did not play. She was important to the work of the office, but most likely not as designer. History needs to record her actual role. Katherine McCoy is a partner with Michael McCoy in both design practice and design education. The partnerships are often between designers in different disciplines: Nancy Skolos (graphic design) and Tom Wedell (photography); Lella Vignelli (industrial design) and Massimo Vignelli (graphic design); and Deborah Sussman (graphic design) and Paul Prezja (architecture).

Women in design have also been business partners or collaborators with male and female significant others. Early in this century, Beatrice Warde separated from her husband and spent many years working with Stanley Morison, both scholars promoting fine and practical typography. Over her career April Greiman has collaborated with her then husband and other male designers, at each stage marking a significant change in her work. And there are examples of female design couples in practice together.

For all the business partnerships that include private relationships, questions about roles, organization, work choices intersect with personal dynamics in ways different from those of romantically uninvolved partners. What is the nature of lives so completely involved with design? The benefits are apparent in the fine work of many designing couples, but there will be deficits of these public/private combinations as well. If design couples part, the female designer may be at more risk for professional fallout. The point is not irrelevant or prurient interest but rather to understand when, and how important, such intimate relationships can be to development and to work.

Independent Designers and Spouses or Significant Others in Design

Another example of sharing lives in design is that of women designers who practice independently, but who have or had spouses or significant others also involved in design. As with partnerships, the shared information, networks, interests can be critically important to the work. Cipe Pineles had a career in magazines independent from her two designer husbands, William Golden and Will Burtin. However, Pineles and Golden are both noted for their use of fine artists as illustrators, she in women's magazines and he for CBS promotions. Same idea, different venues; it makes more sense if you know they were married. Paula Scher and Seymour Chwast use historical reference as an important part of their work, and were among the first revivalists. Louise Fili and Steven Heller share an interest in graphic design history; she resurrects old typefaces for her book jackets, he writes and organizes conferences, and they have recently collaborated on two design history books (on Dutch Moderne and Italian Art Deco). Lorraine Louie and Daniel Pelavin are both noted book jacket designers. When studying the work and its conceptual and stylistic provenance, it is useful to know where a designer studied, with whom, where a designer has worked, with whom and who might be at home.

Female and Female Working Collaborations

A separate category is women designers who are professional partners. Ruth Ansel and Bea Feitler collaborated for several years on *Harper's Bazaar*. Muriel Cooper and Jacqueline Casey spent almost whole careers designing for MIT, much of the time in the same office. Are there special benefits from this interaction? Interactions might differ from female/male ones. Work place organization and working styles may be different. Female collaborators may be able to confront larger institutions more effectively together. Mentoring relationships may be more important for women and different between them. Lorraine Wild and her partners at ReVerb would be a contemporary example for study.

Women Designers Who Leave Design

The focus has been on successful designers, their partnerships and how these intersect with personal relationships. What about those design careers that are abandoned because of such conflicts? Women may leave design for many reasons, but one is competition with a spouse in the same or a related field. There were some cases written about in the mid-1970s where women's careers were overshadowed by men's careers.[25] Has there ever been an article titled 'Husbands of Artists'? What happens to shared design practices when parenthood is chosen, but one is designated to have the baby?

Defining 'design' as mainstream design, leaving design may be a conscious strategic move. There are different kinds of leaving. Designers leave the corporate design world for the freedom of independent practice or for a change of scale in problem-solving. There are many recent reports that many African-American designers find the corporate world useful for training but not comfortable for the long haul; they are creating their own business, business that may be out of the mainstream. Another way to move to the margins is to find or invent new territory within the borders of graphic design that is distant from dominant structures. Some current examples are new technical areas and cultural areas: Women and African-Americans are entering the field at the margin through video production and music promotion.[26]

The study of conditions for failure (or leaving) are as important as conditions for success. Nochlin, in discovering the answer to her question, was able to describe the path to success for women artist.[27] What is the route to success for women designers at different periods in graphic design history?

Women in Design Business

Women Who Run Husbands' Design Businesses

The professional design world is supported by legions of staff who, while they do not directly put pen to paper or mouse to pad, are closely connected with design work and design decisions. The first employee beyond design assistant that any owner/designer hires is a bookkeeper or financial manager. This person is most often female, may ease into this position unsalaried, may be the wife of the designer, and may even be educated as a designer herself. Linda Hinrichs ran Hinrichs et al. through several permutations; Valerie Richardson runs Richardson or Richardson; Dixie Manwaring is the business manager for her husband; Sonia Tscherny runs George's practice. Perhaps this is the more accurate category for Ray Eames. What is the nature of the influence that such women exercise in such positions? There are many historical antecedents; study should be made of how this role has changed; when and how it is acknowledged, in credits, in name, and/or in salary.

Unacknowledged Partners and Supporters

Some illustrations of the phrase 'behind every man (designer) is a woman' are available. These are women who worked alongside men and are unsung but crucial to the creative work. Dorothy Abbe was devoted to helping W.A. Dwiggins; Carla Binder assisted Joseph. Dorothy Beall aided Lester playing the common and traditional role for women of the period, hostess to professional clients. However, given the location of Beall's practice in rural Connecticut and the corporate nature of his clients, this was more than occasional dinner parties. She was a partner in the business enterprise, if not in the design.[28] Roles, even if traditional, cannot be dismissed on those grounds, and are important to design success. If conventional history acknowledged male business partners of designers, how would that history and our understanding have been different? We might also be looking for a man managing a woman designer's practice and what this means.

Women in Education

Though the institutions and structures are the same for women and men, their experiences within them are frequently at odds, and their responses different. Among AIGA members, women designers have tended to have more formal education than men. This response could be due to the lack of opportunity through the 'trade route' and/or a response to other conditions, such as the perception that a woman has to be 'better' to be considered equal. The last decade witnessed a huge increase in the number of women students in design schools; the number of women faculty increased, and at the same time many graphic design programs were and are headed by women (Cranbrook, co-chair Katherine McCoy; CalArts, April Greiman and then Lorraine Wild; Otis-Parsons and Yale, Sheila Levrant de Bretteville: Northeastern, Mary Anne Frye; North Carolina State University, Meredith Davis). General 'demographics' may explain some of this; more importantly, it is the result of the women's movement and changing roles for women and professional women.

Educational institutions provide a valuable route for women's success. Universities and schools are a platform for women's research and ideas, and may offer opportunities much earlier than less egalitarian private industry.

Women as Teachers

It is only in the last ten years that women have significantly joined the ranks of graphic design teaching; there were some earlier pioneers, such as Cipe Pineles at Parsons from 1963 to 1987. Like their male counterparts, women graphic designers have often combined teaching with practice. Teaching careers have been useful for professional women needing flexible time for private responsibilities. With a growing community of female program heads as well as female teachers, more exchange and support occurs. There is greater likelihood that courses will include the work and experiences of women designers.

Are women different as teachers? As design teaching commonly includes more collaborative work than is found in traditional educational paradigms, the presence of women in the classroom may make less difference in graphic design education. However, the conduct of critiques and juries can be a place where differences could be found. It could be expected that given their design experiences, women faculty will prepare students (especially women) differently for the marketplace.[29] The study of AIGA members showed that very few designers currently practicing had been taught by a woman in design school.

As mentors, what have women faculty offered? Mentorships are expected in education. Later, in the professional world, such relationships will encompass broader issues. In what ways have women in design helped younger designers of either gender? Patterns of sponsorship may have developed. When the paths for success for women designers are better known, mentoring will have more solid ground.

Women as Students

The recent influx of women to design schools and then into practice and education will do the most to change the profession. Female students come to design with different expectations, different interests, different strengths and weaknesses. Has this been acknowledged in the past and in the present? How does graphic design education respond to any differences among students, by gender or by race? Based on observation and reading, women students in more technical and mechanical design fields than graphic design (architecture and industrial design) have greater problems: fewer women teachers, more conventional attitudes and prejudices still in place, more hierarchical educational practices in use.[30]

Women as Critics, Historians and Theoreticians

Are communication ideas gendered? In the 1970s, having read feminist and literary theory, Sheila Levrant de Bretteville developed a strategy she called 'feminist design' that was also an implicit critique of the hegemony of modernist (male) design. Based on the principles of 'bringing more of the human attributes associated with women... into the public and professional sphere', she described four design methods: the inclusion of several perspectives on a subject; the posing of questions without providing answers; the use of evocative rather than explicit views of subject matter; and the provision of a contradictory gap between word and image. Such a strategy was to encourage an exchange of ideas rather than a purely objective transmission of information.[31] Why was there so little response to these ideas?

Interestingly, at about the same time, other American designers were also reading French literary criticism and applying linguistic and semiotic research and analysis to design. There evolved design strategies based on the same philosophies and bearing visual similarities to 'feminist design', but without the association with feminism. Cranbrook Academy of Art, where much of this activity took place, and its 1980s graduates, became influential in design and design education.[32] Was de Bretteville's label limiting or damaging? Was it important that a woman was co-head of design at Cranbrook? The answer to this latter question is 'no'. The theory and criticism studied was largely by male philosophers and the students, coming from art and film criticism, art history and literature were mostly male as well. What may be more significant is the multidisciplinary, research-oriented atmosphere of the graduate program that welcomed the broad synthesis ideas; an atmosphere created by the co-chairs, Katherine and Michael McCoy. Perhaps it was more important for their dissemination that these ideas had the validation of an educational institution. Of added significance is that these same ideas are now a very useful component of multicultural design.

The critic of today is the historian of tomorrow. Women have operated as writers, critics and theoreticians since the early modern era of graphic design. Beatrice Warde was commenting on typefaces and contemporary typography in the 1920s, when she also put forth her theory of typographic form in 'The Crystal Goblet.' De Bretteville's writing, design, and teaching have acted as criticism, and 'feminist design' was theory as strategy. The curatorial work of Ellen Lupton (often with her husband Abbott Miller) for Cooper Union and now the Cooper-Hewitt Museum has been directed by critical theory. Frances Butler, always on the margins and usually between design disciplines, has written frequently in all these areas with great erudition.[33] Lorraine Wild was among the first graphic design historians of Modernism in America and has written extensively about design practice and education. Karrie Jacobs, writing for *Metropolis*, is one of the few women in design journalism and has maintained a high profile. She is joined by Chee Perlman of *I.D.*, and Carol Stevens and Julie Lasky of *Print*. Maud Lavin has been an independent scholar and curator, producing an exhibition on montage and recently an excellent critical study of Hannah Höch.[34] Artist and critic, Barbara Kruger qualifies as a woman designer who has 'left' the field of design for the fine arts, contributing extensively to cultural criticism.[35] Educators have been responsible for much early writing and publishing. All of these women have been important contributors to the discourse of graphic design history and criticism, and most have brought a distinctly different perspective.

As stated, the focus of this paper has been on women graphic designers, with 'designer' defined broadly. Closely related, but not possible to discuss here for reasons of space, are several categories of 'women in design' that would also benefit from further research. With the growing presence of women in leadership positions in business and institutions, they will increasingly become design clients. How they approach a project, the selection of a designer, the client/designer relationship, are worthy of study. Closely related to making is consuming. Women have been targeted as consumers through the reception of images and visual messages. The impact has been well-documented.[36] Beyond this, more can be discovered about female audiences. What has been the history of critical response on the part of women, especially of women of different classes and races? Perhaps the most obvious category missing is the one most extensively explored, but hardly exhausted: women as representational subject. There appears to be an unending supply of representations to discuss, connections to be made with other image-making disciplines and new theories to supply the discourse. Work in feminist theory, feminist art history, film criticism, reception theory and literary theory have all affected positively the critical climate.[37]

So, where is the design, the artifact? Design is a social, economic and cultural activity. The proposal here is to study design activity, to study design roles, to study response to design, rather than to concentrate on individual designers and their artifacts and use these as the sole filter for graphic design history. By using a typology such as the one suggested here, graphic design history can be enlarged by the inclusion of women and their particular experiences. Historians must discover the conditions under which design and designers flourish, and the reasons either may wither. This is the social history of graphic design, a perspective that demands the inclusion of a broad range of activities, people and objects, and the application of ideas and methods from many areas of historical and cultural study. It is complex, it is undefined, it is messy, but the rewards will be great.

Martha Scotford is Professor Emeritus of Graphic Design at the College of Design,
North Carolina State University, Raleigh.
First published in *Visible Language*, vol. 28, no. 4, 1994.

1   Julie Lasky, 'The Search for Georg Olden', *Print*, XLVIII: 2 (1994), p.21–29, 126–129. See this, finally, for information about an African-American pioneer.

2   Cheryl Buckley, 'Made in Patriarchy: Toward a Feminist Analysis of Women and Design', *Design Issues*, 3:2 (1986), p.3–14. This is one of the best feminist analyses so far of the problems of design history. Buckley is writing from the context of British design history which is more fully developed than in this country, and which uses a broader definition of design, which includes the decorative arts and crafts.

3   Buckley, 'Made in Patriarchy', quoted from Griselda Pollock, 'Vision, Voice and Power: Feminist Art History and Marxism', *Block* (1982), p.6.

4   Buckley, 'Made in Patriarchy', p.3.

5   Linda Nochlin, 'Why Have There Been No Great Women Artists?' in *Art and Sexual Politics*, Thomas B. Hess and Elizabeth C. Baker, eds. (New York: Collier Books, 1971).

6   Martha Scotford, 'Is There a Canon of Graphic Design?' *AIGA Journal of Graphic Design*, 9: 2 (1991), p.3–5, 13.

7   Philip B. Meggs, *A History of Graphic Design* (New York: Van Nostrand Reinhold, 1992 2nd rev ed.).

8   Meggs, op.cit., p.ix.

9   Meggs, op.cit., p.x.

10 The absence of women in the historical record has been addressed in the three most recent 'Modernism and Eclecticism' symposia on graphic design history. Directed by Steven Heller and sponsored by The School of Visual Arts in New York, the symposia have been an annual event since 1988. Karrie Jacobs discussed 'lost' women designers and Teal Triggs presented new information on Beatrice Warde. Oral history was served when Estelle Ellis discussed creating magazines for teenage girls. There have been a few publications: Liz McQuiston, *Women in Design* (New York: Rizzoli; Supon Design Group, 1993). *International Women in Design* (Washington, DC: SDG, International Book Division); and an exercise in 'self-publishing' following the example of several male designers: April Greiman, *Hybrid Imagery: The Fusion of Technology and Graphic Design* (New York: Watson-Guptill Publications, 1990). In fairness, Meggs' second edition has increased the exposure of women designers' work by 250 percent.

11 The scholarly work on the representation of women (primarily in advertising, some in general mass media) has been by authors with a variety of approaches. John Berger, *Ways of Seeing* (Harmondsworth: Penguin, 1972) uses a Marxist approach. Judith Williamson, *Decoding Advertisements* (New York: Marion Boyars Publishers Inc., 1984) uses semiotics and post-structuralist theory. Erving Goffman, *Gender Advertisements* (New York: Harper and Row, Publishers, 1976) employs a sociological approach to create a typology of position and gesture in images. Carol Wald, *Myth America* (New York: Pantheon, 1975) studies the construction of feminine myths. Sally Stein, 'The Graphic Ordering of Desire: Modernization of a Middle-Class Women's Magazine 1919–39', in *The Contest of Meaning*, Richard Bolton, ed. (Cambridge: MIT Press, 1989), analyzes and diagrams the structure of women's magazines in a longitudinal study. There are several useful methodologies here; and the books are historical documents themselves representing specific periods of design criticism.

12 The effects of design products (more industrial than graphic) on women in the domestic and professional spheres have been studied, written about and exhibited by Ellen Lupton and Abbott Miller (Ellen Lupton and Abbott Miller, *The Bathroom, the Kitchen, and the Aesthetics of Waste* (Cambridge: MIT List Visual Arts Centre, 1992); and Ellen Lupton, *Mechanical Brides: Women and Machines from Home to Office* (New York: Cooper-Hewitt National Museum of Design, 1993).

13 Throughout all of this discussion, it is important to keep in mind that design is more than the physical presence of artifacts or the connection of people to those artifacts through making. Design is what comes before the artifact and what happens after the artifact is part of the cultural and social world. Design history must be where it is explained how and why each artifact exists and what difference the existence makes. Design history is also about design ideas that have no material presence; it is about design education; it is about audience and societal values. Historians have depended on physical evidence: artifacts from which to read, literally and figuratively, the texts that provide facts and allow understanding and interpretation. Especially privileged have been verbal/ written texts and through them the cultures, groups and individuals they helped to explain. The methodology of collecting and validating historical evidence through oral history has developed, permitting the inclusion of peoples without tradition based in print, or of people not comfortable with written communication. People such as designers? Designers tend to be more visual than verbal; if verbal, more oral than written (though this is changing for the better). As a nod toward future historical work attempting to capture our past, we should be collecting and preserving oral histories about all aspects of designers and design activity, on video and audio tapes. Some exist in archives such as the Graphic Design Archive at Rochester Institute of Technology, while Anne Ghory-Goodman has been making video tapes of design educators. In a field of enlarging media, all resources should be employed for the archiving of information and materials. It would be refreshing, as well, if graphic design history could be based on more egalitarian records and types of distribution than those which currently must depend on publication (and, therefore, on markets and patriarchal power).

14 The past aside, even today one of the most frequently reported problems for women in graphic design is the demeaning treatment by men representing the necessary technical support services.

15 Perhaps it is time to discover 'Judith Gutenberg'. You will remember the 'sister' conceit, 'Judith Shakespeare', in Virginia Woolf's *A Room of One's Own*.

16 See reports on the AIGA Miami 1993 conference that complained of sexist behaviour and presentations, as well as very few presentations by women. For example: Paula Scher, 'The Devaluation of Design by the Design Community', *AIGA Journal of Graphic Design*. 11: 4 (1994), p.4–5; Elizabeth Resnick, 'Fighting for Recognition', *AIGA*

Journal of Graphic Design, 11:4 (1994), p.12; Julie Lasky, and Tod Lippy, 'AigABC's', *Print*, XLVIII:1 (1994), p.112; and Deborah K. Holland, 'Nero Fiddles While Rome Burns', *Communication Arts*, 36: 1 (1994), p.14–18.

17 Martha Scotford, *Survey of membership of American Institute of Graphic Arts*, part of research on women in graphic design supported by a grant from the National Endowment for the Arts, 1992.

18 Janet Higgins, 'And the Wife Helped Also', *Southeastern College Art Conference Review*, XI: 3 (1988), p.201–206.

19 Mary Catherine Bateson, *Composing A Life* (New York: The Atlantic Monthly Press, 1989).

20 Carolyn Gold Heilbrun *Writing a Woman's Life* (New York: Ballantine Books, 1988).

21 Ann de Forest, 'Women in Graphic Design: Building a Velvet Ghetto?' *AIGA Journal of Graphic Design*, 6:3 (1988), p.1, 14. Moira Cullen, 'Beyond Politics and Gender – The Hillary Factor', *Communication Arts*, 35:3 (1993) p.24–30. Stephanie Streyer, 'Designer Moms', *Communication Arts*, 34:2 (1992) p.28–30.

22 Whitney Chadwick, and Isabelle de Courtivon, eds., *Significant Others: Creativity and Intimate Partnership* (London and New York: Thames & Hudson, 1993).

23 Janet Higgins, 'And the Wife Helped Also', p.201.

24 Marilyn and John Neuhart, and Ray Eames, *Eames Design* (New York: Harry N. Abrams, 1989).

25 Valerie Brooks, 'The Wives of the Artists', *Print*, 29:2 (1975), p.44–49, 86.

26 For discussion of contemporary African-American graphic design practice see: Cheryl D. Miller, 'Black Designers: Missing in Action', *Print*, XLI:5 (1987), p.58–65, 138 and Tonya Locke, 'In the Voices of My Sisters: African-American Women in Graphic Design', Unpublished master's thesis (Raleigh, NC: North Carolina State University, 1994).

27 Linda Nochlin, 'Why Are There No Great Women Artists', p.30–37.

28 Roger Remington, conversation with author, based on his research on Lester and Dorothy Beall, manuscript pending publication (1992).

29 Comparative studies would be useful. See the different conditions in architecture discussed in: Sherry Ahrentzen, and Linda N. Groat, 'Rethinking Architectural Educations: Patriarchal Conventions and Alternative Visions from the Perspectives of Women Faculty', *Journal of Architectural and Planning Research*, 9:2 (1992), p.95–111. Karen Kingsley, 'Gender Issues in Teaching Architectural History', *Journal of Architectural Education*, 41:2 (1988), p.21–25.

30 Sherry Ahrentzen, and Kathryn H. Anthony, 'Sex, Stars and Studios: A Look at Gendered Educational Practices in Architecture', *Journal of Architectural Education*, 47:1 (1993), p.11–29. Mark Paul Fredrickson, 'Gender and Racial Bias in Design Juries', *Journal of Architectural Education*, 47:1 (1993), p.38–48.

31 A general critical discussion and early expression of her ideas is found in: Sheila Levrant de Bretteville, 'A Re-examination of Some Aspects of the Design Arts from the Perspective of a Woman Designer' *Arts in Society*, 11:1 (1974), p.115–123. The strategy is outlined in: Sheila Levrant de Bretteville 'Feminist Design'. *Space and Society*, 6:22 (1983), p.98–103.

32 Lorraine Wild, 'Graphic Design', *Cranbrook Design: The New Discourse* (New York: Rizzoli, 1990).

33 Frances Butler, *Light and Heavy Light: Contemporary Shadow Use in the Visual Arts* (Berkeley: Poltroon Press, 1985). This is one example; there are others.

34 Maud Lavin, *Cut with the Kitchen Knife: The Weimar Photomontages of Hannah Höch* (New Haven: Yale University Press, 1993).

35 Barbara Kruger, *Remote Control: Power, Culture and the World of Appearances* (Cambridge: MIT Press, 1993).

36 Adrian Forty, *Objects of Desire* (New York: Pantheon Books, 1986) also Carol Wald, *Myth America*, and others, including Lupton and Miller, previously cited.

37 To name only a few: Judy Attfield, and Pat Kirkman, eds., *A View from the Interior: Feminism, Women and Design* (London: The Women's Press, 1989). Norma Broude, and Mary D. Garrard, eds., *Feminism and Art History: Questioning the Litany* (New York: Harper & Row, Publishers, 1982). Laura Mulvey, *Visual and Other Pleasures* (Bloomington: Indiana University Press, 1989). Griselda Pollock, *Vision and Difference: Femininity, Feminism and the Histories of Art* (London: Routledge, 1988). Susan Rubin Suleiman, *Subversive Intent: Gender, Politics and the Avant-Garde* (Cambridge: Harvard University Press, 1990).

DESIGN
WRITING
RESEARCH

WRITING
ON
GRAPHIC
DESIGN

ELLEN LUPTON
ABBOTT MILLER

PHAIDON

DECONSTRUCTION AND GRAPHIC DESIGN

ELLEN LUPTON AND ABBOTT MILLER
1994

Since the surfacing of the term 'deconstruction' in design journalism in the mid-1980s, this suggestive word has served to label practices in architecture, graphic design, products and fashion that favor chopped-up, layered and fragmented forms, often imbued with ambiguous Futuristic overtones. This essay looks at the reception and use of deconstruction in the recent history of design, and then considers the place of typography within the work of Jacques Derrida, who initiated the theory of deconstruction. Derrida described deconstruction as a mode of questioning through and about the technologies, formal devices, social institutions and central metaphors of representation. Deconstruction belongs to both history and theory. It is embedded in recent visual and academic culture, and it describes a strategy of critical form-making which is performed across a range of artifacts and practices.

Derrida introduced the concept of deconstruction in his book *Of Grammatology*, published in France in 1967 and translated into English in 1976.[1] Deconstruction became a banner for vanguard literary studies in the US in the 1970s and 1980s, scandalizing departments of English, French, and comparative literature. Deconstruction rejected the project of modern criticism, which had been to uncover the meaning of a literary work by studying the way its form and content communicate essential humanistic messages. Deconstruction, like critical strategies based on Marxism, feminism, semiotics, and anthropology, focuses not on the themes and imagery of its objects but rather on the linguistic and institutional systems that frame their production.[2]

In Derrida's theory, deconstruction asks how representation inhabits reality. How does the external image of things get inside their internal essence? How does the surface get under the skin? Western culture since Plato has been governed by such oppositions as reality/representation, inside/outside, original/copy, and mind/body. The intellectual achievements of the West – its science, art, philosophy, literature – have valued one side of these pairs over the other, allying one with truth and the other with falsehood. Deconstruction attacks such oppositions by showing how the devalued, negative concept inhabits the valued, positive one.

Consider, for example, the opposition between nature and culture. The idea of 'nature' depends on the idea of 'culture' in order to be understood, and yet culture is embedded in nature. It is delusionary to conceive of the non-human environment as a pristine setting untouched by the products of human endeavor – cities, roads, farms, landfills. The fact that Western societies have produced a concept of 'nature' in opposition to 'culture' reflects our alienation from the ecological systems that civilization depletes and transforms. Another inside/outside construction is found in the Judeo-Christian concept of the body as an external shell for the inner soul, a construction that elevates the mind as the sacred source of thought and spirit, while denigrating the body as mere mechanics. In the realm of aesthetics, the original work of art carries an aura of authenticity that its copy lacks – the original is endowed with the spirit of its maker, while the copy is mere empty matter.

Derrida asserted that an intellectual system (or *episteme*) built on the opposition between reality and representation has, in fact, depended on representations to build itself:

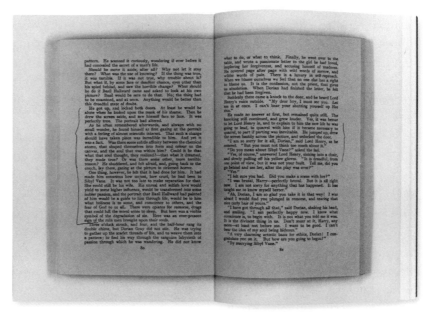

Top: Brochure, designed by Herbert Bayer, 1934. Republished in *Gebrauchsgrafik*, April 1936. This Nazi publication uses the structure of a book-within-a-book. The shield-like book appears against backgrounds depicting the 'folk' masses and Germany's natural and industrial resources. **Middle**: *The Reign of Narcissism*, by Barbara Bloom, 1990. Wurttembergischer Kunstverein Stuttgart. Bloom presents a literary source as a physical artifact. **Bottom**: Catalogue, California Institute of the Arts, designed by Barbara Glauber and Somi Kim, 1993. A cartoon-like icon of a book occupies the spine of the layout.

External/internal, image/reality, representation/presence, such is the old grid to which is given the task of outlining the domain of a science. And of what science? Of a science that can no longer answer to the classical concept of the *episteme* because the originality of its field – an originality that it inaugurates – is that the opening of the 'image' within it appears as the condition of 'reality: a relationship that can no longer be thought within the simple difference and the uncompromising exteriority of 'image' and 'reality: of 'out-side' and 'inside: of 'appearance' and 'essence' (33).

A crucial opposition for Derrida is speech/writing. The Western philosophical tradition has denigrated writing as an inferior copy of the spoken word. *Speech* draws on interior consciousness, but *writing* is dead and abstract. Writing sets language adrift, un-tethering it from the speaking subject. In the process of embodying language, writing steals its soul. Contrary to this view, deconstruction looks at writing as an active form of representation. Writing is not merely a bad copy, a faulty transcription, of the spoken word; writing invades thought and speech, transforming the sacred realms of memory, knowledge and spirit.

SPEECH	WRITING
interior to the mind	*exterior to the mind*
requires no equipment	*requires equipment*
spontaneously learned	*culturally constructed*
natural	*artificial*
original	*copy*
present subject	*absent subject*

According to Derrida, any memory system can be called a form of writing, since it records information for the purpose of future transmissions. The spoken language itself shares writing's characteristic alienation from interior consciousness, since its function depends on the repeatability of signs, and thus on a split between thought and expression, between the originality of the spontaneous utterance and the familiarity of the copy.

Derrida used the term *grammatology* to name the study of writing as a distinctive form of representation. This rather cumbersome word serves to title the book whose more infamous legacy is deconstruction. Derrida proposed grammatology as a field of inquiry for which deconstruction is a crucial mode of research, a manner of questioning that frames the nature of its object. Falling within the domain of grammatology are the material forms and processes of typography and graphic design.

If writing is but a copy of spoken language, typography is a mode of representation even farther removed from the primal source of meaning in the mind of the author. The alphabet, in principal, represents the sounds of speech by reducing them to a finite set of repeatable marks; typography is but one of the media through which this repetition occurs. The letter *a* might be carved in stone, written in pencil, or printed from an engraved block, but only the last is, properly speaking, typographic. Typographic production involves composing identical letters into lines of text. The characters might be generated from relief surfaces made of wood, metal or rubber or from a photographic negative, a digital code or a paper stencil. The art of typography includes the design of letterforms for reproduction and the arrangement of characters into lines of text. Typographic features include the choice of typefaces; the spacing of letters, words, lines, and columns; and the pattern formed by these graphic distinctions across the body of a document. We will return to Derrida's own engagement with typographic forms later in this essay, but first, we will look at the life of deconstruction in design culture.

Deconstruction belongs to the broader critical field known as 'poststructuralism' whose key figures include Roland Barthes, Michel Foucault and Jean Baudrillard. Each of these writers has looked at modes of representation – from the conventions of literature and photography to the design of schools and prisons – as powerful technologies that build and remake the social world. Deconstruction's attack on the neutrality of signs is also at work in the consumer mythologies of Barthes, the institutional archaeologies of Foucault, and the simulationist aesthetics of Baudrillard.[3]

The idea that cultural forms help fabricate such seemingly 'natural' categories as race, sexuality, class and aesthetic value had profound relevance to visual artists in the 1970s and 1980s. Post-structuralism provided a critical avenue into 'Post-Modernism', posing an alternative to the period's nostalgic returns to figurative painting and neo-classical architecture. While Barbara Kruger, Cindy Sherman and Victor Burgin were attacking media myths through their visual work, books such as Hal Foster's *The Anti-Aesthetic* and Terry Eagleton's *Literary Theory* delivered post-structuralism to artists and students in an accessible form.[4]

Graphic designers in many US art programs were exposed to critical theory through the fields of photography, architecture, and performance and installation art. The most widely publicized intersection of poststructuralism and graphic design occurred at the Cranbrook Academy of Art under the leadership of co-chair Katherine McCoy.[5] Designers at Cranbrook first confronted literary criticism when they designed a special issue of the journal *Visible Language* on contemporary French literary aesthetics, published in the Summer of 1978. Daniel Libeskind, head of Cranbrook's architecture program, provided the graphic designers with a seminar in literary theory that prepared them to develop their strategy: the students disintegrated the series of essays by progressively expanding the spaces between lines and words and pushing the footnotes into the space normally reserved for the main text. *French Currents of the Letter* rejected the established ideologies of problem-solving and direct communication that constituted 'normal science' for modern graphic designers.[6]

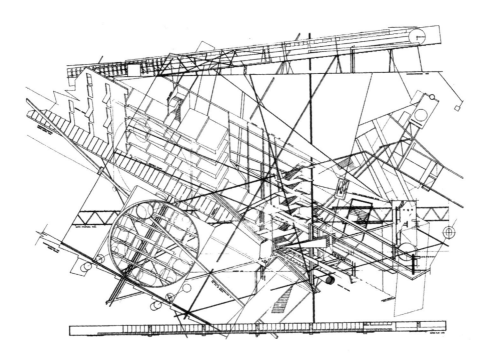

Sections and exploded axonometric of structure and circulation, *City Edge*, designed by Daniel Libeskind, 1987. Featured in the Museum of Modern Art's 1988 exhibition *Deconstructivist Architecture*.

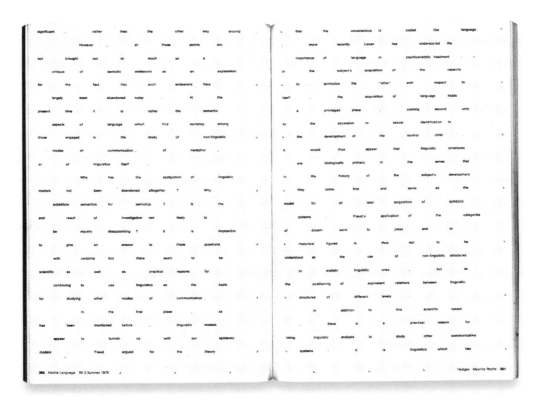

Visible Language, 'French Currents of the letter', designed by Richard Kerr, Alice Hecht, Jane Kosstrin, Herbert Thompson, and Katherine McCoy at Cranbrook Academy of Art, 1978. This collection of essays on French literary theory was designed as a student project. The conventional relationship between inside and outside, figure and ground, is inverted as the spaces between lines and words progressively expand and the footnotes move into the area normally reserved for the central text.

Post-structuralism re-entered discussions at Cranbrook around 1983. McCoy has credited Jeffery Keedy, a student at the school from 1983–85, with introducing fellow course members to books by Barthes and others.[7] The classes of 1985–87 and 1986–88 also actively engaged with critical theory; students at this time included Andrew Blauvelt, Brad Collins, Edward Fella, David Frej and Allen Hori. Interaction with the photography department, chaired by Carl Toth, fostered dialogue about critical theory and visual practice.[8] Post-structuralism did not serve, however, as a unified methodology at the school, even in the period of its strongest currency, but was part of an eclectic gathering of ideas. According to Keedy, his peers at Cranbrook were looking at everything from alchemical mysticism to the 'proportion voodoo' of the golden section.[9]

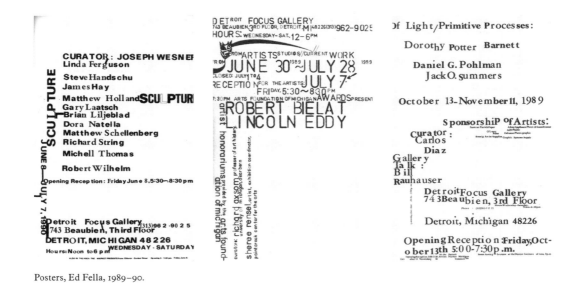

Posters, Ed Fella, 1989–90.

McCoy recalled in a 1991 interview: 'Theory had become part of the intellectual culture in art and photography. We were never trying to apply specific texts – it was more of a general filtration process. The term 'deconstructivist' drives me crazy. Post-structuralism is an attitude, not a style.'[10] Designers at Cranbrook expressed this 'attitude' in formal experiments (visual and verbal) that played with conventions of reading, and in projects that used theory as a direct source of content by collaging together quotations from various sources. Theory thus provided both an intellectual background for abstract expression and a subject for research. Hori's 1989 poster *Typography as Discourse*, designed to announce a lecture by McCoy, is a manifesto for a design practice informed by literary theory. Hori's typography challenges the traditional opposition between seeing and reading by treating the surface as both theoretical content and sensual form, as both text and texture. Rather than deliver information directly, Hori's poster expects the reader to work to uncover its messages.

The response to post-structuralism at Cranbrook was largely optimistic, side-stepping the pessimism and political critique that permeates the work of Barthes, Foucault and others. McCoy used the architectural theory of Robert Venturi and Denise Scott Brown as a 'stepping stone' to post-structuralism, enabling her to merge the Pop appreciation of the commercial vernacular with post-structuralism's critique of 'fixed meaning'.[11] McCoy's preference for formal celebration over cultural criticism is echoed in Keedy's comment: 'It was the poetic aspect of Barthes which attracted me, not the Marxist analysis. After all, we're designers working in a consumer society, and while Marxism is interesting as an idea, I wouldn't want to put it into practice.'[12]

Post-structuralism's emphasis on the openness of meaning has been incorporated by many designers into a romantic theory of self-expression: as the argument goes, because signification is not fixed in material forms, designers and readers share in the spontaneous creation

158

of meaning. Interpretations are private and personal, generated by the unique sensibilities of makers and readers. This approach represents a rather cheerful response to the post-structuralist theme of the 'death of the author', which asserts that the interior self is constructed by external systems and technologies. According to the writings of Barthes and Foucault, for example, the citizen/artist/producer is not the imperious master of language, media, education, custom and so forth; instead, the individual operates within the grid of possibilities these codes present. Rather than view the production of meaning as a private matter, post-structuralist theory tends to see the realm of the 'personal' as structured by external signs. Invention and revolution result from tactical aggressions against the grid.[13]

'Deconstructivism' catapulted into the mainstream design press with MoMA's 1988 exhibition *Deconstructivist Architecture*, curated by Philip Johnson and Mark Wigley.[14] The curators used the term 'deconstructivism' to link a range of contemporary architectural practices to Russian Constructivism, whose early years envisioned form and technology in chaotic upheaval rather than rational resolution. The MoMA exhibition located a similarly skewed variant of Modernism in the work of Frank Gehry, Daniel Libeskind, Peter Eisenman and others. Wigley wrote in his catalogue essay:

> A deconstructive architect is … not one who dismantles buildings, but one who locates the inherent dilemmas within buildings. The deconstructive architect puts the pure forms of the architectural tradition on the couch and identifies the symptoms of a repressed impurity. The impurity is drawn to the surface by a combination of gentle coaxing and violent torture: the form is interrogated (11).

In Wigley's view, deconstruction in architecture asks questions about Modernism by re-examining its own language, materials and processes.

Although the MoMA show described deconstruction as a mode of inquiry rather than a repertoire of mannerisms, the curators nonetheless framed their exhibition around a new 'ism' and thus helped canonize the elements of a period style, marked by twisted geometries, centerless plans, and shards of glass and metal. This cluster of visual features quickly emigrated from architecture to graphic design, just as the icons and colors of neo-classical Post-modernism had traveled there shortly before. While a more critical approach to deconstruction had reached graphic designers through the fields of photography and the fine arts, architecture provided a ready-to-use formal vocabulary that could be adopted more broadly. 'Deconstruction', 'deconstructivism' and just plain 'decon' became design-world clichés, where they named existing tendencies and catalyzed new ones in the fields of furniture, fashion and graphic design.[15]

In 1990, Philip B. Meggs published a how-to guide for would-be deconstructivists in the magazine *Step-by-Step Graphics*. Following the logic of the MoMA project, Meggs' story begins with Constructivism and ends with 'deconstruction'; unlike Wigley, however, Meggs depicted early Modernism as a purely rational enterprise.[16] Chuck Byrne's and Martha Witte's more analytical piece for *Print* (1990) describes deconstruction as a 'zeitgeist: a philosophical germ circulating in contemporary culture that influences graphic designers even though they might not know it'. Their view corresponds roughly to McCoy's sense of post-structuralism as a general 'attitude' responding to the 'intellectual culture' of the time. Byrne's and Witte's article identifies examples of deconstruction across the ideological map of contemporary design, ranging from the work of Paula Scher and Stephen Doyle to Lucille Tenazas and Lorraine Wild.

Today, in the mid-1990s, the term 'deconstruction' is used casually to label any work that favors complexity over simplicity and dramatizes the formal possibilities of digital production. The term is commonly used to invoke a generic allegiance with Cranbrook or CalArts, a gesture that reduces both schools to flat symbols by blanketing a variety of distinct practices. Our view of deconstruction in graphic design is at once narrower and broader in its scope than the view evolving from the current discourse. Rather than look at deconstruction as a historical style or period, we see deconstruction as a critical process – an act of questioning.

Having looked at deconstruction's life in recent design culture, we will now locate design within the theory of deconstruction. The visual resources of typography are instrumental to Derrida's dissection of Western art and philosophy. Derrida's critique of the speech/writing opposition developed out of his reading of Ferdinand de Saussure's *Course in General Linguistics*, a foundational text for structuralist linguistics, semiotics and anthropology.[17] Saussure asserted that the meaning of signs does not reside in the signs themselves: there is no natural bond between the signifier (the sign's material aspect) and the signified (its referent). Instead, the meaning of a sign comes only from its relationship to other signs in a system. This principle is the basis of structuralism, which focuses on patterns or structures that generate meaning rather than on the 'content' of a given code or custom.

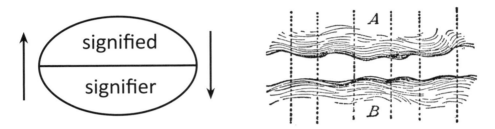

Left: Diagram, *structure of the sign* Right: Diagram, *language taking form out of the shapeless mass of sounds and concepts.* Both from from *Course in General Linguistics* by Ferdinand de Saussure.

Saussure argued that because the sign has no inherent meaning, it is, taken by itself, empty, void, absent. The sign has no life apart from the system or 'structure' that frames it. Language is not a transparent window onto pre-existing concepts, but instead actively forms the realm of ideas. The base, material body of the signifier is not a secondary copy of the elevated, lofty realm of concepts: both are formless masses before the articulating work of language has sliced them into distinct pieces. Rather than think of language as a code for passively representing 'thoughts', Saussure showed that 'thoughts' take shape out of the material body of language.

Derrida's *Of Grammatology* points out that although Saussure was willing to reveal the emptiness at the heart of language, he became infuriated when he saw the same principle at work in writing, the system of signs created to represent speech. Saussure viewed writing as a copy of speech, an artificial technology for reproducing language. While the alphabet claims to be a phonetic transcription of spoken sounds, codes such as written English are full of irrational spellings: for example, words that sound the same but are spelled differently (*meet/meat*) and letter combinations with spurious pronunciations (*th-, sh-, -ght*). The tone of Saussure's critique escalates from mild irritation at the beginning of his argument to impassioned condemnation of the alphabet's violation of an innocent, natural speech: the 'tyranny of writing' distorts its pristine referent through 'orthographic monstrosities' and 'phonic deformations' (30–32).

Saussure launched his attack on *phonetic* writing, the paradigmatic medium of communication in the West. He explicitly excluded pictographic and ideographic scripts from his critique. In Saussure's words, Chinese ideograms have fewer 'annoying consequences' than the alphabet, because their users clearly understand their role as secondary signs for spoken words and not as language itself (26). The power (and seductiveness) of phonetic writing lies in its economy: a small number of characters can represent an infinite series of words. Unlike pictographic or ideographic scripts, phonetic writing represents the *signifier* of language (its material sound) rather than the *signified* (its conceptual meaning or 'content'). Whereas an ideogram depicts a concept, phonetic characters merely indicate sound. The alphabet thus embraces the arbitrariness of the sign by considering the signifier independently of its meaning.

The alphabet cleaved language into an inside and an outside: the destiny of phonetic writing is to occupy and define the outside, to serve as a mechanical copy of the signifier that leaves intact a sacred interior. According to Derrida, the interiority, the fullness, of speech relies on the existence of an exterior, empty representation – the alphabet. Similarly, the notion of 'nature' as an ideal realm separate from human production could only emerge as 'civilization' was despoiling the ecological systems on which culture depends. To 'deconstruct' the relationship between speech and writing is to reverse the status of the two terms, but not just to replace one with the other. Deconstruction aims to show that speech is, at bottom, characterized by the same failure to transparently reflect reality, by the same internal emptiness. There is no full or innocent speech.

The fact that our culture developed a phonetic writing system – one that represents the material *signifier* in isolation from the sacred *signified* – is indicative of our primary alienation from the spoken language. Phonetic writing, because it exploits the gap between signifier and signified, is not simply a secondary reflection of language, but is a symptom of language's own lack of presence, its lack of interior self-completeness.

Derrida's final attack on the notion of writing as a secondary copy of speech is to claim, perversely, that 'phonetic writing does not exist' (39). Not only does writing inhabit speech, transforming its grammar and sound, and not only does phonetic writing function as language's 'own other', an 'outside' manufactured to affirm its own illusory 'insideness', but this model of the 'outside' continually fails to behave in the manner expected of it. Thus where Saussure had claimed that there are only two kinds of writing – phonetic and ideographic – Derrida showed that the frontiers between them fluctuate.

Phonetic writing is full of non-phonetic elements and functions. Some signs used in conjunction with the alphabet are ideographic, including numbers and mathematical symbols. Other graphic marks cannot be called signs at all, because they do not represent distinct 'signifieds' or concepts: for example, punctuation, flourishes, deletions, and patterns of difference such as roman/italic and uppercase/lowercase. What 'idea' is represented by the space between two words or a dingbat at the opening of a line? Key among these non-phonetic marks are various forms of spacing – negative gaps between the positive symbols of the alphabet. According to Derrida spacing cannot be dismissed as a 'simple accessory' of writing: 'That a speech supposedly alive can lend itself to spacing in its own writing is what relates to its own death' (39). The alphabet has come to rely on silent graphic servants such as spacing and punctuation, which, like the frame of a picture, seem safely 'outside' the internal content and structure of a work and yet are necessary conditions for making and reading.

Derrida's book *The Truth in Painting* discusses framing as a crucial component of works of art.[18] In the Enlightenment aesthetics of Kant, the frame of a picture belongs to a class of elements called *parerga*, meaning 'about the work': or outside/around the work. Kant's list of *parerga* includes the columns on buildings, the draperies on statues and the frames on pictures. Kant describes such framing devices as ornamental appendages to the work of art: they touch the work but remain safely outside it. Kant's aesthetics form the basis of modern art criticism, which proclaims the wholeness and self-completeness of the object.

According to Derrida, the 'quasi-detachment' and apparent self-effacement of the picture frame and other *parerga* serve both to hide and reveal the emptiness at the core of the seemingly autonomous object of aesthetic devotion. Like the non-phonetic supplements to the alphabet, the borders around images or texts are at once figure and ground, positive element and negative gap, expendable appendix and crucial support. In Derrida's words:

The *parergon*
is a form that has,
as its traditional determination,
not that it stands out
but that it disappears,
buries itself, effaces itself,
melts away at the moment it deploys its greatest energy.
The frame
is in no way a background...
but neither
is its thickness as margin a figure.
Or at least it is a figure which
comes away of its own accord (61)

Spacing and punctuation, borders and frames: these are the territory of typography and graphic design, those marginal arts that render texts and images readable. The substance of typography lies not in the alphabet as such – the generic forms of characters and their conventionalized uses – but rather in the visual framework and specific graphic forms that materialize the system of writing. Design and typography work at the edges of writing, determining the shape and style of letters, the spaces between them and their placement on the page. Typography, from its position at the margins of communication, has moved writing away from speech.

The history of typography and writing could be written as the development of formal structures that have explored the border between the inside and the outside of texts. To compile a catalogue of the micro-mechanics of publishing – indexes and title pages, captions and colophons, folios and footnotes, leading and line lengths, margins and marginalia, spacing and punctuation – would contribute to the field that Derrida called *grammatology*, the study of writing as a distinctive mode of representation. Such a history could position various typographic techniques in relation to the split between form and content, inside and outside. Some conventions have served to rationalize the delivery of information by erecting transparent 'crystal goblets' around a seemingly independent, neutral body of 'content'. Some structures invade the sacred interior so deeply as to turn the text inside out, while others ignore or contradict the internal organization of a text in response to external pressures imposed by technology, aesthetics, corporate interests, social propriety, production conveniences and so on.

Left: *Campanus Opera*, by Johannes Antonius, printed by Eucharius Silber, Rome, 1445.
Right: *Latin Bible*, printed by Anton Koberger, Nurenberg, 1497.

Robin Kinross' *Modern Typography* (1992) charts the progressive rationalization of the forms and uses of letters across several centuries. Kinross' book describes printing as a proto-typically 'modern' process, that from its inception mobilized techniques of mass production and precipitated the mature arts and sciences. The seeds of modernization were present in Gutenberg's first proofs; their fruits are born in the self-conscious methodologies, professional-ized practices and standardized visual forms of printers and typographers, which, beginning in the late seventeenth century, replaced an older notion of printing as a hermetic art of 'black magic', its methods jealously guarded by a caste of craftsmen.[19] If Kinross' history of modern typography spans five centuries, so too might a counter history of deconstruction, running alongside and beneath the erection of transparent formal structures and coherent bodies of professional knowledge.

Derrida's own writing has drawn on forms of page layout from outside the conventions of university publishing. His book *Glas*, designed with Richard Eckersley at the University of Nebraska Press, consists of parallel texts set in different typefaces to suggest heterogeneous voices and modes of writing. *Glas* transforms the scholarly annotations of medieval manuscripts and the accidental juxtapositions of modern newspapers into a deliberate authorial strategy.

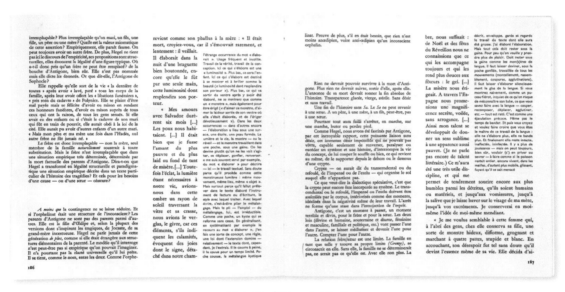

Glas by Jacques Derrida. French edition, published by Éditions Galilée, Paris, 1974.

A study of typography and writing informed by deconstruction would examine struc-tures that dramatize the intrusion of visual form into verbal content, the invasion of 'ideas' by graphic marks, gaps and differences. The pages at top left represent two different approaches to framing the text. In the first, the margins are a transparent border for the solid block that domi-nates the page. The lines of classical roman characters are minimally interrupted, preserving the text as a continuous field of letters. The second example draws on the tradition of scribal marginalia and biblical commentary. Here, typography is an interpretive medium; the text is open rather than closed. The first example suggests that the frontiers between interior and exterior, figure and ground, reader and writer, are securely defined, while the second example dramatizes such divides by engulfing the center with the edge.

Another comparison comes from the history of the newspaper, which emerged as an elite literary medium in the seventeenth century. Early English newspapers based their structure on the classical book, whose text block was designed to be read from beginning to end. As the newspaper became a popular medium in nineteenth-century Europe and America, it expanded from a book-scaled signature to a broadsheet incorporating diverse elements, from reports of

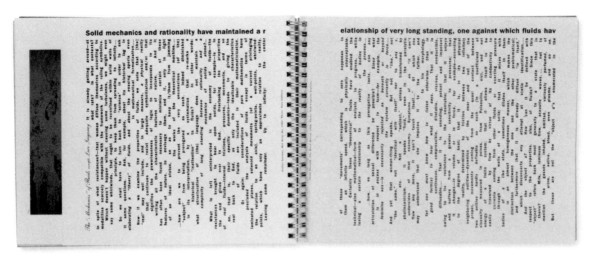

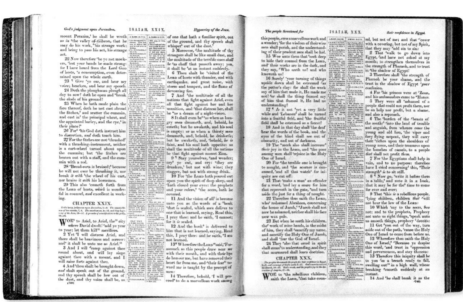

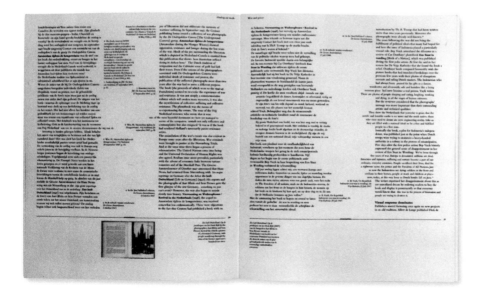

Top: *Strange Attractors*, designed by Marlene McCarty and Tibor Kalman, 1989.
Middle: *The Imperial Family Bible*, 1854. Blackie and Son, Glasgow. Marginal commentary runs down the center of the page.
Bottom: *Photography Between the Covers: The Dutch Documentary Photobook after 1945*, designed by Fred Struving, 1989.
Fragment Uitgeverij, Amsterdam. In this bilingual book, footnotes and other marginalia occupy the center.

crime and scandal to ads for goods and services. The modern illustrated newspaper is a patch-work of competing elements, whose juxtaposition reflects not rational hierarchies of content but struggles between editorial, advertising and production interests. While the structure of the classical news journal aspired to the status of a coherent, complete object, the appearance of the popular paper resulted from hasty compromises and arbitrary conditions.[20]

Left: *Publick Occurrences Both Foreign and Domestick*, Boston, 1690.

Right: *The Daily Inter Ocean*, Chicago, 1881. Reproduced in Robert F. Ravolevitz, *From Quill to Computer: The Story of America's Community Newspapers* (Freeman, South Dakota: National Newspaper Foundation, 1985).

Visual 'dictionaries' of page design featuring schematic diagrams of typical layouts have been a common theme in the trade literature of twentieth-century design. Jan Tschichold's 1934 manifesto 'The Placing of Type in a Given Space' charts a range of subtle variations in the location of headings and body copy, while Don May's 1942 manual *101 Roughs* depicts variants of commercial page design. While Tschichold charted minor differences among clearly ordered elements, May accommodated the diverse media and competing messages found in advertising. Both theorists presented a series of formal containers for generic bodies of 'content', but with a difference: Tschichold's structures aspire to be neutral frames for dominant textual figures, while May's patterns are active grounds that ignore conventional hierarchies. Included among May's deranged structures are '*Four point:* The layout touches all four sides of the space once and only once' and '*Center axis:* The heading copy, illustration and logotype flush on alternate sides of axis.'

If one pursued the study of grammatology proposed by Derrida, the resulting catalogue of forms might include the graphic conditions outlined above. In each case, we have juxtaposed a coherent, seemingly self-complete artifact with a situation where external forces interfere with content. A history of typography informed by deconstruction would show how graphic design has revealed, revised or ignored the accepted rules of communication. Such interventions can represent either deliberate, critical confrontations or haphazard, casual encounters with the social, technological and aesthetic pressures that shape the making of texts.

In a 1994 interview, Derrida was asked about the purported 'death' of deconstruction on North American campuses. He answered: 'I think there is some element in deconstruction that belongs to the structure of history or events. It started before the academic phenomenon of deconstruction, and it will continue with other names.'[21] In the spirit of this statement, we are interested in de-periodizing the relevance of deconstruction. Instead of viewing it as an 'ism' of the late-1980s and early-1990s, we see it as part of the ongoing development of design and typography as distinctive modes of representation.

Pig Iron Produced

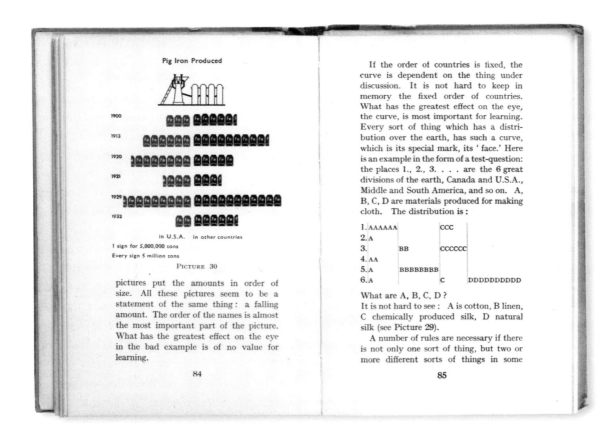

in U.S.A.   in other countries
1 sign for 5,000,000 tons
Every sign 5 million tons

PICTURE 30

pictures put the amounts in order of size. All these pictures seem to be a statement of the same thing: a falling amount. The order of the names is almost the most important part of the picture. What has the greatest effect on the eye in the bad example is of no value for learning.

84

If the order of countries is fixed, the curve is dependent on the thing under discussion. It is not hard to keep in memory the fixed order of countries. What has the greatest effect on the eye, the curve, is most important for learning. Every sort of thing which has a distribution over the earth, has such a curve, which is its special mark, its 'face.' Here is an example in the form of a test-question: the places 1., 2., 3. . . . are the 6 great divisions of the earth, Canada and U.S.A., Middle and South America, and so on. A, B, C, D are materials produced for making cloth. The distribution is :

	A	B	C	D
1.	AAAAAA		CCC	
2.	A			
3.		BB	CCCCCC	
4.	AA			
5.	A	BBBBBBBB		
6.	A	B	C	DDDDDDDDD

What are A, B, C, D ?
It is not hard to see : A is cotton, B linen, C chemically produced silk, D natural silk (see Picture 29).

A number of rules are necessary if there is not only one sort of thing, but two or more different sorts of things in some

85

relation to one another. Some examples :
Iron produced in U.S.A. and other countries

    1900 UUUOOOOO
    1913 UUUUUUOOOOOOOOOO
    1920 UUUUUUUOOOOO

The changes will be made much clearer in this way :

    1900   UUU   OOOOO
    1913   UUUUUU   OOOOOOOOOO
    1920   UUUUUUU OOOOO

(See Picture 30).

Births and deaths. Here it is important to see by how much one amount is greater than the other.

1.   BBBBBBB
          DDDDD

2.   BBBBB
       DD DDDDD

3.   BBBBB
          DDDDD

1, more births than deaths : greater number of men ;

2, more deaths than births : smaller number of men ;

3, the same number of births and deaths : no change in the number of men. There are less births in 3, than in 1, and the same number of deaths, and so on (see Picture 31, and, for comparison, Picture 36).

86

Births and Deaths in Germany in a Year

1911-14

1915-18

1919-22

1923-26

1 red sign for 250,000 births a year
1 black sign for 250,000 deaths a year

PICTURE 31

87

Otto Neurath, *International Picture Language.*

But deconstruction also belongs to culture: it is an operation that has taken a name and has spun a web of influence in particular social contexts. Deconstruction has lived in a variety of institutional worlds, from university literature departments to schools of art and design to the discourse of popular journalism, where it has functioned both as a critical activity and as a banner for a range of styles. We will close our essay with an example of graphic design that directly critiques contemporary media.

Magazine cover, *NYQ*,
designed by Vincent Gagliostro,
New York, 1991.

Vincent Gagliostro's cover for *NYQ*, a gay and lesbian news magazine, was designed in November, 1991, in response to basketball star Magic Johnson's announcement that he is HIV-positive. Gagliostro imposed *NYQ's* own logo and headline over a *Newsweek* cover of Magic Johnson, his arms upheld in a gesture of saintly sacrifice and athletic vigor. 'He is not our hero', wrote *NYQ* over the existing text. While Gagliostro's layering and splicing of type and image are shared with more aestheticized, individualized gestures found elsewhere in contemporary design, his design did not aim to trigger an infinite variety of 'personal' interpretations but instead explicitly manipulated a cultural artifact. Gagliostro's act of rewriting is a powerful response to the ubiquity of normative sign systems, showing that the structures of mass media can be reshuffled and reinhabited. The *NYQ* cover reveals and exploits the function of framing as a transformative process that refuses to remain outside the editorial content it encloses.

Spacing, framing, punctuation, type style, layout and other non-phonetic structures of difference constitute the material interface of writing. Traditional literary and linguistic research overlooks such graphic forms, focusing instead on the word as the center of communication. According to Derrida, the functions of repetition, quotation and fragmentation that characterize writing are conditions endemic to all human expression – even the seemingly spontaneous, self-present utterances of speech or the smooth, naturalistic surfaces of painting and photography. Design can critically engage the mechanics of representation, exposing and revising its ideological biases; design also can remake the grammar of communication by discovering structures and patterns within the material media of visual and verbal writing.

Ellen Lupton is Senior Curator of Contemporary Design at Smithsonian's Cooper Hewitt National Design Museum, New York, and Director of the Graphic Design MFA at Maryland Institute College of Art, Baltimore. Abbott Miller is Partner at Pentagram, New York.
First published in *Visible Language*, vol. 28, no. 4, 1994 and then in *Design Writing Research*, Phaidon, 1996.

1   Jacques Derrida, *Of Grammatology*, trans. Gayatri Chakravorty Spivak (Baltimore: Johns Hopkins University Press, 1976). See especially Chapter 2, 'Linguistics and Grammatology', p.27–73.

2   Jonathan Culler explores the impact of deconstruction on literary criticism in his book *On Deconstruction: Theory and Criticism after Structuralism* (Ithaca: Cornell University Press, 1982).

3   Post-structuralist texts widely read by students of art and design during the 1980s include Roland Bathes, *Mythologies*, trans. Annette Lavers (New York: Farrar, Straus & Giroux, 1972); Michel Foucault, *Discipline and Punish: The Birth of the Prison*, trans. Alan Sheridan (New York: Random House, 1979); and Jean Boudrillard, *For a Critique of the Political Economy of the Sign*, trans. Charles Levin (St. Louis, MO: Telos Press, 1981).

4   Books that helped popularize post-structuralism include *The Anti-Aesthetic: Essays on Postmoden Culture*, Hal Foster, ed. (Port Townsend, WA: Bay Press, 1983), and Terry Eagleton, *Literary Theory: An Introduction* (Minneapolis: University of Minnesota Press, 1983).

5   *Cranbrook Design: The New Discourse* (New York: Rizzoli, 1990), with essays by Katherine McCoy, Lorraine Wild, and others. See also Katherine McCoy, 'American Graphic Design Expression', *Design Quarterly* 148 (1990), p.4–22.

6   *French Currents of the Letter* includes essays on the typography and deconstruction. See Andrew J. McKenna, 'Biblioclasm: Derrida and his Precursors', *Visible Language* XII (Summer 1978), p.289–304

7   Katherine McCoy, interview with Ellen Lupton. February, 1991.

8   Communication with Andrew Blauvelt (June 1994).

9   Jeffery Keedy, interview with Ellen Lupton (February 1991).

10 Katherine McCoy, interview with Ellen Lupton (February 1994).

11 Robert Venturi, Denise Scott Brown and Steven Izenour, *Learning from Las Vegas* (Cambridge: MIT Press, 1972).

12 Jeffery Keedy, interview with Ellen Lupton (February 1991).

13 Robin Kinross has blamed post-structuralism for contemporary designers' retreat into personal visions of typographic form and function. Although theory has been used this way by some designers, the post-structuralist view of the power of signs is profoundly social, yielding a critique rather than a celebration of hurnanist notions of taste and originality. See Kinross, *Fellow Readers: Notes on Multiplied Language* (London: Hyphen Press, 1994).

14 Philip Johnson and Mark Wigley, *Deconstructivist Architecture* (New York: Museum of Modern Art, 1988).

15 Michael Collins and Andreas Papadakis include a chapter on 'Deconstruction, Deconstructivism, and Late Modernism' in their book *Post-Modern Design* (New York: Rizzoli, 1989), p.179–95. The book is a survey of furniture, jewelry, and other decorative arts.

16 Essays on deconstruction and graphic design include Philip B. Meggs. 'De-constructing Typography', *Step-by-Step Graphics* 6 (February 1990), p.178–181 and Chuck Byrne and Martha Witte, 'A Brave New World: Understanding Deconstruction', *Print* XLIV (November/December 1990), p.80–87.

17 Ferdinand de Saussure founded structural linguistics with his *Course in General Linguistics*, trans. Wade Baskin (New York: McGraw-Hill, 1959). See 'Graphic Representation of Language', p.23–32, and 'General Principles', p.65–100. On Saussure and critical theory, see Jonathan Culler, *Ferdinand de Saussure* (Ithaca: Cornell University Press, 1976).

18 Derrida presents a theory of the frame in *The Truth in Painting*, trans. Geoff Bennington and Ian Mcleod (Chicago: University of Chicago Press, 1987).

19 Robin Kinross, *Modern Typography: An Essay in Critical History* (London: Hyphen Press, 1992). Johanna Drucker writes about the experimental and transgressive – rather than rational – side of Modernism in side *Visible Word: Experimental Typography and Modern Art, 1909–23* (Chicago: University of Oticago Press, 1994).

20 On the history of the the newspaper, see Allen Hutt, *The Changing Newspaper: Typographic Trends in Britain and America, 1622–1972* (London: Gordon Fraser, 1973).

21 Mitchell Stevens, 'Jacques Derrida', *The New York Times Magazine* (January 23, 1994), p.22–5

MEGGS

**Making
Graphic
Design
History**

METHODS AND PHILOSOPHIES
IN DESIGN HISTORY RESEARCH

PHILIP B. MEGGS
1994

Some years ago an advertising circular for the then-new design magazine *HOW* arrived in my mailbox; I longed for a new design magazine entitled *WHY*. As we pursue our busy daily schedules as designers, educators and students, we rarely have time to pause and ask, WHY? Unlike the French post-Impressionist Paul Gauguin, we seldom confront the questions in the tille of his 1897 painting, 'Where do we come from? What are we? Where are we going?' Like Gauguin, I know some tough questions; it's the answers that elude me. As the social anthropologist Bengt Danielsson noted in his biography of Gauguin: 'All who persist, as do rational Westerners, in trying to understand and analyze everything, including the problems of life and death, inevitably grow unhappy, while animals, children and 'savages' [I need not dwell on the cultural bias of Danielsson's term for persons from other societies; he would probably be embarrassed by it today] ... are happy for the very reason that it never enters their heads to reflect on metaphysical problems to which there are no solutions.' (Quoted by Jay Jacobs, 'Anatomy of a Masterpiece: 'Where do we come from? What are we? Where are we going?" *Horizon*, Summer 1969, p.65.)

History is in large measure a myth, because the historian looks back over the great sprawling network of human struggle and attempts to construct a web of meaning. Oversimplification, ignorance of causes and their effects, and the lack of an objective vantage point are grave risks. When we attempt to record the accomplishments of the past, we do so from the vantage point of our own time. History becomes a reflection of the needs, sensibilities and attitudes of the chronicler's time as surely as it represents the accomplishments of bygone eras. As much as one might strive for objectivity, the limitations of individual knowledge and insights ultimately intrude.

The evolution of graphic design history over the past quarter-century has generated a series of viewpoints and philosophies that don't replace the earlier views or render them obsolete; rather, they have added new levels of complexity and meaning. The efforts of some commentators to discredit other viewpoints are unfortunate, for they seek to deny an emerging richness and pluralism that strengthens the study of graphic design history.

Graphic design history has not yet emerged as a full-fledged discipline with appropriate educational preparation and certification. It remains anarchic and incohesive. Issues I wish to discuss today are:

1. The Art History Dilemma
2. Graphic Designs as Collectibles
3. The Unified Design History Theory
4. The Problem of Style
5. The Cult of Individualism
6. Pedagogic Imperatives
7. From Feminism to Eurocentrism and Multiculturalism:
   Politically Correct Graphic Design History
8. Whose Design History?
9. Design as Ideology

The Art History Dilemma

In the beginning – of this rapidly fading century, anyway – was Art History, with a capital A. The concept of art for art's sake, a beautiful object that exists solely for its aesthetic value, did not develop until the nineteenth century. Before the Industrial Revolution, the beauty of the forms and images that people made were linked to their function in human society.

Twentieth-century art history has been largely under the spell of art historian Bernard Berenson, an American living in Italy who set out to become the most important connoisseur and authority of Italian Renaissance painting during his day.

Berenson, endowed with a phenomenal memory and keen reasoning ability, put great faith in the personal response to the work under scrutiny. Berenson believed art must be life-enhancing. 'In order to be life-enhancing', he wrote, 'an object must appeal to the whole of one's being, to one's senses, nerves, muscles, viscera, and to one's feeling for direction, for support and weight, for balance, for stresses and counter-stresses, and for the minimum of space required for one's indispensable bodily autonomy – an autonomy so precious that to yield an iota of it is to be a lover, to be compelled to surrender even an inch is to be a de-individualized prisoner' (Bernard Berenson, *Aesthetics and History* (New York: Doubleday, 1954), p.67–68.)

Berenson certainly had a late-Victorian flair for the dramatic. His lofty ideal for aesthetic experience sounds like a combination of orgasm and winning an Olympic gold medal. It transcends everyday experience; yet graphic design by definition is rooted in the ordinary human discourse of information, persuasion, and entertainment.

The traditional research methods of art historians do not fully take into account the complexities of graphic design. A focus upon individual artists, organized into schools or movements, with their masterpieces and unique contributions identified, cannot adequately address graphic design history. Often new developments are shaped by technology, such as the invention of lithography or phototypesetting, or evolve over time as a public dialog by graphic designers eclectically influenced by one another's work.

Graphic design involves a premeditated three-part human relationship between the designer, the client with a communications need, and the intended audience. Add in photographers, illustrators and printers, and the situation becomes even more complex. These relationships, along with the limitations and capabilities of production, create a context vastly different from the fine arts.

My latest reminder of the gulf existing between the traditional art historian and graphic design occurred last month when an art historian at the university where I teach – Dennis Halloran – and I were both placing slides in adjacent display cases so that our students could review the images shown in his art history class and my design course. Professor Halloran sniffed: 'I certainly hope that material you're putting on display won't get mixed in and corrupt my slides.'

Yet, the model of the Berensonian connoisseur with a genuine and informed response to a work with the whole of his or her physical and mental being, cannot be totally abandoned. The aesthetic dimension of graphic design must not be abandoned to the forces of marketing or functionalism. Nikolaus Pevsner believed that 'design for the masses must be functional, in the sense that they must be acceptable to all and that their well-functioning is the primary necessity. A chair can be uncomfortable and a work of art, but only the occasional connoisseur can be expected to prefer its aesthetic to its utilitarian qualities.' (Nikolaus Pevsner, *The Sources of Modern Architecture and Design* (New York: Thames & Hudson, 1968), p.9)

But utility and aesthetics are not mutually exclusive. In 1935, Jan Tschichold wrote: 'Plain utilitarianism and modern design have much in common but remain two different things. Fitness of purpose and usefulness are prerequisites for good work but the real value of a work lies in its spiritual content. The new movement aims to produce a new beauty which 'is more closely bound up with its materials than earlier methods, but whose horizons lie far beyond.' This feeling for materials and proportion can transform the merely functional into a work of art.' (Jan Tschichold, trans. Ruari McLean, *Asymmetric Typography* (New York: Reinhold and Toronto: Cooper and Beatty, 1967), p.72.) The challenge for graphic design and the study of its history must remain a dual one, committed to both the aesthetic and functional dimensions of design.

The value of the scholar/connoisseur is best exemplified in the work of early twentieth-century scholars of typography, including Beatrice Warde and Stanley Morison. Warde's research into the origins of old style typefaces served not only to correct the mistakes of the past, but to create a renewed appreciation of typographic form and nuance. Their scholarship significantly influenced the evolution of typeface design and the formal vocabulary of the twentieth century. The quality of our typographic communications today are greatly improved by their research; this is a paradigm of how design history research can upgrade professional practice and the typographic experience within an entire culture.

Graphic Designs as Collectibles

A wide interest in graphic design artifacts as collectible commodities has emerged, from posters of the avant-garde that sell for thousands of dollars in exclusive galleries, to flea market trafficking in Victorian holiday cards. Is the motivation for this aspect of design history commercial opportunism? Clive Dilnot speaks disparagingly of 'junk antiques'. Marketing expert Irma Zandl says anthropologists relate the human impulse to collect to ancient activities of gathering, foraging and hunting. They also note the differences between men and women in collecting and acquiring. Men seek to complete the whole set, while women seek the outstanding specimens. Zandl believes these differences relate to different roles of men and women in the survival of the primeval community. (Conversation with the author, Washington, DC, 19 May 1993.)

Lick'em and Stick'em. Though often superficial in scholarship and lacking any cohesive philosophy, the collectibles movement provides some useful functions. Artifacts and ephemera are preserved that might otherwise be lost, material is documented and catalogued. Information about design is disseminated and a popular audience for design history, however shallow, is created.

The Unified Design History Fallacy

Some seek to approach design history from a unified viewpoint, combining architecture, graphics, fashion and product design into a unified design history discipline. I believe that this does a great disservice to the cause of graphic design history. A design by definition has a function, and this functional aspect is central to the history of a design discipline. When we consider function, a vast gulf opens between the design disciplines. Shelter; work; communicate: architectural, product, and graphic design exist to serve different needs. While visual attributes might be similar at a given historical moment, such as Renaissance ornament appearing on buildings and book title pages, the real meaning of the cathedral and typographic book lie far apart.

The ephemeral nature of graphic design, combined with its life within the social, economic, and cultural spheres of a society, creates a diversity beyond the range of architecture or industrial design. What architectural or product design equivalences exist to the posters of First World War or Second World War? Or protest posters from the 1960s? Or recent underground or protest graphics addressing pressing social issues of the 1990s? A unified design history excludes artifacts that don't fit a categorical evolution, such as: Victorian to Art Nouveau to Modern to Postmodern. Stylistic evolution denies the dualistic nature of graphic design as graphic form and social message.

Architectural history is so well established that a unified design history inevitably leads to graphic design history becoming an appendage to architecture: This is not an acceptable situation, given graphic design's continuing struggle to gain professional status.

Research methodologies for studying the various design disciplines should vary. Architects produce a relatively small number of buildings and inevitably leave a trail of drawings, models, blueprints and correspondence, providing a rich depository of collateral research materials, while graphic designers produce hundreds of designs and frequently do not retain their process material. Architecture is often studied as artifact and process; graphic design is studied as artifact and for its social and political role.

Of course, a strong relationship exists between various design disciplines and should not be ignored. Graphic design is sufficiently significant to deserve isolated study apart from other disciplines. Its relationship to painting and languaging are at least as significant, if not more significant, than its relationship to architecture and product design.

The Problem of Style

Anyone who sees graphic design as a mere chronicle of style misunderstands graphic design. Today the word style is often used to define superficial surface characteristics, dictated by marketing considerations. Its original meaning – distinctive excellence of artistic expression achieved by appropriate forms and their relationships to one another in space – has been corrupted. While the visual attributes of graphic design are critical and should receive appropriate emphasis in the study of design history, we must be equally concerned about designers' underlying philosophical viewpoints, the meaning graphic design holds for its culture and audience, and the signification of forms and their syntactic relationships. In some eras, such as late-nineteenth- and early-twentieth-century Art Nouveau, a pervasive style becomes an umbrella for the era. In other instances, such as the broad range of work produced in Europe between the two World Wars, formalists and propagandists were poles apart. Efforts to create order by organizing graphic design history solely according to visual attributes forces the elimination of important works falling outside the visual parameters.

Graphic design educators have embraced semiotics, the study of signs and sign-using behavior, in an effort to understand a visual communication. In 1938, the behavioral semanticist Charles Morris divided semiotics into three branches: pragmatics, concerned with how signs are used; semantics, concerned with the relations between signs and their meanings; and syntactics, concerned with signs apart from their meanings, including their physical forms and how they are related into a structure. There are problems from a total reliance upon semiotics for design theory. As the *Encyclopaedia Britannica* points out: 'Although this three-fold division has been widely adopted by logicians, and more recently by linguists, there is considerable disagreement as to the precise definition of pragmatics in relation to semantics, as also of such key terms as sign, symbol, and signal.'

A graphic design isn't just a sign, it is an amalgam of signs, images and visual elements configured to deliver a complex message that is visual/verbal/nonverbal. The ambiguity and disagreements among semioticians has permitted some graphic design researchers to reshape the meaning of pragmatics, semantics, and syntactics into components of graphic design: form, message and operation, used here to mean how the graphic design operates upon people and within societies.

Perhaps form, message and operation are too lucid for scholarly discourse: figuration, impartation, operancy might be more precise and esoteric. With semiotics as a part of the foundation, I believe the time has come for a theory of graphic design, rather than continuing the past practice of piggybacking on other disciplines such as perceptual psychology, semiotics, architecture and art history.

The Cult of Individualism

There have been calls for a rejection of design history based on the accomplishments of individuals; instead, it is proposed that a collective evolution be substituted. In some periods, a collective vision and imagery evolve which cannot be easily attributable to specific individuals. Design involves a creative process; designs are usually made by an individual or a small collaboration. When we are unable to determine the authorship of historical artifacts such as the director's chair, the designer is not anonymous or collective, but merely unknown to us. George Tscherny has noted that the matter of dates is absolutely critical in graphic design history. Sometimes the time span between an original innovation and the host of imitations is perilously short, making the task of identifying the original from the imitation difficult. An apparently collective outbreak can almost always be traced to a source.

Those who seek to deny the role of seminal individuals – and call for a collective view of design history – produce an equally biased vision. There are pivotal individuals who shaped the direction of graphic design in their times by inventing new typographic and symbolic forms, innovative ways to structure information in graphic space, pioneering imagery, and original methodologies for signifying messages. It would be foolhardy to deny the unique contributions to our graphic heritage by such individuals as John Baskerville or El Lissitzky. During the 1960s, Tschichold wrote of Lissitzky: 'His indirect influence was widespread and enduring... A generation that has never heard of him... stands upon his shoulders.'

Careful analysis of dates of similar works often proves that seemingly collective directions do in fact have an identifiable point of origin; however, when a collective evolution such as popular vernacular Victorian graphics does occur, many works typify the essence of the direction and time period, many artisans contribute to the collective evolution.

Concurrent analysis from two historical points of view – synchrony and diachrony – can help steer an exploration of graphic design around many pitfalls. Synchrony is simultaneous occurrence; while diachrony is a study of phenomena as they occur and change over time. Adolphe Mouron Cassandre's first poster serves as an example. One can examine its synchronic relationship to other graphic designs of its time, then examine it in relationship to the graphic designs preceding and following it. This poster appears to be unlike other graphic designs of its immediate time and its antecedents: but it significantly influenced work by Cassandre and others in the months and years following its publication. Because the concepts embodied in this poster drew inspiration from advanced art, an understanding of Cubism and Futurism is needed to fully comprehend this poster. This poster gains significance in the historical evolution of post First World War French advertising art due to its profound influence.

Due to the rampart plagiarism and eclecticism in mass communication, synchrony and diachrony are critical to the design historian's efforts to separate an innovator from his or her army of imitators.

A real dilemma surrounds issues of influence and plagiarism, for the evolution of graphic design has often been a continuum, evolving over time. The evolution of seventeenth-century European typography design, from Old Style to Transitional to Modern, is but one example of a dialog transcending decades and national boundaries. A building process enabled designers to achieve a gradual transition from Renaissance design to this modern epoch.

Pedagogic Imperatives

Design educators have maintained a focus upon students and to a lesser degree professional designers, while ignoring the need to educate the larger society – the general public, the business community, governmental decision makers – to the value of graphic design.

Dilnot strikes to the heart of this problem when he asks: 'When historically does society begin to recognize consciously that things are designed rather than that they simply are?' ('The of Design History, Part I' *Design Issues*, no. 1. Spring, 1984.) The design history movement should expand its mission, developing strategies for educating the public and clients. This would serve the needs not only of the design profession, but of society at large.

Feminism, Eurocentrism, and Multiculturalism:
Politically Correct Graphic Design History

Great waves of controversy about political correctness have swept through society in the US during the last few years. Universities and academics have been at the center of this maelstrom, with many universities adopting codes of behavior and speech, some of which have been struck down by the courts for violating the constitutional right of free speech.

It is not surprising that graphic design and its history have become embroiled in the political correctness controversies. Unlike fine art, which is often birthed from an internal necessity on the part of the artist, a graphic design comes into being as a direct result of a social, cultural or economic need. It is loaded with the attitudes, biases and values of the designer and/ or her client.

The feminist branch of the design history movement seeks an interpretation of past attitudes toward women and an understanding of women's experiences. The line of demarcation between design history and social/political history is a fuzzy one, prone to leakage. This is how it should be, because graphic design almost always has a co-presence of perceptual form and societal message on the same surface, creating a duality of meaning and interpretation. Those who reject the feminist approach due to its narrow focus upon one aspect of the design fail to realize that this topical research is one of the few efforts to address the content and social influence of graphic design. Hopefully, the feminist wing of the design history movement will develop theory and methodology that can be applied to a range of social and political issues.

The feminist design history movement should aspire to the fate of the Easter Seal Society, which struggled for years in the battle against the dreaded disease, polio. When the Easter Seal Society finally triumphed and effective vaccination virtually ended polio, it lost its reason for existence. But, it turned its expertise toward new problems, notably birth defects. Although I have expressed this optimistic view, recent events such as media hysteria surrounding the Bobbitt trials convinces me that a vaccination against sexism, etc., is probably a long way off.

Eurocentrism is defined as the tendency to focus upon European culture while excluding other cultural traditions. Multiculturalism means an expanding understanding of the rich diversity and values inherent in many cultures. I believe the design history movement should embrace multiculturalism as one of the most important philosophical issues today. It can bring the human community toward greater unity and understanding. Advanced communications and transportation technology are shrinking spaceship earth into Marshall McLuhan's 'global village' at an ever-increasing pace. We are evolving a pluralistic, international culture, and the need for cross-cultural understanding has never been greater.

During the mid-1970s, when I was researching and writing the first edition of my graphic design history text, the publisher placed a contractual limit of 300 pages and 600 images.

I reduced my material based on their evolutionary linkage to contemporary design practice in the US. The regrettable result was an overemphasis upon European traditions, while vital topics such as Persian manuscripts and the Korean alphabet were not included. Perhaps my criteria were appropriate based on the vantage points of the 1970s, but I fairly cringe at some of the oversights and biases not clear to us at that time. I hope to rectify some of these problems in the next edition.

In the reaction against Eurocentrism, two cautionary notes are in order. Expanding our research and teaching to embrace and include multiple cultures should not be accompanied by a denunciation and rejection of the European culture heritage. Significant contributions of European culture should not be slighted or ignored in a quest for balance, for the finest impulses of multiculturalism are inclusionary rather than exclusionary. Zealots – whether feminists, multiculturalists, animal rights activists, Modernist (or Postmodernist) designers, etc. – can become fascists if they lose their sense of balance and proportion in a drive to correct inequities or right past wrongs.

Whose or Who's Design History?

Diverse philosophies, attitudes and biases of various components of the design history movement bring us to one of the most perplexing dilemmas of all. How shall we define the parameters of graphic designs we admit into our history? The range of graphic design artifacts spans postage stamps, to comic books, to art posters by Picasso and Matisse. Each of these subcategories have their own history, traditions and museums, such as the Postal Museum in Washington and a Museum of Comic Art in New York state. The astounding range of graphic design expression makes this fragmentation unavoidable.

The graphic design history movement has focused upon significant designers and their works, rather than the audience or the overall cultural impact of design activities. This design-history approach has been closely bound to the training of young designers, who desperately need a system of values, philosophical underpinnings and a sense of professional worth. Those who seek to discredit this approach to design history fail to recognize the continuing predicaments of graphic design.

Design as Ideology

Every designer is an ideologist, even in situations where he or she does not even realize it. The history of graphic design is filled with symbolic cues about the attitudes and beliefs of client, designer and audience. This ideological aspect becomes the potent link between design history and social history. The corporate designer embraces a philosophy of capitalism, the advertising designer advocates consumption, the social activist designer protests and demands action. The designer who does not see himself or herself as an ideologue is a sleepwalker oblivious to his or her social role.

Just as we may never know with full certainty whether or not the toxic herbicide commonly known as Agent Orange – unleashed into the environment during the Vietnam War in such massive quantities that it now resides in every living creature on the planet, each of us in this room being a walking depository of Agent Orange – is the direct cause of the cancers and chronic skin ailments plaguing Vietnam War veterans and their offspring, we also may never be able to determine the culpability of Beavis and Butthead in the fire set by a six-year-old viewer that killed his baby sister, or the degree to which Joe Camel encourages teenagers to use lethal tobacco products. The possible link between graphical images and audience behavior should motivate us toward a continual examination of the ideology of graphic communications.

A bias-free communication is virtually impossible. Even benign designs, or movements that sought neutral, objective visual communications, are laden with potent ideologies

'When one says sentimentality', Berenson observed, 'one wants to denounce a sentiment in which one is no longer participating... When we say for example that Millet is sentimental it simply means that we are reacting against a sentiment that is no longer fashionable, and because of that reaction we forget to appreciate the value of Millet's paintings: solid noble painting which rank with the best of the nineteenth century.' (Umberto T. Morra and Florence Hammond, *Conversations with Berenson* (Boston: Houghton Mifflin, 1965), p.259.) In the study of graphic design history, the sentiment and attitudes embedded in the artifact can be interpreted in the terms of its time or of our time. We run the risk of revisionist history where we warp and bend the work of an earlier time to suit the values and biases of today.

The final of Gauguin's three questions is: 'Where are we going?' Certainly, technology is a driving force continually reshaping how visual communications are delivered to the audience, who creates them, and what they mean for creators and consumers of visual messages and images. The current circumstance of the human community and planet Earth appears to be entering a crisis phase. Quite possibly we have the power to confront and even solve interlocking problems such as exploding population growth, resource depletion and environmental degradation; the question is, do we have the will? Are our political and economic institutions sufficiently viable to enable us to confront these dilemmas? For the graphic design profession the pivotal question is: are our communications methods capable of delivering the right messages? Can we provide the public and the political decision-makers the information needed to respond to looming crises? For the practice of design in the twenty-first century, I advocate a philosophy of planetary humanism. Planetary, because we are imperiling the fragile ecosystems – that frail envelope of air, those shallow bodies of water, and that precious thin layer of topsoil – upon which all life on this planet is dependent. Humanism, because the graphic design community must awaken from the award-oriented, materialistic attitudes of the 1980s where graphics was treated as a beautiful surface, and address the needs of the people who receive and use the visual messages we create.

Perhaps one could argue that this challenge is beyond the scope of graphic design, but we must define graphic designers not as decorators, stylists or form arrangers, but as activists making powerful messages capable of touching people's lives.

In what direction should the design history non-movement go? I've always believed that history was in the understanding business. Graphic design has a pervasive impact upon people's lives. We should reject the narrow definition of scholarship as a closed and exclusive club of esoteric scholars talking to themselves. If we understand how and why our forms, concepts, and imaging techniques emerged, and what graphic artifacts meant to the people of their time, we are in a better position to confront the looming challenges of the twenty-first century. A duality of approaches, addressing both the problem of form and the content of graphic artifacts, can help create the awareness needed to help renew both human and aesthetic values in mass communications. The resulting breath of understanding can help visual communications professionals, students and audiences to define their discipline, their work and their potential for contributing positively to the evolution of the emerging international culture and society.

Philip B. Meggs, (1942–2002), Richmond, was an influential graphic designer, professor, historian and author.
Lecture presented at the Universidad de las Americas Puebla, Cholula, Puebla, Mexico (February 28, 1994).
First published in *Meggs: Making Graphic Design History*, John Wiley & Sons, Inc., 2008.

GRAPHIC DESIGN

Edited by **Steven Heller and Georgette Ballance**

HISTORY

KMcC

AS

AH

PBM

MR

JL

CM

AF

NP

THE BEGINNING OF HISTORY

STEVEN HELLER
2001

Who are Robert Massin, Merle Armitage, Georg Olden and Thomas Maitland Cleland? What are *Fact, The Bald Soprano*, the NKF Catalog and *For the Voice*? If these questions were asked on an exam, would you be stumped? If you were, would you know where to locate the answers? Do you understand that these answers relate to the history of your profession? Do you realize that graphic design even has a history?

Lest ignorance overshadow talent, graphic designers should be literate in graphic design history. Being able to design well is not always enough. Knowing the roots of design is necessary to avoid reinvention, no less inadvertent plagiarism. Although not all professionals are required to study the histories of their respective fields, many fields – and graphic design is certainly one of them – are built firmly upon historical foundations. Although graphic design history is routinely inserted as an afterthought or footnote in some histories of art and culture, it is a significant component of mass communication, from producing advertising to defining zeitgeist.

Granted, the word 'history' sounds a bit musty, and designers, particularly young ones, are more interested in creating for the moment than learning about the past. Yet studying history should not be a chore.

When history is recorded with verve and presented with passion, it enlightens and nourishes. What is history if not a collection of narratives that comprise a legacy? What is a legacy if not a foundation on which to build and transform? Given the legacy of graphic design, it is clear that the intersection of applied and fine arts has enriched this field as well as the broader culture.

A compelling case has been made through recent conferences, magazine articles and books, for the centrality of graphic design history in the education of all graphic designers. During this formative period in the digital age, when new media is altering traditional notions of graphic design practice, it is even more important that designers have the grounding provided by historical knowledge. Arguably, design history courses should continue throughout the undergraduate and graduate years, just like typography and computer skills, but this is often thwarted by small budgets and other priorities.

Philip B. Meggs and Richard Hollis each authored general history books – *A History of Graphic Design* and *Graphic Design: A Concise History*, respectively – which provide basic narratives that chart a continuum. Mildred Friedman's 1989 *Graphic Design in America: A Visual Language History* and Ellen Lupton's 1998 *Mixing Messages* offer supplementary commentaries on specific historical themes. Yet a well-rounded graphic design history program must consistently provide more in-depth analysis of an ever increasing subject range. Although it is useful to master the historical chronology, including where and when movements, schools and styles, as well as pioneers, are found in time, this is but the armature around which more detailed research is presented. Graphic design history cannot be taught without the basic textbooks (and the pictures reproduced therein), but unexplored (and sometimes arcane) areas must be frequently introduced in order to enliven history.

History is only as engaging as the talents and skills of those who record it. The most potentially engrossing stories can be as dull as actuarial tables if historians rely on jargon. While jargon is a common shorthand for communicating to like-minded people, it can be stultifying and stupefying for the uninitiated. For graphic design history to be exhilarating – and particularly for students who would rather make design than read about others who preceded them – it must be presented in ways that underscore design's cultural resonance. A poster must not simply be a lesson in formal or theoretical practice, although this is indeed important, but rather a component of a larger context wherein it functions. A typeface should not be viewed only as an instrument for conveying words and sentences, but as representative of the particular period when it was created and the aesthetics of those who created it. A school like the Bauhaus, a movement like Constructivism and a style like Psychedelia cannot be isolated from the societies (as well as the political milieus) in which they were founded. History must show that graphic design is not the product of a hermetically sealed environment.

Yet graphic design history does have its own heroes and villains, icons and eyesores, apart from other arts. While design historians must use cultural and political histories as backdrops, ultimately the stories they tell must be rooted in issues of design. The challenge is, therefore, to find pegs on which to hang design history so that it is relevant beyond the design ghetto. Many of the stories in this book are relevant outside of conventional graphic design areas of interest; in fact, some stories are possibly more significant outside the design universe. For example, the histories of *Avant Garde* and *Fact*, two smartly art-directed and editorially sophisticated political/cultural magazines that challenged current mores and taboos in ways that placed the publisher in jeopardy. The story is as much about these assaults on convention as it is about typography. Of course, other publishing stories, such as the origin of *Emigre* magazine, the evolution of *Fortune* and the art direction of *Esquire* are more about design, but can also be mined for insights into fashions, trends and mores that affect the lives of everyone. Another example of cross-cultural interest is the story about Olden, the first African-American graphic designer to work on the national stage as an art director for CBS television. It could have been written merely as a professional profile focusing on his best work, but as history it is more important to understand how Olden functioned within an all-white media corporation and the effects of racial prejudices on his career. While one can be color-blind with an analysis of his work, Olden's professional and creative lives are more compelling when seen through a sociocultural lens.

Preferences and prejudices determine how a historian presents a story. Some writers are solely interested in the facts of a professional life or commercial fashion or aesthetic movement. Some weave all kinds of details into a more inclusive, interconnected fabric. Other historians interpret the facts through an ideological filter – feminism, Marxism, consumerism, anticonsumerism, or are connoisseurs of certain objects in a fetishistic way. Others focus on the means and results of production as a way of exploring larger issues of design and its impact on society. And still others combine scholarship and journalism into an engaging hybrid. As an example, Olden's life gave Julie Lasky an opportunity to investigate how one man had the strength to overcome racial prejudice, but at the same time become a victim of other forces that ruined his career. Lasky's research began as a journalistic pursuit that resulted in a historical document. But not every designer's biography is this dramatic. The profiles of Massin, Fortunato Depero and Lester Beall are more conventionally focused on their professional accomplishments, yet are no less important to design history. At this stage in the development of design history, all discoveries and approaches are requisite building blocks.

The essays in this book follow a variety of methodologies, yet each provides insight into the work or works while establishing relative significance in the world of design and cultural environment.

Graphic Design History is the first 'reader' of the 'graphic design history movement.' Herein are various selected contributions to the collective literature, originally published in a variety of design periodicals, among them *Print, Communication Arts, Eye, Upper and Lower Case, Critique,*

Graphis and *Design Issues*. Yet the essays selected for inclusion suggest the catch-as-catch-can nature of graphic design history practice. There is no single wellspring, and despite invoking the term 'movement', there is no central organization that encourages historical research.

As editors who also teach design history courses, we believe there is a need to create a bank of writing that has surfaced over the past decade or two. This book is an initial stab at making existing essays accessible. We have organized the material into the areas that are most frequently addressed, at least in magazines and journals. The overarching themes are theory and practice. The majority of the essays herein, however, deal with practice. We begin with essays that scrutinize how history is researched, taught and written in 'Legacy Considered'. Then we segue to specific topics, including the history of magazines and periodicals in 'Between Covers', critical and professional profiles of practitioners in 'Designed Lives', avant-gardes and their offshoots in 'Avant-Gardes', and commercial cultures in 'Mass Communications'. We end the book with an epilogue, diverging from our essay format with an original interview with Louis Danziger, the founder, as it were, of the 'movement' and the most influential teacher of graphic design history in the US. In addition to his overview of the subject, we end with his own syllabus.

Over the past decade there has been more research, shedding increased light on graphic design. And as the literature grows, so does literacy. Nonetheless, despite the core history text-books mentioned above, as well as a handful of supplementary books, graphic design history is currently in the formative developmental stage. New research must be encouraged, outlets must grow, funding must be available, and courses must be endemic to all design programs. Most importantly, young writers should be motivated to raise graphic design history from a parochial recounting to an invigorating drama that informs and inspires us all.

Steven Heller is co-chair of SVA/NYC MFA Design: Designer as Author + Entrepreneur, the 'Visuals' columnist of the New York Times Book Review and author of *The Daily Heller*. First published in *Graphic Design History*, Allworth Press, 2001.

GRAPHIC DESIGN

KMcC

AS

AH

PBM

MR

Edited by Steven Heller and Georgette Ballance

JL

CM

HISTORY

AP

NP

INTERVIEW WITH LOUIS DANZIGER

STEVEN HELLER
2001

Lou Danziger was one of the first historian-cum-practitioners to introduce a class in graphic design history. In this interview he talks about the practice of design history and shares his continually evolving syllabus.

Steven Heller: Where did your interest in graphic design history come from?

Lou Danziger: I started reading design books and journals including *Gebrauchsgraphik* as far back as 1934 or 1935. The Bauhaus had closed only shortly before I started my interest in 'commercial art'. My interest in design history was nurtured while much of the material was current, not yet history. From my earliest days of teaching in 1952, I made reference to the various modern art movements and to the pioneer designers and artists that were part of this history. I encouraged my students to read and research and to be aware of art, architecture, film, etc. It was simply part of the way I teach.

When did you begin teaching graphic design history? Had there been a course of this kind before, that you are aware of?

I began teaching a course called the History of Graphic Design at CalArts, in 1972 or 1973. It was a course begun by Keith Godard a year earlier and it was to my knowledge the only course of its kind at the time. It all began because Keith and I, who were colleagues at CalArts, would often commiserate about how difficult it was to teach students who had no knowledge of the design pioneers. Keith thought we should do something about it, and put the thought into action. As far as I know, Keith should be given the credit of teaching the first course in graphic design history that was listed in a school's catalog; it was an official part of the curriculum. He put a lot of work into the course and it was very effective. When he left CalArts for New York City, I picked up and greatly elaborated the course over the next twenty-five years, teaching it in one form or another at other schools as well as doing synopsis lectures at a variety of universities and institutions. I taught it at Harvard almost every Summer from 1978 to 1988, where many graphic designers and design teachers were exposed to this material. A number of people who are currently teaching graphic design history took that Summer class as a stimulus for their own subsequent efforts.

Other than the obvious value of understanding the past, what additional benefits do students derive from having a historical grounding?

One thing that I have observed is that the students develop a greater commitment to their work, which they now see as part of a continuum. They see themselves as part of something, perhaps the next contributors to this history. They also begin to understand the connections between industrial and social change and how these changes play a role in the shaping of designers' work. The connection between their work and the milieu from which it springs.

How do you teach history? Are you linear? Episodic? Anecdotal? Theoretical?

The course is structured both episodically and in a somewhat linear way and is largely anecdotal. Document 1 is an introduction, which describes the course fully and sets the stage for the lectures. It should provide the greatest understanding of what I am up to. Document 2 is an outline of the course and makes the structure clear as well as indicating the points made and the thrust of the course. Document 3 is a partial list of the people mentioned during these lectures as my course focuses quite a bit on the individuals that played their role in this history. Although I believe in the importance of contexts and historical imperatives, I think that, particularly in design history, the idiosyncratic personality is of prime importance. Different people, a different history! I don't know whether he ever talked to you about it, but Paul Rand was greatly impressed with my history course. Here's a direct quote from a letter to me: 'Your history is very impressive. I perspire at the mere thought of the hours you put into producing the stupendous outline. And what's more, it is extremely well done.' He did think that I included some people like Stephen Dohanos and other illustrators that needed to be edited out. He dismissed them as 'cornballs'. I had them in there to make a point about the difference in the way illustrators dealt with problems and the way that graphic designers deal with the same problem. The difference having to do with showing the fish or the fishness. He also felt that there were some important people left out but he never said who. He then asked me if I would do a synopsis history lecture at Yale, which I did.

What would you describe as the ideal way to impart history? And should it be integrated, somehow, into practice?

I'm not quite sure how to answer this. My own experiences vis-à-vis graphic design history are quite unique in several ways. For one thing, I am always talking to designers or future designers; for another, unlike most people that I know of who are teaching the subject, I have gained my knowledge incrementally over a very long period of time and through direct experience. So many people who are teaching the subject today gained their knowledge through extensive and concentrated research over a relatively short span of time. That's very different, and leads to different kinds of understanding and thinking. Furthermore, so many of the trade journals used for research, particularly American design journals, are full of inaccuracies, as they were not of very high caliber. I know what is wrong, as I was there, so to speak; the fairly recent comers to the subject would have no way of knowing. There is a real dearth of reputable material on design history. As a result, my own teaching can't be extrapolated as a model of how to do it. I think each person teaching the subject tries to find ways to optimize their pedagogic capabilities. I don't know if there is an ideal way. There are simply too many variables to speculate about that. As for integration into practice, I believe that is inevitable. Even if you do not intentionally make the effort, such as assigning history assignments in studio classes, the consciousness of design history, the practitioners and the concepts will have a direct impact on the students' work.

How do you determine what is, in fact, historically important? Conversely, what do you ignore or reject?

I deal primarily with the Modern movement, as I believe the ideas fundamental to good design are there (remember, I am directing my teaching to designers in an effort to enhance their performance). It is also the area in which I feel I have the most to offer. I use my own judgment to select material that they need to know about, material that elucidates particular concepts, or demonstrates something of value. I often select things not necessarily because they are important historically but rather because they make a point. I sometimes select material because I find it amusing or interesting for whatever reason. One doesn't want to lull the students to sleep.

I'm sure you are interested in the growth of design history as a discipline. What do you feel is wrong with how it is taught, and what do you feel is right?

A discipline which conducts research, asks questions, gathers credible information and leads to greater understanding of a subject is of value for general cultural and intellectual reasons irrespective of whom that material is addressed to or to what specific purpose that research is directed. Having said that, I think that in graphic design history particularly, the distinction between the academic historian and the practitioner-cum-historian presents problems. I believe they look at the same material with different eyes. This is inherently problematic. Ideally, I think the research, writing and teaching would be collaborative. On very rare occasions there are people like Ellen Lupton, for example (there are others), who I think do good objective history and can also see. One can write a chapter on what it means to see. An educated eye is like an educated palate. You don't get it from eating, you have to cook. Seeing, too, has to do not only with looking but with making.

If you had it to do all over again, how would you structure a history course?

My own course was evolved over a period of more than twenty-five years. I continued to modify it as I taught and as opportunity presented itself (finding new material or some new insight). I honed and polished it as I went. I often made modifications based on suggestions from students. One thing that I found to be particularly interesting was the fact that when I first started the course in the early seventies, most of the students had direct experience with the 1960s. The lecture on the graphics of the counterculture was one of the most popular lectures. The students loved it! It was like a high school reunion for them, pure nostalgia. I didn't have to tell them anything about the 1960s. It was their home turf. As the years went on apace, that all changed. The students now were not yet born in the 1960s. Now one has to set the stage, one has to do a lot of explaining. And of course it is impossible, no matter what one shows or talks about, for the students of the beginning new millennium to understand emotionally how truly revolutionary and nation-transforming the 1960s were. At the moment I am no longer teaching the course, but were I to do it again tomorrow, I would do it the same way. Based on continuous feedback, it worked well, had a positive impact on the students and kept me continuously learning and examining my thoughts about what designers do and have done and, even more importantly, what I think they should be doing.

Steven Heller is co-chair of SVA/NYC MFA Design: Designer as Author + Entrepreneur, the 'Visuals' columnist of the New York Times Book Review and author of *The Daily Heller*.
First published in *Graphic Design History*, Allworth Press, 2001.

THE CRITICAL 'LANGUAGES' OF GRAPHIC DESIGN

JOHANNA DRUCKER
2001

This paper addresses the history of attitudes towards criticism in design within nineteenth and twentieth century intellectual contexts and looks to the contemporary condition of design in electronic formats and platforms as a way of asking the question: 'How are we to conceptualize what is graphic about graphic design?' This question is a subset of the larger inquiry that begs illumination, even in the early twenty-first century – how to establish a foundation for graphesis, or visual representation as a field of knowledge? And what are the critical and theoretical approaches appropriate to it?

Theoretical and critical approaches to graphic design rely heavily – and paradoxically – upon analogies between visual forms and language. The phrase 'languages of design' inscribes that analogy in such familiar terms that the assumptions underlying it almost disappear. The paradox results from the fact that the fundamental visuality of graphic design is sacrificed when its specificity is subsumed within a critical framework premised on concepts of language.

The censored form of a 1898 poster by French artist Alfred Choubrac makes this paradox apparent. When informed that his can-can dancer was apparently displaying too much of her lace underclothing for so public an image, rather than redraw the image, Choubrac reworked the poster with a banner over the offending portion that proclaimed: 'This part of the image is banned.' A text thus stands in for that segment of the image that is not to be viewed. Read another way, this statement makes clear that the function of text is not only to cover what can't be seen, but that in doing so, text covers and conceals visual form. What is always rhetorically the case in critical writing about design is here demonstrated graphically. Critical writing substitutes language for image, basically swapping out text for visual elements in exactly the manner Choubrac's redrawn image made explicit. The special case of the censored poster is in fact a demonstration of the general case of critical language in its relation to images.

Much graphic design criticism not only attempts to use language for discussion of visual form, but also pushes the use of linguistic analogies. In so doing, it engages in a sleight of discourse, substituting not only a word for an image, but a linguistic premise for a visual one. Graphesis, the idea that knowledge can be represented in visual form as a distinct mode of symbolic communication with its own rules and systems, is always at a disadvantage because criticism functions most effectively and familiarly in language. These analogies between 'languages' of visual communication and language as a system of verbal communication have repeatedly reinforced the perception that this is a useful, logical and even truthful way to understand graphic design from a critical perspective. But is it?

The phrase 'the language of graphic design' is part of a very specific history of approaches to graphic form. It conjures associations of systematic principles ordering visual elements with maximum effectiveness and streamlined elegance. This is classic twentieth-century Modernism, the International Style of mid-century, in which the lucid presentation of visual material was organized to seem like the natural order of communication. Exemplary – even emblematic – of such work is the well-known 1950 publication, *Sweet's Catalogue Design Progress* by Ladislav Sutnar and K. Lundberg-Holm. The striking project that forms the center of this piece is their graphic redesign of the *Techron* catalogue. Through an integration of content analysis and graphic presentation, their work epitomizes this rational sensibility and its communicative efficacy. Starting with a catch-all, randomly sequenced arrangement of time-pieces, text and jumbled page layout designed half a century earlier, Sutnar and Holm developed an approach to design that was systematic and generalizable rather than project-specific. Though they linked their concept of systematicity to an image of traffic and information flow, the more fundamental idea of ordered rules functioning as a 'grammar' of design underlies their text.

The use of the analogy between language and visual forms in graphic design, or in discussions of pattern and visual art, has precedents in the nineteenth century (earlier in architecture). This analogy is suggested by the title of the monumental volume by Owen Jones published in 1856, *The Grammar of Ornament*, another significant landmark in the field of design history. The use of this analogy between language and visual forms in graphic design participates in broader attempts to formalize and systematize areas of human knowledge and their representation. Such efforts are the product of nineteenth-century attempts to rationalize areas of humanistic inquiry aligning them with the perception that scientific knowledge has greater truth value and thus greater cultural authority than humanistic disciplines whose methodologies are largely descriptive and subjective, qualifiable rather than quantifiable. Scientific thought provided models for rational order as a governing principle of the natural world. The cultural authority that attends to such disambiguating methods continues to predominate in our contemporary culture. Though the elusive dream of a systematic approach to graphic design, grounded in principles that function according to an analogy with language, now bears a nostalgic stigma, the primacy of language has been reinforced by another type of authority, that of formal languages in digital technology.

In the twentieth century the concept of the 'languages of design' and its parallel formation, 'theories of visual communication', became a commonplace notion that circulated widely through the profession and its training ground in curricula and textbooks for the graphic designer. The approach had many assumptions in common with those of Modernism in the visual arts, in particular, a drive to articulate a set of universals that would always hold true within formal, visual expressions. The attempt at creation of a rigorous visual system, such as that developed in the Bauhaus curriculum through the work of, among others, the influential figure Josef Albers, was an almost unquestioned desideratum of the design world in its moves towards definition and professionalization. The systematic approach was premised on the belief that a formal system of rules for effective design could transcend historical circumstance. The principles of formal relations were conceived to be absolutes, governing visual elements in a scheme that had parallels in the project of formalization of natural languages in many fields. The influence of analytic philosophy, mathematics and formal logic in the early decades of the twentieth century established a foundation for asserting the benefits of formal methodologies for the *production* of works of visual art and graphic design as well as for the critical analysis of visual art. After mid-century, these principles bore mature fruit in the visual form, organizing principles and international influence of Swiss design, on the work of Josef Müller-Brockmann, Anton Stankowski, Paul Rand and legions of others.

These systematic approaches and their basis in formalist methodologies, as well as their attendant ideological baggage, came under attack in the 1970s. Feminist theory, cultural studies, the principles of deconstructionist criticism and post-structuralist analyses called attention to the complicity between claims to universal truth-values within objective-seeming formal systems and the institutionalization of power relations in social and cultural institutions. Perversely, in this same decade, the effect of semiotics on many humanistic fields – including graphic design – was to conceive of every available artifact (visual, aural, material etc.) as a 'text'. The overwhelming projection of the linguistic paradigm onto every area of symbolic discourse went forward at the same time as deconstructionist attacks were aimed at the 'logocentric' premises of western philosophy.

By the 1980s, erosion of such predominant models was in part effected through the capabilities of new technology. Digital media encourages an easy blurring of the boundaries of image/text through production methods that are radically different from those of more traditional/conventional production methods grounded in hot type, mechanical/darkroom photography and photomechanical methods of production. The emergence of an aesthetic of 'illegibility' – the famously unreadable work of designers like David Carson or P. Scott Makela in the late 1980s and early 1990s – seems an utterly consistent expression of a moment in which the authority of language is undermined through theoretical attacks on logocentrism that coincide with the exuberant exploitation of the hybrid capabilities of digital media. The celebration of simulacral modes coincided with the simultaneous erosion of the legibility and credibility of language in an apparent undercutting of its critical authority. But critical approaches within the context of Cranbrook Academy and the McCoys, for example, or Lorraine Wild before and after her move to CalArts, and the important work of Ellen Lupton and Abbott Miller relied heavily on semiotic and linguistic theory in their attempts to grapple with the problems of visual graphic form. Meanwhile, lurking in the wings was yet another incarnation of the persistent trope of formal systematicity – now in the form of the mathematical underpinnings of digital media. If natural language, with all its flawed idiosyncrasy, had been held up for generations as the model of potentially systematic representation of thought within human expression, then formal language – logic-based, computational, and unambiguous – would present the most extreme version of this promise. But is it a promise fulfilled? Would we wish it to be?

There are unexamined premises within this inquiry that require another backtrack through the historiography of graphic design history before they can be addressed, one that looks at the connections between the stylistic rhetorics within design discourse and the critical rhetorics that establish criteria of their success. Cultural authority resides within that set of connections – between the rhetorical expectations of design and the terms on which it is assessed. The cultural authority that attends to design in our current moment is grounded in very specific values, familiarized to the point of invisibility. The process of defamiliarizing these premises puts them into relation with a longer, historical perspective – in which this is merely one moment in the history of graphic design and its critical discourses.

A very brief, almost telegraphic overview of earlier moments in design history will have to serve to invoke these various points within the modern history of graphic design before concluding with a return glance at the opening questions about the critical frameworks that address the graphic character of design.

Manuals for the printing trade served as the sole repository of written information about design up until the late nineteenth century. Precious little self-conscious discussion of design found its way into these publications, which were meant to provide technical instruction to the production staff in a print shop. The emphasis in such texts was on efficiency, and suggestions to create sketches or mock-ups on paper in advance of actual setting of type were supported largely by an argument that such preparation could spare the compositor the time and effort of resetting. Considerations such as spacing, choice of display or body type were dictated almost entirely by availability. The structure of public notices, title pages, book and page layout proceeded according to classical rules of proportion, largely absorbed as habit and convention rather than as articulated precepts. Publications like *The Inland Printer* introduced aesthetic considerations chiefly on the grounds of efficiency and communicative efficacy. Semantically driven hierarchy, which would appear to be commonsense, nonetheless took time to come to the fore as a design consideration. Little or no design 'discourse' to be found even reading between the lines of these instrumentally oriented manuals. The field remained as flat, as literal in its approach, as the relation of relief surface to paper in the transfer of ink.

While pragmatism dominated the trade publications, a concept of aesthetic design emerged slowly within the world of book and poster activity that synthesized principles from such major movements as Impressionism and Post-Impressionism in France, the Arts and Crafts movement in Scotland, England and the US, as these intersected with work in commercial venues. Graphic design and book production, particularly fine print work, are quite different zones of activity. But attention to the qualities of composition, organization and formal features of presentation in practice and its discussion found considerable support in the precepts of late nineteenth-century aestheticism. The influence of Thomas Cobden-Sanderson on William Morris and in turn on Will Bradley were not without impact in the broader commercial field. The rhetoric of such productions was pitched against the numbing effects of industrialization; the components of hand-made or crafted form, though often put at the service of mass-produced items (print publications, shoes, light bulbs, soap and so on), suggested aesthetics were an alternative to industrial mechanization. But aesthetics was and would continue to be a secondary consideration in the advertising realm where the link between communication and marketing was paramount. No trade manual or codification of the design profession would have been likely to pose its production as an opposition to the forces of mass-produced commercial activity. Likewise, aesthetes isolated their ideas from mass-market concerns. Walter Crane's *Line and Form*, for instance, made no reference to 'communication' in the commercial sense, focusing instead on concepts closer to the principles of classical architecture such as proportion, or to the musical analogies dear to the sensibility of nineteenth-century Symbolism and its aesthetic precepts. Thus the sinewy organic lines, elegant earth-toned colors and finely drawn images that show up in the work of the Beggarstaffs, on the pages of *Ver Sacrum* or in the advertising imagery of Lucian Bernhard have a common root in the visual order according to which the natural world is set apart for distinction from the industrial underpinnings on which such productions operate and whose interests they actually serve.

In the early twentieth century the evangelical tone of reform movements and socially progressive campaigns produced a righteous promotional approach to consumer culture. A work like *Jesus was an Ad-Man*, its title meant un-ironically, exhibits the curious combination of faith and capitalist zeal as a foundation for advertising rhetoric. Increased capacities for production brought about a need for increased consumption, and the creation of artificial (or at least, enhanced) desire found itself in lockstep with the development of scientific methods for advertising design. Graphic design received a boost from the world of commercial advertising that differentiated it from the craft of book production and from the aesthetic attention lavished on artist-drawn posters. The American advertising professional, no longer an 'artist', focused on sales in the name of moral 'uplift' while design rode a wave of production and prosperity cycles in the 1910s and 1920s. Civic and moral virtue went hand in hand with hard work and honest consumption in this rhetoric. And the graphic style that accompanied such ideals was declamatory and directly promotional.

While American design stressed marketing, with organization and legibility, brand name recognition and standardization as its hallmarks, Soviet and European designers established some of the first systematic curricula for the teaching of graphic design. With the establishment of the Bauhaus, as well as parallel institutions within the newly formed Soviet Union, a shift occurred that had major implications for the design profession as we know it today. Drawing on the radical use of abstract forms in visual art that had been one of the signature elements of the avant-garde, Herbert Bayer, El Lissitzky, Joost Schmidt, and their counterparts in the Soviet context, developed a concept of design grounded in principles of visual order and systematic precepts. The explosion and then taming of avant-garde innovation, coinciding as it did with a self-conscious search for 'languages' of abstraction in visual fine art, created the first rationalized foundation for design as a discourse with its own rules. Building on such works as Wassily Kandinsky's *Point and Line to Plane*, educator-designers such as Georgy Kepes and Laszlo Moholy-Nagy created manuals that outlined organized principles of communication. Pragmatism and moralizing ceded to clean efficiency and systematic organization. These formal 'languages' of design would dominate the graphic field and its critical self-conception throughout the rest of the twentieth century. The emphasis on formal properties within such systematic discussions allowed them to lay claim to an ahistorical universality while establishing a stylistic basis for the Modernism that linked avant-garde abstraction to corporate identity systems.

American design in the 1930s, still fraught with moral and reform sensibilities, engaged another set of concerns that would last through the Depression years, the Second World War and into the 1950s – an emphasis on normative imagery in vignettes and scenarios of family and civic life. By embedding products within illustrations or photographs that communicated a narrative of everyday dependability for the average and increasingly upwardly mobile American family, advertisers knit the public and private spheres of business and domestic life into a finely wrought fabric whose pattern justified spending on the basis of hygiene, independence, security and style. Design publications specialized along lines that reflected segments of a market – outdoor advertising, print campaigns and, eventually, television spots. Public service campaigns, such as the famous series of posters for Rural Electrification produced by Lester Beall, had much in common with those of their European and Soviet counterparts in the field of propaganda campaigns. Exceptions to this abound, of course, and the highly stylized and elegant work of designers like Edward McKnight Kauffer or Adolphe Mouron Cassandre borrowed heavily on the fine art traditions of Modernism to promote goods and services in quotidian as well as luxury markets. As a profession, graphic design came into its own, intent upon aesthetic validation as well as integrity, and the two reinforced each other's legitimacy.

The hiatus in normal activity caused by the Second World War, accompanied as it was by a massive intensification of production in all sectors, left a legacy of infrastructure and affluence. Propaganda, recruitment, war bond campaigns and other graphics associated with the war gave way in peace time to an unprecedented level of professionalism in graphic design. The full-blown development of an International Style, associated with Swiss design, matured in the 1950s, carrying in its abstract and geometric minimal codes all the signs of a neutral aesthetic. Organization, legibility, elegance – these were all characteristics of a 'cool' Modernism, with its unfussy sans-serif typography, its semantically neutral seeming forms with templates and grids conspicuously grounded in rational aesthetics. Design took on the aura of a profession closer to architecture and engineering than drawing and painting. The rhetoric that came to the fore in this period became the stock in trade of design schools and organizations. The predominance of a publication like *Graphis*, the awarding of prizes in professional arenas, the integration of corporate and cultural sensibilities – all sustained an integrated approach to systematic design style, unremittingly self-serious, important as an aspect of the international, 'one-dimensional' (to use Herbert Marcuse's apt contemporary term) culture it served.

1960s self-consciousness introduced a critical reflection into the design world. Cuteness, playfulness, an awareness of the 'pop' function of advertising art and of its impact twisted the solid International Style rhetoric on its edge. Though the grinding out of textbooks for 'communications' programs continued (and to some significant extent, still does) to use the rhetoric of 'visual language' as a dominant, if unexamined, motif, the practice of design shifted gears through introduction of a certain clever irony. Taking the system less than seriously, the work of designers like Quentin Fiore (in his work with Marshall McLuhan) or prominent and very successful firms such as Doyle Dane Bernbach, demonstrated the viability of undercutting the systematic 'language' of design with quips, quotes and asides with a nod to a knowing audience. The incorporation of this audience, an admission of complicity with the consumer/viewer, broke the purely formal frame that had been a premise of visual organization throughout the earlier decades of the twentieth century. The acknowledged 'textuality' of visual images came under semiotic investigation in the 1960s as well, with the critical contributions of Roland Barthes, as well as McLuhan, so that a critical case for 'reading' images took its place beside the use of 'languages of design' as the basis of production.

The other legacy of the 1960s was a political counterculture, alternative and aggressive, and focused on control of symbolic systems as a crucial site of strategic intervention into mainstream venues. The consumerism of the 1970s, somewhat chastened by contrast to 1960s exuberance (and Vietnam era affluence), was in continual dialogue with the identity politics issues raised by the Civil Rights and Women's movements. Semiotics became increasingly popular as a way of decoding the ideology of style, and the concepts of structuralism informed design and visual art through their connection to academic critical theory. The cost-effective, bottom-line graphics of the 1970s, with their rather bland corporate identity campaigns and somewhat diluted International Style sensibility, began to show the influence of photographic systems for typesetting. Though desktop publishing didn't prevail until the mid-1980s generations of Macintosh computers made equipment widely available and economically accessible, the automation of aspects of book production, distribution, management and conceptualization reoriented the industry towards an information systems approach to design and away from graphic display or its aesthetics. The proto-deconstructionist impulses of Neville Brody, for instance, fueled design's self-conscious self-examination from within even as the edge of the digital technology began to appear on the horizon of the aesthetic field.

As cultural studies forged one active area of 1980s design discourse, pushing concerns about identity, AIDS, activism and subcultures to the fore, another powerful force undercut the old formal paradigms of graphic design in the name of deconstruction. By demonstrating the alignment between hegemonic forces and an International Style, critics of design revealed the complicity between modern design and systems of power whose repressive agendas could not be wished away. Even as firms like Chermayeff and Geismar might push their 'daring' and 'innovative' facility to create logo designs and elaborate corporate identity systems, the street graphics industry worked to promote AIDS awareness through direct, smart campaigns aimed at communication and self-empowerment. The development of a cult of illegibility within various subcultural environments, such as *Ray Gun*, and the archly self-conscious always inventive and re-inventive publication *Emigre*, exhibited a clear desire to 'diss' the established tenets of graphic design. Design theory became a trendy field of study, and the semiotic disease broke out among the students and faculty of major institutions. Theory proved to be a hungry beast, and a rapid succession of intellectual frameworks was required to keep its insatiable cravings at bay. The effect of such work on graphic design was more academic than practical, with a sub-industry of critical writing and languages working feverishly to deconstruct the logocentric premises of symbolic practices while at the same time aggressively promoting the need for critico-theoretical discourse. Why? Graphic design seemed disadvantaged without some kind of scaffolding to support its productions. There was a sense that the profession no longer simply needed organizations and awards for fine, slick, clever or successful campaigns, but needed a metalanguage of self-conscious critique in order to decode its complicity and contradictions as another among many simulacral artifacts in contemporary life. April Greiman, the McCoys, Cranbrook, CalArts and other nodal points of critical activity epitomized the complex factors of Postmodern design in its first theoretical and practical formations.

The rise of the celebrity designer in the 1990s, coinciding with a major boom cycle in American consumer industries fueled, at least in the public imagination, by the dot.com phenomenon, deposed the critical languages focused on 'display' and simulation with a new vocabulary of interactivity and interface. Illegible, provocative work by David Carson promoted him to star status while writing about his work created new expectations at the intersection of style, celebrity and design. The aesthetic of digital manipulation became riddled with the hybrid, morphing manipulations that eroded all boundaries between media of input. Specificity of tool and media – pen, pencil, brush, paint, stroke or water-based pigment – no longer held. Nor did the age-old distinction between text and image. Medium-enforced but more deeply distinguished in aesthetics, philosophy and other systems of belief, this distinction had enabled a phrase like 'languages of design' to resonate with meaning generations earlier – when language held the upper hand in appearing systematizable, stable and ordered according to rules of grammar. Syntax and semantics, formal and meaning-based registers seemed to exist as a paradigmatic condition of language, extractable as a system of principles that might be usefully applied to visual elements in graphic design. Such premises were hard to sustain in a moment when the fungible character of all data leveled their identity in a digital environment. Enacted stylistically by Carson and others as an exercise in illegible form, this elision of categories at the level of display produced other anxieties about the need or possibility of ever communicating effectively in a noise-filled environment.

Theory-speak also created tensions of its own, alienating professionals from their academic counterparts, inventing a critical elite and seeming to elevate obscurantism to the level of insight. Too bad, since what was lost in this debate was what was at stake in a politics of public discourse – one that might have at least introduced some level of discomfort into the engines of complicity that were driving the publicity machine of celebrity orientation so relentlessly into the design field. Theory, after all, did have the tools to reveal very basic aspects of the design field and the designer's condition. Whose interests were being served? How was the most 'naturalized' imagery culturally loaded? And how were surface rhetorics concealing or enabling values other than those they appeared to espouse? What are the ideological underpinnings of any particular discursive formation? How are they to be named? How are they put into operation? How are we complicit with them? These are crucial aspects of any representational activity (which, by definition, is ALL of human activity). But in a mad rush to professionalize theory as an aspect of design curricula, these basic issues seemed – at least momentarily – to be lost. The languages of design as a set of formally based premises for production have the potential to become clearly stated – but as languages of insight about design, and about the function and performance of visual forms as a cultural system.

To that end, the current condition of graphic design deserves its moment of attention here at the end. For the critical languages that encode new observations and prescriptions for the role of the designer within electronic media also has its tropes and metaphors, as well as concealing certain agendas under yet another naturalizing set of terms. Only now these are the terms of informatics. No longer interested merely in finding rules for predictable effects in relations of visual elements, the theory of design practice will now necessarily grapple with such issues as content analysis, information architecture and the design of interactive processes such as navigation. Dynamic data sets, files that have real-time parameters in them, multi-authored and browser-specific environments – these all introduce variables that cannot be controlled in the same way that type on a page or layout in a page sequence can. And after all, even that, simpler-seeming task, turned out to elude the disciplinary legislation of a set of 'rules' – even if fundamental parameters for legible and pleasing aesthetics were generalizable into principles. Design, like any other form of human expression, turns out to partake of universals only to the extent that any historical moment of its manifestation is part of a larger pattern of symbolic communication. The specificity of any expression is precisely proportional to its capacity to serve as an index to that set of conditions that participate in its production – and to which it returns its meaning as effect. Any universal 'language' will always stop just short of where real communication begins – in difference, deviation and distinction.

In summary: the analogy between language and visual form became a commonplace in twentieth-century criticism and design curricula. The term comes into common currency in visual art and graphic design in the early decades of the twentieth century – most specifically within the context of those now historic efforts to establish systematic premises for the use and understanding of visible forms. Such concepts have their precedents within earlier attempts to perceive, or create, systematic structures within architectural, visual or decorative forms. And they have their triumphant moments in twentieth century activity – when a rhetoric of scientificity permeated all manner of humanistic and aesthetic disciplines – all of which aspired to the condition of authority that had come to attend to the natural, physical sciences in that era. Highest on the truth chain, such disciplines appeared to reveal transcendent, rather than contingent facts. Visual artists took up inquiries that mimicked those of their contemporaries in the lab, struggling to research the laws that might govern composition according to an inviolable and absolute set of design principles. Later, these principles became a garden variety of terms and approaches to design, not necessarily incorrect, but oddly quaint-seeming to our contemporary sensibility – since court decorum, though adorable in small doses, hardly suffices for our daily communications or behaviors. Such extremes of formalism had in them a utopian aspiration that has not only been abandoned, but whose precepts no longer seem either necessary or desirable as goals – the establishment of absolute terms for successful design. Such activity had been a manifestation of rationalized aesthetics, of a 'logic' that did not see itself as a rhetoric, but as an articulatable system of fixed parameters of graphic production.

And now? A whole new world of possibilities, in the simplest creative sense, but also a change of heart and a change of technological possibility. The meta-data metalanguage of design, program and display, code and data, the relation of style sheets and xml-tagged artifacts, of DTDs and mark-up borrows heavily from the world of computer science. Computational methods, grounded in formal logic and its constraints, carries its own ideological baggage. The cultural authority that attends to such methods is weighted heavily by the validation accorded to scientific discourses, and their supposed foundation on quantifiable and therefore unambiguous (read 'truthful') grounds. Natural language, once subject to the rational regimes of a science-oriented linguistics, has been replaced in the critical hierarchy with formal languages and their logic-based orientation. Should the old trope of the 'languages' of design be revived now, it would require a whole new set of caveats and cautions – lest we fall into an even more absolute-seeming trap with yet another layer of authority attendant upon it.

The critical languages that have accompanied the development of graphic design as a field will, no doubt, continue to refine themselves in concert with the development of new tasks and structures, new stylistic manifestations and their underpinnings. What is 'graphic' about graphic design continues to need elucidation – as the evolution of whole new realms of information visualization and visual interfaces to the management and organization of information are integrated into our functions of daily life in entertainment, business and education. The denaturalization of these as truth-functions will require the same critical attention as did those earlier forms of display – and we ignore the visual characteristics by which these forms communicate only at peril of a profound ignorance and blindness, since it is through their visuality that they communicate. This paper has examined the search for a set of systematic precepts as a foundation for an aesthetic of display, but it has barely touched on the question of the way this concept both benefited and constrained the exploration of visuality. Perhaps now, as greater fluency develops in the broad population for visual symbol-making and -manipulation, an era in which a significant fluency for grasping the bases of meaning production in graphic design will emerge.

Johanna Drucker is the Breslauer Professor of Bibliographical Studies at UCLA, Los Angeles.
Presented at *Looking Closer: AIGA Conference on Design History and Criticism*, February 2001.

print

INCLUDING NEW VISUAL ARTISTS REVIEW

America's Graphic Design Magazine

Calligraphy Under Glass

Airport Annuals

Vibe on a Roll

Purely Letterpress

Paris Below

Student Cover Winners

$12.00US $15.00CAN
04>

0 71658 01776 4

$12 US • $15 Canada Print LVII:II

A COLD EYE: THE WRONGS OF RIGHTS

STEVEN HELLER
2003

Graphic design historians are often prevented from reproducing visual materials essential to their narratives.

It is much easier to write a graphic design history than to reproduce artifacts to illustrate that history. Ask any scholar attempting to construct a viable historical record of any aspect of graphic design and you'll hear the same complaint. Permission to show a known designer's work is increasingly harder to secure, and more costly, too.

While a historian or critic has the right to publish whatever can be supported as fact (or viable theory), the right to reproduce the physical evidence is not inalienable. Sometimes the original creator's ego, greed or misplaced priorities are major obstacles to access, rendering dire the implications for scholarship.

Intellectual property rights are obviously a good thing. Designers (and historians, for that matter) should have protections that will not allow their ideas to be vulnerable to theft by plagiarists and unscrupulous profiteers. Yet IP (intellectual property) is big business in all media, particularly for lawyers, and this has had a deleterious effect on graphic design scholars and historians (even students), since we tend to require visual material to support what we've written. Forget the old refrain by the likes of design eminences like Massimo Vignelli that in order for graphic design to be taken seriously as a profession, it must have a codified history. While most designers would agree with this assertion, some of them, nonetheless, try to micromanage how they are portrayed, to the point of claiming the right to choose in which histories they will and will not appear. Certain publicity-conscious designers prefer to write their own histories.

I've experienced little difficulty gathering physical evidence for my books. Fragile though graphic design ephemera may be, examples are fairly easy to obtain. But acquisition is only part of the story. Many publishers are wary of reproducing living or even deceased designers' work without permission because there are no clear directives from the courts as to what is actually permissible for publication. The slightest hint of litigation unnerves them. Even when the responsibility for obtaining permission is shared by a publisher (not always the case), the process can still be time-consuming and frustrating, the end result often being a skewed history.

Sometimes the roadblock is exorbitant reproduction and rights fees. Five years ago, I had to cancel a contract for a book on the history of film-title sequences I had been working on for almost two years. I'd already completed over a dozen interviews with designers and filmmakers and had written a few draft chapters. While the film title designers were pleased to be represented and gave me access to their work, my problem was that about half of the film companies who owned the rights demanded prohibitive reproduction fees. They couldn't care less about the history and rebuffed any attempt to negotiate fairer prices. Oddly enough, the remaining companies generously granted permission and a few even waived the fees. Nonetheless, I decided I couldn't produce a book with only half the historical material needed, so I pulled the plug on it. I understand other writers have tried to tackle this same subject and had a similar experience. To date, a full-fledged history of film titling has yet to be appear in print.

Money is, however, only one part of the problem and not the most insurmountable one. What has become more troublesome in recent years is obtaining permission from the rights holders. It is one thing for living subjects or an estate to withhold information from a writer – alternative sources can always be found – but withholding reproduction rights to images for which there are no substitutes ultimately damages the credibility of a historical work.

Years ago, for my book *The Savage Mirror: The Art of Contemporary Caricature* (Watson-Guptill), I wrote a chapter on Edward Sorel, one of the genre's most original artists. And although I had written articles about him and included him in two of my previous books, on this occasion he declined to grant permission. I was left with three options: eliminate his chapter, retain it without visuals or use his work without his permission. The first option was untenable and the third was unethical. So I chose the second option, as unsatisfactory as it was, because I reasoned it would be worse to ignore him altogether in a book that included all his contemporaries. The result was a work that left a gaping hole and puzzled a lot of readers, despite an explanatory disclaimer.

(I ought to add that I had a fourth option: I might have been able to show the work in the context of the page on which it was originally published. But the format of my book was to run artwork by contemporary artists that was precisely free from the context of its original use.)

I harbor no ill will toward Sorel. He had legitimate reasons for the position he took – he felt the drawings I wished to show had been seen too often in various anthologies and, moreover, he was looking forward to publishing a monograph that would possibly contain the same material. While I can't fault him, I nonetheless believe that a serious historical work was denied full scope.

Another artist I know similarly refused to grant rights to an editor of a book that included over a dozen critical essays focused entirely on his work. He didn't much like the essays and refused to turn over most of the large number of images that were requested, knowing that the editor could not, without permission, use more than a small percentage of those on the list. The artist told me he regretted being a spoiler, but he could not be expected to support a project about himself that he did not believe in. The editor had no recourse but to publish the book with sparse visuals.

When a creator actually owns his work, the answer to grant permission to use it is very clear – yes or no. But another situation frequently arises when a creator, usually a graphic designer or typographer, grants rights that he does not possess. Conversely, a creator may deny use when the rights to a work are not his to control. As a rule, designers, typographers and art directors are engaged in work for hire, which means that everything they design is owned by some overarching entity, even if the entity is no longer in business. Routinely, however, when seeking permission to show an item, I make sure the designer is contacted and, if permission is freely granted, I consider that sufficient, because creators usually have the right to use their work for 'publicity' purposes, which includes annuals and histories. Of course, if permission is denied, problems ensue.

Recently, a designer categorically refused to allow me to reproduce his work for a critical history I was writing, stating: 'There are many histories and I choose to be erased from yours.' Presumably he was angry over something I had written about him in the past that was unrelated to what I was writing about now – in fact, my evaluation of his work was quite favorable. His refusal caused my publisher sufficient anxiety that I was asked to eliminate the particular section that addressed his work. Of course I refused, because the section was essential to the historical narrative. As a result, I spent the next two months attempting to prove that the designer did not actually hold the rights to the items in question. I spoke to a couple of company heads with whom he had worked and each of them confirmed my opinion – they even signed the permission forms I sent them. Yet, because of the designer's vehement refusal, my publisher remained wary about using the material. Eventually, the publisher relented, though not without lengthy legal consultations.

Did my experience with the recalcitrant designer set a precedent for other publishers? No. For the past three years, I have been writing a history of magazines titled *Merz to Émigré and Beyond: Avant-Garde Magazine Design of the Twentieth Century.* Having written books on magazine design, and as a frequent contributor to *Print*'s 'Magazine Watch' column, I wanted to explore the role of experimental and alternative periodicals through the lens of design. My study covers hundreds of small journals – some unknown and many that are cornerstones of twentieth-century modern art, as well as Modern and Postmodern typography. While my text provides a critical perspective, I am interested in placing these journals in the context of politics, culture and technology. In other words, *this is a scholarly work with an educational purpose.*

I italicize the preceding phrase because my IP lawyer advises that, given this purpose, I am entitled to fair-use visual materials as are necessary to substantiate the history. But this so-called 'fair use' notwithstanding, I am still compelled by my publisher to obtain permissions (or to make a good-faith attempt to obtain some) from virtually every presumed rights holder of the publications represented in my study (which goes back over 100 years). At best, this procedure is intensively time-consuming; at worst, it is an exercise in futility, necessitating trying to find the publishers of long-defunct journals that may not have been copyrighted in the first place.

Some lawyers argue that fair use does not pertain to books, but simply grants newspapers and magazines the right to publish photos or documents that relate directly to the story at hand. I recently consulted another IP lawyer who advised that books are indeed a murky area because even the most scholarly of them are usually produced for financial gain, which is the line he drew in the sand. Even for books with an educational purpose, fair use is questionable. Some publishers agree that without a definitive legal precedent – the pursuit of which would be very costly – the only safe course is to obtain permissions. But this merely compounds the problem.

Artist rights organizations that claim to represent many artists' (including graphic designers') estates routinely charge high, at times prohibitive, fees for reproduction rights. While I am diligent about getting my own materials, most scholars obtain reproducible copies or transparencies by going to yet another source, for yet another fee. And given that books of this nature use hundreds of images, the fees mount up, and publishers rarely budget enough to cover them.

How, then, can a serious scholar create a viable history without a license to use historical materials within reasonable parameters? In literature and music, legally sanctioned numbers of lines or lyrics can be reproduced without seeking permission. With visuals, it is not so clear. However, my IP lawyer tells me that as long as I do not take a work out of context (i.e., crop out or blow up details for decorative or non-essential purposes), and as long as I do not use too much of any one designer's work in relation to the other contents in the book, and as long as this work has direct relevance to the book as a whole – then I am in the ballpark of fair use. But this advice is not etched in stone anywhere, and therefore scholars and historians will have to continue to move cautiously as they grapple with the vagaries – and the roadblocks – along the way.

The writing of graphic design history is not as high on most publishers' priorities as it is for the scholars engaged in this activity. While not an oppressed minority, we are often hampered in our efforts to contribute to the field because of the issues surrounding rights. A standard needs to be created that allows the scholar access to needed materials without impinging on the prerogatives of the creator. With graphic design research accumulating every day, it would seem that the time for these issues to be resolved fairly is now.

Steven Heller is co-chair of SVA/NYC MFA Design: Designer as Author + Entrepreneur, the 'Visuals' columnist of the New York Times Book Review and author of *The Daily Heller.* First published in *Graphic Design History*, Allworth Press, 2001.

ISSN 0952-4649

Journal of
Design History

Volume 19 Number 4 2006

www.jdh.oxfordjournals.org

Special Issue: *Oral Histories and Design*
Editor: Linda Sandino

OXFORD JOURNALS
OXFORD UNIVERSITY PRESS

LOCATING GRAPHIC DESIGN HISTORY
IN CANADA

BRIAN DONNELLY
2006

The study of graphic design in Canada suffers from a scarcity of written sources and collecting institutions. Interviews conducted by one researcher suggest that, far from preventing the formation of an active design industry or any sense of a historical canon, Canadian designers draw on international examples from a variety of sources and pass on values in a largely unrecorded fashion, almost like that of an oral tradition itself. Canadian designers have a largely coherent and shared, if vernacular, sense of which works and individuals are of historical importance. Because the process of gathering and recording graphic design history in Canada currently leans heavily on recording oral histories, it is framed by many designers' memories and collections, in interaction with critical and practical analysis of what design history is. The implications of the theory and practice of oral history for design are explored, as is the importance of maintaining the difference between memory and history. Locating that existing, vernacular canon, it is suggested, is the best way to locate and study the postwar history of graphic design in Canada.

Appropriately, this article will begin with a variation on a story I have told before:

> Harold Kurschenska (1931–2003) was a typographer and book designer, and he began working as an apprentice at the University of Toronto Press in 1957. I interviewed him in his small apartment in Toronto in 1999, just before he moved on to retirement in British Columbia. As always with designers, my interview with Harold was lively, wide ranging and surprising. The biggest surprise, however, came as I was leaving: Harold asked me if I would take his papers. He had collected, sorted, filed and labeled the highlights of a long career – in effect, his life's work – and packed them in seven boxes. Now, he insisted that I load them in the trunk of my car.[1]

Kurschenska was the designer of, among many other books, the first edition of *The Gutenberg Galaxy* (University of Toronto Press, 1962), Marshall McLuhan's aphoristic pastiche on print and technological change, subtitled *The Making of Typographic Man*. Although Kurschenska worked at the centre of print culture in Canada, and with one of its gurus, it seems no one else had ever come to talk about his work, and there was apparently no institution willing to take the written records of his history. This is not because Kurschenska was a 'minor' figure in a design history being actively written about other, more important, careers. Except for his careful act of self-archiving, his story is typical: there literally was no place for his history.

For the past ten years, off and on, as time and funding provided, I have been engaged in a process of interviewing graphic designers in Canada, almost a hundred to date, about their history, their work and their understanding of the postwar development of design. Without thinking of it as such, this has involved conducting an oral history project among articulate, educated and literate professionals working at the fulcrum of print culture. The individual designers chosen have all proved very willing to talk, but only a scant few have had work collected somewhere, or themselves preserved representative archival records of their work, much less written about it.

Harold Kurschenska, cover
of *The Gutenberg Galaxy*
by Marshall McLuhan
(Toronto: University of
Toronto Press, 1962).

In the near-complete absence of any collecting institutions dedicated to graphics and the paucity of other sites of memory such as written texts, the material history of graphic design, although reproduced in mass quantities in the recent past, has almost disappeared from view, or just disappeared altogether.

Beyond the obvious irony to be found in producing an oral history of the very designers of our massive print culture, there is another twist in my story. This research has been supported by several different grants and funding initiatives, all of which have been for digital and online projects, funded by governments and organizations wanting to swim with the electronic current by stimulating production of digital information on Canadian culture. The history of 'typographic man', at least in Canada, is being captured largely by 'pre-' and 'post-' print technologies – that is oral and digital, but not in print itself – because the printed and written basis for compiling a written history of print is so rare as to be almost non-existent.[2] The graphic design tradition in Canada, then, could be said to be an oral tradition in two senses: it has been informally transmitted, primarily through studios, schools and periodicals, without having been permanently collected, curated or canonized in print or by institutions, and it is only now being gathered up again as an oral history from the practitioners themselves.

In considering design history in Canada as an oral history, then, we encounter some interesting questions, not primarily about 'who' made this history or when it occurred, but rather where our history is. Canadian communications theorist Harold Adams Innis noted that some social media were based in time: lasting sculptural or architectural monuments, for example, or religious and educational institutions that draw their meaning from their endurance over the years. He distinguished these from media that were highly mobile and diffuse, working across – having a bias in, or being bound by – space. Foremost among these was print culture, ascendant since Gutenberg.[3] (Innis was an important influence on McLuhan, his University of Toronto colleague, in both style and content.) Graphic design extends this notion further, because it is not a medium at all, but a practice that reaches across several media, from print to screen to digitization, each of which accelerates this spatial bias by moving faster through broader channels and across greater distances. The state of design history in Canada, then, remains dispossessed because it has not been formally established or preserved through time. (In this sense the medium of print, in the form of canonical texts, can provide relative permanence and a bias toward time.) Further, it has evolved as a result of many different determining factors drawn from several influences and traditions, many of which are not Canadian at all. Its location, then, is radically decentred, and this paper will look at what theories of oral history and memory can do to help us locate this history.

Design History in Canada

After 1945, graphic design in Canada developed as part of the general, international design discourse, shared in particular among more industrially developed nations. Because of the relative lack of design studies in Canada, however, design institutions here never established broadly ideological claims regarding this country's unique or national design culture, as was so often the case elsewhere and in other fields (such as literature or art). Canada, in other words, has never merited a chapter in Meggs.[4] A recent economic study done in the province of Ontario, *Design Matters*, suggests that, in all fields (including architecture and industrial, interior and graphic design) there are some 40,000 designers in Ontario alone.[5] These industries, with the arguable exception of architecture, function largely without written record of their own history. (Architecture, like painting and sculpture, is studied in art history departments and has more of a published and preserved record.) Obviously, all those designers are working with a clear picture of what they believe design is; where do they get it?

Oral evidence suggests that the picture designers have of their own national disciplines comes from the few national trade magazines (in graphic design, *Applied Arts* has played this role in English; a number of publications, including *G* and *grafika*, have served in French); from whatever local histories are preserved in the companies they work for, in the form of portfolios and self-promotional material; particularly from whatever few Canadian images they have exposure to in schools (often haphazardly captured in the form of an individual instructor's slide collection; small wonder that students attend so closely to the passing flow of contemporary images in advertising and the media). Although Canada possesses a highly developed professional and institutional framework of companies, professional associations, competitive exhibitions, contemporary publications and educational institutions, nonetheless the retained historical record of all that design has depended largely on the unrecorded self-understanding and self-selection of its practitioners. Oral history, then, does have an appropriate role to play in a country where much design history is, by default, transmitted in an informal, largely oral tradition.

One interesting fact of design in Canada is that the dominant visual influences – what designers see in print and construe as the canonical basis of their profession – have come from outside the country, largely from the US and Europe. To note this is not to adopt a nationalist perspective, to raise the flag or posit some crisis of identity or loss in urgent need of salvage and redress. It is to assess the objective reality that the history of design in Canada is not entirely, or even fundamentally, a Canadian history. This can be seen, positively, as the realization of the internationalism and idealism that marked graphic design thinking generally in the postwar period. Remarkable international exhibitions held here after 1945, such as *Typomundus 20*, held in Toronto in 1966, and *Expo 67* in Montreal, were defining moments for Canada's designers – many of whom were trained in and emigrated from Britain, West Germany, Austria or the US in any event. Thus, the national (or perhaps notional) space of 'Canadian' design is, quite literally, an arbitrary line around parts of a much larger intellectual and visual territory.

Scanning is one interesting metaphor for how history might approach this vast space. Scanning emerged from cybernetic theory in the 1950s, and Claude Shannon's original idea was itself based on a spatial metaphor for communicating information: divide up a surface into discrete blocks and average out the visual information in each of them, thereby reducing the smooth surface of the world to manageable, defined, digital pixels. Scanning also implies, however, that the results obtained will depend on the algorithm that defines in advance what is scanned and how. One of the few historical texts, *Great Canadian Posters* (1979) by Canadian designer Theo Dimson,[6] employs a chronology that goes from the early days of colour lithography through to the early 1940s, but then jumps to the late 1960s. In other words, it skips twenty-five years, missing the 1950s completely. Dimson had great success as an illustrator of fantastic, lively fantasies in that decade, and his later work is associated with a highly recognizable, very sophisticated neo-Art Deco style. It appears though that the style of the 1950s, which he did so much to define, was (at least when he wrote this book) no longer to his taste; he therefore scanned accordingly.

Cover of *Great Canadian Posters* by Theo Dimson (Toronto: Oxford University Press, 1979).

Throughout history, aesthetic judgements like these have often been used to erase not the detail of images (all scanning involves choices, sampling, lowering the resolution of the picture), but eliding entire parts of the image. A scan, however, bears a resemblance to the original only to the extent that it attempts to average across all of what is there. Scanning does not involve making judgements or digitizing only selected areas. In instances such as Dimson's book, when a designer's aesthetic and design thinking have been captured in print, the result tends to appear very conservative and selective. Possibly the clearest example of this is Canadian typographic writer Robert Bringhurst, whose book, *The Elements of Typographic Style* (2004), speaks romantically of the deep roots of the dense forests of type and stresses many highly technical rules for the use of hanging punctuation, titling figures and so on.[7] In my experience, design students use this advice in the most enlightened way possible: not as the literal rule, nor even as a set of generally helpful guidelines, but as a manifesto of an individual's historically over-determined and highly specific taste.

In contrast to such highly selective, aesthetically based historical scans, there is a broader and more positive example of a selection process, the one that has been employed directly by designers themselves. When asked to be interviewed about their careers, designers all reach for their 'book', their portfolio of designs, a working tool carefully edited over time and containing largely those works that have been in exhibitions, won awards, drawn the most attention when shown to prospects, clients or other designers or simply those that felt like the best and most sturdy examples over time. The time spent by individuals, working collectively in design firms

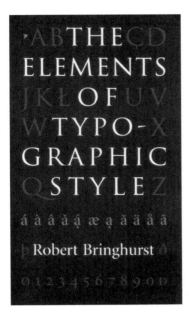

Cover of *The Elements of Typographic Style* (first edition) by Robert Bringhurst (Vancouver: Hartley and Marks Publishers, 1992).

or assembling personal slide libraries in design schools, refining and reconsidering the best (or most readily available) examples of the history, is in fact a large, highly diffuse and self-defining process on which to base the visual history of graphic design in Canada. This heteroglossia or diverse set of practices, with its complex and multiple kinds of codes and purposes, is both more and less than a fixed language or grammar. It is more, in that it permits, stimulates or even requires a high level of creative originality from its practitioners; but it is also less, as it does not presume to contain any binding rules or any notion of a 'correct' grammar for visual images. (For this reason, it is misleading to suppose that a 'visual language', per se, exists at all.) Further, this diversity suggests that the visual culture of graphic design is, in practice, located too broadly for a focused, selective scan to capture. A broadly inclusive oral history project, therefore, seems the only way to record this work and map it into an accurate history.

These memories, narratives and, above all, self-curated professional collections of graphic design show that such a history can define and create itself (as it has) without having occurred in, and without having been directed from, any single place. The memories of designers in Canada have clearly been organized and shaped in comparison with a vast range of images and reproductions. The early efforts of art historians, beginning in the nineteenth century, focused on the identification and collection of the most important images, on the assumption that only specific standards of beauty merited display, in museums, as reproductions in books or as slides in school libraries. Given the present rate of digitization of virtually every fragment of visual culture, however, the very success and scale of this enterprise creates new and different opportunities. Susan Buck-Morss discusses the potential of a visual memory that escapes local containment:

Images are the archive of collective memory. The twentieth century distinguishes itself from all previous centuries because it has left a photographic trace. What is seen only once and recorded, can be perceived any time and by all. History becomes the shared singularity of an event. The complaint that images are taken out of context (cultural context, artistic intention, previous contexts of any sort) is not valid. To struggle to bind them again to their source is not only impossible (as it actually produces a new meaning); it is to miss what is powerful about them, their capacity to generate meaning, and not merely to transmit it.[8]

Precisely because it is not thus bound within national boundaries, nor to any single, dominant narrative or aesthetic, Canadian graphic design might be said to be a powerful generator of meaning and one which opens several questions about the very location of histories and meanings.

Memory and History

My intention in recording and teaching this history is to attempt to lengthen professional memories, beyond immediate experience of the contemporary environment and beyond individual preferences or available business records. Writing and lecturing about that history inevitably shapes memory; the production of new meaning alters existing meanings, changing their metaphorical valence or voltage. History changes how designers and students consider the past by getting beyond their pasts, and thus changes how they imagine their future. But memory, importantly, is not history; history must act as the collective reconsideration and reflection upon the written and remembered record. At a recent conference, 'New Views: Repositioning Graphic Design History', at the London College of Communication, a number of participants very clearly asserted that memory and history were not identical; in the words of Judith Williamson, 'memory masquerades as history'.[9]

Others have written about this important distinction, notably Pierre Nora. In his studies of France's many *lieux de mémoire*, its realms or sites of memory, Nora examines the way that ideas and values adhere to things, both material and immaterial – locales, images, buildings, symbols and so on. His work analyses 'the construction of representations',[10] the richly symbolic stories that make up the imagined, remembered community of a place. This process comes about, he argues, because 'there are no longer any ... settings in which memory is a real part of everyday experience'.[11] The loss of memory, of lived, daily ritual and continuous shared traditions unique to any single place, results in a mania for the past, for collecting and hoarding things, in an attempt to fill the void left by 'churches, schools, families, governments [that] no longer transmit traditional values as they once did'.[12]

Nevertheless, however important the study of such ideological sites – the Eiffel Tower, a painting by Eugène Delacroix, a tri-coloured flag – in suggesting that history is a pale substitute for living memory other, greater problems arise. Nora suggests a specific metaphor for memory: 'memory is life, always embodied in living societies'.[13] This is a dangerous choice of words, as though a national 'body', or any body, were some natural, authentic or organic site for memories, or that memory might be outside history, prior to those social institutions or collections that only sever memory from its original, true site. (Anyway, do we want 'traditional values' transmitted as they once were?) Tony Bennett suggests that 'the opposition at work here is profoundly disabling'.[14] He argues instead that 'all memory is necessarily archival and technical'.[15] While carried in the body, it is nonetheless shaped and socially organized by the media, mechanics and technologies of memory in any given society (and the prevailing powers that employ them). This is not entirely a limitation or loss, either, for it is 'only through their detachment from an immanent tradition that cultural artifacts can become the objects of self-conscious theoretical attention'.[16] For this reason, memory and history must be kept distinct. Yet, they need not be seen as strictly opposed; because they work to frame and shape each other, a collected or contested, but above all public historical account should be seen as the realization of memory, generating common visible traces that in turn provide the armature for further remembering.

Graphic design history in Canada, in its oral, uncollected state, might be said to be apocryphal: not false, but not yet publicly captured or verifiable either, questionable or dubious, perhaps, but not simply wrong. Edward S. Casey distinguishes between kinds of human memory: individual memories (which may be unique, but not created in isolation from or without reference and responsibility to other kinds of memory); social memories (shared by a linked group, without necessarily having wide dissemination); collective memories (broadly shared by several individuals without any conscious link or proximate relationship) and public memories (which include all of the above in an active, open, shared and above all 'contested' resource).[17] In its unformed state, graphic design history in Canada leans rather more toward the former two than the latter pair. Only the last, public memory, by virtue of its openness, is capable of generating history. It will be through the creation and expansion of the public institutions and technologies of collection and history that designers' memories can be made public, placed within a historical narrative, theorized and kept 'alive'.

Given that a public sharing of memories is the key to establishing their historicity, there is also a body of collectively developed principles for assessing the historical truth of what oral historians record. Is a given statement valid, does it stand comparison with other known, external sources? Is a given source internally reliable, is it consistent with itself? Is the information verifiable, can it be authenticated or checked? Are the memories from direct, first-hand experience, or are they hearsay? Is the speaker generally of sound mind?[18] Finally, though not least, what was the role of the interviewer in shaping the questions, as this inevitably introduces an entirely new set of variables? How have the questions been framed? (It is worth noting in this context that large corporate research firms, in addition to polls and surveys, have begun tracking the vast range of unasked opinion that mushrooms daily on the web, in chat rooms and blogs, because 'participants in discussion groups can say anything they like, whereas people answering a survey answer only the questions that researchers think to ask'.[19]) Histories, unlike memories, must be open to the active cross-examination of all these issues. As Paul Thompson notes, one can ask a farmer 'precisely how he handled his horses while ploughing, and it will be very, very rare for him to be wrong'.[20] Professional details and specifics of the trade are not likely to be subject to intense scrutiny or hotly contested; what matters is the historical framework that emerges when writing oral memory into design history.

Of course, despite our best efforts to establish veracity, memories vary. The distinction between different kinds of memory is parsed out by Elizabeth Loftus in her essay 'Tricked by Memory'.[21] Semantic memory, for example is the recollection of specific details and factual information, such as times tables, and is generally more heavily reinforced and reliable. Episodic memory, by contrast, is the narrative flow of a life or career and, while also reinforced over time, tends to be altered or polished by repeated reflection, in consideration of an individual's changing needs and in light of later events. Different kinds of memory require different reconsideration. There is also the (mis)shaping of memory by the desire to write a certain kind of history. The story is often told of how the Canadian National railways (CN) logo, a totemic image in the Canadian Modernist narrative, was drawn on a napkin in a moment of inspiration by Allan Fleming. Sketches in the National Library confirm another story: that the design involved many rough and intermediate sketches, by Fleming and others, in a process art directed by James Valkus, a designer brought in by CN from New York. Fleming played an important design role, but the napkin anecdote must finally be said to be folklore. As such it is, finally, not true; but the story can play more than a negative or obstructive role nonetheless. It is a perfect example of a *lieu de mémoire* in Nora's sense, and its mythical status usefully points to widely held ideas about design, throwing common beliefs – about the sanctity of the creative individual, or the highly personal nature of creativity – into sharp relief. In discussing the work of Fernand Braudel, Bill Schwarz notes that certain interior memories or narrative explanations might be studied in the same way as shamanism or mysticism: they might 'become the object of history, but never the means by which history itself is explained'.[22] The story of the CN logo-on-a-napkin tells us about how design sees its history, but does not tell us the history itself.

In 'Believe it or Not: Rethinking the Historical Interpretation of Memory',[23] Paul Thompson refers to collective memory as the means by which literate societies record, shape and reuse events (and non-events, such as Fleming's imagined moment of solo genius), and he equates this process to the oral traditions of non-literate societies. He defends oral history, arguing that memory is not simply shaped to serve the needs of the present (or by such needs in the past, whence memories come). Functional or instrumental distortions of memory can be overcome with sufficient application to detail, he argues. Memories play an important part in the construction of history, as remembered events and traditions do have genuine links to the past in ways that make them useful to the historical record. Thompson gives the example of apprentice bakers recounting years of hardship, while those who become masters tell of their wonderfully useful and productive training. This suggests that different accounts of history may come from the same general experience, depending on the outcome and the present perspective of the narrators, without either being false. History must capture both of these lived spaces.

Those graphic designers whose work is singled out by other designers in Canada for recognition and historical importance are, of course, the masters (both male and female) of their trade, and their narrative accounts will be similarly affected, whether denigrated or enhanced. Reading back against the grain of what is actually said, checking it against other sources, recognizing the subject position of the source, paying attention to specific factual details and getting beyond personal myth and received ideas are all essential to assembling such interviews and opinions into a more reliable historical record. Alex Callinicos describes history as 'provid[ing] a framework within which [culture] can be understood, not as a free-floating process, but as the ways in which human beings located in contradictory relations of production seek to make sense of the world, and develop strategies for coping with, and sometimes for changing it'.[24]

Issues in Oral History

Oral history in design is motivated by different circumstances from those found in histories of folklore, which make up the majority of oral histories. Folklore is that set of common practices, everyday information and habit spread by informal communication, but which specifically excludes professional or mass-produced, popular cultures (and hence the study of design).[25] Design history is hardly a history of the illiterate or the oppressed, but of individuals highly literate in both verbal and visual means. Indeed, in some accounts of oral history, professional graphic design is counted among the enemy. If oral history is defined as a political tool that finds a voice for marginalized groups, 'a tool for clarifying the past and reshaping the present',[26] then design's easy proximity to mass media make it, to some, part of the problem. As Michael Riordan sees it, the battle to establish a dominant mode of vision is imbalanced: 'in a media-soaked culture, they simply stupefy us'.[27] So oral history, in its application to design, must take into account that its subject places it outside some of the most common purposes for which oral history is employed.

Nonetheless, there are also useful similarities among otherwise very different uses for oral history. In discussing *The Artists Behind the Work, a Study of Four Alaskan Artists*, William Schneider notes that 'Native art has a social, ceremonial and utilitarian role that is different from Western art',[28] which is overly concerned with display and spectacle. He contrasts this with the practical, hands-on and everyday uses of Native Alaskan media such as masks, blankets and bead-work. Artists in small-scale communities display a continuing interest in such concerns as craft or manual skill, the use of objects as gifts and exchange or of such exchanges as markers of status and symbols of identity, and a preference for group standards and collaborative assessment rather than competition over individual creativity or innovation. Interestingly, Schneider might here be said to be inadvertently also describing many of the values retained in the practice of contemporary designers. The strong affinity of design with such visual cultures marks it as an applied, non-art, something to be used, in common, and through openly commodified exchanges of visual and material value. This description also captures how design, like the traditional arts of small-scale cultures, is best understood as positioned outside the dominant visual discourse, that of the fine arts.

Nonetheless, despite all similarities, it must be accepted that the scale and nature of modern mass media have changed the usual goals in the gathering and recording of oral traditions. The ethnography of Franz Boas, to take on originary example, was known for its extraordinary cultural relativism and inclusiveness and for breaking open the collecting habits of Western museums. Design studies research, on the contrary, can all too easily demonstrate an enormous visual variety. Variety is precisely what professional marketing and communications demand, and the design field is indeed highly varied. Neither can design in any way be described as a 'vanishing' culture, as has often been the case with anthropological studies. (The idea of small-scale cultures as 'primitive' or in need of isolation or preservation has been strongly rejected in any event.[29]) Design history is, to borrow a term from Eric Hobsbawm and Terence Ranger, evidence of an invented tradition, one which claims a long and antique history (from cave walls and Mesopotamian markings to Renaissance Europe), but which is, instead, largely a relatively recent product of the industrial revolution, mass marketing and the enormous rise in technological scale of the last century and a half.[30] It does not fit neatly with the goals of even a progressive anthropology.

Because design is a profession, collecting such oral histories could perhaps best be described as 'elite oral history', a category discussed by Eva M. McMahan.[31] She observes that such interviews are transactional, subject to the wilful intent of both interviewer and subject. Political or cultural elites do command social position and power, such that they can create and foster 'a lore that justifies their attempts to control society'.[32] The elite subject cooperates in order to control interpretation. McMahan notes that interpretation is central to human existence; however, in the 'new hermeneutics'[33] that she applies, neither the researcher nor the narrator controls the 'real' meaning. The search is not for authorial intention as the final, correct interpretation: the researcher/author of the history and the narrator/author of the original designs probably have differing, even opposing, intentions in any event.

There are also important implications in the values inherent in designers' descriptions of their own work. Like an ethnographer's system of ethnopoetic notation, designers share a formal language to describe the visual: terms such as 'freshness', for example, or 'originality', which both mark the extraordinary importance of innovation in the design field. This loose verbal system makes frequent reference to shared markers, in particular the work of other well-known designers (many of whom are international, of course), and above all the single great reference point for the description of postwar design, the International Style, which still figures prominently even in the memories of those designers born long after its eclipse. Such terms and their transcription into history provide an opportunity to critically examine the normative biases built into language. For example, could postwar graphic design in Canada be usefully described and historicized without any reference to the 'modern'?

Modernism has been seen as many things, of course: as the inevitable aesthetic response to capitalist modernity; as the best means of rebuilding a better, brighter, more functional world or as the nightmare of a technocratic and monolithic class culture imposed from above. Nonetheless, its primary use in contemporary visual cultural studies remains as a marker of historical originality and canonical importance. The most 'advanced' work is assumed to be the most original and the most important. Interestingly though, the concepts of 'modernism' and the term 'modern' do not figure prominently, if at all, in the interviews I have conducted. This is not to say that we are lacking any consensus on who are the most important designers. The same local and Canadian names recur in designers' recorded narratives, within cities but also across the country. This has been confirmed to me by the steady repetition of particular names – 'oh, have you interviewed…?'; 'do you know the work of…?' It speaks to a continuing, immanent process of canon formation, one which is, crucially, more than the product of individual or centred, institutional judgements of taste or quality. The canon of Canadian design, in other words, is not bounded by any simple, clearly stated principle, such as 'modernism', or its relative state of 'advance'. It would logically follow that we require a broad process of discovery to locate it.

There is, then, even within the limitations of memory and oral tradition, an extensive shared vocabulary and canonical consensus within the country about the main players in that history. This consensus is also shared to a remarkable degree between English-speaking Canada and the distinct national culture of Québec. Such a broadly agreed, largely oral tradition also goes a considerable way towards establishing a history based on something more stable than aesthetic choices. It suggests a mutual assessment of importance based on many factors, a collective judgement or even just grudging acknowledgement that draws on more than visual standards of pleasure: knowledge of others' clientele, jobs and positions held; their role in educational or other institutions; those with whom they worked in the past; the success of their designs for their clients' purposes and so on. The history that emerges from the memories and oral accounts of Canadian designers itself suggests that design is inherently an important counterpart to the concerns and practices that have shaped visual collections and institutions to date. Because it forms the basis of cultural capital in the profession of design, and because it establishes and enforces actual markers of social position, identifying a visual canon is a necessity, one recognized and defended as such by Canadian designers, however unconsciously, in their verbal narratives.

The canonical visual record of modern design is often selected for its simplicity, or its disciplined control of typography, forms, shapes and images. Since the idea of the modern as simplicity [34] does not adequately cover our understanding of the present, it should be possible, in fact necessary, to write a history of design, post-1945, which does not use the terms 'Modernist' or 'Modernism'. (As a term for the dominant social fact of our age, it cannot similarly dispense with 'modernity'.) It could simply be argued, however, that design history is made up of a succession of professionally selected, abstract visual devices, historically determined but with no particular logic of their own. It should be possible, in effect, to 'sample' the field as the designers themselves have sampled it, as a heteroglossia, locating as significant those works that practitioners themselves have found significant for a variety of reasons. These will not be necessarily the most obviously *avant-garde* works, nor those that best represent the aesthetic of simplicity, difficulty or any other single visual value. Any canon does reduce the field, but it need not be filtered through any single aesthetic, nor even, in all cases, through the aesthetic per se, at all. The method of visual cultural studies, in design as in any visual production, must be to place aesthetic affinities in their context, not to exalt or isolate them (which is only to distort the aesthetic in any event). To do so, we must be 'meticulously attentive to the local, the contingent and the conjunctural'. [35]

Conclusion

As a method of investigation, oral history attends quite closely to the local, even as it works to understand it in its increasingly global context. It reports on the judgements of interest and importance as formulated by a diverse and broad association of practitioners – in the case of design, by designers consciously sharing a tradition and a profession, often at a distance from each other, but living in the shared space of design, professionally linked across the borders of any one country. It is therefore necessary to use oral history to sample the visual field of design history as broadly as possible, to arrive at a widely inclusive and plural history. The assumption that extraordinary, difficult, *avant-garde* practices might be the only oppositional space in culture, powerful as it has been, remains a fantasy.[36]

In trying to locate Canadian graphic design, then, the process has necessitated a reconsideration of the methods of visual culture and some reflection on the location and meaning of memory and history. Understood for its apocryphal content, the stories told by designers are not necessarily always true (although most are), but they do yield evidence that points to important truths. The best means for the study of design is close attention to the forms it takes and the understandings of its practitioners, their arbitrary visual selections and their supporting myths. Such ideas are all evidence of design's usefulness, its location – even its absolute necessity – for the reproduction of capital in a world of images. In scanning across the surface of graphic design in Canada, we can get a picture, albeit in somewhat reduced resolution, of a space far larger than just design.

Brian Donnelly is a professor in the York/Sheridan Joint Program in Design, at Sheridan Institute, Oakville. First published in *Journal of Design History* vol. 19, no. 4, 2006.

1   Brian Donnelly, 'Reading Kurschenska: On the Centres and Boundaries of Design History', unpublished paper delivered at the Universities Art Association of Canada annual conference, Montreal, October, 2001.

2   It should be noted that the province of Québec, with its distinct national history, has produced some important exceptions, in particular *L'Affiche au Québec* (Montréal: Les Éditions de l'Homme, 2001) and the section on graphic design in *Le Design au Québec* (Montréal: Les Éditions de l'Homme, 2003) both by Marc H. Choko, director of the Centre de design at the Université du Québec à Montréal. Posters, in particular, have been covered; see Robert Stacey, *The Canadian Poster Book: 100 Years of the Poster in Canada, Toronto* (Toronto: Methuen, 1979). There have been a number of focused historical articles, which usefully go beyond posters (and beyond Québec), particularly in the journal *DA (Devil's Artisan)*, the trade journal *Applied Arts* and the *Graphic Design Journal*, published by the Society of Graphic Designers of Canada.

3   Besides Innis' own late works on communication, notably *Empire and Communications* (1950), and *The Bias of Communication* (1951), an excellent short introduction is provided in 'The Communication Thought of Harold Adams Innis (1894–1952)', ch. 3 of Robert E. Babe, *Canadian Communication Thought: Ten Foundational Writers* (Toronto: University of Toronto Press, 2000).

4   Philip B. Meggs, *Meggs' History of Graphic Design*, 4th edn (Toronto: John Wiley & Sons, 2005).

5   Design Industry Advisory Committee, DIAC Design Industry Study, Toronto, 2004, *www.dx.org/diac.html*

6   Theo Dimson, *Great Canadian Posters* (Toronto: Oxford University Press, 1979).

7   Robert Bringhurst, *The Elements of Typographic Style*, 3rd edn (Point Roberts, WA: Hartley & Marks, 2004).

8   Susan Buck-Morss, 'Visual Studies and Global Imagination', *Papers of Surrealism*, no. 2 (Summer 2004), *www.surrealismcentre.ac.uk/publications/papers/journal2*

9   Author's notes, from panel discussion on 'Memory and History', including Anne Bush, Judith Williamson, Val Williams and Kerry William-Purcell, Saturday, 29 October 2005.

10 Pierre Nora, *Realms of Memory*, Lawrence D. Kritzman, ed., trans. Arthur Goldhammer (New York: Columbia University Press, 1996), p.xxi.

11 Ibid., p.1.

12 Ibid., p.2.

13 Ibid., p.3.

14 Tony Bennett, 'Stored Virtue: Memory, the Body, and the Evolutionary Museum', in Susannah Radstone and Katharine Hodgkin, eds., *Regimes of Memory* (New York: Routledge, 2003), p.41.

15 Ibid., p.52.

16 Ibid., p.42.

17 Ed Casey, 'Public Memory in Place and Time', in Kendall Phillips, ed., *Framing Public Memory* (Tuscaloosa: University of Alabama Press, 2004), p.17–44.

18 William Schneider, … *So They Understand: Cultural Issues in Oral History* (Logan: Utah State University Press, 2002), p.129.

19 'Listening to the Internet', in *Technology Quarterly* (supplement, *The Economist* (11 March 2006), p.8.

20 Paul Thompson, *The Voice of the Past: Oral History*, 3rd edn (Oxford: Oxford University Press, 2000), p.158.

21 Elizabeth Loftus, 'Tricked by Memory', in Jaclyn Jeffrey and Glenace Edwall, eds., *Memory and History: Essays on Recalling and Interpreting Experience* (Lanham: University Press of America, 1994), p.17–32.

22 Bill Schwarz, 'Already the Past': Memory and Historical Time', in Susannah Radstone and Katharine Hodgkin, op.cit., p.141. Schwarz notes that, for Braudel, memory was to be seen not only as distinct from history but also as its enemy.

23 Paul Thompson, 'Believe It or Not: Rethinking the Historical Interpretation of Memory', in Jaclyn Jeffrey and Glenace Edwall, eds., op.cit., p.1–16.

24 Alex Callinicos, 'Marxism and the Crisis of Social History', in John Rees, ed., *Essays on Historical Materialism* (London: Bookmarks, 1998), p.25–40.

25 Martha Sims and Martine Stephens, *Living Folklore* (Logan: Utah State University Press, 2005), p.1 ff.

26 Michael Riordan, *An Unauthorized Biography of the World: Oral History on the Front Lines* (Ontario: Between the Lines Press, 2004), p.6.

27 Ibid., p.2.

28 William Schneider, 2002, op.cit., p.95 ff.

29 See James Clifford, Minh-Ha Trinh and Virginia Dominguez, 'Of Other People's: Beyond the "Salvage" Paradigm', in Hal Foster, ed., *Discussions in Contemporary Culture* (New York: Bay Press, 1987), p.121–50.

30 While their examples tend to the social, as, for example the British monarchy or Scottish tartans, it is a concept usefully applied to design. It might be especially useful in understanding what great significance is assumed to be attached to contemporary design by tracing its roots to the shapes of ancient alphabets and other pieces of distant or pre-modern history. See Eric Hobsbawm and Terence Ranger, eds., *The Invention of Tradition* (Cambridge: Cambridge University Press, 1983).

31 Eva M. McMahan, *Elite Oral History Discourse: A Study of Cooperation and Coherence* (Tuscaloosa: University of Alabama Press, 1989).

32 Ibid., p.xiv.

33 Ibid., p.2.

34 This narrative has been recently and cogently summarized by Paul Greenhalgh in *The Modern Ideal: The Rise and Collapse of Idealism in the Visual Arts* (London: V&A Publications, 2005).

35 Ibid., p.39.

36 This argument has recently been remade by Hal Foster, in *Design and Crime* (New York: Verso, 2002).

REORIENT: GRAPHIC DESIGN HISTORY FROM A GLOBOLOGICAL PERSPECTIVE

WEN HUEI CHOU
2006

Abstract

To counter East Asia's marginalization in graphic design history, this research looks at graphic design history in Taiwan as an example and argues for a reconsideration of design history from deeper historical and globological perspectives. The meta-discourses of Euro-American Modernism and Post-Modernism constitute the roots of privileged and prejudicial knowledge in relation to the history of graphic design, establishing Western development as the yardstick for the production of design history. Substantive frameworks for shaping design history are necessary; however, such frameworks are, like historical conditions, subject to change. The recent rise of East Asian economies focuses attention on their culture, including their cultural heritage, which has had a world historical influence over fields as diverse as writing, printing and design. Acknowledging this historical influence is fundamental to the development of East Asian localities as distinctive graphic design spheres, while widening the scope for culture-based knowledge and understanding to reorient aspects of homogenous Western design.

The objective of the present research is to encourage debate and offer a critique of the classification methods and focus of mainstream design history, especially as it reflects on the past, present and future circumstances of Taiwanese graphic design.

Westernized Design History

William Addison Dwiggins first used the expression 'graphic design' in 1922 to address the seeming lack of professionalism of commercial art (Meggs, 1998). In particular, the phrase was meant to signify that Dwiggins' work had gone beyond mere graphic printing and employed professional rules of design and principles of visual styling. Since Dwiggins distinguished graphic design's need for professional recognition, and from its beginnings in printing and commercial promotion, graphic design has morphed into a range of specialties, creating new terminology as it diversified into brand, communication, identity, interface and information design.

The comparative newness of the term 'graphic design' has had important ramifications for the construction of graphic design history. As John A. Walker posits in *Design History and the History of Design* (1989), before design was considered a distinct professional field it was conventionally classified under the category of 'art' – a classification that influenced many research methodologies and historiographic perspectives of design history.

Over the last two decades, other writers have called for those perspectives and approaches absorbed into design history from art history to be reviewed. Such writers include Tony Fry, whose work *Design History Australia* identified the dilemma of historical exclusion for all national design cultures considered peripheral to the economic, technical, cultural and geographic axis of Euro-America.

In his influential work, Fry argues that due to Australia's geographic position removed from the 'centre of the world', relatively small population, low market output and limited internationalization, it has been seen as a nation almost devoid of design. Fry urged design historians and students to take into account Australia's unique perspective on the material world in which it is embedded and that it transforms.

Fry's point did not fall on deaf ears, prompting considerable reflection on the integrity of Australian design and the development of Australian design history as a postcolonial project. Fry himself, in his paper 'A Geography of Power: Design History and Marginality' (1989), specifically discusses the marginalization, if not outright neglect of Australian design past and present, arguing for a systematic and regionally specific design history to be conducted in response to the territorial biases of general histories of design. In contrast to the canonical account of design presented in such a histories, an Australian design history would explore the nature and nurture factors that enabled the rewriting of design history specific to Australia, simultaneously uncovering the reasons for why its history has been ignored. Bradford R. Collins further argues that after Post-Modernism, issues of bias against women and minorities in art historical research have been sufficiently challenged to invalidate the tendency to establish categorically exclusive canons of design and designers (1995). Collins concludes that the preference for aesthetics (in the case of connoisseurship), or authorial intent and art historical forces (in the case of canonization), has been so extensively questioned as to require much greater inclusiveness and reflection in the narration of design history, especially given its significant impact on contemporary design thinking and activity.

Design history and criticism, however, continue to be influenced by three main hypotheses of cultural change: art history (art archaeology, monography, autobiography and style); Modernism (capitalism, industrialization, functionalism, technology and progress); and social science (material culture). Histories of design are still mainly accounts of the *oeuvres* of single designers or design or manufacturing companies, or works of connoisseurship. For Ellen Mazur Thomson, the focus in design history on particular designers' stories severely skews the knowledge of broad cultural forces that design history should provide (2001). The cultural imperialism of a large part of the corpus of design history is beyond doubt, written as it is precisely by those who constitute the discipline. But this does not mean that artifacts and an associated system of values have not developed in other cultures. Quite the contrary: each and every culture has its unique perspective on the material world in which it is embedded and that it transforms.

Graphic Design History in Globalization

The effects of globalization at the end of the twentieth century enjoin us to beware of the domination of capitalism and Modernism – which exerted such powerful influence on research in numerous fields – leading to a clearer direction and adding support to often neglected areas of research. Many recent seminars held by the *Design History Society Annual Conference* indicate a will to expand the geographic horizons of graphic design history, as did the 2002 *International Conference on Design History and Design Studies* entitled 'Mind the Map: Design History beyond Borders', while journals such as *Design Issues* and *Journal of Design History* have pointed out the urgency and importance of redrawing the map of world design and rethinking design history. Jonathan M. Woodham sparked debate on design history and set the tone for subsequent research by arguing that it should be aimed at what was 'missing' or 'never been seen' in mainstream surveys of design (Woodham, 2005; see also Chou, 2005). As François Furet has emphasized, however, the history of graphic design is different, as present values influence the framing of knowledge of the past and especially the understanding of historical facts (Furet, 1985). Analysis of the 'present' has to include historical investigation at different levels. Current research has indicated the importance of the unique contribution other visions would bring, and which set of values they would foster, especially from those regions that have been considered marginal for so long. Although, as Arjun Appadurai has argued, culture in late capitalism is tied to broad global forces, the traffic is not all one way, with the central tension in the contemporary world being that between 'cultural homogenization and cultural heterogenization' (1996). Appadurai confirms that a substantial amount of empirical evidence can be marshaled to demonstrate the influence of Euro-American, and especially American cultures as the hegemonic force the early 21st century, through the influence of their economies and media. But external forces are rapidly localizing in one or more dimensions and, as Appadurai argues, Americanization is not always the most pressing hegemonic force. In the case of Taiwan, one only has to consider the power and influence of China, although the former's sense of marginalization from the world at large (and consequent interest in Euro-American cultures) is exacerbated by its political exclusion from the World Trade Organization and other supranational institutions. For the health and development of Taiwanese design, it is critical that we rebuild our design characteristics and capabilities from scratch on the basis of solid historical research into what Taiwanese design has been.

Taiwanese culture can no longer be seen through centre-periphery structures. As Terry Eagleton proposes, 'global perspective' or 'global thinking' does not necessarily mean the centralization of global power, but rather the integration of domestic and indigenous criteria into global networks against a tide of irreversible loss (2005). The situatedness of Australian design is relevant here: Simon Jackson observes that Denmark, Italy, Japan and Sweden have been much more successful in developing economically sustainable and culturally specific design traditions than Australia (2002). He attributes this to the design traditions of those nations starting earlier than Australia, and their strong desire to present their cultural individuality to the world. For Jackson, however, Australia enjoys a certain natural and geographic uniqueness, which led to the early pioneers adapting tools, for example, to their particular environmental conditions. Jackson underscores the value of this focus on design expertise; for example, he suggests that 'Australian industrial design' should be called 'design activity in Australia'. This shift would move the emphasis towards the design needs and related fields in Australia, and away from mimicry of mainstream trends.

These observations on the fostering of uniqueness in Australian design are applicable, I would argue, to Taiwanese design and design education.

Design History in Taiwan

According to Wendy Siuyi Wong (2001, 2005), Chinese design history is hardly heard or seen, beginning in earnest only in 1979. Matthew Turner – one of the few historians to consider Chinese design history – adds that the design history of Hong Kong before 1960 'was believed not to exist' (1995). Wong believes the reason modern Chinese design history had not been taken into account by the West prior to this date was because before the 'open gate' policy of China, enforced in 1979, most design took the form of communist propaganda, whereas design activity in Taiwan was seen to be inspired and influenced by Hong Kong, and the main area of development was between Hong Kong and Mainland China (Wong, 1995). If we look at the past thirty years of design theory and activity in Taiwan, most of the salient examples are of 'modernist design', reflecting an eagerness to adopt the style of the capitalistic metropolis and

European society. Moreover, the design history of China and other Asian countries (with the exception of Japan) is considered an imitation of the cultural value systems of Western industrialized countries. Focusing on this imitative aspect has led Western nations to neglect the development and value of design in these areas (Chou, 2005; Wong, 2001). Worse, these industrialized countries considered the output of developing Asian nations as of their own making, as duplicating and producing design for/from them.

Aside from this cultural bias, graphic design history research in Taiwan faces another challenge. Although the first design association was founded in 1962, and despite a small number of relevant design associations – including the Packaging Design Association, Graphic Design Association, Designers Association, Poster Design Association, and the Chinese Institute of Design – graphic design history research in Taiwan has lacked sufficient peer cooperation and resources. On the one hand, current graphic design history research in Taiwan has been understood as a subsection of architectural history and fine art history, or subsumed under cultural and social research. Until recently, research in the fields of architecture, industrial design, and craft history could afford to make statements on behalf of graphic design history, which contributed to stunting the development of Taiwanese graphic design history in contrast to the rapid expansion of graphic design practice. On the other hand, within the field of graphic design history itself, three debilitating factors can be isolated. First, there is a shortage in existing Taiwanese graphic design history circles of communities to share and discuss information. Very few researchers and educators who have dug up rare sources of information and completed study projects have made their contributions available to the public. Second, the research itself has directed graphic design history towards capitalism or histories of style, out of lack of accurate knowledge of graphic design history. In fact, much uncovered historical evidence goes against some of the main principles of modern graphic design history, which researchers desperately want to establish. Finally, efforts to establish a professional field of graphic design history research in Taiwan have so far not been profitable.

Not only do we need to shift the focus of graphic history research away from marginalization, but we need to bring the quality of design principles (as opposed to the splendor of artworks or new technology) into full view. For this, we must recognize that design activity and behavior are inevitable products of commercialized and industrialized society. Indeed, since it is now given that design activity is imbedded in its social context, it is impossible to investigate the development of existing graphic design history by completely excluding or denying the great impact of modernization, industrialization and capitalism. Yet after being blinded by the latter for so long, we finally have the chance and capability to reveal their hegemony over our cultural discourses. In the case of Taiwan, contending with the force of (post)colonial influences, while also investigating modern acculturation and seeking multiple approaches to historical interpretation, brings us to the native literature debates of the 1970s. The arguments of this controversial movement have left lasting marks in areas as diverse as literature, fine art, music and dance. It helped loosen the autocratic authority of imported regimes, and enriched and hastened the hybridisation of Taiwanese culture. The native literature movement is clear evidence of Pieterse's interpretation of 'postcoloniality', in which we endeavor to recognize the inevitable hegemony and absolute essentiality of primordial ties, both endogenous and exogenous, while rebuilding the energy and character of contemporary culture (Pieterse, 1995; Conces, 2005).

To study the history of graphic design and education in Taiwan, we must therefore understand the history of the early migrants from the Southern mainland, the living conditions and utensils used by aborigines, the influences of fine art design and the industrial revolution under Japanese rule, of coastal cities and Hong Kong, and take race, colonialism, manufacturing and production practices, as well as the shifting political environment, into consideration. At the same time, we must tie our research into the current industrial structure, economical development and cultural and political status of Taiwan. Only when this has been realized can research into Taiwanese graphic design history get away from the limited interpretations based on the effects of 'mass production', 'style analysis' and the 'canon' of Modernism, and arrive at a deeper history of graphic design in Taiwan from a globalized viewpoint. It is vital – especially as it is now profitable to produce work on design history from within 'marginalized' areas – that this history not be based merely on a historical viewpoint of the past and that it should encapsulate new viewpoints and research methods.

As I have argued, design is the product of Modernism and industrialized society, and historical research cannot dismiss the fact that graphic design history perspectives and methodologies have been shaped by Euro-American hegemony (Kaelble, 2005). While such attitudes may now appear biased, they have inevitably conditioned the information upon which we base our research. On the other hand, emerging nations have for a long time endeavored to pursue and imitate Western cultures, hoping to get a chance for presentation, expression and recognition. Once at the epicenter of power, Western powers must be alarmed that the world no longer corresponds to their own image, since they could not see the design from the non-industrialized, non-capitalist world coming. Countries like Taiwan – but also Turkey, Mexico, India, Brazil and Cuba – are now in a position to rewrite and reinterpret their own their local design cultures and histories (Margolin, 2005). After deconstructing Western approaches to research, we are now in a position to return to the native cultural characteristics specific to particular, once 'marginalised' nations (Uriarte, 2005).

This will enable graphic design history research to be undertaken with self-determination according to the culture's design activity and socio-cultural factors, and to outlast its status as the latest hot topic of globalization.

Wen Huei Chou is Associate Professor at National Yunlin University of Science and Technology, Taiwan.

Home ›

THE ART OF DESIGNER BIOGRAPHIES: AN INTERVIEW KERRY WILLIAM PURCELL

Article by Steven Heller December 26, 2006.
Filed Under: ,

Kerry William Purcell, author of the Phaidon books on Alexey Brodovitch, Josef Müller-Brockmann, as well as an unpublished text on Herbert Matter, has been writing about designers and photographers (Weegee) for many years. His thorough texts document the lives of these storied practitioners, but do they go further than to build a glorified resume? In this interview, Purcell examines and critiques the art and craft of writing professional biographies, and the problems that arise when the families of the subjects do not authorize the works.

Steven Heller: How and why did you become a graphic design biographer?

Kerry William Purcell: Well, firstly, I wouldn't really define myself exclusively as a "graphic design biographer." Although I have now written three design biographies (one remains unpublished), my background was originally one of sociology and cultural theory. However, I have found that having a education that is not rooted solely in graphic design has proved of immense help in writing about design, especially in my book reviews and essays.

As to how I came to write these design books, it all started when I was an archivist at The Photographers' Gallery, London. Many students and researchers would come in to look at books and essays on such photographers as Robert Frank, Richard Avedon and Ted Croner. When going through this material, Alexey Brodovitch's name kept cropping up as an important influence in these figures lives. A friend of mine at the

THE ART OF DESIGNER BIOGRAPHIES:
AN INTERVIEW WITH KERRY WILLIAM PURCELL

STEVEN HELLER
2006

Kerry William Purcell, author of the Phaidon books on Alexey Brodovitch, Josef Müller-Brockmann, as well as an unpublished text on Herbert Matter, has been writing about designers and photographers for many years. His thorough texts document the lives of these storied practitioners, but do they go further than build a glorified résumé? In this interview, Purcell examines and critiques the art and craft of writing professional biographies, and the problems that arise when the families of the subjects do not authorize the works.

Steven Heller: How and why did you become a graphic design biographer?

Kerry William Purcell: Well, firstly, I wouldn't really define myself exclusively as a 'graphic design biographer.' Although I have now written three design biographies (one remains unpublished), my background was originally in sociology and cultural theory. However, I have found that having an education that is not rooted solely in graphic design has proved of immense help in writing about design, especially in my book reviews and essays.

As to how I came to write these design books, it all started when I was an archivist at The Photographers' Gallery, London. Many students and researchers would come in to look at books and essays on such photographers as Robert Frank, Richard Avedon and Ted Croner. When going through this material, Alexey Brodovitch's name kept cropping up as an important influence in these figures' lives. A friend of mine at the gallery, the photographer Ed Dimsdale, shared this curiosity about Brodovitch, and we decided to make a documentary film of his life. So, entirely self-financed, we contacted Brodovitch's remaining family, colleagues and students, and traveled to New York and Paris to interview them. Unfortunately, once we returned to London, we had no funds left with which to continue the project. As the tapes gathered dust, I decided to write an article for *Baseline* magazine on Brodovitch. Karen Stein at Phaidon spotted my essay, and subsequently commissioned me to write a biography.

Photography has been your field, you even did a biography of Weegee. Where is the nexus between photography and design, and are the subjects you address always engaged in the two?

Well, as I came to graphics via photography, it has always been a particular interest of mine to know how designers use the photograph as an object in the design process (and frequently fail to credit the photographer!). Yet, while there have been a few 'how-to' books and brief histories of the image in design, it always amazes me that there has never been a comprehensive history of 'photo-graphics'. In fact, such an absence becomes all the more remarkable when we see that the development of graphic design as a profession intersects with the growing use of photography in print. Admittedly, this has begun to change with such works as Gerry Badger's and Martin Parr's two-volume study of the photobook. However, an analysis that explicitly examines the relationship between graphic design and photography is still missing.

My essays for *Baseline* on such publications as *Photographie* and *Camera* have been my small attempt to address this. In addition, my biographies on Brodovitch, Herbert Matter and, to a much lesser extent, Josef Müller-Brockmann, have touched on this broader history and attempted to document the lives of its key pioneers.

So far, and this is not meant as an insult, I have yet to read a real page-turner biography of a designer. At best, they are sprightly and at worst, academic, but the stories are all professional. How are design biographies different, say, from those on film stars, politicians and poets?

No insult taken! In fact, I am now very critical of my biography on Brodovitch. It was very much my apprenticeship, and I now see its many deficiencies. Although I received many wonderful reviews for the book, alongside a marvelous letter from Richard Avedon, knowing what I know now, I wish I could rewrite it. In principle, however, I would say that there should be no qualitative difference between a biography on, for example, a filmmaker, and one on a designer. Good writing is good writing, whatever the subject.

Still, there are some problems unique to graphic design biographies. One is that they are often part critique, part showcase of the designer's work. In terms of the layout of the book, you are often required to talk more directly about the work and less about the life. As such the personal/professional analysis is often a difficult balancing act. Maybe one of the reasons for the dearth of 'real page-turner' design biographies is that designers, rather than writers, have written many of them. I'm not saying designers can't write! But the level of research needed for a comprehensive biography is truly daunting, and the demands of a busy design workload would be an obstacle to any real engagement with the subject. Then again, I'm talking here as if we are inundated with biographies on graphic designers, and we are not!

In researching and writing a biography like that of Brodovitch or Müller-Brockmann, how much research do you do into the private lives of these figures? And once examined, how much to you cull from your final manuscript?

Well, this relates to the question above. If anyone is going to write a good biography, I feel nothing should be out of bounds. If the subject is still alive, or the family/estate is protective of the person's reputation, then, admittedly, you have to take this into account – you are often forced to take this into account! Yet, I believe if a biographer is going to write a comprehensive and engaging work, they must fundamentally disrespect their subject. What I mean by this is that to stop a work from becoming a mere promotional puff piece, a measure of critical distance is required that will preclude any easy rapport with your subject. With all the biographies I have written, people I interviewed told me stories about the designer that I knew the families would not want to be made public. As long as the interviewee was not harboring some personal resentment and the information was relevant to my account, then I have always used it. In my book on Müller-Brockmann, his widow did ask for a handful of her own quotations to be edited out. On this occasion, I was more than happy to do this since their removal did not damage the book as a whole.

When writing the 'authorized' biography, does an author have a kind of contract with either his subject or his subject's family? When you wrote your books, did you have to get approval from the wives, children and so on?

With Brodovitch, there was no estate as such. His collection was scattered across Europe and the US. This was partly as a result of Brodovitch giving his work away when old students used to come to visit him towards the end of his life. The only family member with any interest in his work was his nephew Michel Brodovitch who lived in Paris. I remember visiting him in his apartment and doing a double take, as he looked so much like his uncle! However, he really never wanted any involvement in the book.

With Müller-Brockmann, it was exactly the opposite. I worked very closely with his widow Shizuko Yoshikawa. She herself was once a designer (she trained at Ulm with Otl Aicher) and from the early drafts of the manuscript through to the layout she wanted to be involved. I was very pleased for her to read through my work, her insights into Swiss design and her late husbands life were extremely helpful.

I understand you finished an entire biography on Matter, but were unable to get rights to publish his work? What happened? As a biographer don't you, a priori, have the fair-use right to reproduce material that supports your text?

Increasingly the families and relations of graphic designers are assuming the traditional role of estates in a manner similar to those of artists or photographers. I feel there are certain problems with this. Unlike a painting or photograph, a graphic design object is often an amalgam. In her or his work, a designer may use a photograph taken by a contemporary photographer, then combine it with a typeface that was released by a foundry in the early nineteenth century, which is all then set by a printer. In addition, the completed design is a 'work for hire' that was bought and owned by the company who originally commissioned the work. Yet many families of designers are looking to retrospectively obtain full copyright control over their relation's work.

In my case, I was researching and writing a book on Matter, when I heard from an archivist at the Fotostiftung Schweiz archive (where they have an extensive Matter collection) that there was another Matter project underway. Of course, I was alarmed to hear this! So wanting to find out more, my editor at Phaidon tracked down this other project and set up a meeting with its initiator Alex Matter, Herbert Matter's son. All was looking positive until, allegedly, Alex Matter requested a sum of money for the reproduction of his father's work. As most design biography sales are, in the words of one editor, 'a bloodbath', the margins on these publications are so slight that the possibility of paying reproduction rights was never an option. Although the Fotostiftung Schweiz owns the copyright on the Matter work (and had previously published a book on Matter with Lars Müller) they were apparently unwilling to go ahead with any project without Alex Matter's say so. This was equally the case for Phaidon. That was nearly three years ago.

Without the Matter heirs' approval, how did you research his life?

As noted, the Fotostiftung Schweiz have a very good collection, including Matter's school books, diaries and early designs up until he left for America in 1936. I also visited Yale and MoMA to view small collections of his work there.

How do you decide who to write about? What factors must be in play for someone to rate a full-fledged biography? And at what point in a designer's life or death is he or she ripe?

Your own prodigious output aside, graphic design history is still a fairly young and under-researched discipline. There are numerous designers, art directors and so on who would be worthy candidates for a biography. Through my research, I have often come across figures I would like to write about in the future. Other key factors are whether there have been any previous books on the designer and how widely known he or she is. However, the real problem is finding publishers interested in pursuing such works. As already noted, in terms of sales, it is widely known that design biographies don't sell in any great numbers.

In recent years there seem to be more biographies, whereas 15 years ago there were none. What accounts for this surge? And do you think it will continue?

As a profession, I think we can trace an arc through the twentieth century, from the emergence of Modernism until the arrival of the computer, which serves as a very neat, self-contained story of graphic design (probably too neat). Within this story, there are numerous figures who played key roles in the development of the discipline. I don't think it's any surprise that, as this story reached its natural end, works began to appear, surmising the central players and periods. It should also be remembered that what we consider to be worthy of historical study today is very much determined by our own contemporary socio-economic and political climate.

History is not some objective thing out there, but is relived and retold with each new generation. Therefore, to know whether designers' biographies will continue to be published depends on many factors from how design is taught to inclinations of the publishing industry.

Unlike figures like Pablo Picasso or Andy Warhol, about whom numerous biographies have been written, there really isn't room for more than one on Brodovitch, Müller-Brockman, etc. In this sense do you feel the responsibility to be as definitive as possible, or do you feel at some point someone else will write another?

To believe one is writing the definitive biography is to suffer delusions of omnipotence! But you're correct to note that there isn't really room for another biography on Müller-Brockmann or Paul Rand. As to whether this makes me feel more responsible? No it doesn't. Maybe as the desire for a different interpretation of Müller-Brockmann's oeuvre arises in ten years time, someone may be inspired to offer a new take on his life and work. As long as the present keeps changing, the need to reinterpret the past will remain.

Steven Heller is co-chair of SVA/NYC MFA Design: Designer as Author + Entrepreneur, the 'Visuals' columnist of the New York Times Book Review and author of *The Daily Heller*. First published in *Graphic Design History*, Allworth Press, 2001.

Pixação:
São Paulo Signature

François Chastanet   Avant-propos par Steven Heller   XGpress

WHAT'S TO BE SEEN: SCRIPTURAL GESTURES

FRANÇOIS CHASTANET
2007

Where can one still find handwriting in use at the beginning of the twenty-first century? What is meant by penmanship today? What tools or specific media characterized the end of the last century in this area? In era, marked by the atrophy of gesture, the contact with the material in a handcrafted mode[1] is gradually disappearing. Handwriting is evidently becoming extremely rare, giving way to retranscription on a keyboard. Computers, electronic agendas and portable telephones have become the most common supports of the written word. Recourse to conventional Western calligraphy, mainly based on the use of a broad nib,[2] has been quantitatively on the way out since the ballpoint pen and the round felt-tip pen won 'hands down' long ago.

However, parallel with the phenomenon of the gradual disappearance of penmanship, there exists another form of contemporary handwriting, extremely robust and worldwide in extension, known as 'tags'. For about twenty years now, these illegal signatures represent a far larger volume than envisaged, very probably now exceeding that of traditional calligraphic production. This vandal handwriting, essentially ornamental, is freed of all functional constraints with regard to readability by the majority. Most of the books and articles dealing with the end of twentieth-century calligraphy note this recent articulation.

The presence and quotations of the tag phenomenon in various introductions,[3] notes[4] or conclusions[5] testify to their extent but unfortunately fail to follow through the analysis from either the historical or visual standpoints. Tags, on the other hand, are practically never considered or presented as examples of calligraphic practice in their own right, complying with their own constraints and conventions: their rejection or omission, the overall refusal to take them into consideration in the graphic arts sphere are clear evidence of this. In the closed circle of calligraphers and type designers, neither the existence nor the extent of the phenomena observed are denied, but they are considered of no real interest. In their vast majority, graphic designers and typographers consider graffiti as a denial of their own design pursuits or, at best, as a degenerate calligraphic practice or a fashionable ornamental texture, a regressive anti-work practice, unworthy of veritable formal interest. This is a prejudicial attitude, since only they would be in a position to describe and analyze the formal calligraphic evolutionary trends to be discovered in the tags.

Written language has become an expected daily part of any urban landscape of any metropolis having reached a certain degree of urban 'maturity'. Competing signals confronting vast urban expanses, from commercial neon signs to the different types of graffiti, together with the relentless pursuit of visibility have become the norm. Like a palimpsest, the tags, these massive serial signatures, have become an acquired characteristic of the worldwide imaginary of metropolises and a reflection of urban ways of life. Yet no extensive analysis based on visual perception exists so far on any graffiti situation, despite the large number of works published on the subject, coming from both the graffiti world itself – a tremendous source of fanzines and books with various attributes[6] – and from the academic world, where a sociological or semiological approach prevails.[7] However, extremely rare pertinent examples are to be noted, deriving form urban geography[8] and architecture.[9] Works published by photographers, such as Martha Cooper and Henry Chalfant, archivists of the New York movement in the

On top of the façade: *pig (os pigmeus)* and *tr nazis (triturador de nazis)* [persecutors of nazis], lower down in black, *antboys* [literally the anti-boys, against rich people], further down, still in black, *bb's and mobi 99 (1999)*, bottom line in white, *os caretas* [the clean guys, the sukers] and again *tr nazis*.

1970s, which notably played a major role in the worldwide spreading of tags, high quality image reproduction, nevertheless don't deal in detail with the writing practices adopted, the new rules and customs, the implementation tactics and stratagems, the importance of tools, the calligraphic skill required, together with the associated formal inventions.[10] All these books, including those, in their vast majority, from the graffiti world itself, focus their attention on the 'pieces' and the frescoes, complex, highly coloured productions, sometimes comprising figurative additions, erroneously thus considered as stylistically and technically superior to the tags and 'throw-ups',[11] with a view to pleasing and seeking the acknowledgement of a vast section of the general public who are totally unaware of what is really at stake in these practices. Only a few rare works have succeeded in putting to the forefront this aspect, representing the plasticity and intrinsic beauty of these signatures in the urban landscape[12] and in analyzing their profound significance.[13]

A rare exception in the graphic design world, the articles of Ken Garland, one of the 1964 founders of the 'First Things First' manifesto, nevertheless paved the way to a dispassionate visual analysis. Going beyond the simple illegal dimension of the act, in any case, less esthetically offensive in his opinion than the excessive visual mediocrity of the publicity overrunning his neighborhood, he concentrates on the shapes produced by tags. This attempt to achieve a formal affiliation, introduction of the tags into the design world via their interrelation with 'lettering' practices,[14] constitutes a veritable graphic survey proposal of graffiti, of vernacular and informal letterings in a visual mode. This standpoint also involves critical questioning as to the basis of the corporate identity idea and the current ubiquity of the transnational logos, together with concerns as to due respect for the 'genius loci'.[15]

These graffiti practices, these 'displayed writings'[16] also denote a return to the initial writing medium, the wall and its verticality, a reversion to pulsatory and gestural forces of the hand, here expressed in signatures. These signatures, these word-images constitute empty significants:[17] in the action of writing, the lesser the significance of the sign, the freer the tracing gesture. It is not so much the significance, which matters, but, on the contrary, the stroke and movement which are essential.[18] This being so, reading doesn't result here on an alphabetic understanding, but on perception of the emotion felt with regard to the plastic elements presented. The interest of penmanship may thus sometimes lie not in what is written, but how it is written. The calligraphic sign sometimes deliberately refuses to transmit meaning, since it is itself the meaning.[19] The primary interest of these urban signatures is not, in this case, their readability or their message, but our appraisal of their formal freedom and inventiveness; to be capable of sharing the visual pleasure component involved in the vernacular construction of the sign inscribed by an aristocracy of vandal scribes. These notions are essential to an understanding of this type of written phenomena.

Tags, these graffitis-signatures, are at the core of the link between metropolis and anonymity. Transgressive appropriation of urban territory, the longing for symbolic control over space, constitute the basic programme of any tag situation in a metropolitan area. Exploration of the world-city and its outward bounds would currently appear to constitute the only remaining great adventure, between nocturnal drifting and excursions in the margins of the city. Graffiti practices, representing a ludic transformation of the daily drabness, often providing a welcome escape from overall moroseness, results in a change in general perception of the daily urban environment on the part of the active minority constituting the 'writers' community. They induce a reappraisal of the town as a continuous backdrop, far removed from sectorizing based on freehold principles, more like a visual common good-support to be encroached upon by the most venturesome and the most intrepid. In this perspective, the town metropolis becomes a playing field, characacterized by its immensity, comprising extended flat surfaces for inscription under ever-changing conditions.

The signature may be defined, broadly speaking, as the stylized autographic apposition of the name, that's to say an identification drawing, a hand-written text where the value of the tracing gesture [20] persists. The writer, in perpetual graphic knocking together of his identity, also presents a body, only apparent from the trace left by the writing. But what is of prime interest here is the definition of the signature as the 'visible trace of a corporal gesture', where the begetting of gesture and form is reciprocal. A gesture is also characterized by a duration: the calligraphy conserves a tangible trace of the creative uplift, enabling the spectator to relive the uplift in its actual duration. [21] As Norman Mailer observed, during a discussion with New York writers saying that 'the name is the religion of graffiti', these names are a weapon, [22] a weapon against the media system and the generalized 'spectacle'. Their beauty lies in the action of writing, the gesture and its trace. These names, even if they are constantly obliterated, are aimed at a timeless and monumental dimension. In order to comply with these requirements, it is necessary to select a hard, vertical architectural support. Criticism of the readability of the tags perceived by a vast majority as a linear entanglement, both indistinct and incomprehensible, is a question constantly raised in descriptions of this type of writing. People tend to refer to 'code languages' (projection of ciphering fantasies, of parallel secret language phantasms), whereas we are simply dealing with the deployment of a new form of Latin scriptural aesthetics. It obeys its own rules, with stylistic criteria common solely to those employing this form of writing, a specialized public accustomed to the mental gymnastics involved in recognition of the letters, enabling further innovations in their own writing conventions, i.e. hermetic communication of the name in a particular environment. These circumstances permit unrestrained calligraphic freedom in the execution of the forms involved. The problem of ease of reading, of legibility [23] disappears from scriptural constraints, to be replaced by the obligation for graphic inventiveness, in competition with the other scribes, where readability is limited to recognition of a name. In other words, a typical present-day programme, currently applicable on a 'one person scale', it involves the fictitious staging of the renown and glory of a name, a public performance of the self, where visibility and repetition are currently the only true measures of success in a world marketing media context based on the ubiquity of the sign. To use Bernard Stiegler's term, our 'primordial narcissism', which requires symbols, is obliterated by the unlimited organization of the consumer society, resulting in the loss of 'individuation'. Invention is a combat, [24] the expression of a necessity: these signatures may be envisaged as a primitive save-all counteroffensive against worldwide publicity and marketing. These narcissistic signatures, enabling one to howl one's ego in public visual space, tell a very short story, that of a writer and his action, here and at this precise spot. [25] The word-image, or rather the name-image thus constitutes the basic visual unit of this 'language', the sole content of these writings, from New York to São Paulo.

The São Paulo urban writings, so far little considered in detail, [26] represent a unique specific case in the worldwide proliferation of the graffiti phenomenon: formal originality of the lettering used and a force of visual encroachment hitherto never observed worldwide. No other megalopolis has been invaded in this way. The extraordinary case of the São Paulo tags would seem to set a precedent in the recent history of the advent of the metropolis as well as in the history of writing, or more specifically in the field of the creation of signs. This 'colonization by signs' situation, in its impressive magnitude, on a similar scale to that of the São Paulo megalopolis itself, may be defined as a technical process for the invasion by writing of the urban space in its entirety. Our purpose is to describe what is rarely mentioned in connection with Brazil: a suffocating, seamy side to the urban setting, far removed from the usual clichés on Rio de Janeiro or Brazilian music, the symbolic colonization by the *favelas* of the entire city, the description of debased post-industrial urban reality, capitalist urbanism grounded on publicity, the consuming of space and image, here destroyed with its own means of offense by the work of the sign, by an all-pervading, destructive handcrafted 'logo-script', reflecting the 'other side' of

Fragment of the name *sp crimes* [são paulo crimes], drawn over a painted political publicity,
Capão Redondo, south zone of São Paulo.

furia ®, the consistency of the line and spacing in this inscription shows
the exceptional calligraphic dexterity of some pixadores.

the current race for economic competitiveness nowadays. Manifestation of major interference with the urban landscape, the history of this illegal vernacular calligraphic movement, proclaimed as such by its active members, provides an opportunity to apprehend this type of writing in another way, i.e. to consider the 'graffiti of names' from the graphic design viewpoint.

The currently prevailing sociological analysis on graffiti questions is, in our opinion, irrelevant, considering the widely differing personal paths of the 'writers', whatever their geographical place of action. The form produced in this case, a specific type of urban calligraphy acting as a deliberately created graphic mask, is the only factor linking them as a homogeneous, and thereby analyzable, object. The genesis of the scriptural shapes themselves and the question of 'how' would appear to be of paramount importance: how we say, how we do, how we build things... The 'how' makes all the difference, the 'how' says who we are. However they may be interpreted by the observer, the true significance of the tags is to be comprehended in the way in which they are produced, not in what they say. Our approach, refusing both sociological considerations and moralistic censuring, proposes an inventory of things and objects. No value judgment is passed on the act in itself, but we shall focus here on analysis of ways of proceeding, on the disclosure of a conception of creation, on resituating the analysis in the design criticism domain, more specifically with regard to 'lettering', the history of forms of handwriting and their conception. Our approach, hitherto little explored, since no exhaustive analysis of the shapes involved, in the manner of palaeographic or epigraphic[27] studies but in a contemporary and urban version, have been published yet. Here, the shape is thus envisaged as the imprint of the gesture, which itself relates practices. How did these forms of writing come to exist? What is their place in the history of the shape of letters? What constructions, what aesthetic fore-shortenings or what cultural collisions and influences gave rise to their appearance, at this particular spot, at this precise moment? We shall thus attempt to reconstruct the stylistic genesis of this writing phenomenon, to understand the workmanship involved in a chronological historical perspective, to reveal the creative process behind this São Paulo 'alphabet'. This approach will enable us to study and analyze the impact of urban conditions on the design of the autographic written sign.

Moreover, the São Paulo urban area is in line with the current perspective of the worldwide phenomenon of metropolization, characterized by the dual simultaneous trend towards concentration around these major cities and spatial extension/dissemination of their urban areas, dominated by a form of international industrial architecture, characterized by its banality and duplicated ad infinitum, whether vertical or suburban. The consequence: a relatively indiscernible object, the town surpasses our perception of it. What image should we use to represent the present day city?[28] Should we intervene and invent arbitrary aesthetics or should we extract from the urban fabric itself its potentialities, what is 'already there', and bring them into play?[29] Certain architectural columnists use the term 'nondescript urban evolutions'[30] when referring to these urban situations, to the profusion factor in the accumulative character of the ordinary megalopolis where distinctive quality and force of exception have disappeared. However, parallel identification constructions seem to appear,[31] emergencies of graphic cultural identities related to the metropolis and based on the forms of the illegal writing of the name, the tags. How are these urban environments with no distinguishing attributes still able to produce difference and in what areas? In this generic world-city context, marked by the relentless economic runaway towards urban sprawl, is not the spirit of the place henceforth more present in the form of illegal writing than in the architectural quality of a site? This unauthorized writing, is it not the ultimate stronghold for expression of a local specificity, if indeed the latter still exists?

François Chastanet is an architect and graphic designer co-founder of the studio TypoMorpho based in Bordeaux and teacher at the Institut Supérieur des Arts de Toulouse / isdaT.
First published in *Pixação: São Paulo Signature*, XGpress, 2007.

1   André Leroi-Gourhan, *Le geste et la Parole, Tome 2* (Paris: Albin Michel, 1965), p.201.

2   Gerrit Noordzij, 'The Seven-times Table', p.36–37 and 'Upsetting The Table. A Dialogue Between Nicolete Gray and Gerrit Noordzij', p.46–50, in *Letterletter: An Inconsistent Collection of Tentative Theories That Do Not Claim Any Other Authority Than That of Common Sense* (Vancouver: Hartley & Marks Publishers, 2000).

3   See Claude Mediavilla's introduction to *Calligraphie* (Paris: Imprimerie Nationale, 1993), p.13.

4   Ladislas Mandel, *Écritures, miroir des hommes et des sociétés* (La Tuilière: Atelier Perrousseaux, 1998), p.213.

5   Gérard Blanchard, 'Nœuds & esperluettes, actualités et pérennité d'un signe', article published in *Les Cahiers de Gutenberg*, no. 22 (September 1995) and *Communication et Langages*, no. 92 (1992), p.85–101.

6   Tarek Ben Yakhlef and Sylvain Doriath, *Paris Tonkar* (Éditions Florent Massot and Romain Pillement, 1991); Olivier Monmagnon, *Sabotage! Graffiti art on trains in Europe* (Florent Massot, 1995); and eds. Markus Mai, Arthur Remke, Robert Klanten, *Writing: Urban Calligraphy and Beyond* (Berlin: Die Gestalten Verlag, 2004); Malcolm Jacobson, *They Call Us Vandals* (2000) and *Overground* (2003) (Stockholm: Dokument Förlag); and Björn Almqvist and Emil Hagelin, *Writers United, The Story about WUFC, A Swedish Graffiti Crew* (Stockholm: Dokument Förlag, 2005). For fanzines, see *Underground Productions* in Stockholm, *Intox* and *Xplicit Grafx* in Paris, *Bomber* in Holland and *Overkill* in Berlin.

7   Craig Castleman, *Getting Up. Subway Graffiti in New York* (Cambridge: The MIT Press, 1982); Joe Austin, *Taking the Train. How Graffiti Art Became an Urban Crisis in New York City*, 'Popular Cultures, Everyday Lives' (New York: Columbia University Press, 2001). See also Staffan Jacobsen, *The Spray-painted Image. Graffiti Painting as Type of Image*, Art Movement & Learning Process, Ph.D, 1996; for France and Paris see Michel Kokoreff, *Le lisse et l'incisif. Les tags dans le métro* (Paris: Iris editions, 1990) and Alain Vulbeau, *Du tag au tag* (Paris: Institut de l'enfance et de la famille and Alizé Productions editions, 1990).

8   Jacques Defert, 'Une topographie transgressive', in *Cartes et figures de la Terre*, exh. cat. (Paris: Centre Georges Pompidou/ Centre de Création Industrielle, 1980); and Alex Alonso, *Urban Graffiti on the City Landscape* (Los Angeles: University of Southern California, 1998).

9   Jacques Jouet, 'Si les tags et autres bombages sont un ornement de la ville…', in *L'architecture d'aujourd'hui*, special issue *Ornement*, no. 333 (March–April 2001), p.101–115. On lettering and architecture, see Nicolete Gray, *A History of Lettering: Creative Experiment and Letter Identity* (Oxford: Phaidon, 1986), *Lettering on Buildings* (London: Architectural Press, 1960) or *Lettering as Drawing (Contour and Silhouette/The Moving Line)* (Oxford: Oxford University Press, 1971); *Architectural Review* (November 1953, April, June and August 1954). Also Alan Bartram, *The English Lettering Tradition: From 1700 to The Present Day* (London: Lund Humphries Publishers, 1986); or *Lettering in Architecture* (London: Lund Humphries Publishers, 1975). More recently, see Phil Baines and Catherine Dixon, 'Exploiting Context', *TypoGraphic*, no. 59 (September 2002), p.8–10; and *Signs: Lettering in The Environment* (London: Laurence King Publishing, 2003).

10 Martha Cooper, Henry Chalfant, *Subway Art* (London: Thames & Hudson, 1984); and Henry Chalfant, James Prigoff, *Spraycan Art* (London: Thames & Hudson, 1987).

11 A 'throw-up' is a contracted signature, consisting of the first letters, or the first and last letter of a name.

12 See Norman Mailer, *The Faith of Graffiti* (New York: Alskog Ind. and Praeger Publishers Inc., 1974); Kevin Heldman, 'Mean Streaks' in *Rolling Stone* (9 February 1995); and Stephen Powers, *The Art of Getting Over: Graffiti at the Millenium* (New York: St Martin's Press, 1999).

13 Jean Baudrillard, 'Kool Killer, or The Insurrection of Signs', *Symbolic Exchange and Death* (London: Theory, Culture & Society and Sage Publications, 1993), p.76–84.

14 Ken Garland, 'Horrible, Horrible?' (1988), *A Word in Your Eye. Opinions, Observations and Conjectures on Design, From 1960 to Present* (Reading: The University of Reading, Department of Typography and Graphic Communication, 1996), p.89–91.

15 Garland, 'Design and The Spirit of The Place' (1995), op.cit., p.149–154.

16 Béatrice Fraenkel, 'Les écritures exposées', *Lynx*, no. 31 (Paris, 1994).

17 '(…) the graffitis (in the sense of tags), which are, in fact, only names, elude any reference, any origin. They alone are untamed, in that their message is void'. Baudrillard, op.cit., p.76–84.

18 Tseng Yu-Ho, *A History of Chinese Calligraphy* (Hong Kong: The Chinese University Press, 1993), or *Chinese Calligraphy* (Philadelphia: Philadelphia Museum of Art and Boston Book & Art, 1971).

19 See Claude Mediavilla, *Calligraphie* (Paris: Imprimerie Nationale, 1993), p.19.

20 Béatrice Fraenkel, *La Signature. Genèse d'un Signe* (Paris: Gallimard, collection 'Histoire des idées', 1992), p.32.

21 Jean-François Billeter, *L'art chinois de l'écriture* (Genève: Skira, 1989), p.223.

22 More in 'The Faith of Graffiti' by Mailer, op.cit.

23 Legibility is linked to reading habits. According to Zuzana Licko, co-founder of digital typefoundry Emigre 'We read best what we read most'.

24 Bernard Stiegler, *Aimer, s'aimer, nous aimer. Du 11 septembre au 21 avril* (Paris: Galilée editions, 'Incises' collection, 2003), p.73.

25 Introduction to Powers, op.cit., p.6.

26 A few rare books do exist: Tristan Manco, Lost Art and Caleb Neelon, *Graffiti Brasil* (London: Thames & Hudson, 2005), p.26–29; Caleeb Neelon, 'São Paulo: Hidden City', *Swindle*, no. 1 (2004), p.94–105; Celia Maria Antonacci Ramos, *Grafite, pichação e cia* (São Paulo: Annablume editions, 1994). Boleta (Daniel Medeiros) and João Wainer, *Ttsss: Pixação, The vatest Art, São Paulo, Brazil* (São Paulo: Editora do Bispo, 2005). See also specialized fanzines such as *1zoz Prophets*; *Fiz*, *Só Pixo* or *Látex* (São Paulo, 1998). Also see 'Pichação' *Eye 56* (2005), p.40–47.

27 Paleography is a science that deals with the deciphering of ancient writings, generally on perishable supports: papyrus, parchment, paper or wax. Epigraphy is a branch of paleography that studies

236

writing on hard supports, such as stone, metal or bone. Paleography and epigraphy each develop their own methods of investigation. One focuses mainly on the visual aspect of the signs, whereas as the other concentrates on their meaning.

28 See *Twin* by Erik van Blokland and Just van Rossum, exploring the the idea of a typeface reflecting the characteristics of a town in Deborah Littlejohn, *Metro Letters: A Typeface for the Twin Cities* (Minneapolis: University of Minnesota Press, 2004).

29 Henri-Pierre Jeudy, *Critique de l'esthétique urbaine* (Paris: Sens & Tonka, collection 10/vingt, 2003).

30 Paul Ardenne, 'Quelques remarques sur le D.U.Q (Devenir Urbain Quelconque)', *Archistorm*, no. 8 (2004).

31 A similar case happened in Los Angeles, where an illegal script was based on shapes used in commercial packaging. On this subject, see Alonso, op.cit.

Graphic
Design History
A Critical Guide

Johanna Drucker
Emily McVarish

A CRITICAL VIEW
OF GRAPHIC DESIGN HISTORY

DENISE GONZALES CRISP
AND RICK POYNOR
2008

For years, anyone who wanted to read a history of graphic design, written in English, had conspicuously few choices. It was either Philip B. Meggs' trailblazing *A History of Graphic Design* (1983, now in its fourth, posthumous edition) or Richard Hollis' more compact *Graphic Design: A Concise History* (1994). It took until 2006 for a heavyweight rival to Meggs to appear in English – French art historian Roxane Jubert's *Typography and Graphic Design: From Antiquity to the Present*. Last year, a fourth, better distributed contender arrived, Stephen J. Eskilson's *Graphic Design: A New History*. The book received some tough criticism in a previous dialogue on Design Observer.

Now, snapping at Eskilson's heels comes yet another historical survey, *Graphic Design History: A Critical Guide* by Johanna Drucker and Emily McVarish (Pearson Prentice Hall). Their critical history differs in some significant ways from its predecessors. 'Graphic artifacts always serve a purpose and contain an agenda, no matter how neutral or natural they appear to be', they explain. Designer and design educator Denise Gonzales Crisp (North Carolina) and Design Observer contributor Rick Poynor (London) have been marking pages, making notes and exchanging views.

Denise Gonzales Crisp: On my first pass through *Graphic Design History: A Critical Guide*, two details distinguished it from other histories. First are the 'Tools of the Trade' listed at the end of each chapter, which are suggestive rather than exhaustive. The lists begin with one spanning 37,000 and 7,000 BCE – items such as knotted cords, mouth and spittle, animal fat and marrow lamps. The last chapter, 'Digital Design: After the 1970s', lists the Wacom tablet, wireless networks and the mouse. The evolution of graphic design technologies, and by extension artifacts, is palpably captured in this factual inventory. Most notable is how categories of things in the first list become actions over time: from sticks, bones and roots at the dawn of civilization, to the drawing, image manipulation, rendering, animation and layout software of our clickable present. Graphic design is presented, first, as a making discipline, shaped by production and reproduction limits and advances. Makers in this volume carry less weight.

Second, the book's design runs statements smack in the middle of nearly every spread like Silent Radio headlines. Most are generalized, quantifiable facts: 'Newspapers began to address the interests of the working class.' Many are provocative: 'Utopianism was gone, along with unwavering faith in progress.' And some downright aggressive: 'In a market driven by opportunism, novelty was worth the price.' 'Working class', 'hegemony', 'codes', 'ideological' and 'pedagogy' are but a few terms staged (in 16 pt. Gothic!) as if such notions were as natural to graphic design practice as Pantone Red.

These two narratives threaded throughout *A Critical Guide* characterize the authorial springboard. Corroborated by the introductory treatise emblazoned on the opening pages – including a ten-point manifesto stating 'critical principles' – the authors put forward design as a 'cultural phenomenon … embedded in institutions … shaped by cultural and historical forces … that operates within a network of constraints.'

You know that moment when somebody articulates an idea that you hadn't quite put together, but as you hear it you say 'em, duh!' Well, that would be the point of this book. A seriously explicit and sharp point, as it turns out, but a vital one in the context of historical surveys on graphic design. Not that such insights haven't been written. The bibliography cites works by Reyner Banham, Maud Lavin, Stuart Ewen and Victor Margolin, historians and critics who have contributed under similar critical terms. But who reads that stuff? Graduate design students, educators and design writers, mostly. *A Critical Guide* is clearly targeted at them and undergraduate students, but also to 'the rest of us', practitioners inclined to read design history.

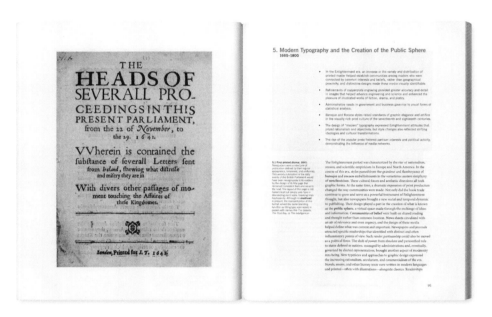

Chapter openings summarize key ideas in a list of bullet points.

Rick Poynor: It certainly seems to have been conceived as a textbook – both authors are teachers – and on the publisher's website there is a blurb describing it as being: 'For one-semester History of Graphic Design and History of Visual Communication courses.' Amazingly, the back cover, consisting of plugs from colleagues, gives no information at all. The publisher isn't presenting the book in a way that suggests it foresees a wide, non-academic readership, and general booksellers aren't going to get too excited by the strangely severe front cover.

I admire the book's critical ambition, as set out in the list of principles. I also agree with Drucker and McVarish that we need more design writing informed by an understanding of critical theory – Drucker, an art historian and book artist, is steeped in it. But what would a raw 19-year-old design student, attending that one-semester course, make of a sentence like this from the preface? 'The capabilities of production always constitute affordances, within which design practices can be received as well as realized.' You need some knowledge of perceptual psychology or interaction design even to begin to grasp the use of 'affordance' there. At moments like this, the authors seem to lose sight of their intended, and most likely, reader. If they are so concerned to unmask the 'exclusionary tactics' of design rhetoric, as they tell us a page later, why snaggle their prose with rhetorical obstructions of their own?

It's curious because in other ways the book is acutely aware of the inexperienced reader's needs. Words marked in bold in the text can be looked up in an excellent 23-page glossary that covers everything from algorithm to x-height. As writing, though, despite the political urgency of its underlying leftist agenda – fight the power! – the text is flatter, more buttoned-up and technical sounding at times than it needs to be. The authors clearly love the subject, so where's the verbal zest? *Graphic Design as Communication* by Malcolm Barnard, a book that's had less attention than it deserves – though it's aimed at the same student reader – explores similar theoretical territory in relation to design (Roland Barthes, Jacques Derrida, Michel Foucault) more explicitly and with greater argumentative vigor.

Crisp: The writing is dense, no question. You bring to mind an issue that bedevils a number of graphic design educators, at least in the US: how to integrate design theories and scholarship – by definition demanding – that instill critical rigor in ways accessible and meaningful (aka applicable) to budding practitioners? Scholarship in graphic design is a fairly recent player compared to other design disciplines, and frequently alien to undergraduate curricula. I can't help but wonder if the book is jam-packed in order to address (with immediacy) some conspicuous oversights.

I do read joy in the surprising illustration choices throughout. This is no parade of aloof 'greatest hits'. Artifacts range from a sobering nineteenth-century slave auction announcement to an elaborate trade 'kalendar' promoting Norris & Cokayne, proprietors of fine printing. Original drawings and notes for Edward Johnston's 1915 London Underground typeface and William Morris' 1892 Troy demonstrate craft as well as ideals. I also appreciate the many humanizing glimpses into graphic design's unsung legacies, for instance the comical 1485 'My Heart Doth Smart' in which a lovesick Casper of Regensburg depicts hearts being 'sawn, hooked, roasted, pierced, stuck in a vice, and wounded in various ways.' Who knew early Renaissance men had a sense of humor? The chapter 'Public Interest Campaigns and Information Design' features Second World War posters designed to educate the US public about army insignias and air raid procedures – refreshingly secular examples compared to the usual relics hawked in design histories.

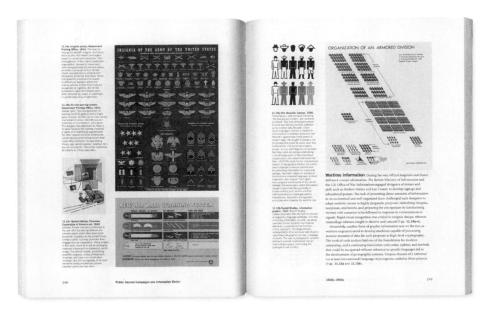

From 'Public Interest Campaigns and Information Design'.

Meditations accompanying every image are sometimes wry and radical, other times a bit dogmatic in an attempt to 'unpack' the work. For instance, the comment 'corporate identity and anonymity combine to reinforce the breachless representation of power' concludes a discussion of the CBS 'eye' logo designed in 1950. Many captions register disconnects between intention and reality that can read as object lessons for the politically correct: 'Circumstances and limiting factors that could affect response (incapacitating illness, age, etc.) are not considered. The poster addresses all citizens as if they were alike.' Also: '… in *real* encounters, signs and shapes were often distorted by speed of movement or partial obscuring of sight lines.' (My emphasis.)

Poynor: The startlingly fresh choice of illustrations is one of the book's pleasures, as you say. The images in the early and middle sections are wonderfully researched and informative, though the authors' formidable searchlight seems to waver as they approach the present, where they rely too much on published sources in their selection of images. The chapter on Post-modernism offers nothing we haven't seen before despite the huge wealth of international examples to choose from. American work dominates the later pages and this chauvinism is out of keeping with the book's iconoclastic critical spirit. A caption accompanying the famous 1960s 'pregnant man' ad for the Campaign for Family Planning forgets to say that it comes from Britain. Isn't nationality a significant contextual factor? How can we fully understand a social information campaign without situating it within the social trends and political program of the nation state that produced it? This vagueness of location is a recurrent problem in the captions that could have been avoided by putting the country of origin next to the date.

The main text carries general analysis, while the discussion of examples is pushed out into the captions, which run in parallel. True, the caption commentary – a kind of slide show – is packed with some exceptional insights, but this treatment of the material makes for a fragmented reading experience. *A Critical Guide* is constantly tugging at your sleeve and saying: 'Come over here.' Many of the more densely illustrated pages read as a patchwork, with as much to absorb in the captions as there is in the text. Often the captions have no direct connection with the sentence that contains the figure number, creating an expectation that a point will be developed by the visual example, which isn't then fulfilled.

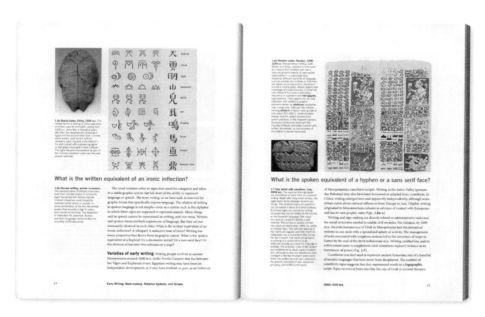

From 'Mass Mediation'.

For all the criticisms of Eskilson's *Graphic Design: A New History*, it's rather more readerly in this respect, and so is Hollis' *Graphic Design: A Concise History*. Their integrated texts allow you to immerse yourself and concentrate. Although Drucker and McVarish hope their book will be used for systematic study, it's a volume that both student and non-student readers are more likely to dip into and skim because that's what its editorial structure and layout encourage.

Crisp: I see your point, and agree that for some readers the multiple entry approach might be problematic. But speaking for multi-tasking hyper-texters such as myself, I appreciate the format and delivery. Aspects you find distracting I welcome as exuberant exhortation, which is not necessarily an impediment to reflection.

Poynor: What do you think about their determination to play down the role of individuals? They avoid quoting designers, denying their voices and discounting their experiences and intentions. With a handful of exceptions (Ruari McLean's study of Jan Tschichold is the most recent), the titles in their otherwise thorough bibliography tend to be general studies and surveys. Did they really not consult any other monographs during their research? Few would argue at this point for a view of design confined to the uncritical celebration of 'great names', but is there a danger of a different kind of distortion? The ex cathedra assertions in this kind of analytical writing are also a form of authority. 'Fabricating an intangible aura of desirability, far beyond any real necessity, graphic designers produced perpetual longing for an imagined life', they write in a chapter about the culture of consumption in the 1920s and 1930s. I believe, as they do, that this is just as true today, but I still want to see it demonstrated with close attention to the activities of actual designers – and for that matter, their clients.

Crisp: Ah. Clients. Now there's a group whose perspectives we could use, if for no other reason than to name producers as design collaborators. In any case, evidence-based texts are a priori 'distortions' of one sort or the other. Creators (and clients) would be the first to cite their intentions as meaningful evidence in support of their respective enterprises, which critics then interpret to fuel conclusions often divorced from what either might have intended.

At first, I did miss the impassioned words of Eric Gill and Frederic Goudy and William Golden. I am a designer, after all, and love hearing ancestors wax theoretical, nostalgic, profound, what have you. Not long ago I sat at lunch with the printer and fine book publisher Jack Stauffacher. He had in tow a stunning photogravure book printed in the 1960s and his face seemed to glow as he described those now lost days of which he was major proponent. Enchanting, truly. Still, his insights revealed little of critical import about the work or its context.

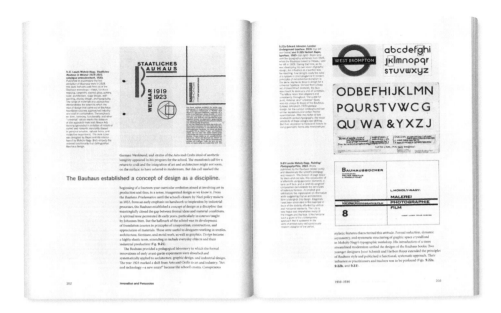

From 'Innovation and Persuasion'.

Seminal philosophies and motivations are implicit throughout *A Critical Guide*. For instance, Herbert Bayer, Laszlo Moholy-Nagy and Walter Gropius are present in the Bauhaus discussion. But the objects of study are artifacts and their surrounds, not designers. In an uncharacteristic moment of reverie, the authors profess their fascination with the work: 'What drove this book more than anything was our genuine enthusiasm for the material. At every stage of research and writing, review and exchange, layout and production, we found ourselves deeply involved with the images in front of us... we were always discovering materials so compelling that we would say, "This stuff is the most interesting of all."'

The very premise of the book seems to preclude designer voices as germane. The authors strive for the meta-view, routinely citing examples as 'typical' of approach or attitude, rather than attributing uncommon artistry to any given individual. I may want and need to believe in genius (sadly, I do), but the writers trump my desire with dogged focus on their proposal: that artifacts reflect the culture and moment they help produce; that they shape cultural expectations and hide assumptions. One thing you have to say about Drucker and McVarish: they are resolute! In this context, designer stories are best left to respective essays, monographs and biographies – a few of which the bibliography names.

Poynor: But arguments have to be made from evidence and the quality of an argument will depend in large part on the quality of that evidence. I'm not calling for a parade of 'geniuses'. I'm suggesting that a fuller understanding of design will come from paying some attention – some – to what designers say they are trying to do and why. We might then conclude, weighing their testimonies against other kinds of evidence and other forms of analysis, that designers don't fully understand, and can't finally account for, their own work. But these testimonies will still contribute to our understanding.

The other point of some judicious quoting is that it gives readers a chance to gauge for themselves the content, tenor and strength of a designer's views, rather than having the authors imply, from a position of assumed authority, that these views can simply be set aside. For a reader new to the Futurist Filippo Tommaso Marinetti, what gives the most effective (or least distorted) sense of what he was about? A well-chosen sample of his actual words? Or someone else's summary of what he was about, filtered through his or her own concerns?

Eskilson's history received a hard time on Design Observer for its lack of footnotes. While this is not necessarily a problem – Ernst Gombrich's hugely readable *The Story of Art* has gone through dozens of reprints without them – in a book that sets store by its critical method, the lack of footnotes raises some questions. The more the authors seek to embed the history of graphic design in other kinds of history – political, economic, business, retail and so on – the more we need to know where their understanding of these areas comes from. For instance, in the chapter on the graphic effects of industrial production, they write that 'The popular press is often seen as an instrument of social control through which the masses consume ideas and values that may run counter to their own interests.' Often seen by whom? A well-established tradition of leftist media criticism from cultural studies and media studies lies behind that claim, but readers just have to take these ideologically loaded accounts of history on trust, with no signposts to relevant further reading.

Not far into a chapter on corporate identities and the International Style, we learn that 'The unified image afforded by a distinctive logo and corporate identity system might well conceal a host of inequities or abuses, even as it functioned with clear, rational effectiveness in strategic communications.' Yes, it might, and this is certainly not the kind of observation that previous histories of graphic design have been inclined to make. So have there been historical or critical studies showing this to be the case with corporations in the 1950s and 1960s? They don't say. The paragraph goes on to mention the CIBA pharmaceutical company and Chase Manhattan bank, as if to substantiate the argument. Certainly, these organizations were geographically dispersed and structurally complex, but the authors provide no evidence of inequity or abuse.

From 'Corporate Identities and International Style'.

Nevertheless, they repeat their earlier point: 'Good visual communication could gloss over irregularities in business activity or accounting practices by constructing an image of smooth operations in a climate of uncertainty. The graphic designer's art sometimes raised ethical questions of accountability.' The figure number takes us to the caption for Chermayeff & Geismar's Chase Manhattan corporate identity (1960) and its placement within the sentence seems to imply that the designers' work on the identity raises ethical questions. This is not developed in the caption and, once again, the assertion – a point fundamental to the authors' critical view – goes unsupported.

Crisp: The book declares more than it debates, from the opening terms of engagement to the droll timelines concluding each chapter, where design-related milestones are listed amid other 'selective and suggestive' cultural and political markers.

I also take the title at face value: a guide to help navigate any number of other sources. A single paragraph under 'Graphic Persuasion and Its Effects', for example, invokes several themes that surfaced between the Wars. 'The field of propaganda studies was born'; the Frankfurt School examined 'how values could so permeate a culture as to make their manipulation almost invisible;' Edward Bernays (Freud's nephew) founded the public relations field in the US; sociologists Walter Lippmann and Paul Lazarsfeld studied and theorized 'the mechanisms by which print media encoded and delivered messages.' Obviously these areas would need the support of more extensive illustrations and deeper discussion in, say, a history of advertising.

The authors don't explain if the book is meant to function as worthy counsel or earnest competitor to fatter, hardbound volumes on graphic design history such as Eskilson's. I expect the former is more likely. Assuming the book is a map of sorts, with a fixed perspective, then providing means for zooming in closer is in order. The recommended texts listed for each chapter promise ample detail for the motivated reader, but they don't always lead one to qualifying sources. The study and analyses of writers and practitioners in the text cited above – background I should think critical to fully grasping the forces at work – are not included.

Meanwhile, I find plenty of insights across chapters that make new sense of existing, perhaps more comfortable, assumptions. The last, 'Digital Design', mirrors an earlier chapter entitled 'Renaissance Design'. This parallel brings to light two periods that on the surface appear to have little in common. However, each brought tremendous technological shifts, and with them far-reaching consequences. The authors point out how the means of production and distribution dramatically altered societal inclusion – moved toward more democratic authorship and readership – and fundamentally changed creator/designer tasks and knowledge. Similar connections pervade the book (see also recurring discussions of information design and photography) and they show how contemporary designers participate in, and are products of, their moment. This is both liberating, as self-knowledge should be, and incriminating.

Many examples and discussions implicate design's role in representing optimism (read: complicity) for commercial gain or 'hegemonic' reinforcement. Chapters such as 'Mass Mediation' and 'The Culture of Consumption' tapped into my inner graphic guilt. 'Modern Typography and the Creation of the Public Sphere' and 'Pop and Protest', on the other hand, give more affirming outcomes their due. The authors abundantly argue that graphic communication reflects and generates societal values. In fact, I now whisper a daily devotion over my morning coffee: 'graphic design is a vital social vehicle.' If we value a certain kind of awareness, *A Critical Guide* just might be our sermon.

From 'Pop and Protest'.

Poynor: In the June issue of *Print* (2008), Drucker accepts the delicate assignment of reviewing Eskilson's rival volume. She acknowledges the difficulty faced by any design history author of writing for 'the many constituencies of practitioners, teachers, students, and academic audiences, each with their own needs and agendas.' The problems highlighted in our discussion underline that challenge. Given Drucker's view, reiterated in *Print*, that 'a history of graphic design provides insight into the way we understand practice today', the book's heavy emphasis on the subject's distant 'pre-history' might be counterproductive. The section titled 'Prehistoric Prelude to Graphic Design: 35,000–2700 BCE' is such a stretch it sounds like a spoof.

From 'Postmodernism in Design'.

A less American, more generously international perspective on recent decades would also have served their critical cause better. It's very noticeable that while many well-known US designers (Muriel Cooper, April Greiman, Tibor Kalman, P. Scott Makela, Paula Scher, Art Chantry, Charles S. Anderson, Elliott Earls) receive at least a name check, the treatment of non-American designers of equal or greater stature is much patchier.

In a book that can find space to tell us, in a timeline, that protozoan life forms began two billion years ago, or that the Black Sox baseball scandal took place in 1921, some might wonder what happened to Henryk Tomaszewski (and the entire school of Polish poster designers), Max Huber, Karl Gerstner, Robert Massin, Ikko Tanaka, Gunter Rambow or Wim Crouwel, to name only a few notable omissions. The national favoritism in the later chapters suggests that the authors are keeping a close eye on the expectations of the book's primary market, the US – it's more worrying to think they just didn't notice their own bias – and it somewhat undercuts their avowed emphasis on artifacts rather than designers, at least for this European reader. Meggs and Hollis, despite his briefer text, are more inclusive in this regard, and so is Jubert's *Typography and Graphic Design*.

Crisp: Don't forget: the year 410, Rome sacked by Visigoths; 1836, Samuel Colt invents the revolver; 1965, Malcolm X assassinated; 1988, Prozac marketed. These odd complements to design milestones put what I often say is 'only graphic design' into perspective. Positioning our game in line with major and minor world events also demonstrates the fact that design bears import and kookiness equal to all human endeavors. I await future editions with entries like 'AIDS cure discovered' and 'Nanodesign degree track introduced at MIT.'

The opening 'prelude' you refer to is worth quoting here because its thesis underwrites other rationales driving the book, and inscribes a poetic connection. 'Deliberate mark-making, the preparation of materials and surfaces, the use of conventional signs, the cultural primacy of communication, and the expression of ideas in form, are the legacy of prehistoric graphic work to the present-day designer.' To the extent that inert stone and bone markings so removed from contemporary experience can have significance, this viewpoint pumps life into these, and ultimately all the dead marks that follow. Design students and non-historians frequently see ancient artifacts as inconsequential (or as awesome visual material for CD covers). As far-fetched as it may sound, the imaginative leap that 'graphic' and 'design' impulses and inventions span millennia adds a bit of healthy color to graphic design activity of every sort.

Poynor: I can see you like these aspects of the book more than I do. For me, the immense sweep of time this study attempts to encompass and condense sometimes blurs its critical focus and necessary detail goes missing. The deep background is interesting, but not essential to the intended exposure of design's hidden agendas. If they had opened, after some nimble scene-setting, with the chapter on mass mediation from 1850 to the 1900s – the period when, as they say, 'commercial artists began to develop a recognizable professional identity' – there would have been more room for their critical investigation of the modern design likely to concern most readers, and of the economic, sociological and technological forces that shaped it. Having said that, despite some almost inevitable flaws, given the huge scope of the task, this smart, challenging, and in so many ways painstakingly researched guide is an important new addition to the design library. The book breaks new ground and raises the stakes. Future histories of visual communication will be obliged to pay it close attention.

Denise Gonzales Crisp is Professor of Graphic Design at North Carolina State University, Raleigh.
Rick Poynor is a writer and Visiting Professor in Critical Writing at the Royal College of Art, London.
First published on *Design Observer* (www.designobserver.com), 2 June 2008.

Women Artists
elles@centrepompidou

IN THE COLLECTION OF THE MUSÉE NATIONAL D'ART MODERNE, CENTRE DE CRÉATION INDUSTRIELLE

PUSSY GALORE AND BUDDHA OF THE FUTURE WOMEN, GRAPHIC DESIGN, ETC.

CATHERINE DE SMET
2009

'She felt in italics and thought in capitals.'
— Henry James, *The Figure in the Carpet*, 1896

'Fun things to do in museums: invade the bookstore. Slap stickers to alter book titles.' Most essays on graphic design would merit a corrective analogous to what the Guerrilla Girls recommend in their *Art Museum Activity Book*, where the proposed stickers are intended to transform the cover of a *History of Art* into a *History of Mostly Male Art*.[1] As a recent discipline, graphic design history might well have been expected to adopt more egalitarian habits from the outset, but even today, the attention paid to women who have worked in the field remains slight. The fact that they were a minority during much of the twentieth century does not explain such treatment, even from a point of view dominated by the most traditional values, exalting the heroic figure of the innovative creator. Indeed, even those women who seemingly complied in every way with the profile required for figuring in the textbooks have nonetheless been excluded. Such is the case of Muriel Cooper: despite the fact that she co-founded the Visible Language Workshop at MIT in 1973 and headed it until her death in 1994, Philip B. Meggs does not mention her in any of the successive editions of his pioneering work *A History of Graphic Design* (in spite of the corrections introduced over the years).[2] Initially published in 1983, this history, which runs from the Lascaux caves to the contemporary period, was the first of its kind and still remains a major reference work.

As a creator, researcher and teacher at a leading institution like MIT, Cooper, a pioneer of interactive design, clearly belongs to the category of influential figures who would normally be cited by those, like Meggs, seeking to provide readers with a survey of the field concerned. She was one of the first graphic designers convinced of the importance of computer technology and immediately sought to introduce high visual standards for the layout of the information presented, and animated, on the screen. In addition, she trained and inspired several generations of students.[3] Meggs' book can be reproached for its Western, English-speaking and more specifically US orientation, but the reasons that might have motivated the omission of the American Cooper must be sought elsewhere. It is also true that Meggs, who had little familiarity with the new technologies, privileged traditional graphic design media, but this second limiting factor still does not allow us to understand the exclusion of Cooper, who was also art director of the MIT Press and as such realised many memorable layouts associating the principles of a functional sobriety inherited from European Modernism with elements inspired by contemporary daily life.[4] Among her notable contributions to editorial creation was the clean, airy layout of the original edition of *Learning from Las Vegas*.[5] Cooper was also responsible for a logo of exemplary visual quality and effectiveness – that of the MIT Press itself. Designed in 1963, it is still

Muriel Cooper,
MIT Press logo, 1963

in use today: seven vertical black bars of equal width, with the two at the far right extended, one upwards, for the ascender of the T, and the other downwards, for the descender of the P. It is only at second glance that the publishing house's initials emerge from the compact geometric image – a remarkable instance of visual economy in the conception of a symbol.

Thus, nothing justifies Meggs' omission – apart from the fact that Cooper was a woman and one who, in addition, did not seek to promote her own name but on the contrary privileged the spirit of collective work which characterises design practice. In fact, integrating Cooper into the pantheon of twentieth-century graphic design as a single individual, duly glorified according to the current criteria, would have betrayed the feminist cause, for which it is indispensable to call into question the tools used in the construction of history. Indeed, the term 'pioneer', which I myself applied to Cooper earlier on, is also suspect. In an article reviewing the feminist positions relative to design in the professional literature, Carma R. Gorman indicates: 'Describing an artist or a designer as a "pioneer" suggests (at least to me) a desire to position that person within a euro-centric, masculinist, modernist canon of "greats".'[6] In support of her argument, she cites a review by Ellen Mazur Thomson denouncing the biographical approach of an essay devoted to graphic designer Cipe Pineles: 'To concentrate on the life of individual designers would appear to distort graphic design history.'[7] Pineles was a magazine art director trained by Mehemed Fehmy Agha at *Vogue* and *Vanity Fair* in the 1930s and a teacher at Parsons School of Design in New York. But she also married two famous graphic designers, William Golden and Will Burtin – information that accompanies the smallest note on her career, whereas, obviously, the reverse is rarely true. Only a radically different perspective would permit an adequate appreciation of women's activity, for it cannot be acknowledged without being associated with other forms of production which have been hidden or marginalised until now, as the fruits of the practice of individuals insufficiently recognised within western society or coming from other cultures, and for whom the idea of the 'author' is not necessarily important.[8] This is what Cheryl Buckley, for example, maintains in her article 'Made in Patriarchy', which calls for a redefinition of design in order to include craft production.[9] Johanna Drucker and Emily McVarish pursue a similar vein in their *Graphic Design History: A Critical Guide*, where they include ephemera – posters and other anonymous signs usually absent from general histories of graphic design – and place the objects, more than individual creators, at the heart of their approach (but without failing to mention Muriel Cooper).[10] If the corpus studied by Drucker and McVarish attests to a desire to modify the conventional perception of graphic design, however, it still remains a prisoner of the Anglo-American or North American geographical sphere, especially for the contemporary period. The decentralising process now underway must also lead, as Buckley, Gorman and others have suggested, to new attention brought to bear on what is happening in countries that have been less well served by historians, without forgetting that such countries may, like France, be located in the West.

The defence of women's rights and feminist demands has, like all social struggles, made use of street posters, the distribution of leaflets and other printed matter and the publication of ads in the press, and they have seized on all the media permitting the combination of text and image, from T-shirts and buttons to cyberspace. In *Suffragettes to She-Devils*, Liz McQuiston explores the women's movement through a visual compendium of its graphics.[11] Whether signed by one person or a collective or strictly anonymous, such works most often draw on the typographic and iconographic vocabulary of their times. Apart from the plus sign surmounted by a circle which became the movement's symbol in the 1960s and underwent multiple manipulations in order to stress its activist intent (in particular, the addition of a clenched fist), no distinctive sign runs through the whole of this production. On the contrary, we often sense the desire to employ the most ordinary communication codes. Thus, the Guerrilla Girls posters, without departing from the rules of professional-quality design, do not show any particular stylistic pursuit, and the subversion of their famous ad 'The Advantage of Being a Woman Artist' recently proposed by the young New York art collective LTTR ('The Advantage of Being a ~~Woman~~ Lesbian Artist', signed Ridykeulous), uses the effects of hand-written correction – heavy, awkward cross-outs, irregular letters – and the raw look of the four strips of masking tape hastily tacked around the edges of the sheet. Such an improvised, do-it-yourself aesthetic is present in the group's other works and often found in the most recent international graphic production.[12]

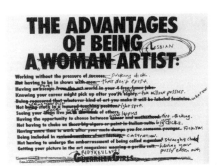

Ridykeulous (Nicole Eisenman + A. L. Steiner), *The Advantages of Being a ~~Woman~~ Lesbian Artist*, 2006.

Graphic designers committed to the women's cause have made use of their skills and means in a specific way. Sheila Levrant de Bretteville, who set up the Women's Design programme at CalArts in Los Angeles in 1971, has developed collective practices based on user participation and the sharing of experiences.[13] In her view, it was clear that 'women designers could only locate and solve design problems in a responsive way if they simultaneously studied their own history, tried to isolate female values and worked cooperatively'.[14] The poster *Pink is Childish* (1974) which she designed at the request of the American Institute of Graphic Design (AIGA) for an exhibition on the colour pink at the Whitney Museum of American Art, illustrates her positions and her concern with bringing out multiple voices. Its patchwork composition – alluding to a woman's craft – reproduces in their original state texts and/or images contributed by different women asked to comment on the significance the colour pink had for them. Two decades later, when the new possibilities of computer graphics were setting off a typographic fervour among graphic designers, Siân Cook, McQuiston and Teal Triggs, associated under the banner of the Women's Design and Research Unit (WD + RU) in the UK, created *Pussy Galore*, a font comprised of different kinds of signs (pictograms, words or expressions, isolated or grouped together) playing on several semantic levels accessed with the computer keyboard. The name comes from the high-powered heroine of the James Bond novel *Goldfinger*, who appears in the 1964 movie version by Honor Blackman.[15] The aim was to provide, with a good dose of irony, an 'interactive tool' which would allow anyone to compose personalised messages by delving into an activist repertory (the project was conceived for an issue of the typographic magazine *Fuse* on the theme of propaganda).[16]

Siân Cook, Liz McQuiston, Teal Triggs (WD + RU), *Pussy Galore*, 1994.

The considerable imbalance between the sexes which prevailed in graphic design until the past few decades seems to be declining.[17] The anecdote about the hiring of typographer and printing historian Beatrice Warde in 1926 – she was approached by the Monotype foundry in London because they thought she was a man, owing to the male pseudonym she used to sign her articles in the journal *The Fleuron* – belongs to the past. Nonetheless, as German font designer Sybille Hagmann indicated in 2005, her profession remains predominantly male.[18] And the visibility of women is still grossly inferior to that of men, as reflected in specialised reviews, magazines, books, conferences and exhibitions. Notwithstanding the risk that the criterion of 'gender' can be used to other ends, the present situation provides a convincing argument for the interest of exhibitions or essays exclusively devoted to the creation of women graphic designers and thus liable to change a persistent discriminatory tendency.[19] Throughout *What is Graphic Design?*, the book's author, Quentin Newark, employs the pronoun 'she' to designate the graphic designer rather than the *conventional* 'he'; in addition to stressing the mixed nature of the profession, this substitution (worthy of the feminist *herstory* of the 1960s) also serves to recall the machismo of lexical uses.

Some authors have attempted to repopulate the history of the book and printing with the women figures that have been unjustly excluded from it, despite the fact that they were active from the fifteenth century on, in a field supposed to be exclusively male.[20] This much-needed research effort becomes even more convincing when the foregrounding of women's work also opens unexpected doors or sheds new light on what were thought to be familiar subjects. As is the case, for example, with Swiss typography specialist and font designer François Rappo: recalling that France, 'in typography as elsewhere, is modern but no longer aware of it', he cites the ('amazing') research of Jeanne Veyrin-Forrer, whose book *La Lettre et le Texte* reveals a 'three-hundred-year field of graphical modernity [...] within the reach of your pencil'.[21] Veyrin-Forrer, director of the Rare Books Collection at the Bibliothèque nationale de France, studied the work of Antoine Augereau, Claude Garamond, the Fourniers and the Didots and was one of the first in France to adopt the principles of the Anglo-American analytical bibliography, which profoundly transformed the history of the book. Going back even further, to the origins of printing, Far Eastern historian T.H. Barrett has devoted a study to the woman he considers the real inventor of printing, towards the end of the seventh century: the Chinese empress Wu – who chose to be called 'Iron Lady', 'Wise Mother', 'Emperor' (in the masculine) or 'Buddha of the Future'.[22] By drawing attention to this remarkable person and stressing the continuity between wooden and lead type, Barrett questions Western knowledge about the history of mechanical reproduction of text, invented seven centuries before Gutenberg, on another continent and under the impulse of a woman. In particular, he insists on the importance of the Chinese religious context of the period for understanding the reasons behind the spread of block printing during Wu's reign and thus broadens our knowledge of the development of a technology with major cultural impact.

Contemporary research on graphic design and the role played by women changes the way we look at the past of the book, writing and printing. Beyond the necessary reintegration of neglected works and creators, it imposes a continuous reappraisal of a history which is all the more open because of the newness of the discipline itself. Women's voices from the past can also help to bring out what is sometimes still difficult to express today and to recall the virtues of otherness for revitalising our ways of seeing. In eleventh-century Japan, the woman of letters Sei Shÿnagon expressed better than anyone else the power of the visual presentation of information. The lists of objects, impressions and feelings in her *Pillow Book* include a category based on the image of words which serves to bring out the importance of such an image for our perception of the world: 'Words That Look Commonplace but That Become Impressive When Written in Chinese Characters: strawberries, a dew-plant, a prickly water-lily, walnut, a Doctor of Literature, a Provisional Senior Steward in the Office of the Emperor's Household, a red myrtle.'[23] An original way of thinking about graphic design.

Catherine de Smet teaches History of Graphic Design at l'Université Paris 8, l'École européenne supérieure d'art de Bretagne-Rennes and L'École nationale supérieure des arts décoratifs, Paris.
Translated from the French by Miriam Rosen. First published in *Elles@Pompidou*, Centre Pompidou, 2009.

1 Guerrilla Girls, *Art Museum Activity Book* (New York: Printed Matter, Inc., 2004), p.12.

2 Philip B. Meggs, *A History of Graphic Design* (1983) (New York: John Wiley & Sons, 1998). I am referring here to the last edition published during the author's lifetime; a new edition, entitled *Meggs' History of Graphic Design*, revised by Alston Purvis, was published in 2005.

3 Among Cooper's students, we can cite John Maeda, who succeeded her at MIT and, through his books, lectures and exhibitions, helped to convince a growing public of the possibilities offered by the encounter of computers and graphic design. On Cooper, see David Reinfurt's extensive study of her work, 'This stands as a sketch for the future. Muriel Cooper and the Visible Language Workshop', 2007 http://www.dextersinister.org/MEDIA/PDF/Thisstandsasasketchforthefuture.pdf (accessed 23 April 2012).

4 For example, Herbert Muschamp's *File Under Architecture*, printed on brown wrapping paper with the text composed on an IBM typewriter, or Edward Allen's *The Responsive House*, where the sub-title *Do Your Own Thing*, roughly drawn in large, irregular white capital letters on the cover, is juxtaposed with the title in Helvetica discreetly placed in the upper portion of the page.

5 Robert Venturi, Denise Scott Brown and Steven Izenour, *Learning From Las Vegas* (Cambridge, MA: MIT Press, 1972). The authors abandoned this layout as of the first new edition, in particular because of the Bauhaus influence they detected and considered unsuited to the content of a book intended to criticise the latter's mark on architectural design. On Cooper's layout and graphic changes between the first and subsequent editions, see in particular Michael Golec, '"Doing It Dead Pan": Venturi, Scott Brown and Izenour's *Learning from Las Vegas*', *Visible Language*, vol. 37, no. 1 (2004), p.266–287.

6 Carma R. Gorman, 'Reshaping and Rethinking: Recent Feminist Scholarship on Design and Designers', *Design Issues*, vol. 17, no. 4 (Autumn 2001), p.72–88.

7 Ellen Mazur Thomson, review of Martha Scottford's *Cipe Pineles: A Life of Design*, in Pat Kirkham and Ella Howard, eds., *Women Designers in the USA,*

1900–2000, special issue of *Studies in the Decorative Arts*, vol. 8, no. 1 (Autumn–Winter 2000–01). Cited by Carma R. Gorman, op.cit., p.76.

8 David Reinfurt's booklet on Muriel Cooper, op.cit., is presented as a 'work-in-progress', which seemed to the author 'like the right approach to Muriel's work'.

9 Cheryl Buckley, 'Made in Patriarchy: Toward a Feminist Critique of Design', *Design Issues*, vol. 3, no. 2 (Spring 1986), p.3–14.

10 Johanna Drucker and Emily McVarish, *Graphic Design History. A Critical Guide* (New York: Prentice Hall, 2008).

11 Liz McQuiston, *Suffragettes to She-Devils* (London: Phaidon, 1997).

12 I would like to thank Sofia Hernandez for having brought the LTTR collective to my attention: www.lttr.org/journal/5/the-advantages-of-being-a-lesbian-woman-artist (accessed 23 April 2012).

13 See the extensively documented article by Benoît Buquet, 'Art, graphisme et féminisme à Los Angeles autour de Sheila Levrant de Bretteville', *Histoire de l'art*, no. 63 (October 2008), p.123–132.

14 Sheila Levrant de Bretteville, 'Some Aspects of Design from the Perspective of a Woman Designer', *Icographic*, no. 6 (1973), p.6.

15 In the film version of Goldfinger, *Pussy Galore*, a pilot at the head of a squadron of young Amazons, declares herself immune to male seduction (which is refuted by what follows in the film).

16 *Fuse 12: Propaganda* (Winter 1994).

17 In 1988, Liz McQuiston, citing an article which had recently appeared in *ID Magazine*, stated that the proportion of women in the field had gone from 25 percent to 52 percent between 1980 and 1985, *Women in Design* (London: Trefoil Publications, 1988), p.6. Thirteen years later, Maud Lavin, in the introduction to her 'Portfolio: Women and Design' *Clean New World* (Cambridge, MA: MIT Press, 2001), p.108, cites a publication of the American Institute of Graphic Design (AIGA) indicating that there are now more women entering the profession than men – but that women are still less well paid.

18 Sybille Hagmann, 'Non Existent Design: Women and the Creation of Type', *Visual Communication*, vol. 4, no. 2 (June 2005), p.186–194.

19 Besides the works by Liz McQuiston and Maud Lavin's 'Portfolio' essay already mentioned, we can cite in particular two essays by Ellen Lupton: 'Graphic Design in the Urban Landscape', in Joan Rothschild, ed., *Design and Feminism: Re-Visioning Spaces, Places, and Everyday Things* (New Brunswick, N. J: Rutgers University Press, 1999), and 'Women Graphic Designers', in Pat Kirkham, ed., *Women Designers in the USA, 1900–2000: Diversity and Difference*, exh. cat., Bard Graduate Center for Studies in the Decorative Arts, Design and Culture (New Haven/London: Yale University Press, 2000) (also available on the author's website: www.elupton.com), as well as Bryony Gomez-Palacio and Armin Vit's recent *Women of Design: Influence and Inspiration from the Original Trailblazers to the New Groundbreakers* (Cincinnati, Ohio: HOW Books, 2008). It should also be recalled that the 2007 Échirolles graphic design festival, in France, included an exhibition entitled '9 Women Graphic Designers'.

20 See in particular Jef Tombeur, *Women in the Printing Trade* (Mons, Belgium: Talus d'approche/Paris: Convention typographique, 2004) and Paul W Nash 'The Distaff Side: A Short History of Female Printer', *Ultrabold*, no. 1 (Autumn 2006), p.12–18.

21 François Rappo, 'Vieille France', *Sang Bleu*, nos. 3–4 (December 2008), available (in English) on the site ianparty.com (accessed 23 April 2012); Jeanne Veyrin-Forrer, *La Lettre et le Texte. Trente années de recherche sur l'histoire du livre* (Paris: École nationale supérieure de jeunes filles, 1987).

22 T. H. Barrett, *The Woman Who Discovered Printing* (New Haven and London: Yale University Press, 2007).

23 *The Pillow Book of Sei Shÿnagon*, Ivan Morris (trans. and ed.) (New York: Columbia University Press, 1967), p.159.

ISSN 0952-4649

Journal of

Design History

Volume 22 | Number 4 | 2009

Special Issue:
The Current State of Design History
Edited by Hazel Clark and David Brody

OXFORD UNIVERSITY PRESS

DESIGNING GRAPHIC DESIGN HISTORY

TEAL TRIGGS
2009

Introduction: The Graphic Artefact

*The National Grid is interested in the artefacts and methodologies of the practitioner –
the designers of everyday things – who seek to transform, in some small way, both
their own and their audiences' experience of the world around them.*[1]

Any approach to the study of graphic design and its history needs to take into account the form of the graphic object just as much as the nature of the content. It is the way that this form and content come together that makes this a unique enterprise. Victor Margolin (1996) has argued for a move away from 'a history of objects... toward a history of practice...' as a way of recognizing that there are multiple histories to consider – whether the product of Postmodernist thinking or not.[2] This was made manifest in the scholarship on self-published graphic design publications that has often been framed around the notion of 'graphic authorship'. Graphic authorship emerged during the mid-1990s and introduced new ways of considering the designer/client role within professional practice. The designers became the originators of the message and in turn adopted their own authorial voice and 'signature style'. Steven McCarthy writes about 'designer-authored histories' and the predominance of self-authorship where he suggests that publications such as *Octavo, Emigre, Fuse, Zed* and *News of the Whirled*, for example, were part of the ways in which contemporary aspects of 'culture, new technologies, and socio-political issues informed the history of the discipline'. At the same time, McCarthy is quick to point out that the history of self-publishing can also be seen in early twentieth-century publications such as *PM, Portfolio, Push Pin Graphic* and *Dot Zero*, and even further back to the typographic books of Eric Gill (1931) and Jan Tschichold (1928).[3]

On the other hand, curator and author Ellen Lupton differentiates between the designer as 'originator of content' and as 'producer' who 'is part of the system of making' a role that she highlights. Lupton also suggests that with the emergence of new 'desktop' technologies, the graphic designer returned to being someone who brought 'production activities back into the process of design'.[4] There is little doubt that designers and art directors, including Tibor Kalman (*Colours*), Neville Brody (*The Face*), Cipe Pineles (*Seventeen*) and Alexey Brodovitch (*Harper's Bazaar*) are firmly part of a history of graphic design and also within a history of visual culture more generally. The difference between these mainstream publications and those produced under the banner of graphic authorship depends, however, on who generates and maintains control over content. Lupton proposes that graphic designers might 'actively mediate between form and content'. If this is the case, then in what way might publications in which the graphic designer is both the producer and author represent an alternative view of history?

Graphic authorship has attempted to legitimize the designer's voice as equal to that of other privileged forms of authorship. The designer is able to exert 'control' over the content of what he or she is designing. Critics such as Michael Rock argue that 'design itself (is) content enough', making the analogy that the film director's work is embedded 'not in the story but the storytelling'.[5] Works written and produced by graphic designers contribute to any discussion of a discipline's 'history' in their essence as designed forms as well as social and cultural documents, but 'little magazines' are closer to the world of fan magazines than anything else. They are not client-driven and they are (in general) not intended for a mainstream readership. Instead, little magazines seek to address a design-literate demographic on its own terms. The job of documenting graphic design history within such publications is done through its content and is analogous to, for example, the horror fanzine (a contraction of 'fan magazine') that documents the history of horror films. In both cases, the design of the object itself is carefully constructed in order to suit its intended context.

Clive Dilnot wrote in 1984: '... defining and explaining design and what a designer does are dependent not only on immersion in design practice, but also on the ability to see this practice in both historical and social perspectives'.[6] I would add to this and suggest that at another level publications identified as little magazines – produced and written by graphic designers – do much more. At once they are not only designed forms but also forms that document graphic design history itself.

A Brief History of Graphic Design History

Graphic design history has often been relegated to discussions in footnotes. It is often viewed outside more established areas of historical study such as architecture, decorative arts or industrial design. In part, this may be due to graphic design's various beginnings in the history of art, printing, typography, photography and advertising.[7] In 1983, the event 'Coming of Age: The First Symposium on the History of Graphic Design', held at the Rochester Institute of Technology, sought to reconsider these histories, calling for 'recognition and formal study of graphic design history'.[8] The symposium's organizers argued that establishing 'graphic design history' would be a step forward for the graphic design profession. A year later, Dilnot's two-part essay on the 'The State of Design History' ('Part I: Mapping the Field' and 'Part II: Problems and Possibilities') appeared in *Design Issues*, and its publication proved a further significant shift in recognizing design history, theory and criticism. To his credit, Dilnot was not oblivious to the role of the graphic design historian or design practitioner. Indeed, he engaged with a discussion on typography and its history in order to reinforce his argument that any methodological armoury is appropriate to the task whatever the research question might be. He bemoaned the fact that some history had become celebratory and, in surveying typographic history, he briefly mentioned British printing traditions and problematized their intellectual positions.

Although the 1980s saw a plethora of books on industrial design and related areas, graphic design in general was not attracting the same attention from historians. The relationship between graphic design history and design history became disputed, and this was no more evident than in mainstream publishing. Dilnot's reference to key books published on industrial design history included titles by Jeffrey Meikle (1982), Arthur J. Pulos (1983), Penny Sparke (1983) and John Heskett (1985).[9] These, he claimed, had established a recognizable foundation for study out of which a series of design histories emerged with a focus on objects and design practices. These histories were also framed by art history, and social and cultural history, as well as material culture, and as a result began to take on 'new' significance for academics and design professionals alike.

In 1983, Nancy Green, the Editorial Director of Van Nostrand Reinhold, remarked: 'Of one hundred and twenty active titles (including about thirty titles in preparation) we have one book on the history of graphic design'.[10] Green explained that most books published on graphic design were practical, 'how-to' guides.[11] Twenty-five years later, little seems to have changed.

The division between histories of the subject and instructional books remains entrenched. This point is not lost on contemporary design critics such as Rick Poynor, who laments the lack of publishing opportunities in the field. He writes:

> When this patchy output is placed beside the numerous books produced by scholars working in, for instance, the fields of art, architecture or film, as it is in any visual arts bookshop, the effect is to confirm that graphic design history as a terrain for intensive and sustained research and study barely exists at all.[12]

Perhaps this ephemerality is the natural consequence of a lack of definition for the subject. Jeremy Aynsley, one of Britain's first historians of graphic design, has acknowledged that the field of graphic design has an inherently broad design remit and therefore that accompanying historical writings will mirror this. Thus

> At its broadest, graphic design, and consequently its history, came to cover anything from the design of a bus ticket to sign systems for motorways, the packaging of cigarettes to the typographical organization of dictionaries, the design of the lead-in to nightly television news to art-directing a magazine.[13]

For the same reason, graphic design history has provided us with a multiplicity of voices. The late historian and educator Philip B. Meggs commented that 'the ephemeral nature of graphic design combined with its life within social, economic, and cultural spheres of a society, creates a diversity beyond the range of architecture or graphic design'.[14] As if in response to this diversity, its history books have followed the format of survey texts, organized chronologically from cave dwellings to digital design, and focusing on establishing 'a' (if not 'the') canon of graphic design. Meggs writes, 'history becomes a reflection of the needs, sensibilities, and attitudes of the chronicler's time as surely as it represents the accomplishments of bygone eras'.[15] In his so-called 'definitive history of graphic communication',[16] Meggs introduces his first edition with a graphic history of prehistoric times and the cave paintings of Lascaux and ends with the subjective viewpoints of Postmodernist designers, illustrated by Kenneth Hiebert's poster for an exhibition by Paul Rand and a symposium on the 'role of art in graphic design'.

In the 1990s, an identifiable canon of graphic design history emerged.[17] The 'heroic' designer monograph appeared, providing a list of 'Who's Who', including David Carson, Paul Rand, Neville Brody, Fuel, and Tomato, with the contribution of women and ethnic role models notably absent. Many of these monographs may also be considered 'object' books – that is, books produced by design studios full of vibrant images of individual projects and studio collaborations. Object books were promotional vehicles for commercial design studios. They were not necessarily self-critical and often presented the designer's history in a chronological fashion without any reflective or critical analysis of the work's social, political or economic contexts. A decade later such an approach has not gone unnoticed in the design press where, for example, one commentator observes about the intent of the designer's monograph: 'Not one speck of self-criticism, historic or artistic contextualisation, nothing too deep, too ambitious, nothing that might inhibit new commissions'.[18]

On the other hand, the way in which designers visualized their own work in these books often challenges conventional ways of reading history. The British design trio of Peter Miles, Damon Murray and Stephen Sorrell of Fuel employed bold image and text juxtapositions in their two published monographs, *Fuel* (1997) and *Fuel Three Thousand* (2000) as a way of exploring authorial positions. A similar, yet more politically charged thematic approach forms the basis of Jonathan Barnbrook's monograph *The Barnbrook Bible: The Graphic Design of Jonathan*

Barnbrook (2007). Commissioned essayists position Barnbrook's work within a historical framework, but at the same time the designer himself has a reputation for contextualizing the historical and political positioning of his own typeface designs. These books can in some ways be seen as taking a Postmodern path. The history on offer is not necessarily linear and involves a variety of entry points. Nonetheless, in terms of critical distance we must ask how much has actually changed.

The issue of copyright and control over visual material is of note here. Any author seeking to take a critical stance on a designer's work will necessarily have to obtain access and permission. As such, any documentation of designer's work within the context of graphic design history is edited and therefore, any narrative history is distorted.

Yet, at the same time, our understanding of graphic design history has been shaped by edited series. For example, Poynor's series of books on typography, beginning with *Typography Now: The Next Wave* (1991), reproduced some of the defining pieces of the 1980s' typographic explosion. Poynor's editorial selection (re)presented an emerging canon of works by typographers such as Phil Baines, Barry Deck and Barnbrook. Steven Heller's range of design anthologies for Allworth Press (e.g. the *Looking Closer* series) reproduced mainly previously published articles and similarly sought to refine the canon.

Other books published during the 1990s were more forward looking. Richard Hollis' *Graphic Design: A Concise History* (1992), for example, took as its starting point the design profession, beginning in the middle of the twentieth century. As author and designer of the book, Hollis creates visual and text-based narratives as viewed from a Modernist's authorial position. David Crowley and Paul Jobling's *Graphic Design: Reproduction and Representation since 1800* (1996) presented a broader historical overview of graphic design, choosing to focus on the social, cultural and political contexts of the graphic artefact. This approach 'fitted' well with any discussion of posters, magazines and other mainstream ephemera where the readers/users of graphic design artefacts were not understood in isolation. Although the book was well researched and written, Victor Margolin pointed out in *Eye* magazine (1997) that the authors 'are too ready to sacrifice design at the altar of an all consuming capitalism, unlike Michael Twyman, Meggs and Hollis, who, as practitioners, convey in their writings a passion for graphic communication that is missing here'.[19]

Bringing things up to date, recent textbooks such as Johanna Drucker and Emily McVarish's *Graphic Design History: A Critical Guide* (2008) explore the potential of establishing other approaches to graphic design history. In their introduction, the authors readily acknowledge the influence of three of their predecessors: Meggs and his 'historical foundation'; Richard Hollis' cultural contexts; and the 'methodological approach' offered by Crowley and Jobling. They go on to suggest a different position on the history of graphic design by contextualizing the 'social forces and conditions of their production' of the work in order to provide insight into the way we understand practice today.[20]

A final mention should be made of Stephen J. Eskilson's book *Graphic Design: A New History*, published a year earlier than Drucker and McVarish's, which was written in order to provide a contrast to the conventional style books and design monographs. Eskilson comments: 'It is my belief that graphic design history has too often been presented through a parade of styles and individual achievements devoid of significant social context, and that this tendency has obscured much of the richness and complexity of its development.'[21] Such an assertion is questioned by Jobling in a review published in the *Journal of Design History* (2008), where he reflects that 'Eskilson's study ends up more or less as a chronological survey, another history of graphic design rather than "a new history"'.[22]

The narratives of graphic design history have thus ranged from the chronological and biographical to the visual and contextual. Yet, as Steven Heller wrote in the introduction to his reader *Graphic Design History* (2001), 'While design historians must use cultural and political histories as backdrops, ultimately the stories they tell must be rooted in issues of design. The challenge is, therefore, to find pegs on which to hang design history so that it is relevant beyond the design ghetto.'[23] It is to this task that we now must turn.

The Little Magazine in Graphic Design History

The relationship of design practice to its history is a continuing theme in Dilnot's writings. For graphic design, he states, 'history seemed to be irrelevant for a discipline in the process of forming itself and attempting to escape the historic limitations of arts-and-crafts attitudes and its commercial art background'.[24] Yet, it is in early publications such as *Typos: International Journal of Typography* (produced at the London College of Printing, and quoted by Dilnot) and other independent publishing ventures that a history of graphic design (and indeed printing traditions) is documented – whether consciously or not. These publications on type might be considered design objects in and of themselves. One way of reconnecting with Dilnot's plea for a historical method 'fit for purpose' could be to consider this extra dimension: in other words, in what ways might the work of criticism function as a designed 'graphic' artefact and hence as a work of visual critique in its own right? This is a view echoed by the curator Freek Lomme in his recent essay on the tensions between industrial and visual design. He writes that visual design '... is not just about form or about content. It is about form of communication that is carved hand in hand along with the material conditions and immaterial paradigms'.[25]

Certainly, this does not discount the celebratory or the aesthetic (see Dilnot's remark that a possible history of the design profession is to be found in the design of the 'glossy pages' of magazines such as *Domus* and *Industrial Design*), but it does offer new possibilities for present-day design criticism and history. Such possibilities, however, require a platform for debate, a way of disseminating information to a broader audience. Dilnot asks 'to what extent can history contribute to the understanding of what design is and what the designer does, and to what extent can history make that understanding public?' It is here where graphic design, as a practice that considers its audience as a primary element of the communication process, is able to contribute more fully.

Graphic design critics such as Poynor, for example, regularly lament the deficiencies of mainstream publishing practices in producing books that focus on the dissemination of a graphic design history.[26] On the other hand, such gaps in publishing have left the field open to a plethora of independently produced graphic design self-published magazines – many emerging out of the 1980s wave of graphic design activity. *Emigre*, for example, began as a fanzine for typographers and gradually emerged as one of the more dynamic documents of 1980s and 1990s graphic design. Despite its eventual absorption into mainstream design practices, the publication's founders, Zuzana Licko and Rudy VanderLans, regularly sought to make it a 'meeting place for ideas' where graphic design stood 'at its very center'. The magazine was about graphic design, 'craft, style, practice, education, theory, history, ethics, as well as its impact on our society.'[27]

British designers were also exploring ways in which little magazines could become venues for discussions on matters of typographic design, both historical and contemporary. Although short lived, with a series of eight issues launching in 1986, *Octavo: An International Journal of Typography*, produced by the British design group 8vo, generated a great interest amongst the design community internationally, at the same time running essays that interrogated issues related to design and typography. For example, Bridget Wilkins' piece 'Type and Image', first published in issue 90.7, questioned conventions of reading, layout and legibility. The design of the essay produced a highly contested space as a result of the visual tension between the page layout and its content. Its producers conceived *Octavo* as a forum for challenging the conventions and accepted practices of typography. Despite its position as a forum for visual experimentation, some critics argued that the journal's design continually 'overwhelmed' the authors' texts. On reflection, the designers explained:

> This was partly driven by what we perceived as a growing expectation (among the audience) of the design and print production with each issue published. But we were the client, and the audience were typographers and designers – we were designing for the visually literate, which of course is not the same as designing, for example, a bus timetable for public uses. We understood the difference and the context.[28]

Octavo emerged out of a growing tradition of self-published magazines in which designers found the freedom to experiment with visual forms and production techniques. A decade later, two other significant publications emerged: *Zed* (1995–2000) edited by Katie Salen, then based at Virginia Commonwealth University, and Peter Bilak and Stuart Bailey's *Dot Dot Dot* (2000–2011) in the Netherlands. These publications reflected a shift in focus by their producers from overt typographic experimentation to an editorial and design policy more akin to the production of a 'fanzine-journal'. Much like the fanzines that emerged in the late 1970s, *Dot Dot Dot* in particular developed out of a keen interest in the process of making. Co-founder Bilak reflects that 'in fact the actual process of making the magazine is the real motivation. For ourselves, *DDD* cannot be defined by a single description. If it does, it becomes stifled and we should do something about it. I suppose it is mainly about the development.'[29] Despite the publication's change in publisher (now Stuart Bailey and David Reinfurt as Dexter Sinister), such process orientation has become even more visible. For example, Dexter Sinister presented three evenings of events held at Somerset House, London (2008), where the content of a forthcoming issue of *Dot Dot Dot* was played out 'live' before an audience, thus 'existing in "real time" before being hardened into printed form'.[30]

During this period, Visual Culture emerged as an area of study, introducing graphic design writers and historians to new ways of framing the visuality of graphic artefacts. *Zed*, for example, framed discussions of designed objects around sociopolitical themes including the politics of design, public and private, design and morality as well as semiotics and pedagogy.

Dot Dot Dot magazine.

Meanwhile, *Dot Dot Dot* questioned the tensions existing between art and design drawing, and a broader context of art practice, music, language, politics, film and literature.

It may be suggested that these publications have gone some way towards documenting the history of the profession and its debates through content as well as 'designed' forms. Thus, they and other little magazines have an impact on the ways in which graphic design is positioned and documented within both theoretical and historical frameworks. Nonetheless, their reach to a broader 'public' audience is still limited. In the case of *Dot Dot Dot*, only 3000 copies per issue were printed in 2004 for example, and although distributed worldwide tended to be read by designers and educators. As such, we must be cautious in claiming that the little magazine has had an impact on the ways in which a broader public might consider a history of graphic design.

The Remaking of Graphic Design History: Little Magazines

Graphic design history has in many ways built upon traditions found in architectural history and its understanding of theory and practice. It is worth looking for a moment at the publishing traditions fostered by architectural little magazines of the early 1960s and 1970s, which exploited potential synergies between graphic designers and architects.[31] These were indeed 'engagements of enquiry' and through collaboration demonstrated the visual and critical richness found at such an intersection of these disciplines.

Such little magazine collaborations were featured in the recently held exhibition at the Architectural Association in London titled 'Clip Stamp Fold: The Radical Architecture of Little Magazines, 196x–7x', which explored how experimental publications such as *Room East 128 Chronicle*, *Archigram*, *Op.cit* and *Connection* affected the development of a postwar architectural culture.[32] The show's curator, architectural historian Beatriz Colomina, argued that these often cheaply produced publications: 'provided an arena for critical discussion of the role of politics and new technologies in architecture and through their dissemination, a global network of exchange amongst architectural students, avant-garde architects and theorists...'[33] Through form and critical discourse, the magazine's specific concerns, and political and/or philosophical positions, reflected a moment on the historical timeline. Disseminated to a like-minded community, the little magazine (and in some cases broadsheet) represented an immediate snapshot of contemporary discourse and sometimes provided a catalyst for action.[34]

For example, issue 1 of *NET* (1975) featured a cover printed in bright yellow and red showing an image of the British-born architectural critic and historian Colin Rowe, juxtaposed with a building by Berlin architect Ludwig Leo. Rowe became best known for his book *Collage City* (with Fred Koetter) and for identifying a 'conceptual relationship between modernity and tradition' in architecture. Here, *NET* publishes the transcription of Rowe's conference piece on 'Conceptual Architecture' (1975), emphasizing the immediacy of the discourse within architectural circles. This 'cut-n-paste' sense of immediacy and urgency was soon formalized. One reviewer in the *New York Times* observed that with the launch of *Oppositions* (1973), both the debates and the design had become mainstream. For instance, the bright orange covers designed by Massimo Vignelli reflected the 'more self-conscious discussion of architectural theory' found inside.[35]

The concept of little magazines permeated a range of cultural discourses throughout the 1970s, in literature as well as fine art practices. In graphic design, self-published magazines were also a feature of design and printing practices (e.g. *Dot Zero*, *Typographische Monatsblätter* (TM) and *Push Pin Studios*) and in art schools (e.g. *Ark* and *Typos*). By the 1980s and into the 1990s critical discourse was more prominent. An interest in graphic authorship combined with the desire to reflect a critical discourse in design and typography was prevalent in, amongst others, *Emigre*, *Octavo*, *Dot Dot Dot* and *ZED*. All these were publications designed and produced by their editors – a set-up that suggested that equal consideration was being given to both form and content generation.[36] Something was happening in the world of design publishing, but it would take another step in its evolution to connect it with the notion of the everyday.

Design History and Popular Cultural Theory

... I guess it [issue 1] reflects a bias towards the practice of graphic design being about documenting culture rather than creating culture.[37]

In Part II of the essay 'The State of Design History' (1984), Dilnot observes that 'the integration of cultural studies with design history has not taken place'. He asks 'what could design historians bring to the study of contemporary material culture?' and goes on to suggest that consideration should be given to accounts of "cultural systems" and the artefacts within them which 'may well be useful for constructing a theory of design history'.[38] It is worthwhile exploring further the way in which Dilnot positions the designed artefact and its context at the centre of the discourse, and what that means for graphic design.

In the UK, the 1980s saw the predominant model of Cultural Studies still informed by the Centre for Contemporary Cultural Studies at the University of Birmingham, which essentially took a Marxist position on culture and saw criticism as a form of intervention. It also pioneered work in subcultural theory, focusing on notions of political resistance. Since then, Cultural Studies has moved on and become less dominated by such critiques and has drifted more towards the study of culture, in its broadest sense. In the 1980s, a new breed of design historian emerged, including Sparke and Meikle, who embraced material culture as an approach to studying the designed artefact, taking into account not only the socio-historical context but also the process of design and production.

In the 2000s, Henry Jenkins and others took this approach even further to argue for an 'emergent cultural studies'.[39] This form of an 'emergent perspective' meant drawing upon culture that forms part of everyday life while at the same time 'reclaiming cultural studies' relationship to popular traditions of criticism and debate'. Thus, in a sentence that echoes the Birmingham School: '... pop culture's politics continue to be formed not only by the historical context and the individual readers who experience it, but also by the ongoing class battle over who determines culture'.[40]

This approach takes into account popular culture 'as a potentially powerful and progressive political force in the battle to define "culture"'.[41] An example would be early British punk fanzines such as *Sniffin Glue*, *Ripped & Torn* and *Chainsaw*, where individuals' voices of opposition played a part in informing an understanding of subcultures. As the 'zines were quickly absorbed into the mainstream, any position of resistance suggested by the visual was subsequently made less threatening. The visual characteristics of 'cut-n-paste' ransom note letterforms, collage and hand-drawn and typewritten texts became commonplace, appropriated by advertisers and large retail chains. A graphic language of 'resistance'[42] once found in the realm of the subcultural emerged as a 'cool' understated message for consumers.

The graphic design publications under discussion in this essay are not oppositional in the sense of being political interventions, but rather express, as the fanzines did before them, the need to be linked to other like-minded individuals and to be considered as an integral part of such a group. The framework that I propose here for examining the phenomenon of designers' publications draws from the recent work of Jenkins and his discussion of the centrality of popular culture; in particular, his work that focuses on fan cultures (the fan scholar) and the manner in which this is contextualized. *The National Grid*, much like the architectural publications of the 1970s, reflects a fascination for crossing disciplinary territories while at the same time documenting 'culture'. This little magazine is challenging perceived notions of what graphic design history should be. It is at once local and international, taking as its cue the perspectives of a new wave of young designers steeped in the culture of music, fanzines and the design of the everyday. *The National Grid's* editors are also the publication's designers, with a commitment to providing a mouthpiece for those voices not normally heard. In doing so, a history of a design culture and design practice is made explicit.

A Case Study
Passionate About Music, Design and Culture: The National Grid

I think it would be interesting if graphic design could look at itself in relation to music rather than architecture or industrial design. Then we wouldn't have to talk about problem solving, and we could talk about resonance instead.[43]

Launched in 2006, *The National Grid* is edited and produced by Luke Wood and Jonty Valentine with the stated intent of plugging the 'void in New Zealand's design discourse'. Its title was chosen at first because they 'just thought it sounded good' but later associations with music were made with the name of a New Zealand recording studio and a Bats album titled *At The National Grid*.[44] Thus, there are obvious echoes of the 'design grid' and of national (New Zealand) consciousness. Yet there is also a desire to speak to an international readership: in issue 1 its editors comment, 'Artefacts are only interesting in as much as they index the rest of the world'.[45]

The National Grid no. 1 (March 2006), front and back cover. Front cover by Luke Wood and Jonty Valentine, back cover featuring a folder belonging to Dylan Herkes.

This correlation between local and global cultural production is reflected throughout many of the essays published thus far in the five issues of the series (prevalent in the work by Steve Kerr and Wood and others). Kerr's essay 'Labels from the Post-Punk Periphery' (issue 2), for example, reflects upon the significance of New Zealand's independent record label 'Flying Nun' as a 'major cultural movement'. Explicit links are made to a broader post-punk music scene but specifically in relationship to an emerging 'do-it-yourself' ethos. New Zealand's geographical position – peripheral, often overlooked – resonates with the 'edgy' post-punk musical and design directions. Kerr remarks: 'Thinking carefully about the connections between local culture and international movements might offer a fruitful approach to understanding New Zealand's pop cultural preferences and its wider society'.[46]

Top: *The National Grid* no. 2 (December 2006), front and back cover. Front cover by Dylan Herkes, back cover featuring the back cover of the album *Clyma Est Mort* by The Dead C. **Bottom:** *The National Grid* no. 3 (July 2007), front and back cover. Front cover by Bruce Russell, back cover featuring a photograph of Geoffrey Walker arranging placards for use during an anti-Springbok tour demonstration in Wellington, 1981 (Evening Post Collection, Alexander Turnbull Library).

The National Grid is an independently produced publication with a relatively small press run, distributed through the web, by word of mouth, and sold in selected specialist bookstores internationally. The first issue was financed by a grant from the University of Canterbury School of Fine Arts with subsequent funding from Creative New Zealand, the government's arts council. The publication is modelled on 'a cheap lo-fi graphic design fanzine' and therefore there is no advertising and, in the first two issues, a reliance on low production qualities to enhance its sense of belonging in the margins. There is a clear nod to the visual referencing of music fanzines in the way text is sometimes crossed out and the subversion of the conventions of traditional layout (e.g. the footnotes appear before the essay). The printing is less than perfect. In fact, the editors connect this to the current conditions of the printing industry in New Zealand, where the debates between 'trade' and 'craft' are current (by issue 3, 'Colour Plates' are highlighted in a separate section at the front of the issue, perhaps indicating increased trust in the ability of the printers). At the same time, the design of the publication takes a 'knowing' approach to the look and feel of the production and layout format of early issues of *Dot Dot Dot*.

On another level, *The National Grid* shares concerns similar to those of the editors of *Dot Dot Dot*. Take, for example, an essay published in issue 3 by Valentine, reflecting on an exhibition he curated of 'commonplace books' – the precursor to modern-day reference books. Valentine quotes from Stuart Bailey's music writings published in *Dot Dot Dot*, as well as those texts written by British historian and Hyphen Press publisher Robin Kinross, who has been a supporter of the Dutch publication from its inception.[47] Thus, he makes the link with Bailey's ideas on 'graphic design as translation' – that is, the transformation from the conceptual to the physical object. The central theme of the exhibition (titled 'Just hold me') and its accompanying essay focuses on an intent to '... showcase (in this case publication) design as a dimension of object making – and in doing, to profile designers as makers'.[48] The author critically evaluates the judging processes of contemporary New Zealand's professional design awards by problematizing the design brief and the resulting discourse, and by making visible the design process.

An emergent Cultural Studies takes into account the shift from 'author' to 'maker' in order to acknowledge the process of generating cultural materials. The notion of the author and the emphasis on authority, which ultimately is relational, takes into account origins, process, aesthetic and ideological goals. Jenkins writes: 'The concept of "Maker" allows us to understand that works have origins, that they are made from earlier works, and that the aesthetic and ideological goals of their makers are relevant to our understanding of their production and circulation'.[49]

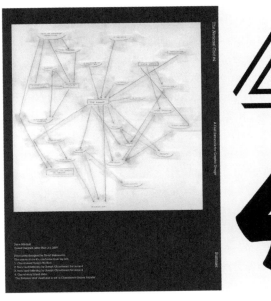

The National Grid no. 4 (December 2007), front and back cover. Front cover by David Bennewith using typefaces by Joseph Churchward, back cover featuring the work *Crowd Diagram*, by Dane Mitchell.

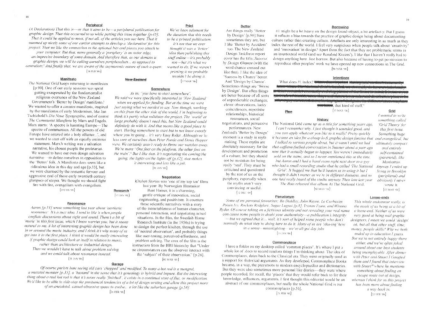

The National Grid adopted a graphic language found in early punk fanzines while also subverting the conventional layout of a design magazine. no. 1 (March 2006), p.38–39.

The editors of *The National Grid* document their early thinking about the rationale behind this direction in a double-page spread located on pages 38 and 39 in issue 1. Citations for the piece are found on the previous page 37, making evident their 'critical map' (based upon Salvador Dalí's 'Paranoid-Critical Method') prior to the reading of the rationale.[50] The double-page spread organizes itself into categories of reflection providing a framework where consideration is given, for example, to the publication's perspective on the 'peripheral'. The producers argue for the idea of being at the 'outer edge' of the dominant design profession in New Zealand. In issue 1, its editors define the magazine's relationship to the peripheral. They explain: '... it [*The National Grid*] aims to be a peripheral publication for graphic design... a periphery is an outer edge, an imprecise boundary of some domain. And therefore that, as our domain is graphic design, we will be calling ourselves peripheralists... as opposed to central-ists.'[51] This is similar to the idea that fanzines are 'below critical radar'.[52] *The National Grid* also represents resistance to the cultural norm in the way the publication fills a conspicuously empty space in New Zealand's design discourse. Like many little magazines, there is a move away, in terms of content, from a reliance on business and client relationships.

Nonetheless, this is not to say that *The National Grid* does not embrace the conventions of writing about graphic design history or theory. Other essays in the publication include his-torical discussions such as 'The Lay of the Case: Putting NZ Communication Design on the Map' or more theoretical positioning of design in 'Graphic Design Needs a Distortion Pedal'. In addition, essays appear that focus on the everyday, such as exterior signs on university build-ings and New Zealand postcards, as well as a theoretical positioning of Michel de Certeau in relationship to counterfeit design.[53]

The commissioned writers on *The National Grid* are normally also design practitio-ners – an approach which the editors hope will encourage writing about design that is 'more speculative, resonant and useful...'[54] in crossing over between the world of popular music, art and conventional design history. The only criterion they have for contributors proposes that '*The National Grid* invites people to design and write about aspects of graphic/visual culture – at home or abroad – that excite their curiosity and keep them up at night'. Jenkins observes that 'the best cultural critics speak as "insiders" as well as "outsiders"'.[55] Much as in the per-sonal fanzines we see today, 'writing about popular culture from an "up close and personal" perspective has brought new issues to the foreground, such as the place of mass culture within personal and popular memory...' [56] Jenkins argues for a 'new relationship between academic and popular modes of engagement that takes the best of both worlds, recognizes and values alternative forms of knowledge production, and seeks to better map the continuities and differences between them'. [57] Any study of documents such as these, however, raises interesting questions about the relationship between historical understanding and material documentation. Michel Foucault comments on this problematic in his book *The Archaeology of Knowledge* where he cautions: 'The document is not the fortunate tool of a history that is primarily and fundamentally memory; history is one way in which a society recognizes and develops a mass of documentation with which it is inextricably linked'. [58]

The National Grid has a circulation of 500. It does get distributed in Europe and the US and has a web presence (www.thenationalgrid.co.nz). It has not yet garnered any publicity in the mainstream design press, so far as I am aware, but its value resides in its attitude. No longer are graphic designers treating history and their subject in a linear fashion: the incorporation of perspectives on popular culture opens up the possibility of looking at the individual, the everyday and the 'cultural object as the primary source of meaning'. [59]

Little magazines have been pivotal in this shift. They reflect a slice of time through their explorations of the social, political and cultural frameworks in which they operate. *The National Grid* is not only a prime example but also takes the discussion further into the realm of design process, method and operating on the 'margins' of mainstream practice. At the same time, *The National Grid* provides a forum to highlight New Zealand's graphic design history and to address the international context in which its history resides. Any written design history and criticism needs to have a critical distance between that which is produced and analysed. I would, however, argue that self-produced design publications provide valuable insights into the theoretical and visual concerns that enrich our understanding of the history of the profession, graphic artefacts and their cultural contexts.

Teal Triggs is Professor of Graphic Design and Associate Dean, Royal College of Art, London.
First published in *Journal of Design History*, vol. 22, no. 4, 2009.

Page spread illustrating an essay on New Zealand's first typographer written by Don McKenzie 'Harding, Robert Coupland, 1849–1916: Printer, Typographer, Journalist'. *The National Grid* no. 4 (2007), p.18–19.

1   Andy Palmer, *The National Grid. The Lumiere Reader* (17 May 2008) lumiere.net.nz/reader/arts.php/item/1704 (accessed 25 May 2009).

2   Victor Margolin, 'Teaching Design History', *Statements*, vol. 11, no.2 (1996), n.p.

3   Steven McCarthy, 'What is Self-authored Graphic Design Anyway?' (1995) www.episodic-design.com/writings/agenda.html (accessed 25 May 2009). A year later, Michael Rock outlined the phenomenon of 'The Designer as Author' for *Eye* magazine *Eye* 20 (Spring 1996), which has been republished on the internet (www. typotheque.com and www.2x4.org) and in the *Education of a Graphic Designer* edited by Steven Heller (1998). In his essay, Rock suggests that the 'designer as author' may be defined as: (1) the designers who are writing and publishing material about design, (2) the designer who constructs other's narratives or (3) the designer who is involved in the 'creation of self-referential statements'. This is also to distinguish it from Rick Poynor's arguments of visual journalism and the 'designer as reporter' in Rick Poynor, 'The Designer as Reporter' in *Obey the Giant* (Basel: August/Birkhauser, 2001), p.185–8.

4   Ellen Lupton, 'The Producers', in Ellen Lupton, Susan Yelavich, Donald Albrecht and Mitchell Owen, eds., *Inside Design Now: National Design Triennial* (New York: Princeton Architectural Press, 2003), www.elupton.com/index.php?id=48 (accessed 25 May 2009).

5   Michael Rock, 'Fuck Content', 2005, www.2x4.org/# (accessed 15 February 2008). McCarthy questions Rock's position, remarking that '… his reliance on post-structural literary theory and film auteur theory served more to retro-fit a definition of self-authorship in graphic design than to discuss why this movement is born of the present moment'.

6   Clive Dilnot, 'The State of Design History, Part I: Mapping the Field', *Design Issues*, vol. 1, no. 1 (1984), p.6.

7   For example, see Lucien Febvre and Henri-Jean Martin, *The Coming of the Book: The Impact of Printing 1450–1800*, trans. David Gerard, Geoffrey Nowell-Smith and David Wootton, eds. (London: Verso, 1957) (republished in English 1976 and 1984). See also Douglas McMurtrie, *The Book: The Story of Printing and Bookmaking* (New York: Oxford University Press, 1943); Warren Chappell, *A Short History of the Printed Word* (New York: Alfred A Knopf, 1970); John Dreyfus, *Into Print: Selected Writings on Printing History, Typography and Book Production* (Boston: David R. Godine, 1995).

8   Barbara Hodik and Roger Remington, 'Introduction', in *Coming of Age: The First Symposium on the History of Graphic Design* (New York: RIT, 1983), p.5.

9   See, for example, Arthur Pulos, *American Design Ethic* (Cambridge: MIT Press, 1983); John Heskett, *Industrial Design* (World of Art Series) (London: Thames & Hudson, 1985); Jeffrey Meikle, *Twentieth Century Limited: Industrial Design in American* (Philadelphia: Temple University Press, 1982); Penny Sparke, *Consultant Design: The History and Practice of the Designer in Industry* (London: Pembridge Press, 1983).

10   Nancy Green, 'Publishing Graphic Design History', in Barbara Hodik and Roger Remington, eds., *The First Symposium on the History of Graphic Design: Coming of Age* (Rochester: Rochester Institute of Technology, 1983), p.32.

11   This is a point taken up again in 2005 by Rick Poynor in his keynote during 'New Views: Repositioning Graphic Design History' held at the London College of Communication. See also the conference review by Alice Twemlow, 'New Views: Repositioning Graphic Design History', *Eye* 70 (Spring 2006). Graphic design history has always had difficulty in being seen as an established field of study. Although typography and book design, perhaps in the way it has developed out of printing traditions, is more firmly represented by a range of historical accounts (e.g. William Irvins (1953); S.H. Steinberg (1996); Lucien Febvre and Henri-Jean Martin (1976)). Dilnot acknowledges this too (1984: 10).

12   Rick Poynor, 'Out of the Studio: Graphic Design History and Visual Studies', ed. Teal Triggs, *Design Issues*, Special Issue: *The History of Graphic Design* (2010).

13   Jeremy Aynsley, 'Graphic Design', in Hazel Conway, ed., *Design History: A Student's Handbook* (London Allen & Unwin, 1987), p.136.

14   Philip B. Meggs, 'Methods and Philosophies in Design History Research', Lecture presented at the Universidad de las Americas Luebla, Cholula, Puebla, Mexico (24 February 1994), reprinted in *Meggs: Making Graphic Design History* (Hoboken: John Wiley & Sons, 2008), p.221

15   Philip B. Meggs, *A History of Graphic Design* (New York: Van Nostrand Reinhold, 1983), n.p.

16   Publisher's promotional blurb in the first edition (*Meggs, A History of Graphic Design*). Even today it continues to be one of the most influential written histories, appearing on class reading lists internationally.

17   For an in-depth discussion of books published in the 1990s, see Teal Triggs, 'The Endless Library at the End of Print', *Eye* 27 (Spring 1998), p.39–47

18   Michael Johnson, 'Thought for the Week: Dreaming about Designer Monographs' (2008) www. johnsonbanks.co.uk/thoughtfortheweek/index.php (accessed 4 May 2009).

19   Victor Margolin, 'Graphic Design: Reproduction and Representation Since 1800 – A Review', *Eye* 25 (Summer 1997), p.83–4.

20   Johanna Drucker and Emily McVarish, *Graphic Design History: A Critical Guide*, Pearson Prentice Hall, Upper Saddle River, 2008, p.xi. Written with the student of graphic design in mind, the approach of this book has been debated on the design profession's blogs – most notably the online discussion between Denise Gonzales Crisp and Rick Poynor for *Design Observer*. Crisp, a design practitioner/educator, and Poynor, a design writer, present a series of musings on this general survey book, drawing the conclusion that the book 'makes an admirable leap in the right direction of adding social context to a social activity'. Denise Gonzales Crisp and Rick Poynor, 'A Critical View of Graphic Design History', in *Design Observer: Writings on Design and Culture*, Michael Bierut, William Drenttel, Jessica Helfund, Julie Lasky, eds. (2008) do3.rubystudio.com/archives/entry.html ? id = 38766 (accessed 5 October 2008).

21   Stephen Eskilson, *Graphic Design: A New History* (London: Laurence King, 2007), p.10.

22   Paul Jobling, 'Graphic Design, A New History', *Journal of Design History*, vol. 21, no. 3 (2008), p.296–8.

23 Steven Heller, 'The Beginning of History', in eds. Steven Heller and Georgette Balance, *Graphic Design History* (New York: Allworth Press, 2001), p.viii.

24 Clive Dilnot, 'The State of Design History', Part 1, in ed. Victor Margolin, *Design Discourse: History Theory Criticism* (Chicago: The University of Chicago Press, 1984), p.218.

25 Freek Lomme, 'Descarting – A Study of the Tension Between Industrial and Visual Design', in *Onomatopee 19: Where Visual and Industrial Design Mutually Attracts and Distract* (Eindhoven: Onamatopee, 2008), p.6.

26 Rick Poynor, 'Reluctant Discipline: Graphic Design History's Protracted Birth', in ed. Teal Triggs, *New Views: An International Symposium on the History of Graphic Design*, London College of Communication (27–29 October 2005).

27 Zuzana Licko and Rudy VanderLans, 'Extract' from *Emigre Exhibition Catalogue* (Nuth: Drukkerij Rosbeek, 1998) www.emigre.com/EB.php?id=93 (accessed 8 November 2008).

28 8vo, *On the Outside* (Baden: Lars Müller Publishers, 2005), p.98.

29 Rudy VanderLans, 'Peter Bilak Founder of Typotheque, Dot Dot Dot' www.typotheque.com/articles/peter_bilak_founder_of_typotheque_dot_dot_dot_areerbuilder.com (accessed 8 November 2008). First published in *Emigre*, no. 67 (2004).

30 'Wouldn't it be Nice: Wishful Thinking in Art and Design' www.somersethouse.org.uk/visual_arts/721.asp (accessed 8 November 2008).

31 This also applied to numerous fine art publications as well as literary little magazines.

32 The show opened in New York at the Storefront for Art and Architecture (February 2007).

33 Introductory panel and press release Beatriz Colomina, organised by AACP/Schumon Basar, 'Clip Stamp Fold: The Radical Architecture of Little Magazines, 196x–7x' held 9.11–7.12.2007), Architectural Association London www.clipstampfold.com (accessed 5 October 2008).

34 Indeed, the importance of publications in maintaining a contemporary discourse is picked up in RoseLee Goldberg's article 'The Word on Art, or the New Magazines', an assessment of a new generation of magazines, which 'want to use the magazine format as a catalyst for attitudes that have slowly emerged in the past few years', unlike those of the previous decade, which she discerns as vehicles for a 'search for a new world' www.clipstampfold.com.

35 Nicolai Ouroussoff, 'Such Cheek! Those Were the Days, Architects', *New York Times* (8 February 2007) www.nytimes.com/2007/02/08/arts/design/08clip.html (accessed 5 October 2008).

36 The only one that continues to be published is *Dot Dot Dot*, which started out as a graphic design magazine (its first issue featured a comprehensive list of all the graphic design publications produced internationally), has now been described as 'twice-yearly 'jocuserious' art journal'. Travis Elborough, 'Masterclasses in arts and crafts', *The Guardian* (9 February 2008), p.18.

37 Luke Wood and Jonty Valentine, eds., 'Index: More Paranoid-Critical Map Than Editorial', *The National Grid*, no. 1 (March, 2006), p.39.

38 Clive Dilnot, op.cit., p.9.

39 Henry Jenkins, Tara McPherson and Jane Shattuc, eds., *Hop on Pop: The Politics and Pleasures of Popular Culture* (Durham: Duke University Press, 2002), p.6.

40 Ibid., p.40.

41 Ibid., p.26.

42 See Teal Triggs, *Generation Terrorists: The Politics and Graphic Language of Punk and Riot Grrrl Fanzines in Britain 1976–2000*, Unpublished PhD thesis (Reading: University of Reading, 2006).

43 Luke Wood and Jonty Valentine, eds., 'Index: More Paranoid-Critical Map Than Editorial', *The National Grid*, no. 1 (March 2006), p.38.

44 In subsequent conversations with Wood, he explained the impact of the Manchester-based Factory Records that had been very influential on the design and music scene in New Zealand. For Wood as an Indy producer, this would manifest itself in the adoption of a visual language for *The National Grid* which drew in part upon with the hard industrial edge of Britain's northern city.

45 *The National Grid* editors acknowledge how they have relied on 'the design-found object' in the first issue (for example, Max Hailstone's book *Design and Designers* (1985), sport scoreboards and postcards) and they admit this results in being a 'bit artefact-y'. Wood and Valentine, eds., op.cit., p.39.

46 Steve Kerr, 'Labels from the Post-Punk Periphery', *The National Grid*, no. 2 (December 2006), p.82.

47 Jonty Valentine, 'Commonplace Books and Other Rhetorical Devices or Just Hold Me', *The National Grid*, no. 3 (2007), p.88.

48 Ibid., p.89

49 Jenkins et al., op.cit., p.161.

50 This form of revealing a mapping of ideas and relationships is an inherent part of the design process. *The National Grid* editors express their interest in the linking or associations of events/ideas that are not normally connected.

51 Wood and Valentine, eds., op.cit., p.38.

52 Roger Sabin and Teal Triggs, *'Below Critical Radar' Fanzines and Alternative Comics from 1976 to Now*, Codex, Hove, 2000.

53 This notion of tactics and resistance is explored by Wood in issue 3 in his essay 'Counterfeit Design: A Tactical Approach', p.44–9. Here, Wood presents the recent case of Rebecca Li, who had set up a design and advertising company near Auckland and was allegedly also engaged in document forgeries.

54 'TBI Tuesday Q&A: Luke Wood of The National Grid', The Big Idea: www.thebigidea.co.nz (accessed 13 February 2008).

55 Jenkins et al., op.cit., p.7.

56 Ibid., p.9.

57 Ibid.

58 Michel Foucault, *The Archaeology of Knowledge* (London: Routledge, 1972) (1997 reprint), p.7.

59 Jenkins et al., op.cit., p.35.

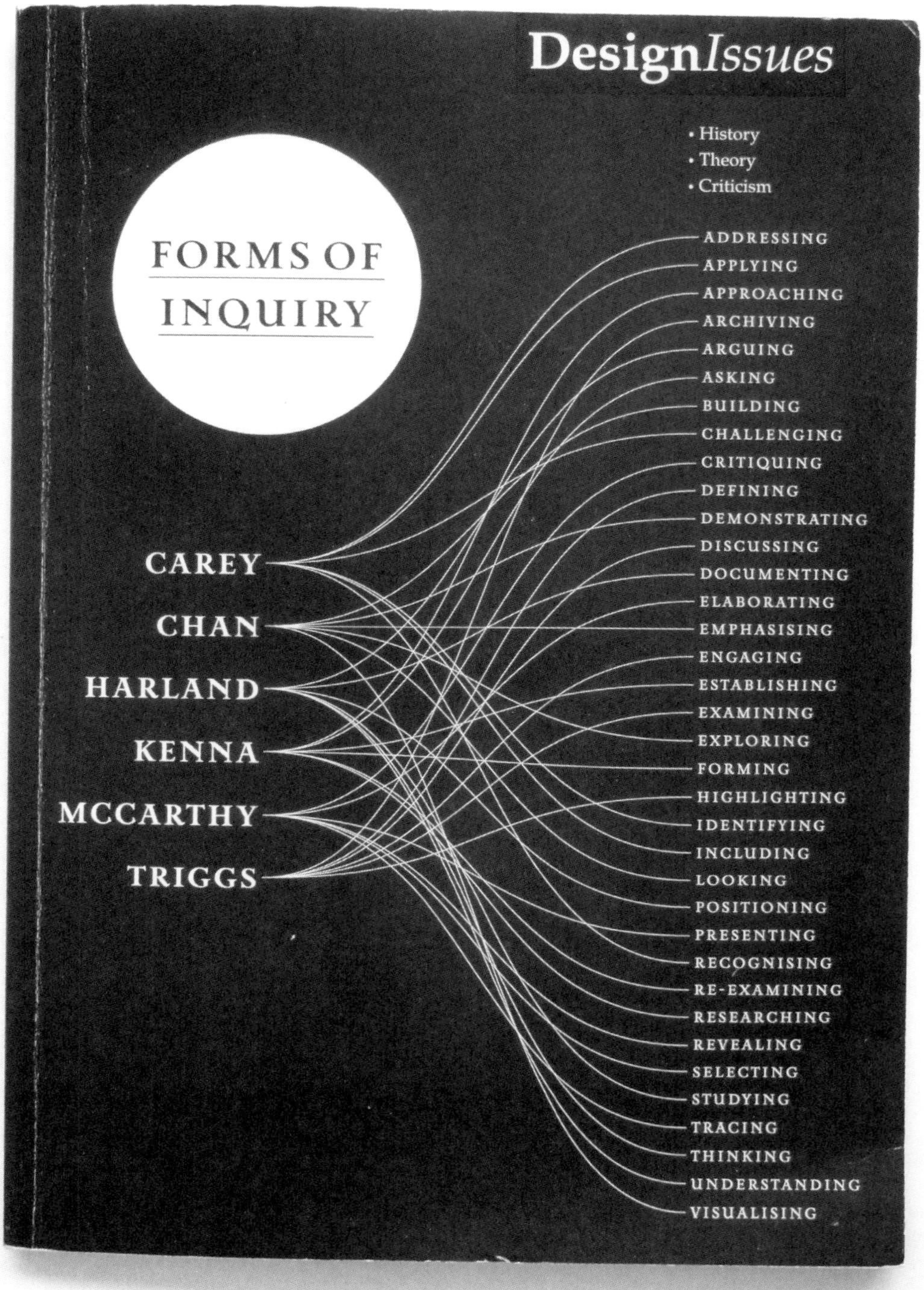

Design*Issues*

• History
• Theory
• Criticism

FORMS OF
INQUIRY

CAREY

CHAN

HARLAND

KENNA

MCCARTHY

TRIGGS

ADDRESSING
APPLYING
APPROACHING
ARCHIVING
ARGUING
ASKING
BUILDING
CHALLENGING
CRITIQUING
DEFINING
DEMONSTRATING
DISCUSSING
DOCUMENTING
ELABORATING
EMPHASISING
ENGAGING
ESTABLISHING
EXAMINING
EXPLORING
FORMING
HIGHLIGHTING
IDENTIFYING
INCLUDING
LOOKING
POSITIONING
PRESENTING
RECOGNISING
RE-EXAMINING
RESEARCHING
REVEALING
SELECTING
STUDYING
TRACING
THINKING
UNDERSTANDING
VISUALISING

FROM THE OUTSIDE IN:
A PLACE FOR INDIGENOUS GRAPHIC
TRADITIONS IN CONTEMPORARY
SOUTH AFRICAN GRAPHIC DESIGN

PIERS CAREY
2011

This essay makes a case for indigenous African graphic systems as appropriate subject matter for inclusion in a history of graphic design in South Africa. The case study describes the range and nature of graphic systems and, by focusing on one example, demonstrates the integral importance of indigenous systems to contemporary communication issues in South Africa. The relationship between specific traditional symbols from the Zulu culture of KwaZulu-Natal province is examined and compared with the conventionalized version of the AIDS ribbon commonly used in many HIV/AIDS awareness campaigns.

In this case, we revisit the work done by the Siyazama Project,[1] which focuses on HIV/AIDS awareness among rural craftswomen. Its relevance here is that its work also demonstrates the importance of graphic symbols in an otherwise oral community. We also briefly explore the social context in which this campaign takes place to clarify the marginality of this community.

The relationship between communication partners in South Africa tends to be characterized by ignorance of the 'marginal' cultures on the part of the dominant and efforts by the 'marginalized' to adopt the dominant culture and abandon their own. For the purposes of this case study, the closer a community is to the traditional, monolingual isiZulu-speaking,[2] non-literate, rural, subsistence end of the scale, the more 'marginalized' it is considered; the dominant, meanwhile, are the Westernized, literate, English-speaking urban populations, regardless of their 'racial' origins.

As a profession in the province of KwaZulu-Natal, graphic design exists primarily in this dominant section of society, and its history is largely defined by this ethos.[3] Thus, both in its contemporary practice and in its history, graphic design in this region, wittingly or not, colludes in this process of marginalization. Such marginalization can only be addressed by designers if they research both the historical and contemporary uses of visual communication among the amaZulu and then integrate this knowledge into their work.

The case study concludes by proposing that, as a consequence of this situation, South Africa's graphic design history, or lack of it, calls for the development of a respectful equality of mutual cultural knowledge as a working method for designers, regardless of their cultural power.

African Graphic Systems

Africa is currently home to approximately 2,000 languages[4] and it is likely that all of the cultures using these languages have had, at one time, some systematic form of graphic communication. In my own research,[5] I have identified over 80 such systems, a figure certainly incomplete. Saki Mafundikwa (2004)[6] has also written on these systems in the context of the African diaspora in his book, *Afrikan Alphabets*, which I believe is the first such study from a graphic design perspective.

Forms of graphic communication include alphabets and syllabaries, easily recognizable as comparable to those used in European or Indian cultures, as well as collections of less comprehensible symbolic pictographs and ideographs. Examples of the former, such as the Ethiopic alphabet of Christian Ethiopia (Figure 1), were accorded a certain respect by European explorers and colonizers, particularly for religious reasons. Pictographic and ideographic systems, unfortunately, were often misunderstood or rejected as being part of 'primitive' cultures, which, in the colonial ethos, were to be either suppressed or 'developed'. The complex pictographic system created by the Bamum people of Cameroon, for example, was developed into a sophisticated syllabary (Figure 2) before its suppression by the French.[7]

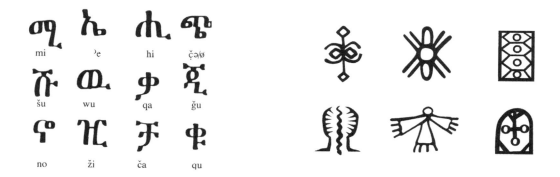

Figure 1 (left): Examples of the Ethiopic syllabary, or syllabic alphabet. Characters combine an initial consonant with a vowel determined by the shape and position of a diacritical mark. **Figure 2** (right): Characters from the first version of the pictographic script produced by the Bamum people of Cameroon in the 1890s. Characters represent, from left to right, top: a white person, truth (representing a spider used in divination), war; bottom: a man under the influence of evil spirits, a large war drum.

Part of the problem also stemmed from the use of forms or substrates in African graphic communication, which were unfamiliar to colonial-era Europeans: the systems might have been inscribed on wood (carvings), the ground (sand diagrams), cloth or the human body (as body painting, tattooing or scarification) (Figures 3 and 4). Because of these dissimilarities, European writers often failed to recognize these systems as texts; nonetheless, they fulfilled that function in their own cultures. The Portuguese explorer, Duarte Lopez, writing at the end of the sixteenth century, refers to Congolese carvings, for example, as 'devil's images cut in wood, in all kinds of horrible shapes: many worship winged dragons, others worship snakes as their gods, others again bucks, tigers or other loathsome and abhorrent animals.'[8]

Figure 3
The Luchazi of North-Western Zambia and related peoples used a complex style of geometrical diagrams called Tusona. This example represents the cosmological relationship between God, mankind and the natural world.

Semiotics provides very broad descriptions of a 'text.' Barthes describes a text as *'a work conceived, perceived and received in its integrally symbolic nature'*[9] and discusses, as examples, professional wrestling, actors' haircuts in a film of Julius Caesar, a new model of Citroën car and so on.[10] Noble and Bestley broaden the definition even further, identifying a text as 'anything that carries meaning and that could be "read" by an audience',[11] as well as any sequential printed or written words.

African graphic systems can be examined in this light, but their use within the societies concerned is intended, as Clémentine Madiya Faik-Nzuji (writing from within Congolese culture) makes clear, to convey a more specific, if not actually, monosemic meaning (Figure 4). In her discussion, the meanings are restricted to a limited and specific range of qualities related to the concept and exercise of chieftaincy.[12]

Figure 4
Chiefs of the Ndengese of the DRC used to wear scarified symbols and patterns such as these to represent their attributes and duties. The symbols and patterns were also carved on statues to represent the chief's authority.

A graphic text might be described as limited to those forms that are produced by the use, within a particular culture or society, of a systematized group of conventionally rendered and recognized marks on a surface. The graphic systems and codes found throughout the African continent fit this definition.

Graphic design itself could then be defined as: the set of visual and technical skills required to render these marks both attractive and effective as communication in the society concerned. Using this definition, the history of graphic design should expand to cover all such mark systems, visual and technical skills, and relevant modes of communication throughout human history. Given the vast amount of material this understanding encompasses, selections would have to be made; but such selection could then be recognized for what it is, and the motivation for the selection could be made explicit. If an emphasis is then laid on graphic design for commercial or any other specific purposes, the bias inherent in such a decision would be more easily identified and, if necessary, contested. Students of the history of graphic design in different countries or cultures would then have a more consistent framework on which to base their selections.

This approach would be consistent with semiological theories of communication, which stress 'the production and exchange of meanings'[13] as defining the process. 'Exchange' implies an equal, two-way process, which can only happen in a context of cultural understanding. Malcolm Barnard describes communication as a 'negotiation', in which designers study a group's beliefs, values, reactions – in other words, its culture – to communicate with the group.[14] This definition further emphasizes the need for equality and understanding. Barnard also argues 'that the study of communication is the study of culture, and that culture is the creation and use of meaningful forms, which would clearly include graphic design.'[15] Thus, the interrelationship between graphic design, culture and communication, and the need to understand the first two to accomplish the third, is established.

According to this logic, African graphic systems are clearly situated in the history of graphic design. They embodied meaning in the culture that produced them, by graphic means. To the level it was culturally acceptable, these systems could be 'read' by the 'literate' in the given society, and so could communicate effectively according to their design. Their study is also important as one small means of validating the history of African societies and cultures and of helping to destroy the myth, still to be found in Western society, that Africa had no writing or history.

African societies are changing rapidly, with the result that many of these traditional systems have become extinct or devalued. However, even in such circumstances, their 'ghosts' linger in contemporary societies and affect the society's understanding of the present. Where the culture has maintained the graphic or symbolic system, of course, the influence is easier to identify and work with, but even a dead system still has influence. The following example illustrates the potential usefulness of such graphic symbols in contemporary communication problems in one South African community.

Traditional Graphic Symbols and the AIDS Pandemic: The Siyazama Project

The HIV/AIDS infection rate in South Africa has been estimated to be between 10.2 percent[16] and 18.8 percent,[17] the latter equivalent to over nine million people. One authority has given the HIV infection rate among new registrations at one local hospital as being 70 percent to 80 percent,[18] although the South African Department of Health claims the rate is 30.2 percent for pregnant women.[19]

A number of publicity campaigns, such as 'LoveLife' and 'Soul City',[20] have focused on various aspects of the pandemic. Unfortunately, it has yet to be shown that any of these broad campaigns have produced significant behavioral change in their intended audience. Most people in South Africa have been exposed to these campaigns and have known a number of HIV/AIDS casualties. Nevertheless, and perhaps because of contradictory government messages, high-risk sexual behavior remains widespread, particularly among those the country can least afford to lose: educated young adults, just entering employment. Claire Keeton, reporting on a survey of current attitudes and a subsequent discussion of the findings among a group of young adults, seeks to explain, or at least make clear, the bizarre contradiction between awareness of risk factors and persistent high-risk behavior: 'Infidelity was normal' (i.e., acceptable), the participants agreed, despite knowing the risks of multiple partners and despite the fact that 15 percent of the survey respondents had lost at least one family member to the disease.[21]

Although we still must hope that success will result, it is noteworthy that none of the campaigns I have seen sought to communicate with its intended audience on the symbolic level – the approach used by the Siyazama Project. Some have not even bothered to 'communicate' in indigenous languages, even in parts of the country where English is almost completely unknown.

The Siyazama Project began in 1999 as a series of workshops specifically addressing the need to provide HIV/AIDS information to rural female bead-workers in the Valley of a Thousand Hills, the Inanda Valley, the Msinga region and the Ndwedwe informal settlements, all in KwaZulu-Natal. Thus, it was much more focused than the other campaigns mentioned. The project has demonstrated how visual communication can make a contribution in a community in which large numbers of people do not look to writing or print for their information.[22] More specifically for this essay, it demonstrates how visual symbols that resonate with the indigenous cultural history can play a part in this communication process.

The project developed a collegial and friendly workshop ethos that allowed rural women to become comfortable seeking and expressing information about previously taboo sexual subjects, including HIV/AIDS and other STDs, abuse and violence. It has enabled them to communicate this information to their communities through the visual medium of beaded dolls and tableaux. The use of a visual medium, in turn, has allowed expression of the issues to the wider society outside the workshops, which would still be taboo to discuss verbally.

A major visual motif in the various dolls and tableaux has been a geometrical version of the AIDS red ribbon. The ribbon was first used as a symbol of awareness and support in the HIV/AIDS struggle during 1991, in the US, by organizations such as Visual AIDS, Broadway Cares and Equity Fights AIDS.[23] Its use spread internationally, and by the mid- to late-1990s, the ribbon was featured widely in South African AIDS campaigns and was becoming familiar in the South African context.

Because of the geometric design structure of most South African beadwork, such as that made in the Siyazama Project, the depiction of the ribbon became very stylized and geometrical and even almost abstract (Figure 5). Abstracted or stylized versions of the ribbon have also become common in the various South African AIDS campaigns. The ribbon itself, or a realistic rendering of it, is not so common, which suggests that the two-dimensional graphic device is what has taken hold in the local culture. This traction might have resulted simply from the repetition of a more easily reproduced version of the symbol, but it seems likely that it results from its cultural resonance.

Figure 5
A poster for an exhibition of the work of the Siyazama Project, showing the type of beaded dolls its members produce, representing traditional costumes of the Zulu people. Note the use of geometric representations of the AIDS ribbon on all three dolls (By permission of Dr. K. Wells/The Siyazama Project).

The cultural resonance refers to a system or group of traditional graphic symbols used by the amaZulu and other South African peoples. Credo Mutwa has described 'Bantu Symbol Writing' as having once been widespread among the black peoples of sub-equatorial Africa but as having 'died out fast as the people learned the European alphabet.'[24] He gives approximately 250 symbols that cover a wide range of meanings, some presented in the form of short texts, others as lists of related concepts. All are linear in execution but vary in style: some are completely abstract; some are simplified pictorial or pictographic representations; some resemble the angular geometric style of Ndebele house decorations (Figure 6).

How many of these symbols are widely understood today is not known, but some clearly do still have currency in isiZulu-speaking culture. They are familiar to many, particularly in the more remote rural areas, where the population remains substantially separate from Westernized South African culture.

Light

Our Land

A Wish
(A Flower in the mind)

The Royal Kraal
or Homestead

Marriage – Love–
Unity of people

Evil

Buck or
Antelope

Lion

Madness
(An Insect under the Skull)

Respect

Figure 6
Examples of the pictographs described by Credo Mutwa as 'Bantu symbol writing' (1998, 664).

In particular, the symbols for 'man' and 'woman' are still known. The conventionalized and geometricized version of the AIDS ribbon, used as a logo in many South African AIDS campaigns, shows a clear and fortuitous visual relationship with the male and female symbols (Figure 7). This resemblance, Kate Wells believes, is a substantial factor in the widespread acceptance of the graphic version of the AIDS ribbon and its preference over the three-dimensional version or its more realistic representation.[25]

Figure 7
The Zulu Male (left) and Female (right) signs. Compare their structure with examples of the geometric version of the AIDS ribbon as used in Zulu beadwork in Figure 5.

This cultural resonance with an older but not quite forgotten visual tradition is particularly important for large numbers of rural people, such as the women of the Siyazama Project. Many of the women are illiterate and speak only isiZulu and thus are excluded from most communication by written or print means. In this society, information is typically communicated orally and in social settings, but women are further constrained by cultural traditions from seeking or expressing information about sexual matters. They are thus doubly excluded from information and counseling about AIDS.

The Siyazama Project workshops encouraged the expression of concerns initially through non-verbal, three-dimensional forms of communication: the dolls and tableaux. Awareness and use of the AIDS ribbon/logo was encouraged, but again, it was the stylized, graphic version that the women preferred, rather than trying to make, for example, three-dimensional bead versions.

According to Wells, combining elements of both male and female, and thus symbolizing their union, with all its joy and pain, allowed the AIDS symbol in this context to 'convey a profound message of life and death, thus effectively triggering awareness of AIDS, promoting care for the sick, and encouraging behavioral change.'[26] Few of its products are considered to be traditional graphic design, but Siyazama's process has communicated the AIDS issues successfully with the bead-working women. Virtually every product of the project incorporates the symbol, and it is broadly understood as a significant element within the overall AIDS message. The women's improved understanding of the epidemic and its associated risk factors has been shown in their three-dimensional illustrations of the various events and issues. Nevertheless, understanding unfortunately has not enabled them to protect themselves better, because of the unequal, traditional power relations surrounding issues of sexuality.[27]

Research has yet to establish the extent to which the effect of this particular symbol could be repeated and expanded across South Africa, either with other symbols or, farther afield, using other systems – or whether this was just a lucky coincidence. What has become clear is that the availability of a symbol that resonates with the audience, and that the audience is able to adapt and assimilate on its own terms, has made a huge difference in the effectiveness of the communication process developed in the project. This case study is just one example of the use in design of symbolism and social concepts that may be unfamiliar to Western (or Westernized) designers, and it could well be repeated many times. If designers, particularly in Africa, wish to communicate with communities or peoples for whom such concepts or symbolism are not only familiar but natural, understanding and valuing the symbols and systems, as well as the cultures from which they spring, becomes vital.

Given the 'Western' emphasis of most South African graphic design, only a conscious effort by both the profession and graphic design educators, as well as intentional research of the several cultures with which they might work in South Africa, can lead to this level of communication. Designers and students do engage in research for particular projects, but this kind of research typically is not written up systematically or published. For example, no graphic communication literature has as yet been located that deals with the visual culture as a whole of either traditional or contemporary indigenous cultures in South Africa. Such a process can only begin if both the education and experience of the designers engage with these cultures. In graphic design education, because of the complete practical domination of the discipline by Western technology, the emphasis is likely to be on history and theory. A history of graphic design or visual communication for South Africa might thus include not simply the visual traditions of the pre-colonial indigenous societies, or the development of 'Westernized' graphic design in the country, but also the range of accommodations and adaptations made between the two types of tradition over time. Given the dearth of existing literature, extensive research will be required.

Conclusion

This article has discussed the case for indigenous African graphic systems as appropriate subject matter for the history of graphic design in South Africa. It has examined the relationship between certain Zulu traditional symbols, the AIDS symbol, and the social context in which the Siyazama Project has taken place. It proposes that a more culturally equal relationship between designer and audience, based on cultural respect and knowledge, actually produces a more effective form of communication than is the current norm. Such a relationship can help to promote a revaluation of indigenous cultures, including languages that are currently under threat from globalization. This relationship is likely to develop among designers only if their experience includes research and study of both historical and contemporary aspects of all South African visual traditions, including the languages and cultures in which they are embedded. This broad scope is therefore proposed as the aim of graphic design history in South Africa, using the Siyazama project to illustrate an investigation of the effectiveness of this type of graphic symbol.

Finally, it must be suggested that the relationship between designer and audience, reflecting as it does the gap in cultural power between dominant and marginalized elements in South African society, is likely to remain unequal; however, both partners may strive toward each other's position. The marginalized may adapt, subvert or appropriate communication material or processes for their own use, but the sheer volume of output from the globalized cultural media makes it extremely difficult for them to relate equally with designers or other cultural producers. This appropriation is possibly the only way for them to gain or maintain some level of control over their cultures, but until this independent control is developed and sustainable, equal relationships between designers and marginalized audiences are likely to remain extremely rare.

Piers Carey is Lecturer in Graphic Design at Durban University of Technology, Durban.
First published in *Design Issues*, vol. 27, no. 1, 2011.

1   The Siyazama Project was previously discussed in *Design Issues* 20:2 (Spring 2004), p.73–89. That article focused on the project's history and scope, and on the effectiveness of beadwork as a mode of expression.

2   As in many African languages, 'Zulu' is the root form of the word, and different prefixes specify meaning. Thus, the Zulu language is properly known as 'isiZulu', and the Zulu people as 'amaZulu'.

3   Graphic design history and research at the Durban University of Technology has recently developed beyond an entirely eurocentric emphasis, although Philip B. Meggs' *A History of Graphic Design* remains the set text. American and British sources generally remain the exemplars for the discipline, and their emphases remain the norm.

4   David Crystal, *Language Death* (Cambridge: Cambridge University Press, 2000), p.3–4.

5   Piers Carey, *African Graphic Systems* (Durban: Durban Institute of Technology, 2004) (unpublished MTech dissertation).

6   Saki Mafundikwa, *Afrikan Alphabets: the Story of Writing in Afrika* (New York: Mark Batty Publisher, 2004).

7   Idelette Dugast et Mervyn David Waldegrave Jeffreys, *L'Écriture des Bamum* (Paris: Mémoires de L'Institut Français D'Afrique Noire, 1950).

8   Duarte Lopez quoted in Pieterse, J.N. *White on Black; Images of Africa and Blacks in Western Popular Culture* (New Haven and London: Yale University Press, 1992), p.69.

9   Roland Barthes, 'From Work to Text', homepage. newschool.edu/~quigleyt/vcs/barthes-wt.html (2001) (accessed 4 January 2008).

10 Roland Barthes, *Mythologies* (London: Vintage, 1991).

11 Ian Noble, and Russell Bestley, *Visual Research – An Introduction to Research Methods for Graphic Designers* (Worthing: AVA Academia, 2005), p.189.

12 Clémentine Faik-Nzuji, *Symboles graphiques en Afrique noire* (Paris: Editions Karthala, and Louvain-la-Neuve: CILTADE).

13 John Fiske, *Introduction to Communication Studies* (London: Routledge, 1990), p.2.

14 Malcolm Barnard, *Graphic Design as Communication* (London: Routledge, 2005), p.85.

15 Barnard, op.cit., p.67.

16 UNAIDS (Joint United Nations Programme on HIV/AIDS (UNAIDS) and World Health Organisation (WHO)) 2006. *AIDS Epidemic Update: Special Report on HIV/AIDS: December 2006* (Geneva: UNAIDS. 11. Lowest estimate).

17 Unicef, South Africa Statistics, www.unicef.org/infobycountry/southafrica_statistics.html.3. (accessed July, 11, 2007).

18 Dr. J. Hartzell, 2006. Personal conversation (July 18).

19 Department of Health South Africa, *National HIV and Syphilis Antenatal Prevalence Survey, South Africa 2005.* Pretoria, Department of Health South Africa. Quoted in UNAIDS, 2006:11.

20 'LoveLife' is South Africa's national HIV prevention programme for youth, and can be found at www.lovelife.org.za. 'Soul City', a broader youth/health organization, is at www.soulcity.org.za.

21 Claire Keeton, 'Is the Aids message getting through?' *Sunday Times* (Johannesburg: Johnnic Publishing, 25–31 March 2007), p.6.

22 For more information, see: Kate Wells, Edgard Sienaert and Joan Conolly, 'The Siyazama Project: a Traditional Beadwork and AIDS Intervention Programme', *Design Issues*, 20:2 (Cambridge, MA: Massachusetts Institute of Technology Press, Spring 2004), p.73–89; and Kate Wells, *Manipulating Metaphors: A Study of Rural Craft as a Medium for Communicating on AIDS and Confronting Culture in KwaZulu-Natal* (Durban: University of KwaZulu-Natal: Unpublished Doctoral Thesis, 2006).

23 Avert.org. History of AIDS from 1987 to 1992. Available from: www.avert.org/his87_92.htm. (accessed November, 9, 2007).

24 Credo Mutwa, *Indaba, My Children* (Edinburgh: Canongate Books, 1998) (First published 1964), 664.

25 Kate Wells, personal conversation (14 August 2006).

26 Wells, Sienaert and Conolly, op.cit.

27 Wells, op.cit.

THE **DESIGN OBSERVER** GROUP

HOME   **OBSERVATORY**   CHANGE OBSERVER   PLACES

Design and Visual Culture

DESIGN OBSERVER
Archive
Books + Store
Job Board
Email Archive
Comments
About
Contact
Log In
Register

OBSERVATORY
Resources
Submissions
About
Contact

DEPARTMENTS
Advertisement
Audio
Books
Collections
Dialogues
Essays
Events
Foster Column
Gallery
Interviews
Miscellaneous
Opinions
Poetry
Primary Sources
Projects
Report
Reviews
Slideshows
Today Column
Unusual Suspects
Video

TOPICS
Advertising
Architecture
Art
Books
Branding
Business
Cities / Places
Community
Craft

Posted 01.10.11 I PERMALINK I PRINT   Comments (22)

Rick Poynor

Out of the Studio: Graphic Design History and Visual Studies

Cover designs by James Victore (left) and Nick Shah (right). Illustration by Michelle Thompson

Introduction: the reluctant discipline

OUT OF THE STUDIO: GRAPHIC DESIGN HISTORY AND VISUAL STUDIES

RICK POYNOR
2011

The Reluctant Discipline

Twenty years ago there was considerable optimism about the possibility that graphic design history would become a fully-fledged academic discipline, despite some unresolved questions about its purpose. Although there has been some progress toward this goal in the past two decades, these developments have taken place at a slower pace than might once have been expected.[1] As a discipline – if this is even the right term to use – graphic design history is still in a state of becoming, and there are good reasons to ask whether, on its present course, it will ever achieve the maturity that some observers hoped for.

This lack of progress might be measured in various ways. Most obviously, in Britain, where I write, there is no such thing as a first degree in graphic design history. Even design history studied as a clearly defined degree subject concerned with largely non-graphic forms of design remains a rarity.[2] The subject is usually combined with art history and sometimes with film history.[3] Art history established itself several decades ago as a coherent academic discipline and as a subject for study with a broad appeal to non-practitioners. Design history has a long way to go to achieve the same stature or pulling power.

The situation is not much better when it comes to graphic design history writing – which is not surprising because the need for such research is inevitably linked to the amount of study taking place in higher education. The key indicator of the discipline's health is book publishing. Although academic papers about aspects of graphic design history are delivered at conferences and surface in publications such as *Design Issues* and *Journal of Design History*, we should be wary of mistaking these occasional expressions of interest in graphic design history for signs of much activity in the field. Perhaps the most striking example of this shortfall is the three issues of *Visible Language* published in 1994–95, which set out to explore the possibility of new 'critical histories of graphic design.'[4]

This ambitious project appeared to promise a dawning era of intellectually challenging, revisionist graphic design history writing that would in time have a significant effect on the field of book publishing – even transforming perceptions of what such writing could be; but this promise did not come to fruition. Only a minority of the 15 *Visible Language* contributors went on to make substantial contributions to graphic design history, in terms of scholarly research that led to the publication of original, authoritative, subject-redefining books.[5] This is not to say that there have been no other significant additions to the graphic design history bookshelf during the past decade, but even in a good year, the additions never amount to more than a few titles.[6] When this patchy output is placed beside the numerous books produced by scholars working in, for instance, the fields of art, architecture, or film, as it is in any visual arts bookshop, it becomes obvious that graphic design history as a terrain for intensive and sustained research and study barely exists at all.

The reasons why graphic design history has failed to develop – and, without a change of direction, will most likely continue to fail to develop – are sometimes acknowledged in passing but are not addressed with any persistence or rigor, perhaps because they point to some unwelcome conclusions for the subject as it is currently situated and being taught. In an attempt to see the problem more clearly, this essay revisits some of these perspectives. The essay's second aim, arising from this review, is to propose an alternative site of production for graphic design history, albeit one that is interdisciplinary in essence rather than located within its own clearly delineated departmental borders. Graphic design history's best chance of development now lies in an expanded conception of the rapidly emerging discipline of visual culture or visual studies.[7] Although this proposal is also problematic, for reasons that will be explored, only in visual studies might graphic design history be able to establish the interdisciplinary connections necessary for it to fulfill its early promise and to grow.

Graphic Design History is for Graphic Designers

Almost all of the early arguments about the need for graphic design history were made from within the discipline of graphic design by informed observers, often graphic designers, who felt that knowledge of graphic design's history and development was essential for any practitioner. This grounding would allow graphic designers to avoid plagiarism and pointless reinvention; it would supply 'inspiration' and give them a legacy on which to build. Steven Heller sets out this position in his introduction to *Graphic Design History*, a book of essays about design history subjects intended for graphic design students:

> A compelling case has been made through conferences, magazine articles, and books, for the centrality of graphic design history in the education of all graphic designers. During this formative period in the digital age, when new media is altering traditional notions of graphic design practice, it is even more important that designers have the grounding provided by historical knowledge.[8]

Andrew Blauvelt, editor of the three 'critical histories' issues of *Visible Language*, put the issue even more strongly; writing two years after the trilogy appeared, he went so far as to assert that the only plausible use for graphic design history was as a tool for educating graphic designers more effectively:

> The notion of design as a field of study without practical application is unlikely and undesirable. After all, it is the practice of graphic design – no matter how wanting or limiting – that provides the basis for a theory of graphic design. [...] The calls for graphic design to be a liberal art – a quest for academic legitimacy – need to be supplanted by strategies which foster 'critical making', teaching when, how, and why to question things.[9]

Indeed, at least one call for design to be considered as a liberal art had been made, but this tendency hardly needed to be supplanted because the design-history-is-for-designers point of view has always dominated discussion.[10] This design studio orientation is only to be expected because those who write about the possibilities of graphic design history are usually graphic designers who, if they also teach, are almost always situated within graphic design departments. However, the idea that design history, pursued as an academic end in itself, could lead to estrangement from the methods and goals of design practice has also been proposed by professional historians who might seem to have every reason to wish to construct design history as a separate enclave. Guy Julier and Viviana Narotzky note 'a yawning gap between the desires of design historians and the actions of designers', suggesting that design history might have made itself redundant as a contributor to essential principles of practice.[11] They conclude: 'We do not question the value of history as discourse [...] But we do ask design history to return to its roots and bed itself with practice.'[12] Whatever relevance this request might have had for historians concerned with industrial design, for graphic design it could be taken as little more than a warning for graphic design history to stay where it was already situated – in bed with practice.

However, this location was by no means as secure, congenial, or productive for the incubation of graphic design history as it might sound. In the way that they are usually constituted and administered, graphic design departments have some profound limitations as homes for historical study. As Heller observes, most American design schools do not use dedicated teachers of design history; in fact, most design history teachers are 'practitioners who have entered the field through the back door', without experience in historical research and publishing, and most design schools, even if they offer a few graphic design history courses, do not have the finances to maintain a dedicated history program.[13]

Louis Danziger, described by Heller as one of the first 'historian-cum-practitioners' to introduce a class in graphic design history, is frank about the limitations of his own design history teaching, acknowledging that it is neither academic nor scholarly and is primarily concerned with helping students to enhance their performance as designers. Danziger claims that practitioners cannot be good historians because their experience 'inevitably introduces biases', and they 'cannot be objective.'[14] The British design educator Jonathan Baldwin has expressed similar concerns about the situation in Britain, where design history is often taught by part-timers on hourly contracts, and studio staff and students see design history as disconnected from the practical side of their courses. 'If [design history] is so unimportant that staff are paid by the hour and only during term-time, it's obviously not [seen as] important at all', he writes.[15]

All of these perspectives begin to explain why, despite the energetic and optimistic support of a few notable proponents, graphic design history has progressed so slowly. For the most part, the subject remains essentially an afterthought, a comparatively minor adjunct to the design studio, conceived by its apologists as a means of molding better-rounded graphic designers but still seen as irrelevant by many students obliged to take these classes, and permanently undernourished by a lack of institutional support.

Publishers are fully aware of graphic design history's lack of presence and status as an academic subject, and the small number that are prepared to take the risk and produce books about graphic design history know from experience that the market for these studies remains small. Such books can only do well if they are placed on course reading lists, but the more specialized the subject matter, the less likely this placement is to happen, leading publishers to favor bland visual surveys with the widest possible appeal. At the same time, the number of teachers with the motivation, talent and pressing career reasons to undertake ambitious research projects is tiny compared to other, better established and more academically grounded visual arts subjects. Graphic designers with commercial practices to maintain, in addition to their teaching duties, have little time to engage in protracted historical research and writing, even if they possess an aptitude for it.

Visual Studies' Mysterious Blind Spot

With graphic design history still not fully formed as a subject, it might seem that continuing calls to reform it, to introduce 'new perspectives' and 'new views', can only fall on stony ground, no matter how well intentioned. Who is to do the reforming, and to what end? Is there any reason to suppose that the personal and institutional factors that have inhibited graphic design history's growth in its unreformed state will not continue to inhibit any widespread adoption and application of new thinking within the field? Or will these new impulses by their very nature somehow succeed in lifting graphic design history – still positioned where it always has been as a studio add-on – to a higher plane of perceived relevance, productivity and academic attainment?

The primary contention of the critiques originating within design is that it is not enough for design history to concern itself with the evolution of graphic styles as seen in the work of a canonical list of heroic (white, male) designers. Philip B. Meggs' *A History of Graphic Design* (1983) is generally cited as the work that enshrines this Pevsnerian view of graphic design history.[16] Many design teachers have drawn attention to the limitations of this approach; two examples will suffice. Baldwin suggests that the slide show parade of 'great' historical moments, with its emphasis on long lists of unfamiliar names, facts and dates that must be committed to memory, is thoroughly off-putting to students, who fail to see its relevance to their studio-based studies and future activities as designers. Instead, he suggests, design history should adopt what he calls 'history-less history', which looks at history as a series of causes and effects with particular emphasis on the systems of production and consumption of design. This perspective allows us to bring in social studies, cultural studies, psychology, audience studies, politics and issues that are often ignored: ethics and human ecology.[17]

Prasad Boradkar, writing in *The Education of a Graphic Designer*, likewise moves the emphasis to the contexts of graphic communication's production, arguing that this theme be 'situated within a variety of venues, including cultural, social, political, environmental, and economic contexts.'[18] Similarly, he invokes a list of adjacent disciplines and areas of study that could function as valuable resources, including visual culture, media and cultural studies, anthropology, material culture and sustainability studies.

Although any of these disciplines might offer methods, perspectives and insights for understanding graphic design history, most of them are clearly unsuitable as alternative resting places for the discipline's study. As Robin Kinross has remarked with obvious irony, in the early 1990s it seemed that, at least in Britain, cultural studies would 'take care of graphic design, seeing it as just one more item in the total menu of "culture".'[19] In the past decade, however, visual studies, rather than cultural studies, has emerged as the discipline with aspirations to take care of every aspect of the visual realm, and it might have seemed inevitable that graphic design's outputs, as omnipresent phenomena in this realm, would fall under its gaze. However, this has not as yet happened. It is rare for books about visual culture to include even the briefest discussion of design, while graphic design usually goes entirely unremarked – an omission that can only be described as astonishing, bearing in mind visual studies' overarching ambitions.[20]

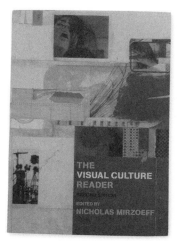

The Visual Culture Reader, edited by
Nicholas Mirzoeff, cover design by Nick Shah,
illustration by Michelle Thompson.

Perhaps the most emblematic example of this oversight is *The Visual Culture Reader,* edited by Nicholas Mirzoeff. This much-reprinted title finds no space for any discussion of graphic design among the 60 texts that fill its 740 pages – not even in the section concerned with 'spectacle and display.'[21] Not a single writer associated with graphic design history, theory or commentary contributed to the book. When visual culture writers summarize the areas that concern the new discipline, graphic design is not one of them. Martin Jay writes that visual culture is 'located somewhere at the crossroads of traditional art history, cinema, photography, and new media studies, the philosophy of perception, the anthropology of the senses, and the burgeoning field of cultural studies....'[22] Margaret Dikovitskaya sees it as arising from the convergence of art history, anthropology, film studies, linguistics and comparative literature after they encountered post-structuralist theory and cultural studies.[23] On the rare occasions when specifically graphic forms of visual culture are discussed, the new discipline's leading lights can sound oddly distant and uncertain, as though they have little precise contextual awareness of the object of study:

[W]hen I look through certain magazines, I am always struck by the manner in which the impact of what is on a page seems to be more due to the images and the typeface and glaring visual stimuli, than to the substance of the arguments and the meanings of the words themselves. However, too much Postmodern writing seems to hide itself behind the pyrotechnics of Postmodern visuality. This may be generational: younger people seem more comfortable with it than older people, since perhaps their greater exposure to computer games and other modern mass media has made them a little more visual.[24]

For anyone located within design, visual studies' failure to acknowledge and address the central role of graphic design as a shaper of the visual environment, alongside the forms of visual culture that it does acknowledge – art, film, television, photography, advertising, new media – must seem unaccountable. What could explain this peculiar blindness among a group of academics hyper-attuned to most forms of visuality?

One point that is immediately clear is that the oversight duplicates a wider public oversight – the oft-remarked 'transparency' or 'invisibility' of graphic communication – that has long been a source of concern among designers. It is still unusual for graphic design to be discussed anywhere other than in professional publications and a few academic journals; in addition, oversight by the media begets oversight by the public (even by academics in neighboring disciplines), so that the vast majority of people are not accustomed to thinking of graphic design as a vital part of culture worthy of continuous (or even sporadic) comment.[25]

Even more significant, however, are the departmental factors discussed earlier. Many of visual studies' leading figures come from art history and evidently lack even the most basic knowledge of design history. Graphic design history's compromised location as an adjunct to the design studio – its lack of full departmental status – denies it the appearance of academic legitimacy. In addition, the inward-looking nature of graphic design history writing and other forms of design discourse, and the continuing assumption among designer writers that the ultimate purpose of such commentary is professional improvement, has created a body of writing that appears from the outside, when it is noticed at all, to be merely of professional interest. If graphic design history books are being consulted by academics working in visual studies, they certainly are not being cited regularly. Before graphic design history writing can connect with a wider academic readership, it needs to orient itself differently – no small task at even the most elementary level of distribution. Bookshops struggle with the idea of interdisciplinarity when it comes to classifying and shelving a book. Even design titles purposefully aimed in part at cultural studies or visual studies readers can end up in the design section, where they are less likely to be encountered by readers who are not designers.[26]

Does Visual Culture Have a History?

Unpromising as its resistance to design might sound, visual studies nevertheless has the potential to offer the most propitious base, outside the design studio, for new critical approaches to graphic design history. To understand how graphic design might fit into visual studies, we need to consider its underlying principles. Any view can only be provisional because, as a new subject, visual studies is in a state of flux and because, despite many shared assumptions, its proponents differ on some key questions. One point they tend to agree on is that culture has taken a 'visual turn': that the visual is ever more dominant in contemporary society, both as a means of communication and as a source of meaning.[27] While this process began with industrialization and accelerated throughout the twentieth century, digital technology pushed the production, dissemination and use of imagery to a new level of reach and saturation. The fusion of media made possible by digital technology mandates the convergence within visual studies of critics, historians and practitioners who reject the received ideas of the established disciplines they come from.[28] Visual studies directs its attention to the visual as a place where, in Mirzoeff's words, 'meanings are created and contested.'[29]

Julier has characterized visual studies as occupying 'the enervated position of the detached or alienated observer overwhelmed by images.'[30] But this complaint underplays the fact that the images are already out there circulating and disregards the possibility that they might be problematic. According to Mirzoeff, 'visual culture is a tactic with which to study the genealogy, definition, and functions of Postmodern everyday life from the point of view of the consumer, rather than the producer.'[31] Far from encouraging enervation, the educational aim of visual studies is, then, essentially positive: to produce active, skeptical viewers equipped to respond critically to the visual imagery that surrounds us. This viewpoint immediately puts the analytical emphasis exactly where many critics of graphic design commentary and history say they wish it to be. Instead of focusing on the designer, a visual culture approach to design would focus on the effects of design as everyday, visual communication on its audiences. As Mirzoeff explains, visual culture is not concerned with the structured, formal viewing that takes place in a cinema or art gallery, but rather with the visual experience in everyday life: 'from the snapshot to the VCR and even the blockbuster art exhibition.'[32]

Although this brief list typically privileges forms of visual material (e.g., photography, film, art) that tend to predominate in visual studies, we might just as plausibly add wall posters, magazine layouts, luxury goods packaging or postage stamps. Graphic design has been overlooked precisely because it forms the connective tissue that holds so many ordinary visual experiences together. We don't usually view a professional photograph in isolation: We view it as part of a page, screen, billboard or shop window display in relationship with other pictorial, typographic and structural elements determined in the design process. These frameworks and relationships are an indivisible part of the meaning.

Where the theorists of visual studies sometimes part company is in their view of the extent to which the field should concern itself with history. Irit Rogoff is emphatic in distinguishing between her work on visual culture and her early approach as an art historian:

The field that I work in [...] does not function as a form of art history or film studies or mass media, but is clearly informed by all of them and intersects with all of them. It does not historicize the art object or any other visual image, nor does it provide for it either a narrow history within art nor a broader genealogy within the world of social and cultural developments. It does not assume that if we overpopulate the field of vision with ever more complementary information, we shall actually gain any greater insight into it.[33]

Such a view might be welcomed by supporters of 'history-less history', but it poses some problems for graphic design history. As Dikovitskaya notes, an academic field is defined by three criteria: 'the object of study, the basic assumptions that underpin the methods of approach to the object, and the history of the discipline itself.'[34] Compared to art history, the project of graphic design history is still at a formative stage, and this is one reason why the subject has low visibility for people in visual studies. Only in recent years, more than two decades after the arrival of Meggs' history, have several similarly scaled rival volumes emerged.[35] By the time radical art historians developed the new art history in the 1970s, with its emphasis on the social production of art, the art libraries of the world were already stocked with conventional art histories. In other words, there was already a structure of basic information and an interpretive framework in place for the new wave of historians to revise.[36]

In the graphic design field, however, historical information is still lacking about even the most notable subjects, 'narrow' as such scholarship might appear. Many significant but lesser known figures are overlooked.[37] Given the difficulties of publication already outlined, the arrival of any well-researched volume of graphic design history signifies a triumph against the odds. Rogoff argues persuasively that it is 'the questions that we ask that produce the field of inquiry and not some body of materials which determines what questions need to be posed to it.'[38] Nevertheless, she also acknowledges the danger that casting aside historical periods, schools of style, and the possibility of reading objects through conditions of production might entail losing a firm sense of 'self location'.[39] Divesting graphic design of its historical sign posts and landmarks would be enormously risky for a subject that is shakily located and barely apparent to those outside the field in the first place.[40]

Mirzoeff notes that graduate students approaching visual studies are sometimes worried about what body of material they are supposed to know; their concern instead, he asserts, should be with the questions they want to generate. The focus then moves to finding the most appropriate methods to answer those questions and to locating the sources that can lead to discovering the answers.[41] In a field as broad, provisional and unstable as visual culture, where visual media and their uses change all the time, the traditional pursuit of encyclopedic knowledge is no longer tenable. The history of modern media must be understood collectively rather than as a series of discrete disciplinary units, such as art, film and television (or for that matter, graphic design).

Nevertheless, in Mirzoeff's view, historical inquiry remains central to an understanding of visual culture because signs are always contingent and can only be understood in their historical contexts.[42] If art history, film studies and media studies are going to be taught together under the heading of visual studies, then new integrative histories of visual media must be written, necessitating much new research. W.J.T. Mitchell, one of visual studies' most influential figures, is similarly committed to the idea of a defined and teachable history, wanting students who take his courses to understand that 'visual culture has a history, that the way people look at the world and the way they represent it changes over time, and that this can actually be documented.'[43] According to Mitchell, the idea that visual studies seeks to take an unhistorical approach to vision is a myth.[44]

Conclusion: History Leaves the Studio?

It should be clear even from this brief overview that there is no intrinsic reason why graphic design history (and graphic design studies) should not form part of visual studies' purview. Every indication suggests that visual studies will become increasingly well established in the years ahead. Economic factors to do with student preferences cannot be ignored, and in the US, the subject attracts students who are not necessarily interested in the specialized forms of knowledge offered by traditional visual disciplines.[45] Visual studies connects with visual media experiences familiar to everyone in a way that art history does not. Its burgeoning introductory literature attests to its popularity, as well as its intellectual vigor. For teachers coming to visual studies from other disciplines, it offers ways of understanding visual media more closely related to the overlapping, interlocking, hybrid nature of contemporary visual experience. It would be a strange oversight – to the point of undermining visual studies' claims of integrative purpose – if its theorists were to continue to overlook and thereby discount graphic communication's central participation in the creation of the image world.

This proposal is not to suggest that graphic design history does not have a place in the studio as an essential part of any graphic design student's understanding of the discipline. History-conscious teachers of graphic design no doubt will continue to argue that the subject be taken seriously and given adequate funding and support within design schools, and they are right to do so. However, a view of graphic design history that sees it as being only, or even primarily, for the purpose of educating graphic designers and that seeks to confine it to the design studio will continue to restrict the development of the subject in the ways described here. If graphic design is a truly significant cultural, social and economic force, then it has the potential to be a subject of wider academic (and public) interest, but it will need to be framed and presented in ways that relate to the concerns of viewers who are not designers – that is, to most viewers. As habitually inward-looking custodians of their own history, few graphic design educators have proven to be effective at this outward-looking, viewer-oriented style of writing and public address.[46]

Design educators need to foster this ability because until graphic design teachers with historical and theoretical insights begin to build a bridge toward visual studies – by writing for its journals and presenting papers at its conferences, and by demonstrating graphic design's interest and significance through the strength of their scholarship – there is little prospect that visual studies will expand to include it. Although there are comparatively few academically trained design historians who concentrate on graphic design history (which is also a matter for concern), they, too, could redirect some of their output toward visual studies.

In the short term, this movement toward visual studies would not mean abandoning graphic design departments as places of 'self location', but it would certainly require self-questioning and self-reinvention, starting with a close engagement with the thinking and literature of visual studies, which has barely been mentioned to date in historical and critical writing about graphic design. There are reasons, in any case, as we have seen, to anticipate that less designer-centric and fact-heavy ways of addressing the subject and investigating its social meanings would make graphic design history more appealing and useful to design students. Only when graphic design as an existing object of study becomes more visible will visual studies scholars who have come from other disciplines begin to see it as a potential field of inquiry alongside more clearly perceived visual media. The study of graphic design surely would benefit from opening itself up to these new interdisciplinary perspectives and investigations from the outside.

It might be argued that the partial absorption of graphic design history by visual studies would involve a crucial loss of autonomy. Art historians have certainly voiced fears that the renegade proponents of the new visual studies risk undoing their discipline.[47] In the case of graphic design history, however, there isn't a unified discipline to undo. Graphic design history exists between the cracks. It is not likely to achieve independence as a department in most institutions anytime soon, and, as things stand, it will continue to camp out in the studio. It is a late-starter with a lot of catching up to do.

Visual studies is an even newer arrival, although it has an energy and sense of purpose that comes from soaking up the strength of other disciplines with a long pedigree and deep theoretical foundations. Yet visual studies also exists in the gaps between other less adaptable fields of study, with an uncertainty, a lack of firm adhesion, that only makes it feel more timely and relevant. If graphic design history could find a second outpost within this territory, the making of the subject could prove – at last – to be a possibility.

Rick Poynor is a writer and Visiting Professor in Critical Writing at the Royal College of Art, London.
First published on *Design Observer* (www.designobserver.com), 10 January 2011.

1 See, for instance, *Journal of Design History* 5:1 (1992), a special issue devoted to graphic design history.

2 In the UK, Brighton University offers a well-established BA in History of Design, Culture, and Society. The Royal College of Art, in association with the Victoria and Albert Museum, offers a well-established MA in History of Design.

3 Examples of combined BA courses in the UK include: History of Art, Design, and Film (Kingston University), History of Art and Design (Manchester Metropolitan University), History of Modern Art, Design, and Film (Northumbria University).

4 *Visible Language*, special issues: 'New Perspectives: Critical Histories of Graphic Design', Andrew Blauvelt, guest ed. 28:3 (1994), 28:4 (1994), 29:1 (1995). See also Andrew Blauvelt, 'Designer Finds History, Publishes Book', *Design Observer* (2010).

5 See Victor Margolin, *The Struggle for Utopia: Rodchenko, Lissitzky, Moholy-Nagy 1917–46* (Chicago and London: University of Chicago Press, 1997); Deborah Rothschild, Ellen Lupton and Darra Goldstein, *Graphic Design in the Mechanical Age: Selections from the Merrill C. Berman Collection* (New Haven and London: Yale University Press, 1998); Martha Scotford, *Cipe Pineles: A Life of Design* (New York: W.W. Norton, 1999).

6 Since 2005 see, for instance, Michel Wlassikoff, *The Story of Graphic Design in France* (Corte Madera: Gingko Press, 2005); Stanislaus von Moos, Mara Campana and Giampiero Bosoni, *Max Huber* (London and New York: Phaidon Press, 2006); Richard Hollis, *Swiss Graphic Design: The Origins and Growth of an International Style* (London: Laurence King Publishing, 2006); Kerry William Purcell, *Josef Müller-Brockmann* (London and New York: Phaidon Press, 2006); Roger R. Remington and Robert S.P. Fripp, *Design and Science: The Life and Work of Will Burtin* (Aldershot: Lund Humphries, 2007); Laetitia Wolff, *Massin* (London and New York: Phaidon Press, 2007); Steven Heller, *Iron Fists: Branding the 20th-Century Totalitarian State* (London and New York: Phaidon Press, 2008).

7 I shall follow W.J.T. Mitchell's distinction and use 'visual studies' for the field of study and 'visual culture' for the object or target of study. Some writers on visual culture, including Mitchell, prefer to use 'visual culture' interchangeably. See Mitchell, 'Showing Seeing: A Critique of Visual Culture' in *The Visual Culture Reader*, ed. Nicholas Mirzoeff (London and New York: Routledge, 2nd ed. 2002), p.87. On visual culture, in addition to the other works cited here, see Block Editorial Board and Sally Stafford, *The Block Reader in Visual Culture* (London and New York: Routledge, 1996); John A. Walker and Sarah Chaplin, *Visual Culture: An Introduction* (Manchester: Manchester University Press, 1997); Malcolm Barnard, *Approaches to Understanding Visual Culture* (Basingstoke: Palgrave, 2001); James Elkins, *Visual Studies: A Skeptical Introduction* (New York and London: Routledge, 2003).

8 *Graphic Design History*, eds. Steven Heller and Georgette Ballance (New York: Allworth Press, 2nd ed. 2001), p.viii.

9 Andrew Blauvelt, 'Notes in the Margin', *Eye* 6 (1996), p.57.

10 Gunnar Swanson, 'Graphic Design Education as a Liberal Art: Design and Knowledge in the University and the 'Real World'' in *The Education of a Graphic Designer*, Steven Heller ed. (New York: Allworth Press, 2005), p.22–32.

11 Guy Julier and Viviana Narotzky, 'The Redundancy of Design History' (Leeds: Leeds Metropolitan University, 1998).

12 Ibid.

13 Heller, 'The Case for Critical History' in *Graphic Design History*, op.cit., p.94.

14 Louis Danziger, 'A Danziger Syllabus' in *The Education of a Graphic Designer*, op.cit., p.333.

15 Jonathan Baldwin, 'Abandoning History', *A Word in Your Ear* (2005). Baldwin delivered a paper on this theme at *New Views: Repositioning Graphic Design History* (London College of Communication, 27–29 October 2005).

16 Philip B. Meggs, *A History of Graphic Design* (New York: John Wiley, 3rd ed. 1998, 4th ed. 2005).

17 Baldwin, op.cit.

18 Prasad Boradkar, 'From Form to Context: Teaching a Different Type of Design History' in *The Education of a Graphic Designer*, p.85. For further discussion of the problems arising from the 'varied discursive locations of visual design activity', see Victor Margolin, 'Narrative Problems of Graphic Design History', *Visible Language* 28:3 (1994), p.233–43.

19 Robin Kinross, 'Design History: No Critical Dimension', *AIGA Journal of Graphic Design* 11:1 (1993), p.7.

20 One exception is the British writer Malcolm Barnard. See *Art, Design and Visual Culture: An Introduction* (Basingstoke: Macmillan Press, 1998). Barnard went on to write *Graphic Design as Communication* (London and New York: Routledge, 2005).

21 Nicholas Mirzoeff ed., *The Visual Culture Reader* (London and New York: Routledge, 2nd ed. 2002).

22 Martin Jay, 'Introduction to Show and Tell', *Journal of Visual Culture*, 'The Current State of Visual Studies' 4:2 (2005).

23 Margaret Dikovitskaya, *Visual Culture: The Study of the Visual after the Cultural Turn* (Cambridge and London: MIT Press, 2005), p.1.

24 Martin Jay (interview) in *Visual Culture: The Study of the Visual after the Cultural Turn*, p.206.

25 A significant public 'breakthrough' moment for graphic design was the international release in 2007 of the feature-length documentary, *Helvetica*, directed by Gary Hustwit. Reviewers with no specialized knowledge of design noted that it had made them look at aspects of the visual environment usually taken for granted with a new level of attention and understanding. See, for instance, the *Metromix Chicago* review (2007).

26 I have personal experience of this classification problem. See Rick Poynor, *Obey the Giant: Life in the Image World* (Basel: Birkhäuser, 2007) and *Designing Pornotopia: Travels in Visual Culture* (New York: Princeton Architectural Press, 2006).

27 See Martin Jay, 'That Visual Turn: The Advent of Visual Culture', *Journal of Visual Culture* 1:1 (2002), p.87–92.

28 Mirzoeff, op.cit., p.6.

29 Nicholas Mirzoeff, *An Introduction to Visual Culture* (London and New York: Routledge, 1999), p.6. See also the substantially revised second edition, 2009.

30 Guy Julier, 'From Visual Culture to Design Culture', *Design Issues* 22:1 (2006), p.76.

31 Mirzoeff, *An Introduction to Visual Culture* (1999), p.3.

32 Ibid, p.7.

33 Irit Rogoff, 'Studying Visual Culture' in *The Visual Culture Reader*, p.27.

34 Dikovitskaya, p.4.

35 Roxane Jubert, *Typography and Graphic Design: From Antiquity to the Present* (Paris: Flammarion, English ed. 2006); Stephen J. Eskilson, *Graphic Design: A New History* (New Haven: Yale University Press, 2007); Johanna Drucker and Emily McVarish, *Graphic Design History: A Critical Guide* (Upper Saddle River, NJ: Pearson Prentice Hall, 2008); and Patrick Cramsie, *The Story of Graphic Design* (New York: Abrams, 2010). For extended discussion of Eskilson, see Alice Twemlow and Lorraine Wild, 'A New Graphic Design History?' *Design Observer* (2007). For extended discussion of Drucker and McVarish, see Denise Gonzales Crisp and Rick Poynor, 'A Critical View of Graphic Design History', *Design Observer* (2008).

36 See Jonathan Harris, *The New Art History: A Critical Introduction* (London and New York: Routledge, 2001).

37 See Andrew Blauvelt, 'Modernism in the Fly-Over Zone', *Design Observer* (2007).

38 Gayatri Spivak quoted by Rogoff, op.cit., p.26.

39 Rogoff, op.cit., p.33.

40 For further reflections on this oversight, see Johanna Drucker, 'Who's Afraid of Visual Culture', *Art Journal* 58:4 (1999), p.36-47.

41 Mirzoeff (interview) in *Visual Culture: The Study of the Visual after the Cultural Turn*, op.cit., p.232.

42 Mirzoeff, *An Introduction to Visual Culture* (1999), op.cit., p.14.

43 Mitchell (interview) in *Visual Culture: The Study of the Visual after the Cultural Turn*, p.cit., p.256.

44 Mitchell, *The Visual Culture Reader*, op.cit., p.90.

45 See Mirzoeff and Mitchell in *Visual Culture: The Study of the Visual after the Cultural Turn*, op.cit., p.227–31, 243, 255–7.

46 Exceptions should be noted, in particular the work of Ellen Lupton, curator since 1992 of exhibitions about graphic design at the Cooper-Hewitt National Design Museum. Lupton's practice as designer, educator, curator and writer provides a paradigm for a more publicly oriented presentation of graphic design. As design director of the Walker Art Center, Andrew Blauvelt also assumed a curatorial role. In 2010, he was appointed chief of communications and audience engagement at the Center.

47 See 'Visual Culture Questionnaire', October 77 (1996), op.cit., p.25–70. In particular, see Thomas Crow, p.36.

INDEX